SOCIETY AND POLITICS IN
WILHELMINE GERMANY

Society and Politics in Wilhelmine Germany

Edited by RICHARD J. EVANS

CROOM HELM LONDON

BARNES & NOBLE BOOKS · NEW YORK
(a division of Harper & Row Publishers, Inc.)

© 1978 Richard J. Evans

Croom Helm Ltd, 2-10 St John's Road, London SW11
ISBN 0-85664-347-5

British Library Cataloguing in Publication Data

Society and politics in Wilhelmine Germany.
   1. Germany — Politics and government —
   1888-1918 2. Germany — Social conditions
   I. Evans, Richard John
   301.5'92'0943   JN3388

   ISBN 0-85664-347-5

Published in the USA 1978 by
Harper & Row Publishers Inc.
Barnes & Noble Import Division

ISBN 0-06-492036-4

LC 77-014746

Printed in Great Britain by
Biddles Ltd, Guildford, Surrey

CONTENTS

CONTENTS

LIST OF ABBREVIATIONS

ABDF	Archiv des Bundes Deutscher Frauenvereine (Deutsches Zentralinstitut für Soziale Fragen, Berlin-Dahlem)
AEG	Allgemeine Elektrizitäts-Gesellschaft
AFA	Allgemeiner Freier Angestelltenbund
AStAM	Allgemeines Staatsarchiv München (Bayerisches Haupstaatsarchiv, Allgemeine Abteilung)
BA	Bundesarchiv (Koblenz)
BA-MA	Bundesarchiv-Militärarchiv (Freiburg)
Bg	Bamberg
BDF	Bund Deutscher Frauenvereine
BdL	Bund der Landwirte
DMV	Deutscher Metallarbeiterverband
DMZ	Deutsche Metallarbeiterzeitung
DNVP	Deutschnationale Volkspartei
FAH	Familien-Archiv Hügel (Krupp)
Gedag	Gesamtverband deutscher Angestelltengewerkschaften
GHH	Historisches Archiv der Gutehoffnungshütte
GLA	Badisches Generallandesarchiv Karlsruhe
GStA	Geheimes Staatsarchiv (Bayerisches Hauptstaatsarchiv München, Geheime Abteilung)
HA	Historisches Archiv (der Stadt Köln)
Hbg	Hamburg
HLA	Helene-Lange-Archiv (Deutsches Zentralinstitut für Soziale Fragen, Berlin-Dahlem)
HStA	Hauptstaatsarchiv
IGBE	Industriegewerkschaft Bergbau und Energie (Bergbau–Archiv, Bochum)
INO	Imperial Navy Office
IZF	Institut für Zeitungsforschung (Dortmund)
KPD	Kommunistische Partei Deutschlands
LB	Landesbibliothek
MInn	Ministerium des Innern
Nbg	Neuburg
PA	Politisches Archiv des Auswärtigen Amts, Bonn
RMA	Reichsmarineamt
RT	Stenographische Berichte über die Verhandlungen des Deutschen Reichstags

SA	Stadtarchiv
SAA	Stadtarchiv Augsburg
SAB	Stadtarchiv Bochum (Acta des Königlichen Landrathsamtes)
SAN	Stadtarchiv Nürnberg
SPD	Socialdemokratische Partei Deutschlands
StA	Staatsarchiv
StAA	Staatsarchiv Amberg
StA Bg	Staatsarchiv Bamberg
StA Hbg	Staatsarchiv Hamburg
StAL	Staatsarchiv Landshut
StAM	Staatsarchiv München
StAN	Staatsarchiv Nürnberg
StA Nbg	Staatsarchiv Neuburg
StAW	Staatsarchiv Würzburg
USPD	Unabhängige Socialdemokratische Partei Deutschlands
VdKdAbg	Stenographische Berichte über die Verhandlungen der bayerischen Kammer der Abgeordneten
WA	Werkarchiv (Krupp)
WWA	Westfälisches Wirtschaftsarchiv (Dortmund)
ZSA	Zentrales Staatsarchiv

1 INTRODUCTION: WILHELM II's GERMANY AND THE HISTORIANS

Richard J. Evans

I

The ten original essays collected in this book have all been specially
written for the occasion and are published here for the first time. The
authors are all British historians of the younger generation.[1] It is hoped
that the contributions in this volume will give some indication of the
wealth and diversity of scholarly research now being carried out in
Britain on the history of Germany between 1888 and 1918. All the
authors have worked extensively on primary sources in German archives.
Their essays make use of unpublished documentary material in East
and West Germany to cast new light on many aspects of Wilhelmine
politics and society, both familiar and unfamiliar. The contributions
are arranged by topic along a political continuum starting with
problems of government and moving from the right wing through
political movements in the middle — peasant populism, political
Catholicism, liberalism — to Trade Unionism and Social Democracy,
ending with a study of militancy and revolution on the far left.
Alternatively, the sequence of essays can be viewed in terms of a
descent down the social scale, beginning with the Kaiser and the
Chancellor and progressing through the industrialists, administrators
and intelligentsia via the urban and rural petty-bourgeoisie to the
workers on the shop-floor and down the mines, taking in other social
groups such as women and youth *en route*. In this way, the book as a
whole tries to give the reader some impression of the range of
political opinions and social groups which existed in the German
Empire between the end of the 1880s and the beginning of the 1920s.
    It is, of course, in no way fortuitous that so many younger
historians in Britain — and there are others besides the contributors to
this book[2] — are now working on the history of Wilhelmine Germany.
For in little over a decade, since the middle of the 1960s, the study of
German history between 1888 and 1918 has undergone a profound
revolution which has made it now one of the most exciting of all
historical areas to be working in. The revolution was set off by the
publication in 1961 of Fritz Fischer's book *Griff nach der Weltmacht*
(published in English in 1967 as *Germany's Aims in the First World*

War). Fischer's book brought a mass of documentary evidence to light on the vast range and extent of German war aims in 1914—18. The most controversial part of the book was its claim that Germany had not only sought to annex much of Europe and dominate the rest *during* the war, but that this had also been the intention of Wilhelm II and his advisers for some time *before* 1914 as well; indeed, they had deliberately launched the war in order to achieve this. Outside Germany these arguments had been familiar to historians for some time. But within the West German historical profession itself they were regarded as little better than treachery to the national cause. Moreover, some of the implications of Fischer's work were even more disturbing. If Wilhelm II's Germany deliberately launched a war of European conquest, then Hitler's 'Third Reich' was perhaps not such a unique phenomenon as German historians had previously professed to believe. It was scarcely surprising, therefore, that Fischer's book aroused a storm of controversy within the German historical profession, particularly since it appeared at a time when the West German Federal Republic was trying hard to establish its credentials as a democratic and peaceful country before a sceptical and mistrustful international audience.[3]

The so-called 'Fischer controversy' was argued out largely within the confines of traditional methods of diplomatic history, with historians hurling newly-discovered documents at one another in support of rival theses, and doing their best to discredit the reliability of the documentation presented by their opponents or to dispute the construction which they put on them. As the controversy subsided, however, it had already become apparent to German historians younger than the chief participants in the debate (nearly all of whom, including Fischer himself, were in their fifties or sixties, and a few of whom, including Fischer's main critic, Gerhard Ritter, were even older) that these methods were of limited value in solving the profounder questions at issue. Moreover, as it became clear that Fischer's main points — the large measure of responsibility of Germany for the outbreak of World War I and the far-reaching aims pursued by Germany during the war — had been substantiated beyond all reasonable doubt, several other implications emerged to strengthen this sense of methodological dissatisfaction among the younger West German historians.[4]

In the first place, if there really were some similarities between Hitler's foreign policy and that of Wilhelm II, then might there not also be some similarities in the *internal* political structure of Germany under Hitler and under the last Kaiser?[5] Indeed, could not some of the longer-term origins of the Third Reich — origins whose existence the older generation of historians had largely denied, ascribing the rise of Nazism solely to the demonic genius of Hitler[6] – lie precisely in developments that took place in Wilhelmine or even Bismarckian Germany? Furthermore, if Germany really did launch the First World War, then must there not have been powerful internal social and economic influences prompting her to do so – influences more profound that the mere incompetence of her diplomacy or the blinkered technical rigidity of her military men?[7] Finally, if it was admitted that Nazism had fairly deep roots in German history, and that the German government had borne the major responsibility for the terrible carnage of the First World War, what implications did this have for the role of historical study in Germany? Clearly the historical profession could no longer go on performing the role it had acquired during the nationalist era of the mid-nineteenth century and retained right up to the 1960s – that of helping Germans acquire a national identity through giving them a sense of pride in their past. At the end of the 1960s, therefore, West German historians found themselves searching for a new role.[8]

These considerations led the younger generation of West German historians to a radical break with the traditions of German historiography as they had been developed by the great historians of the past, from Ranke to Meinecke; and it is this, rather than the Fischer controversy itself, which constituted the real revolution in German historiography. Traditional German historical writing placed the State at the centre of the historical stage, and argued that its major policies were dictated by its position in the world of nation states.[9] The younger generation turned this thesis of the so-called 'primacy of foreign policy' (*Primat der Aussenpolitik*) on its head and argued instead for the 'primacy of internal policy' (*Primat der Innenpolitik*) in determining matters of war and peace. As they turned their attention in the wake of the Fischer controversy to the internal politics of Bismarckian and Wilhelmine Germany, they began to take a much more critical view of the German Empire than their predecessors had done. In this process of reassessment, the younger German historians began to discover neglected radical predecessors who had taken a similarly critical view in previous decades (and had been cold-shouldered by the historical profession for precisely this reason) – most notably, perhaps, Eckart Kehr and Hans Rosenberg.[10] More important still, they also began to reach out to the social sciences for new concepts and methods with which to make sense of the new past they were discovering: it was in social history, as they came to believe,

that the key to the internal structure and development of Imperial
Germany was to be found.[11]

It was here too that the new role of the historical profession could
be carved out: in helping people to understand the need for formal
democratic institutions to be underpinned by a genuine democratisation
of society,[12] as they had not been in the Weimar Republic. This need
was dramatically revealed by the political crisis of the West German
state in 1967—70, with neo-Nazism gaining ground in the elections
and a massive student revolt taking place against traditionalist
authoritarianism in the German University, a revolt with many
features of which the younger generation of historians, as young
lecturers or postgraduate students, undoubtedly sympathised. Not
surprisingly, therefore, an element of 'New Left' Marxism was also
added to the conceptual armoury of these younger historians, through .
the influence of philosophers and sociologists such as Jürgen Habermas.
It informed their approach to problems such as the legitimation of rule
by oppressive or undemocratic groups in society. But these elements
of Marxism were harnessed, as we shall see, to a concentration on the
responsibility of pre-industrial élites for the misfortunes of Germany
in the nineteenth and twentieth centuries that was fundamentally
alien to the main emphasis of more consistently Marxist work on the
role of the capitalist system and big business in the origins of the First
World War and the rise of fascism.

The reason for this peculiar slant given to Marxist concepts by the
new German historiography lies in the fact that the general reorientation
of German historiography of which it was in part was really a reflection
of a seismic shift taking place in West German society as a whole, from
the era of reconstruction under Adenauer in the 1950s to the period
of stability and maturity that the Federal Republic has been enjoying
under the Social Democratic-liberal coalition governments of the
1970s. A major aspect of this shift has been the recognition of the
existence of East Germany as a separate state; and the process of self-
definition which this involved for West Germans also left its mark on
the younger generation of West German historians, who had to come
to terms with East German historiography as well as with the interpretations evolved by their own predecessors.[13] The explicit role
played by Marxist-Leninist theory in East German history books
provided an example to West German historians, helping to provoke
them into giving theory a similar role in their own work. But it has
also been a deterrent, forcing them — unlike their radical contemporaries in Britain and America — to give Marxist ideas a strictly

subordinate role; the proximity of the East German model of Marxism to West German historians has meant that the latter have equated Marxism purely with East German Marxist-Leninism, and have virtually ignored other variants of it, rather as 'Euro-Communism' on the Italian model has been a non-starter in West Germany because of the identification there of Communism with the East German regime. As a result, West German historians have largely sealed themselves off from the influence of alternative models of Marxist theory and historiography as developed in Italy, France or Great Britain. A certain theoretical parochialism has been the consequence, and West German historians have tried to mitigate this by turning to the United States, and to the disciplines of political and social science as they have evolved there, above all under the inspiration of the sociological theories of Max Weber, for concepts and approaches. It is not only in the physical aspect of its cities and the structure and dynamism of its economy that West Germany is the most Americanised of European countries; its intellectual life, too, is more heavily influenced by America than that of any other European country. At the same time, as the historical paths of West and East Germany have slowly diverged, the proximity of the East German model has also ensured that historical monographs in West Germany have come more and more to resemble a kind of social-democratic mirror-image of their East German counterparts, with empirical material being sandwiched between two slices of theoretical discussion — and, as often as not, effectively unrelated to either of them.[14] Similarly, the West German historians' preoccupation with history as a form of political education can also be seen as a parallel to the explicitly didactic conception of historical writing favoured by the East Germans.

By the middle of the 1970s, the historiographical revolution in West Germany had more or less run its course. Its major proponents had moved into senior academic posts, produced a long series of important monographic studies, founded their own historical journal — *Geschichte und Gesellschaft* ('History and Society', subtitled 'A Journal of Historical Social Science') — reprinted many of the works of rediscovered predecessors such as Eckart Kehr, issued many collections of essays and readings and begun to produce works of synthesis which summed up the views they had developed.[15] Perhaps the most important of these syntheses has been Hans-Ulrich Wehler's *Das deutsche Kaiserreich 1871–1918* (Göttingen, 1973), a general history of the German Empire under Bismarck and Wilhelm II which may be taken as representative of what the American scholar James J. Sheehan has recently termed the 'new orthodoxy' in German historiography.[16] In the following section I shall attempt to summarise the main conclusions of this novel, challenging and immensely exciting account of German history from 1871 to 1918 before going on in the final part of this introduction to outline the relationship in which the contributions to the present volume stand to it.

II

Imperial Germany, in the view of this 'new orthodoxy', was dominated by the problem of

> the defence of inherited ruling positions by preindustrial élites against the onslaught of new forces — a defensive struggle which not only became ever sharper with the erosion of the economic foundations of these privileged leading strata but also created ever more dangerous tensions because of the success it achieved, and stored up an evil heritage for the future.[17]

The dominant preindustrial élite was the Prussian landed aristocracy, a feudal-military caste which controlled the destinies of Prussia through the bureaucracy, officer corps and Prussian Parliament (particularly the House of Lords but also the Chamber of Deputies, whose electors were divided into three classes according to a property qualification, the two richest classes electing most of the deputies even though they constituted only a small fraction of the population). The German Empire, founded through the defeat of Austria and the South German states in 1866 and the victory against France in 1870–1, represented in military reality as well as in political effect the conquest of Germany by Prussia. The position of German Emperor was always to be filled by the King of Prussia; the German Army was effectively under his command — formally so in time of war; the exiguous ministerial and administrative organs of the Empire were staffed by Prussian bureaucrats; the formal government of the Empire, the Bundesrat, representing the Heads of State of the federated Kingdoms, Principalities, Grand Duchies and City Republics of the Empire and alone possessing the right to initiate legislation in the Reichstag, the Lower Chamber of the Imperial Legislature, was dominated by Prussia, whose representatives could in practice always outvote the others. The pre-eminence of Prussia was underlined by the fact that in size and in economic strength it surpassed all the other states of the

German Empire put together.[18]

Wehler and other historians of the 'new orthodoxy' argue that the feudal-military aristocracy which ruled Prussia, and, through Prussia, Germany, retained its power by a number of techniques of political and social control. The Empire was not a constitutional monarchy; it was, rather, a 'pseudo-constitutional semi-absolutism'.[19] The Reichstag's powers were strictly limited. Ministers were neither elected nor responsible to it. It could not initiate legislation. Governments were appointed by the Kaiser, who also had sole control over the declaration of peace and war. All that the Reichstag could do was to hold up the budget or the military estimates. Under Bismarck, the government got round even this limited power of delay by drumming up a foreign policy crisis every time the military estimates were due — which was not very often — and by turning to secure support in this way and reduce the power of the liberal opponents of his policy, Bismarck had established the Reichstag elections on the basis of universal manhood suffrage. It is for this reason that German historians have recently come to characterise Bismarckian Germany as a 'plebiscitary dictatorship' on the lines of Napoleon III's Second Empire in France; and to describe Bismarck's technique of rule as 'Bonapartism' or 'Caesarism'.[20] No-one, neither the erratic Kaiser Wilhelm II nor the Chancellors who succeeded Bismarck — the well-meaning Caprivi, the senile Hohenlohe, the pliant Bülow and the grey bureaucrat Bethmann Hollweg — could fill the gap left by Bismarck after his departure in 1890. Instead, the 'traditional oligarchies' ruled Germany through the 'anonymous forces of authoritarian polycracy', consisting of 'rival centres of power' in the bureaucracy, the army and navy, the court and in the growing number of nationalistic and economic pressure-groups which exerted an increasingly powerful influence on affairs in the era of Wilhelm II. Though there was no longer any German Caesar, the élites continued to rule through a 'Bonapartist strategy' and to develop the techniques of control first elaborated by Bismarck.[21]

The most overt of these methods — according to these historians — was that of *repression*. Civil rights and freedoms were, they argue, drastically curtailed in the Germany of Wilhelm II. Even if oppositional political parties were not formally outlawed, as the Social Democrats were under Bismarck from 1878 to 1890, they were discriminated against by the exclusion of their members from political power and social influence. No Social Democrat could become a schoolteacher or university professor, no liberal or democrat could join the officer corps in the Prussian army. An elaborate apparatus of police controls and censorship laws severely restricted freedom of expression. There were few Social Democratic newspaper or magazine editors who had not served several terms in prison for permitting seditious or anti-monarchical opinions to be printed; often prosecutions of this kind were made on the merest pretext. Policemen were in attendance at all public meetings, empowered to dissolve them should disloyal or 'immoral' phrases pass the lips of the speaker, or the suspicion be aroused that the meeting might degenerate into disorder. These powers were not used sparingly. Nor were judges, ultra-conservatives to a man, inclined to be lenient towards radicals or Social Democrats or indeed anyone accused of criticising the authorities in any way. Strikes and industrial disputes almost invariably ended in arrests; lockouts and dismissals were commonplace; many industries — above all, those controlled by the government, such as the railways, or those closely connected with government interests, such as the armaments or iron and steel industries — dismissed union members and circulated blacklists of known 'agitators'. Beyond this system of 'class justice'[22] loomed the threat of martial law should the position of the ruling élites ever seem seriously endangered. The country was divided into areas, each under a military commander, with powers to suspend civil liberties, arrest 'trouble-makers' and override civil government in times of 'emergency'. Detailed plans were actually drawn up for such an eventuality. The ultimate threat was that of a *Staatsstreich* or *coup d'état* from above, which was seriously and openly canvassed by Wilhelm II and his advisers at various critical junctures and hung over the constitution like the sword of Damocles, constituting a permanent reminder to opposition politicians of what would happen if they carried their opposition too far.[23]

In addition to repression, the ruling élite, it is argued, also employed the tactic of *manipulation*. The political parties, which posed perhaps the most serious threat to the continuation of the Bonapartist-dictatorial régime, were drawn through a skilful policy of manipulation away from political coalition on the basis of shared beliefs and reduced to mere vehicles of economic interests. A classic example of this was the way in which Bismarck split the liberals, perhaps his most dangerous political opponents in the 1860s and 1870s, by exposing the contradictions between nationalism and con-stitutionalism in liberal ideology through unifying Germany without liberalising it (1866—71) and then (1878—9) through introducing protectionism combined with a further curtailment of civil liberties in the Anti-Socialist Law. By the 1890s the National Liberals, representing heavy industry, were at odds with the South German liberals, representing peasants and petty-bourgeois townsfolk, and various groups of North German left-liberals backed by professional men or light industrialists. Similarly, the Conservatives were tied to the Agrarian League by the mid-1890s, the Social Democrats to the Trade Unions, and so on. This dissolution of political parties into competing pressure-groups, and their inability to emerge from their respective provincial or social *milieux* to combine, further enabled the government to manipulate the groups and prevent them from forming a viable majority in the Reichstag for constitutional reform.[24]

Another form of political manipulation practised by the ruling élite, it has been claimed, was that of the *diversion* of emancipatory and reformist impulses into enthusiasm for foreign conquest, empire and international prestige: the so-called technique of 'social imperialism'. With the encouragement of the government, organisations such as the Navy League, the Colonial Society and the Society for the Eastern Marches set about mobilising the masses behind a programme of nationalist enthusiasm and political conservatism.[25] This tactic was backed up, particularly with reference to the working classes, by a policy of *compensation* for loyalty to the ruling élite in the form of social insurance and welfare policies.[26] The loyalty of the masses was further cemented through a concerted policy of *indoctrination*, through the encouragement of deferential modes of thought and traditionalist monarchism in the schools, the legitimation of the social and political status quo by the State-controlled Protestant Church, the formation of a wide range of voluntary organisations such as the League Against Social Democracy whose aim was to win the masses away from subversive ideas through counter-propaganda, and the provision of anti-democratic models of behaviour in the authoritarian father, the Prussian army officer or the social élite of the student duelling corps.[27]

Finally, the ruling élites themselves, it is alleged, were kept together despite their apparently divergent economic interests by the political device of *negative integration*, that is, by portraying certain groups in society — the socialist working classes, the Catholic South Germans, the Polish, Danish and French national minorities, the Jews — as so subversive and dangerous that the possessing classes had to close ranks in order to survive against the threat which they posed.[28] The counterpart of negative integration was the so-called *Sammlungspolitik*, the policy of gathering together in one political camp all the social and political groups of the right — the 'productive classes' in one formulation, or, more classically, the classes which were said to support the state (*staatserhaltend*). In the first place this meant the owners of heavy industry and the landed aristocrats. At the end of the 1890s the bargain between these two groups was sealed through the aristocracy's agreement to support industry's demand for a big navy, which meant lucrative contracts for armaments manufacturers and iron and steel producers, and a 'world policy' (*Weltpolitik*), which meant the diplomatic search for new markets in competition with the British Empire. Heavy industry in turn agreed to give the landed aristocracy a *quid pro quo* in the form of higher import tariffs on grain (to cushion them against foreign competition).[29] More generally they continued to acquiesce in the social and political status quo. The industrialists' support for the continued dominance of the landed aristocracy in State and society was facilitated by the phenomenon which German historians have dubbed the 'feudalisation of the bourgeoisie' — the adherence of the middle classes, above all the 'barons' of heavy industry, to modes of thought and action that were preindustrial rather than middle-class or liberal after the example of the English bourgeoisie. Industrialists such as Krupp behaved towards their employees much as a medieval baron might towards his serfs, with a mixture of paternalism and despotic ruthlessness; while the social prestige that attached to the position of an officer in the army reserve was so great that wealthy bourgeois gladly conformed to the feudal standards of behaviour expected of them in order to secure appointment.[30]

In sum, then, if these views are correct, it is clear that the techniques of rule through which the Wilhelmine elite hoped to stay in power were formidable in their range and effectiveness. Wehler and those whose views he has synthesised claim that they enabled the Prussian aristocracy, with the aid of the barons of heavy industry, to maintain the status quo intact not only until the Revolution of 1918 — though the situation had been desperate enough to cause them to launch the First World War as a last fling of social imperialism in 1914 — but even afterwards. Just as the élites had mobilised the petty-bourgeoisie behind their social imperialist ideologies before 1914, so as things got worse for them during the Weimar Republic they eventually had recourse to the encouragement of the far more dangerous (but essentially similar) forces of National Socialism. They it was through whose agency Hitler was brought to power in 1933.

Only when it was too late did they realise that Nazism was a force they could not control. By the time they came to revolt, in 1944, their power was almost at an end; Hitler's savage reprisals after the failure of their plot removed them once and for all from the historical scene. 1944—5 thus marks the real end of the élite's dominance, and constitutes therefore the only really major discontinuity in recent German history,[31] despite the superficial appearance of sharp breaks in 1871, 1918 and 1933. And seen in a wider perspective the élite's work lived on even longer; its manipulations had been responsible for preventing the spread of democratic ideas among the middle classes, and, perhaps even more decisively, for fatally weakening the determination to succeed of the one truly democratic force in the *Kaiserreich*, the Social Democrats.

Although the Social Democrats were, superficially at least, implacably opposed to the social and political status quo in the Wilhelmine Empire, in reality as time went on, it is argued, they became progressively more reluctant to translate this opposition into action. Instead, frightened in case they would be outlawed altogether, and increasingly dominated by pragmatic trade unions who were even more terrified at the prospect of losing their assets and destroying years of hard organisational work by courting total repression in the form of a *Staatsstreich* or a revival of the Anti-Socialist Law, they became steadily more passive in their political tactics, encouraged by the inexorable growth of their electoral support to believe that one day they would secure a majority of seats in the Reichstag and so be able to assume the mantle of government. 'Negative integration', in other words, is seen as having affected not only the élite by keeping it together, but also the Social Democrats, by cowing them into submissiveness. Moreover, the conservative and nationalistic education through which the great majority of SPD members passed in the State primary schools was, it is argued, a further influence in weakening the allegiance of the party to peace and democracy. The result of these influences was not only full Social Democratic support for the war in 1915 but also a marked reluctance on the part of the SPD leaders to push through the Revolution of 1918 to a more radical conclusion, and, finally, a legalistic passivity in the face of authoritarian and Nazi attacks in 1932—3 which finally proved the party's downfall.[32] In the long term, then, the policies of the ruling élite of Wilhelmine Germany not only weakened the commitment of the middle classes to democracy, it weakened the working classes' commitment to it as well; and it is in overcoming the effects of this legacy in the present day that many West German historians now see their mission.

III

Such then − in an inevitably abbreviated and an unavoidably over-
simplified form − is the view of recent German history held by most of
of the present 'middle generation' of German historians. The reinterpretation of German history which it involves is stimulating and exciting,
and represents an enormous advance on the work of the 1950s and early
1960s; and it is in the light of this interpretation that the present volume
should be read. It would be fair to say that most of the contributors to
this book were stimulated into turning their attention to the history of
Wilhelmine Germany through coming into contact with some or all
of the views which I have outlined in section II of these introductory
remarks. Of course, the authors of the present collection approached
this new interpretation from different angles and with different
questions in mind. They in no sense form a 'school' or 'group'. Their
interests in Wilhelmine Germany, their methods and their views on
particular issues are certainly far from identical, and in some respects
are even opposed. The reader searching for a unified and identifiable
'line' on Wilhelmine Germany among the essays in this book will
search in vain. However, the authors do come from a common background in the British University system, as a glance at the notes on
contributors at the conclusion to the book will verify, and they have
experienced a common training in the British tradition of historical
scholarship. The difference of emphasis and approach between British
historiography and its West German counterpart is what gives this
book its coherence; it also forms one of the major reasons for having
brought the contributors together in such a collective enterprise in
the first place. This difference has little to do with national prejudice
or rivalry; apart from anything else the authors of this book are too
young to have experienced the events which have coloured the
attitudes of more senior British historians towards German history.[33]
The difference is really one of method, concerned with the way in
which historians in the two countries approach the past in general.

Broadly speaking, German historians have always approached history
from above, either through the philosophical principles expounded by
the great thinkers of the past, or through the institution of the nation
state. The international history of Germany was understood in terms
of the influence of ideas or through the action of international conflict
and *raison d'état* on national politics − the 'primacy of foreign policy'.
The State, of course, has always played a particularly large part in the

history of Germany and above all in the history of Prussia, so it should not be surprising that German historians have always placed it at the centre of their concerns.[34] What *is* a little surprising, perhaps, is the extent to which this is still the case. The new approach to German history still concentrates on high politics. It claims to be 'historical social science'. But as George Iggers, perhaps the most authoritative external observer of the German historiographical scene, has remarked it is not so much social history as it is understood in Britain, France or America, as the *social history of politics*.[35] Political processes, changes and influences are perceived as flowing downwards – though now from the élites who controlled the State, rather than from the socially vaguer entity of the State itself – not upwards from the people. The actions and beliefs of the masses are explained in terms of the influence exerted on them by manipulative élites at the top of society. The German Empire is presented as a puppet theatre, with Junkers and industrialists pulling the strings, and middle and lower classes dancing jerkily across the stage of history towards the final curtain of the Third Reich.[36]

While German historians continue to concentrate on high politics and 'history from above', the British historiographical tradition has been developing in quite a different direction. British historians have come increasingly to emphasise the importance of the grass roots of politics and the everyday life and experience of ordinary people. It is worth noting, perhaps, that this trend has taken place across a whole range of historical subjects, political opinions and methodological approaches and has been expressed in many different ways. It can be seen in the tendency over the last two decades for studies of the English Civil War of the seventeenth century to get away from events at the centre, in London, and reach a new understanding of the most profound of all political conflicts in British history through detailed study of provincial society, where the great majority of English people spent their lives – a tendency that has been explicitly developed in reaction against the Marxist interpretations of the 1950s.[37] It has also manifested itself in the development of a new school of 'people's history', written by working people and arising directly from their experience of work; the studies produced by this school, in their books and pamphlets and in their journal *History Workshop*, are enabling us to see the history of British society in the last 150 years in a new light.[38] Other students of nineteenth-century history have opened up very different perspectives on the Victorian political system by leaving Whitehall and Westminster and going into the country to look at the

shaping of national politics at its most basic, fundamental level.[39] Nor
has this approach been confined to students of British history; British
historians such as George Rudé and Richard Cobb, though working
in very different ways, have been instrumental in advancing our understanding of the French Revolution through detailed examinations of
riots, protest, crime and other expressions of discontent among the
common people.[40] 'History from below' in this very broad sense, encompassing a wide variety of methods and opinions, does not mean a
history without theory, though it would be true to say that British
historians tend to integrate theory with empirical study rather than
separate it out and so make it more obvious and more explicit in the
way that German historians do.[41] Nor does it mean 'history with the
politics left out'. Rather, it means an enlargement of the definition
of politics to include many areas of life which German historians,
continuing to equate politics with high politics, tend to assign to the
category of the 'unpolitical'.[42] In this widened concept of politics,
social and political history find their meeting-place. That is why this
book has been given the title *Society and Politics in Wilhelmine
Germany*: it is not just about society, nor simply about politics, but
concerns itself with the relationship between the two, from the
politics of everyday life to the social foundations of political and
administrative processes at the highest level. When the history of
Wilhelmine Germany is approached from below, in this way,
familiar features appear in an unfamiliar light. The picture that
emerges is different from that portrayed by the 'new orthodoxy'
among German historians. In some respects it contradicts it; in
others it complements it through illuminating aspects of the
Wilhelmine Empire which it has left obscure. In their different ways,
all the essays in this book provide an illustration of these points.

For example, one of the great strengths of British historiography
lies in its tradition of local history, a subject which has no real
equivalent in Germany, where local historical studies are still often
antiquarian in character. Mainstream German historiography concentrates overwhelmingly on Prussia; indeed, one of the many terms
which it uses to characterise the Wilhelmine Empire is 'Prussia-
Germany', implying not simply the unassailable dominance of
Prussia over the rest of the Empire but even the virtual identity of
the two. This is certainly the way it looks at the top, in the Reichstag,
the General Staff, the Imperial Court or the Government Ministries.
But if we shift our focus down to the level of society, to the ordinary
people, the picture changes. There was another Germany besides Prussia,

south of the Main; indeed, Prussia itself was in many ways a composite, artificial entity, containing a wide variety of social and political formations. Germany was an even more variegated and diverse society than France, the richness of whose local and provincial traditions historians have long been engaged in exploring. A number of the studies in this volume reflect this diversity by looking at social and political conditions at a regional level, in Bavaria (the contributions by Robin Lenman and Ian Farr), in other parts of South Germany (David Blackbourn) and in distinctive areas of Prussia (Stephen Hickey's article on the Ruhr). Robin Lenman's essay on that state and the *avant-garde* in Munich in particular reminds us that the sweeping generalisations often made about State repression of intellectual freedom in the Wilhelmine Empire must be qualified by more specific reference to the great variety of local and regional conditions. In Munich, for instance, the authorities seem to have taken a relatively tolerant attitude towards the literary and artistic *avant-garde*, and the legal system seems to have favoured intellectual freedom to an extent that compared favourably with other countries.[43]

Looked at from another angle, Robin Lenman's essay falls into another category of the contributions to this book, apart from local and regional studies; it also addresses itself to the problems of government and the State. A second contribution on this theme, looking at the centre of power in Berlin rather than at government on a regional level, is Terry Cole's essay on Wilhelm II's relations with his Chancellor, Bernhard von Bülow. Terry Cole's contribution suggests that when the ruling élites of Imperial Germany are approached through a close study of their constituent parts rather than from an overall organising concept such as that of *Sammlungspolitik*, their internal instability begins to come sharply into focus. At the top level of government, as Terry Cole shows, there was considerable dissension, which went far deeper than mere differences of opinion about tactics and personalities, extending indeed to fundamental disagreements on the aims and purposes of Government policy. The relations between the Kaiser and his Chancellors were dictated not merely by the clash of personalities; they arose from the constitutional situation of the Chancellor himself, so that even a man as initially subservient to Wilhelm II as Bernhard von Bülow, Chancellor from 1900 to 1909, soon came, as Terry Cole shows in an important revision of previous assessments of Bülow's political personality, to make a concerted effort at reducing the Kaiser's power. It was not a question of Kaiser and Chancellor, constituting 'rival centres of power', pursuing essentially compatible aims but competing for the right to put them into effect; on the contrary, when the actual day-to-day operation of Government is looked at in detail, it becomes clear that more was involved in the struggle between Kaiser and Chancellor than mere ambition for power.[44]

The second contribution to this volume, by Richard Owen, discusses the stability and internal coherence of Wilhelmine Germany's ruling élites from a rather different angle — the relationship of government and heavy industry. The problem is usually discussed by West German historians under the general heading of 'organised capitalism'. This concept has been developed in an effort to work out an alternative model to that put forward by East German historians under the term 'state monopoly capitalism'. Organised capitalism has been described as 'a concentrated and bureaucratised economic order, organised in voluntary associations (*Verbande*) and assured the capacity to function by a variety of governmental measures'. In place of free competition, industry constructed cartels and monopolies. These were backed by controls introduced by an increasingly interventionist State in an attempt to manage the economy so as to minimise social tensions created by economic crises. Most of the historians who have developed the idea of 'organised capitalism' have used it as a general theory encompassing the whole development of the German economy over a long period, rather than actually carrying out any detailed research with its aid or selecting any specific problem of State-industry relations as a test case of its value and utility. One of the few people to have attempted a consideration of 'organised capitalism' in the light of detailed original research, the American historian Gerald Feldman, has found the concept too vague to be of much use in his study of the German iron and steel industry from the outbreak of the First World War to the great inflation of 1923. In his contribution to the present volume, Richard Owen offers another detailed case study, in the shape of a discussion of the relationship of State and industry in the construction of the German battle fleet, concentrating particularly on the firm of Friedrich Krupp. Most historians have approached this subject from the perspective of the government, using official sources; in Richard Owen's essay, however, the problem is seen with the help of the archives of the Krupp firm itself, as well as through the medium of Government documents. In the 1890s, it is clear, declining foreign markets were forcing Krupp to concentrate more and more on domestic outlets for its products. The firm thus had good reason to press for the construction of a big German navy — all the more so since it had secured its position through a series of takeovers and other arrangements which gave it a monopoly on the production of armour-plating. By the time the construction of the battle fleet began, Krupp was thus able to boost its profits by charging the government exorbitant prices. Tirpitz and the Navy Office tried to get the better of Krupp and force his prices down by a variety of means, some of them not very scrupulous, but the traditionally trained bureaucrats of the Navy Office were no match for sharp businessmen such as the members of the Krupp Board. The relationship between Krupps and the Government was by no means a harmonious one. There can be no doubt that Krupps managed to get more out of it than did the government, despite the firm's increasing dependency on naval contracts for its continued profitability. Far from consciously manipulating the economy in the interests of social stability, the government seems to have been uncertain and unsure in the employment of the new powers of economic management it was gaining through the placing of huge naval orders.[45]

Both these essays suggest, then, that it is perhaps time to question the assumption of any real unity of purpose between top members of the ruling élites. The continuity and stability of the *Sammlungspolitik* and the alliance of heavy industry with agrarian landownership through the three decades of Wilhelm II's reign remains in many respects an unproven hypothesis. Even the central bargain of navy and *Weltpolitik* in return for import duties and continuation of the social and political status quo is, as Geoff Eley showed in an important article published in 1974, a theory which has little supporting evidence to recommend it.[46] In his contribution to the present volume, Geoff Eley extends this critique to the way in which the unity and persistence of anti-democratic élites has been made the central explanatory concept for a whole period of German history by the present 'middle generation' of German historians — covering the entire course of Germany's development from the middle of the nineteenth century to 1933. His essay is particularly concerned with two major problems which arise from the idea that the political manipulations of industrialists and agrarians were responsible for almost everything that went wrong with German history in this period, including the launching of the First World War and the advent of the 'Third Reich'. First, like the cruder ideological variations on the theme of continuity in German history, which depended on the identification of certain constant traits in the German character or the German 'frame of mind', this theory of continuity also largely banishes the complex dialectic of historical change from the scene; a feature, incidentally, which is particularly apparent in Hans-Ulrich Wehler's study of Imperial

Germany, which rejects the narrative approach for a 'problem-oriented structural analysis' and in so doing conveys the impression that in its fundamentals the political and social structure of Germany hardly changed at all between 1871 and 1918. Yet this was a period in which Germany underwent cataclysmic social and economic changes and suffered the trauma of a rapid transition to industrial maturity. Given the nature and extent of this transformation the idea that the political superstructure of German society remained basically unchanged seems implausible, to say the least. It is an opinion which can only be held through allowing one's view of German history to be structured by the perspectives of 1933. A second major weakness of recent German interpretations of the *Kaiserreich*, closely related to the first, is their portrayal of politics in terms of the manipulation of the masses by small élites. In his contribution to this book, Geoff Eley argues that economic and social change was mobilising new social groups *from below*; and the pressure on the political system exerted by the stage-by-stage process of the political self-mobilisation of the petty-bourgeoisie played a major and much-neglected part in the progressive creation of a mass fascist movement.

Even here, however, there is an important qualification to be made; for not all petty-bourgeois groups which mobilised themselves in this way contributed towards the development of National Socialism. As Ian Farr shows in his essay on Peasant Leagues in Bavaria, there can be no doubt about the parallels between the political mobilisation of the Bavarian farmer and the simultaneous creation of radical movements of the right among petty-bourgeois groups in the North. Like the political awakening of the artisans or white-collar workers, the entry of the Bavarian peasantry onto the political scene, as Ian Farr points out, was far more a response to economic pressures acting from below than a result of political manipulation acting from above. The influence of the major 'manipulative' group in agrarian politics, the Junker-dominated Agrarian League, was strictly limited in Bavaria, where it was largely restricted to Protestant enclaves in Swabia and Franconia. The bulk of Bavarian peasants, solidly Catholic in religion, rejected the Agrarian League as the representative of the Protestant Prussian aristocracy. They also rejected the militarism of the Agrarian League, because it meant that they would have to pay higher taxes. 'Social imperialism' cut little ice with tight-fisted Bavarian peasants. The formation of Peasant Leagues in the 1890s was as much as anything else a result of the lack of sympathetic response to the peasants' economic plight by the Catholic Centre

Party; and as soon as the Peasant Leagues began to make serious inroads into the party's electoral support, it responded by forming its own pressure-groups for small farmers, with a programme remarkably close to that of the Peasant Leagues themselves. The Catholic groups soon succeeded in reducing the influence of the Leagues and in winning back most of the support which the Centre Party had lost. In this way, the peasant populism of the 1890s — militant, stridently anti-Semitic and strongly opposed to the dominance of aristocratic élites — radicalised the Catholic Centre Party in Bavaria, just as the petty-bourgeois right was being radicalised in Protestant areas. The result, paradoxically, was that the Catholic peasantry in Bavaria was in part immunised against the influence of fascism in the 1920s and early 1930s because it had already been injected with a smaller dose of the same thing in the 1890s and 1900s; it was only in Protestant Franconia that the peasantry voted for Hitler in really large numbers in the Weimar Republic.

Relatively little attention has been paid either to the peasantry, often dismissed as 'backward', or to the Catholic Centre Party, usually regarded as 'clerical' or 'opportunist'; and by focusing on an aspect of Wilhelmine society that has generally been neglected by historians, Ian Farr's contribution points to the fact that by approaching Wilhelmine Germany through the concept of continuity and treating it in terms of the prehistory of the 'Third Reich', a great deal of recent German historical writing not only tends to underestimate the social and political changes which took place between 1888 and 1918 but also slants our perspective on the *Kaiserreich* so as to draw our attention away from features of Wilhelmine society and politics that fit awkwardly into the model of historical continuity so constructed. On the political scene, perhaps the outstanding example of this distortion of perspective is the extraordinary neglect suffered by the Catholic Centre Party. We have tried to give an accurate reflection of the central importance of this party to the Wilhelmine political system by making it a major focus of no less than four of the ten contributions to this volume, those by Ian Farr, Robin Lenman, Terry Cole and David Blackbourn. The party's significance derived in the first place from the fact that it was the largest political group in the Reichstag until 1912. Without its support, it was virtually impossible to put together a workable Reichstag majority. No government in Wilhelmine Germany could hope to get its legislation through in the absence of such a majority to support its proposals. The one brief attempt to do so, the so-called 'Bülow Block' of 1906–9, ended in failure. Despite all this, however, the Catholic Centre Party has barely been studied by German historians of the period.[47] The problem is that the Centre does not really fit most of the generalisations which have become common-place about the Wilhelmine political system. It has not really been possible to portray it as the mere representative of some organised economic interest. It is not easily classifiable in terms of right and left. It was clearly not a political vehicle of the élites; but neither was it brought over to support the system by 'social imperialism' – on the contrary, it went into opposition in 1906 objecting violently to some of the more unpleasant features of Germany's imperial adventures. Theories about Wilhelmine politics which do not fit the most important political party are clearly in need of some revision.

In the *Kulturkampf* of the 1870s, the Catholic Centre Party had been a political pariah, subject to the kind of official hostility and persecution that was reserved in the Wilhelmine period for the Social Democrats. Yet for most of the years with which this book deals – the exception being the period of the 'Bülow Block' from 1906 to 1909 – it was the major support of the government in the Reichstag. Conventional explanations ascribing this to mere political opportunism are too vague and superficial to be convincing. In his contribution to this volume, David Blackbourn shows that the changing political alignments of the Centre Party can only be understood by approaching the problem from below, through a study of the Catholic community's place in the social system of the *Kaiserreich*, and through a careful examination of the social and geographical distribution of the party's active and passive support. When this kind of study is carried out, it emerges that a number of important changes were taking place in the late Bismarckian and early Wilhelmine period which provide the clue to the party's move from an oppositional to a governmental position in the Reichstag. The party was rapidly losing its clerical character and becoming a middle-class party, led by lawyers and supported by the urban and rural petty-bourgeoisie of southern Germany. As the representative of a social sub-culture as all-embracing as that of the Social Democrats, in which members could pass their entire public lives within the hermetically sealed confines of Catholic social, political, economic and recreational associations, the Centre Party underwent the same kind of spontaneous process of 'negative integration' as affected the organisational super-structure of the labour movement. Discriminated against in countless ways in Wilhelmine society, Catholics came ever more eagerly to seek a way out of their subculture into the mainstream of German public life, and their competitive striving for 'insider status' led them to try to prove their national reliability by supporting the government in the Reichstag. Peasants, petty-bourgeois and middle-class Catholics looked to the Centre Party to affirm their social worth. It was this, rather than manipulation from above, that kept the Centre away from the Left-Liberals and Social Democrats with whom it was ultimately to cooperate in the Weimar Republic. It was, perhaps, frustration at being disregarded by the government in matters such as the duelling question which led the party, spurred on by its emergent radical wing, to break with the government in 1906; and its pivotal position in the calculations of the government at this time forms a focal point of Terry Cole's essay on Bülow and the Kaiser at the beginning of this volume. Finally, the radicalisation of Catholic Centre politics through the emergence of peasant populism in Bavaria, a process which Ian Farr discusses in his essay on the Peasant Leagues, was also one of the main influences in producing the decline of Munich as a cultural centre – a decline which was to give Berlin a virtual monopoly over *avant-garde* artistic production in the Weimar Republic. Populist Catholicism, as Robin Lenman shows in his contribution to this book, was hostile to the moral libertarianism of Munich's artistic community. It was popular pressure from below that brought about the decline of artistic freedom, as much as any kind of manipulation or repression from above.

Artists and intellectuals such as those about whom Robin Lenman writes are not always easily classifiable in political terms, and perhaps for this reason historians have usually found it difficult to integrate their account of artistic production into their general view of Wilhelmine society. In the majority of textbooks, art and literature appear, if they appear at all, as extras, unrelated to their social and historical context. Yet the degree of freedom allowed to artists and intellectuals does give at least some indication of the extent to which a society is governed by liberal values. Much the same sort of generalisations may be made about the status of women. Indeed, one German historian, Hans-Günter Zmarzlik, in a lengthy discussion of the 'pessimistic' view of Wilhelmine Germany put forward in Wehler's study *Das deutsche Kaiserreich*, has singled out the emergence of an organised feminist movement as evidence that liberal and progressive developments were also taking place in Germany before 1914. Zmarzlik has pressed this and other similar features of Wilhelmine society into the service of an alternative model of continuity in German history, leading not to 1933 but to 1969. Seen in a longer perspective. he argues, the most important aspects of Wilhelmine Germany were not

those which prefigured the development of the 'Third Reich', but those
which looked forward to the creation of a 'social-liberal' society in
Germany in the 1970s. The major social changes which took place in the
1890s and 1900s were not those which led to the triumph of National
Socialism in 1933, but those which led in the longer term to the triumph
of the Social Democratic-liberal coalition in the Federal Republic in
1969. Wilhelmine Germany should, he concludes, be seen in terms of
the prehistory of the present day, at least as much as in terms of the
prehistory of the 1930s.

In my own contribution to this book, I take the example of the
feminist movement, cited by Zmarzlik, as a test of these two theories of
continuity, and suggest that it fits neither of them. It is difficult to see
the growth of feminism as evidence of Wilhelmine Germany's contribution to a progressive continuity in German history, because when
it reached the stage of a mass movement − after the legalisation of
women's participation in politics by the *Reichsvereinsgesetz* (Imperial
Law of Association) in 1908 − it very rapidly became conservative
and illiberal, losing most of its interest in the emancipation of women.
On the other hand, it is also difficult to explain the feminists' abandonment of liberalism in terms of concepts such as 'social imperialism' or
the diversion of emancipatory forces into nationalist enthusiasm. Indeed,
it was the emancipatory legislation of the *Reichsvereinsgesetz* that
provided the catalyst for the movement's swing to the right by removing
the stigma of illegality from the feminist movement and thus enabling
the recruitment of large numbers of conservative women who had hitherto stayed aloof from political activity. In fact it is to the effects of a
rapidly industrialising economy on the social position and status of the
middle-class women who formed the mass basis for the quarter-million
strong German women's movement that we must look if we are to
understand the movement's changing political beliefs. The picture that
emerges when we approach the history of feminism in this way is a
more complex one than either that of an emancipatory movement
pointing forward to 1969 or that of the diversion of middle-class
liberalism into authoritarian and nationalistic channels leading to 1933.
Perhaps, then, it is time that Wilhelmine Germany ceased acting as a
battleground for rival theories of continuity and became instead a
subject for historical research in its own right.

The final three contributions to this book are concerned with what
was undoubtedly the largest of all movements of social and political
emancipation in the Germany of Wilhelm II − the labour movement. In
some ways the growth of the Social Democratic Party and its allies the

'free' trade unions constituted the most striking political development of
the Wilhelmine period. Research has concentrated overwhelmingly on
the organisational and ideological aspects of this process. The central
problem is the shift of the SPD from revolutionary Marxism, as emphasised in the Erfurt Programme of 1891, to a reformist political
practice which enabled it to support the German war effort in 1914.[49]
This shift has been explained by recent German historians mainly by
reference to the techniques of repression, political manipulation and
'negative integration' operated by Germany's ruling élite.[50] As Stephen
Hickey suggests in his essay on miners in the Ruhr, however, a more
fruitful way of approaching this problem, and the development of the
German labour movement in general, lies in the study of the concrete
realities of life as experienced by the workers who formed the bulk of
the SPD's membership. Seen from this angle, the labour movement
appears to have been shaped not by the operation of the State and the
political élite, but by the experience of working people themselves.
Miners, like other workers, tended to protest against their conditions
and pay in ways that were mostly spontaneous and unorganised –
absenteeism, job-changing and above all, small-scale unofficial and
frequently futile strikes, the significance of which has been obscured
by historians' concentration on the few really big strikes which made
national political headlines. Study of class relations at this detailed
local level reveals the overwhelming importance of specific workplace
concerns in industrial conflict. It also demonstrates the existence and
depth of divisions within the working class – divisions of language,
geographical origin, religion, culture and politics as well as divisions
between occupational groups and generations. Just as it is too simple
to view the ruling élite in Wilhelmine Germany as a united reactionary
monolith, so the view of the working class as an essentially homogeneous
social group needs further analysis and revision. The failure of attempts
to induce greater working-class unity – whether through tightly
disciplined reformist organisations or through ultra-militant spontaneity
– itself illustrates the degree to which social and political diversity
characterised even the most oppressed sections of Wilhelmine society.

The great majority of young workers in Wilhelmine Germany were
probably, as Alex Hall notes in his contribution on the early history of
the socialist youth movement, even worse off than the young militants
down the mines; and it was as a spontaneous reaction to this situation
that the Social Democratic youth movement was founded in 1904. The
attitude of the SPD hierarchy to these adolescents was deeply ambivalent. On the one hand, it desperately wanted to recruit them as

early as possible to the socialist cause, and so immunise them against
the reactionary influences to which they were exposed when they
came to do their military service. On the other hand, it was highly
suspicious of the young workers' spontaneous militancy, and also felt
that a separate youth movement was divisive. The SPD wanted youth
to join them, but they also wanted them to be strictly subordinate
once they were in the party. It was perhaps in the ambivalence of this
attitude, as Alex Hall suggests, and in the desire to suppress the
sponteneity of the reactions which had led to the creation of the youth
movement in the first place, that the SPD lost the allegiance of
proletarian youth and prepared the way for the mass defection of
young people to the Communist Party, which left the SPD in the
Weimar Republic largely a party of the middle-aged.[51]

Both these contributions suggest that while the SPD and Union
hierarchies may have become reformist and lost their militancy by
1914, the same cannot be said of important sections of the working
class, which these organisations claimed to represent. Although the
political ideas of the left-wing radicals won the overt support of only a
small minority of the working class as a whole, industrial militancy,
usually on a small scale but potentially with mass participation,
remained an ever-present possibility. The conclusion that the working
class as a whole became integrated into the Wilhelmine political system
can only be reached through confusing the proletariat with the organisation which it sustained but which, as Stephen Hickey points out in
the case of the unions, represented only a minority of workers. When
labour history is tackled from below, through the work experience, the
extent of the confusion which has resulted from looking at the subject
from above, through institutions and ideas, becomes clear. In the
final contribution to this volume, Dick Geary applies these insights to
the problem of the Revolution in which Wilhelm II was overthrown.
In fact, to confine our attention to the formal constitutional changes
of November 1918 is to underestimate vastly the scope and extent
of the German Revolution. Far from being a product of war-
weariness,[52] losing its drive and power once peace had been achieved,
the mass uprising which set off the events of the 'November
Revolution' were really only a stage in the wider process of worker
radicalisation which began before 1914 and went on until 1923. The
militancy of young workers, and especially of metalworkers, was
already expressing itself in large-scale industrial unrest, often against
the wishes of the official trade union and Social Democratic leaders,
before the outbreak of the war; in 1917—18 it cut across party

boundaries, and in 1919–23 it expressed itself in the creation of mass movements to the left of the SPD and in militant uprisings such as that of the *Ruhrkrieg* in 1920.

It seems, then, that when the German working class under Wilhelm II is examined not through its political organisations but rather through its *social* components, the picture which the 'new orthodoxy' in German history has painted of a relatively passive, socially integrated proletariat, bought off by social insurance and cowed into submission by State repression, stands in need of some modification. If the elements of an alternative continuity to that of the radical right are to be found anywhere in recent German history it is surely here, rather than in more socially conservative and politically conformist groups such as the women's movement. Of course, there is still much work to be done on the history of the German working class under Wilhelm II and in the Weimar Republic. Theoretical as well as empirical questions remain to be resolved; and the reader will notice in particular an implicit contradiction between the essay in the present volume by Stephen Hickey, who finds the coalminers of the Ruhr active and militant indeed, but concentrating their attention on bread-and-butter issues arising from their experience of work, and the contribution by Dick Geary, who argues that industrial militancy, particularly among metalworkers, involved political radicalism as well. But what both contributions do indicate is the enormous diversity of experience and attitudes among the German working class, involving not only strong contrasts between formal organisations and the rank-and-file but also sharp differences between the workers of one trade and another, and wide variations between different regions and towns or even across different parts of the same city.[53] Indeed, this diversity of experience and attitudes, characteristic of many industrialising societies, can also be established for other social classes in Wilhelmine Germany, most notably perhaps the petty-bourgeoisie, whose political position could vary from radical liberalism to right-wing extremism, as the essays in this book illustrate.[54] One lesson of this present volume, therefore, is that Wilhelmine Germany was a society of enormous complexity, a society in the throes of a very rapid transformation or series of transformations, where complicated cross-currents of social, economic and political change produced patterns of thought and action not easily comprehended in terms of a few simple formulae. It is this, indeed, that makes it such a fascinating subject for the historian. A major purpose of this book is to rehabilitate Wilhelmine society as an object of study in its own right, to demonstrate its diversity and to show something of the wealth of political and social processes that were taking place in it. Of course, it is unavoidable that some important areas have been left out of consideration; we are limited by the number of younger British scholars working on the period, and ten people cannot cover every facet of Wilhelmine society within the compass of a book devoted to presenting the results of detailed research. It is particularly to be regretted perhaps that we have no study of the Junker landowning class of East Elbian Prussia and that there are no essays in this book on institutions such as the Protestant Church or the educational system. Foreign policy, the most intensively-studied area of Wilhelmine history, has been omitted to allow for concentration on less familiar themes;[55] and it is also perhaps necessary to reiterate that the essays in the present volume concentrate on the relationship between society and politics, rather than on social history as such. All the same, despite the inevitable omissions, this book does, I believe, offer a wider coverage of German society and politics in the Wilhelmine era than any comparable collection in either English or German. More important still, the reader will find in this book discussions of most of the key concepts of the new German historiography, from *Sammlungspolitik* and social imperialism to negative integration and organised capitalism. Finally, by approaching politics from below, through the study of society, and by taking in many important areas generally neglected by historians, this book hopes to offer a broader view of Wilhelmine society and politics than is customarily presented in historical surveys or symposia, and, in doing so, to widen the scope of the debate currently in progress about the nature and significance of this crucial period in recent German history.

Notes

1. For notes on contributors, see below, pp. 287—9.
2. Further information on research into German history by British scholars can be obtained from the lists circulated by the German Historical Institute, 26 Bloomsbury Square, London.
3. For an account of the 'Fischer controversy' in English, see John A. Moses, *The Politics of Illusion* (London, 1975). Perhaps the clearest German account is by Imanuel Geiss, in his *Studien über Geschichte und Geschichtswissenschaft* (Frankfurt, 1972), pp. 108—98.
4. For an acute discussion of the 'Fischer controversy', see Arnold Sywottek, 'Die Fischer-Kontroverse', in Imanuel Geiss and Bernd-Jürgen Wendt (eds.), *Deutschland in der Weltpolitik des 19. und 20. Jahrhunderts* (Düsseldorf, 1973), pp. 19—74.
5. It is worth noting, perhaps, that not all historians who accepted the first argument went on to concur in the second; cf. the remark by John Röhl,

From Bismarck to Hitler: The Problem of Continuity in German History (London, 1971), p. xiii, that 'if precise comparisons (i.e. between Bismarckian, Wilhelmine, Weimar and Nazi Germany) are relatively easy to make when dealing with the foreign policy of German statesmen, they are virtually impossible in the field of ideas or social change'.

6. Cf. the classic exposition of the 'anti-continuity' thesis in the late Gerhard Ritter's contribution to the collection of essays issued by UNESCO under the title of *The Third Reich* (London, 1955).

7. Fischer went on to explore these reasons in his second book, *War of Illusions* (London, 1975); first published as *Krieg der Illusionen* (Dusseldorf, 1969).

8. This problem inspired a great many theoretical essays published during this period. They include Imanuel Geiss, 'Kritischer Rückblick auf Friedrich Meinecke', in Geiss, *Studien*, pp. 89–107; Wolfgang J. Mommsen, *Die Geschichtswissenschaft jenseits des Historismus* (Düsseldorf, 1971); Arnold Sywottek, *Geschichtswissenschaft in der Legitimationskrise* (*Archiv für Sozialgeschichte*, Beiheft 1); V. Rittner, 'Zur Krise der westdeutschen Historiographie', in I. Geiss *et al., Ansichten einer künftigen Geschichtswissenschaft* (Munich, 1974); Reihart Koselleck, 'Wozu noch Geschichte?', *Historische Zeitschrift* 212 (1971), pp. 1–18. This list is by no means exhaustive. The crisis came to a head in the debate over the proposal by the authorities in Hessen to abolish history as a separate subject in schools; see K. Bergmann and H.-J. Pandel (eds.), *Geschichte und Zukunft* (Frankfurt, 1975).

9. For the history of German historiography, see George Iggers, *The German Conception of History* (Middletown, Conn., 1968). For an interesting comparison between present-day English and German historical scholarship, see V.R. Berghahn, 'Looking Towards England', *The Times Literary Supplement*, 5 November 1976, p. 1401.

10. Eckart Kehr, *Der Primat der Innenpolitik. Gesammelte Aufsätze zur preussisch-deutschen Sozialgeschichte im 19. und 20. Jahrhundert*, ed. Hans-Ulrich Wehler (2nd ed., Berlin, 1970).

11. Hans-Ulrich Wehler, *Geschichte als Historische Sozialwissenschaft* (Frankfurt, 1973); Jürgen Kocka, 'Theorieprobleme der Sozial-und Wirtschaftsgeschichte', in Hans-Ulrich Wehler (ed.), *Geschichte und Soziologie* (Köln, 1972), pp. 305–30; Jürgen Kocka, 'Theorien in der Sozial-und Gesellschaftsgeschichte: Vorschläge zur historischen Schichtungsanalyse', *Geschichte und Gesellschaft* Vol. 1, No. 1 (1975), pp. 9–42; also some of the works cited in note 8, above (e.g., Mommsen).

12. For example, Dieter Groh, *Kritische Geschichtswissenschaft in emanzipatorischer Absicht* (Stuttgart, 1973); Hans-Ulrich Wehler, *Das deutsche Kaiserreich 1871–1918* (Göttingen, 1973), p. 12; and Geiss, *Studien*.

13. East German historians have also been prolific critics of the German tradition of historiography: see for example Joachim Streisand (ed.), *Studien über die deutsche Geschichtswissenschaft* 2 vols., (East Berlin, 1963–5).

14. For an example of this, compare Siegfried Mielke, *Der Hansa-Bund für Gewerbe, Handel und Industrie* (Göttingen, 1976) with East German research monographs on this period.

15. The only approach to a synthesis by a member of this school in English so far has been V.R. Berghahn, *Germany and the Approach of War in 1914* (London, 1914); some essays have been printed in English translation in James J. Sheehan (ed.), *Imperial Germany* (London, 1976).

16. *Journal of Modern History*, Vol. 48, No. 3 (September 1976), pp. 566–7; Sheehan also comments in this review on the continuing concentration of German historians on the 'commanding heights' of politics.

17. Hans-Ulrich Wehler, *Das deutsche Kaiserreich 1871–1918* (Göttingen, 1973), p. 14.
18. See the summary in Berghahn, chs. 1–2; and Martin Kitchen, *A Military History of Germany from the Eighteenth Century to the Present Day* (London, 1973).
19. Wehler, *Das deutsche Kaiserreich*, p. 60.
20. Ibid., pp. 63–9.
21. Ibid., pp. 69–72.
22. See Klaus Saul, *Staat, Industrie, Arbeiterbewegung im Deutschen Kaiserreich* (Düsseldorf, 1974), for a comprehensive detailed survey; in English, see Alex Hall, *Scandal, Sensation and Social Democracy* (Cambridge, 1977).
23. There is a brief explanation of *Staatsstreichpolitik* in Berghahn, Ch. 1, esp. pp. 13, 18, 22.
24. For the idea of political 'milieu' in Wilhelmine society, see M. Rainer Lepsius, 'Parteien und Sozialstruktur: Zum Problem der Demokratisierung der deutschen Gesellschaft', in Gerhard A. Ritter (ed.), *Deutsche Parteien vor 1918* (Köln, 1973), pp. 56–80. More generally, see Wehler, *Kaiserreich*, Ch. III.2.1. ('Ohnmacht der Parteien').
25. Wehler, *Kaiserreich*, pp. 172–9.
26. Cf. the account in ibid., pp. 135–40, entitled 'Entschädigungsleistungen zur Loyalitätssicherung. Sozialversicherung statt Sozialreform'.
27. Ibid., pp. 118–35.
28. Ibid., pp. 105–18.
29. The classic exposition of this interpretation is Eckart Kehr, *Battleship Building and Party Politics in Germany 1894–1901* (ed. and trans. P.R. and E.N. Anderson, Chicago, 1975).
30. See Kehr, *Primat der Innenpolitik*, pp. 53–63.
31. Wehler, *Kaiserreich*, pp. 227–39 ('Eine Bilanz').
32. Elements of a reinterpretation of SPD history along these lines may be found in Hans Mommsen (ed.), *Sozialdemokratie zwischen Klassenbewegung und Volkspartei* (Frankfurt, 1974).
33. Cf. the remark of A.J.P. Taylor in the preface to the 1961 edition of his book *The Course of German History*, that 'I have almost reached the point of believing that I shall not live to see a third German war; but events have an awkward trick of running in the wrong direction, just when you least expect it' (p. x). The different approaches of American and French historians might well result in a comparable shift of perspective in yet another direction if these historians were to engage in an exercise similar to the present work.
34. Cf. Iggers, *op. cit.*
35. George Iggers, *New Directions in European History* (Middletown, Conn., 1975).
36. This image was used by Hans-Gunter Zmarzlik, 'Das Kaiserreich in neuer Sicht?', *Historische Zeitschrift* 222 (1976), pp. 105–26.
37. For a synthesis of this research, see J.S. Morrill, *The Revolt of the Provinces* (London, 1976).
38. See the introduction to Raphael Samuel (ed.), *Village Life and Labour*, History Workshop Series, Vol. 1, (London, 1975).
39. E.g., the combination of local and national studies in J.R. Vincent, *The Formation of the Liberal Party 1857–1868* (London, 1966).
40. George Rudé, *The Crowd in the French Revolution* (Oxford, 1961); Richard Cobb, *The Police and the People. French Popular Protest 1789–1820* (Oxford, 1970).
41. E.H. Carr, *What is History?* (Harmondsworth, 1961), which has influenced the ideas of a whole generation of British historians, contains a useful discussion

of the role of theory.

42. See e.g. the categorisation of social history adopted in the various methodological articles by Jurgen Kocka (see note 11, above).

43. For legal and other constraints on art, writing, etc. in Victorian England in
the name of morality, see Eric Trudgill, *Madonnas and Magdalens* (London,
1976).

44. The attitude of subsequent historians is well conveyed in Kehr, *Primat*,
pp. 279–83 (a review of Bulow's memoirs).

45. For 'organised capitalism' see H.A. Winkler (ed.), *Organisierter Kapitalismus*
(Göttingen, 1974), esp. the contribution by Gerald Feldman. The definition
quoted is on the back cover.

46. Geoff Eley, '*Sammlungspolitik*, Social Imperialism and the Navy Law of
1898', *Militärgeschichtliche Mitteilungen,* Vol. 15, No. 1 (1974), pp. 29–64.

47. Thus the only two recent scholarly books on the Wilhelmine Centre Party
have been by Americans: John K. Zeender, *The German Center Party 1890–
1906* (Philadelphia, 1976) and Ronald J. Ross, *Beleaguered Tower: The
Dilemma of Political Catholicism in Wilhelmine Germany* (Notre Dame, 1976).

48. Zmarzlik, *art. cit.*

49. The classic account of this process is Carl E. Schorske, *German Social
Democracy 1905–1917: The Development of the Great Schism* (Cambridge,
Mass., 1955). I use the word 'emphasised' advisedly: the Erfurt Programme,
of course, deviated from classical Marxist theory in a number of crucial areas.

50. For an extended exposition of the implications of 'negative integration' for the
SPD, see Dieter Groh, *Negative Integration und revolutionärer Attentismus*
(Berlin, 1973).

51. Richard N. Hunt, *German Social Democracy 1919–1933* (New Haven, 1964).

52. F.L. Carsten, *Revolution in Central Europe 1918–1919* (London, 1972).

53. Cf. the introductory essay in Raphael Samuel (ed.), *Miners, Quarrymen and
Saltworkers* (History Workshop Series No. 2, London, 1977) for a detailed
discussion of this diversity in a British context.

54. Cf. David Blackbourn, 'The *Mittelstand* in German Society and Politics 1871–
1914', *Social History* 4 (1977), pp. 409–33.

55. Readers might like to note that this will be dealt with in a forthcoming book
on Anglo-German relations before 1914 by our colleague Paul M. Kennedy
(born 1945), of the University of East Anglia.

2 KAISER VERSUS CHANCELLOR: THE CRISIS OF BÜLOW'S CHANCELLORSHIP 1905–6

Terry Cole

I

Throughout the history of Wilhelmine Germany it was the relationship between the Kaiser and his successive Chancellors which lay at the heart of the constitutional system. This should not be taken to imply any ambitious claims about the role of the individual in history, nor to underestimate the fundamental importance of social and economic forces or the clash of ideologies. It is simply to recognise that, with a ruler of Wilhelm II's personality, convictions and aspirations working within – or rather confronting – a political structure which was becoming increasingly subject to democratic pressures, the Chancellor was the one man capable of maintaining some sort of constitutional equilibrium. In so far as he was successful in performing a balancing act between the autocratic tendencies of the Kaiser and the democratic tendencies of the Reichstag, a tolerable degree of political stability could be ensured. Whenever this balancing act became impossible, the political stability of the Second Reich was gravely threatened.

The attempts of successive Chancellors to maintain this equilibrium frequently induced in them moods ranging from frustration to despair. This is understandable in view of the intractable nature of the problem they faced. They had been appointed and could at any time, theoretically at least, be dismissed by a monarch who was convinced not only of his divine right to rule but also of his superhuman ability to do so on a personal basis. A precondition for the avoidance of dismissal was therefore the enthusiastic endorsement and promotion of the concept of the Kaiser's personal rule. At the same time the Chancellor's most important task was to find majorities in the Reichstag to support the passage of government legislation. This was never easy in a multi-party system in which the composition of the government in no way reflected the composition of the Reichstag. In an era when the social and political effects of industrialisation were producing in ever greater numbers Reichstag deputies who were radically opposed to the prevailing power structure, the task became more difficult. And even though the Reichstag was not exactly awash with democratic sentiment, the habits of parliamentary scrutiny and sometimes obstructionism had become well established over a generation, so that the government could hardly hope for an easy run even from its normal supporters. In their attempts to win majorities for legislation in the Reichstag, Chancellors were inevitably driven to wheel and deal with party leaders, to negotiate political compromises with them and often to associate with them on more or less informal terms in pursuit of their legislative objectives. But in so doing they were constantly in danger of awakening in the Kaiser the suspicion that they were straying from the path of vigorous monarchical rule, that they were becoming dangerously infected with parliamentarianism. If they attempted to allay the Kaiser's suspicion by indulging in celebrations of monarchical rule, they were likely to provoke the hostility of substantial sections of Reichstag opinion. Finding majorities for legislation could then become even more difficult, and the Chancellor's ability to govern was jeopardised. This was the brutal dilemma in which successive Chancellors during Wilhelm's reign found themselves trapped.

No Chancellor experienced this dilemma more acutely than Bernhard von Bülow. He was appointed Secretary of State in the Foreign Office in 1897 and he took over the Chancellorship from the aged and exhausted Hohenlohe in 1900. More than any other leading statesman in Wilhelm's reign, Bülow exhibited at the time of his appointment a firm determination to uphold the principle of monarchical rule in the way the Kaiser favoured. But within a few years he had been driven to deploy an intimidating array of weapons in his battle with the Kaiser. He began his Chancellorship with an attitude of almost obsequious servility towards the Kaiser; he ended it by mounting a campaign of almost treasonable proportions against him.

Bülow's dramatic change of attitude stemmed primarily from his realisation in 1905 and 1906 that the conduct of the Kaiser was a common element running through most of the difficult problems he faced at this time. For the Chancellor it was a period when troubles came not as single spies but in battalions. In foreign affairs, in the Reichstag, among his closest advisers and subordinates, in the court camarilla, in the streets of Berlin, he faced acute difficulties. This was a period when it became increasingly difficult for the Chancellor to maintain the constitutional equilibrium which alone made the Second Reich governable. It was for this reason that he was driven to desperate measures in an attempt to restore the viability of his Chancellorship. An analysis of the multifarious crises he faced should expose not only the motives behind Bülow's fascinating experiments with political reform in the years 1907—9 but also those features of the constitutional structure of the Second Reich which constantly threatened to lead to political paralysis.

II

In the hectic atmosphere which prevailed in Berlin in the early months of 1906, when the Moroccan crisis was drawing to its humiliating conclusion, it was not surprising that the government should be accident-prone. A blunder which occurred in January provided an ominous foretaste of the difficulties which the Chancellor was soon to encounter in his relations with the Catholic Centre Party. An interpellation had been put to Bülow by the Centre Party deputy Roeren concerning duelling in the officer corps. Distracted by so many other apparently more important matters (some of which we shall be dealing with below), Bülow asked for his reply to the interpellation to be drafted for him by an *ad hoc* committee composed of Einem, Nieberding, Posadowsky and a number of members of the Kaiser's military cabinet.[1] When they arrived at an agreed statement, it was submitted to Bülow who, clearly unaware of its controversial nature, merely initialled it without bothering to read it.[2] This statement, which was read out on the Chancellor's behalf in the Reichstag by Einem, ended with the words: 'As long as duelling is recognized by wide circles of society as a means of rehabilitating one's honour, the officer corps will be unable to tolerate in its ranks anyone who is not prepared to defend his honour with weapon in hand'.[3] This declaration was in direct conflict with the religious and moral principles of the Centre Party deputies and, if it accurately reflected the policy of the officer corps, would mean that all orthodox Catholics would necessarily be excluded from its ranks. The Centre Party was outraged that Bülow should, as they mistakenly thought, go out of his way to commend this state of affairs. Prince Arenberg, a prominent Centre Party deputy who was on close terms with the Chancellor and who played an important role as unofficial liaison officer between his party and the government, immediately drafted a letter to Bülow telling him that he had made a serious mistake in issuing this declaration. The letter was never in fact delivered because Arenberg met Loebell, Bülow's Chief of Chancellery, and was able to give him his opinions on the matter for oral transmission to the Chancellor. Arenberg said he felt that he should have been consulted in advance on the wisdom of this policy declaration, as he had been on so many others, and that if similar statements were likely to be made in the future, he would appreciate foreknowledge of this fact as he would then immediately resign his membership of the important budget committee of the Reichstag and terminate his activity as honest broker.[4] If Arenberg were to carry out his threat, Bülow would lose a powerful ally.

The reaction of Bülow's old friend, together with the fury which the Reichstag statement had provoked throughout the Centre Party, drove the already overburdened Chancellor into a state of near-despair. The influential Centre Party leader Carl Bachem reports him as having expressed himself in private in the following terms: 'If the Centre party now leaves me in the lurch, I'll be quite unable to carry on. I cannot govern without the Centre, and if I am to be treated by them in this way, I'd prefer to go.' He added that he had no children, that he valued his independence, that he had a private annual income of three hundred thousand Marks, that he had already held office for five years, and that his wife continually reminded him of the fate suffered by Richthofen, the Secretary of State in the Foreign Office, who had recently died of a stroke brought on by overwork.[5] Bülow was particularly incensed at the accusation of not being a Christian statesman; he had been brought up a devout Christian, he said, and he remained one. Neither his wife nor Loebell was able to pacify him. In subsequent private interviews with Arenberg and with the party leader Spahn, he again complained bitterly about the way he had been treated by the Centre Party, and he repeated his wish to resign. But when Spahn pointed out that not only Catholics but also many devout Protestants had been dumbfounded at the acerbity of the Reichstag statement, Bülow admitted that the last sentence had been indefensible, that it was 'an entirely irresponsible stupidity', and that if he had read it he would never have signed it. Finally Spahn was able to calm the Chancellor somewhat by offering the assurance that the Centre Party did not wish to create too many difficulties for him over this affair, and that it could be readily smoothed over if an early opportunity were taken to make it clear that Catholics would not be excluded from the officer corps or officer reserve.[6]

This episode was relatively trivial in itself. In the whole of 1905 there had only been one duel involving members of the officer corps.[7] Furthermore the outrage amongst Catholics could easily be dispelled by issuing a revised statement as Spahn had suggested. But in the longer term, as a pointer to the future, the row was of greater significance. In his interviews with the Centre Party leaders, Bülow may well have exaggerated his anger; and his threats to resign had a hollow ring about them. This was no doubt a tactical ploy to bamboozle them into restoring tranquillity in their party. But at the same time this episode served to bring home to Bülow how dependent he was on the Centre

Party, and how problematical a withdrawal or even diminution of their support would be. The key to the first five years of his Chancellorship had been friendly relations with the Centre Party. It had been with their support that he had succeeded in passing most of his important legislation through the Reichstag. If these relations were to be severely disrupted, he would require some wholly new parliamentary strategy to preserve his ability to govern. With the balance of parties in the Reichstag as it stood, however, it was evident that he had to do all he could to ensure that the Centre Party remained in the government fold. There was no alternative available in the current Reichstag, and at this stage a dissolution was not under consideration. It was therefore true, as Bülow had said, that he could not govern without the Centre. But two main factors militated against an indefinite prolongation of these friendly relations. The first was that the sort of blunder which had recently led to the row over duelling was always liable to recur, and each recurrence was likely to produce an increasingly bitter confrontation. This was especially the case in the early months of 1906 when the Centre Party went on nursing its grievance to some extent, and when Bülow was working under the strain imposed by the vicissitudes of foreign policy. The government had therefore to guard against alienating the Centre Party by accident. But the second factor making it unlikely that the previous good relations could be preserved was one over which Bülow or the government could exercise very little control.

Throughout 1905 and 1906 the ideological tone of the Centre Party was being transformed. For many of the older members of the party and for a majority of its leaders, memories of the *Kulturkampf* were still vivid. Their foremost wish was to avoid a return to the bitterness of that era. They tended to play down their special position as Catholics because they wanted to merge as far as possible into the ranks of the respectable majority. Any signs of militancy in the party could easily undo in weeks the work of years in building up their image as a group of responsible men of affairs. But that image was now being challenged from within the party as a new generation of deputies, many of them from the South or South-West German states, were rising in prestige and influence. For these younger and more radical deputies the *Kulturkampf* had faded into distant recollections of their youth; it was not locked in their minds as a permanent warning against imprudence. Nor did many of them wish to achieve the positions of respectability so eagerly sought after by their older colleagues. Liberated from the past which so dominated the minds of the party establishment, they were a brash and above all professional group of politicians who disagreed profoundly with the party leadership about the most effective ways of exercising political influence.

Pre-eminent among these younger Centre Party deputies was Matthias Erzberger. This energetic, able and intensely ambitious politician from Württemberg, destined to play a prominent role at a number of turning-points in German history, had first entered the Reichstag in 1903. By 1906 he was managing to create alarm and indignation in his own party leaders, and in the government, in approximately equal proportions.[8] A typical example of the bitterness which was developing in the party, largely as a result of Erzberger's activities, occurred in March. In a Reichstag debate on the colonial budget Spahn corrected Erzberger on a number of points he had made in his speech, and he then went on to repudiate on behalf of the party the campaign which Erzberger was currently mounting against the colonial administration. He said that Erzberger spoke on these matters purely on his own account, to which the latter's prompt reply was that this was precisely the case for Spahn as well.[9] Erzberger and his associates were furious at what they regarded as the authoritarian and peremptory tone which Spahn had adopted in public towards a fellow Centre Party deputy, and they made their feelings known at a caucus meeting held immediately after the debate.[10] To the party leaders, however, Spahn's magisterial rebuke had seemed fully justified:

> Privately and in caucus meetings people have for months been desperately trying to exercise an influence over Erzberger. This seems to have had no results and consequently the older, more sensitive members of the caucus all agreed that Spahn had been right when he finally moved against Erzberger. For the moment this seems to have had some useful effect but I fear it won't last long.[11]

Whether or not Spahn's rebuke had been justified, Bachem's fear that its effects would be short-lived certainly was. These divisions in the Centre Party were increasingly finding their expression over colonial policies, and the assault being mounted on them by the radical wing of the party led by Erzberger.[12] Within a few days of the altercation between Erzberger and Spahn this issue again came to the fore, and this time, while intensifying the internal party squabble, it also had important repercussions within the government.

III

On 21 March 1906 the budget committee of the Reichstag rejected a
government proposal to establish a separate Reich office for colonial
affairs with its own Secretary of State.[13] Bülow had tried to secure a
majority for this proposal for two main reasons: first, he felt that from
a technical point of view the efficiency of the colonial administration
would be improved if it was removed from the responsibility of the
Secretary of State in the Foreign Office, a view with which the new
and over-burdened incumbent of that post, Heinrich von Tschirschky,
was in full agreement.[14] Second, Bülow was aware of the rumours
currently circulating, possibly spread by the Erzberger circle, that
the Kaiser's favoured candidate for the post of Secretary of State in
the proposed Colonial Office, Prince Ernst zu Hohenlohe-Langenburg,
who was at this time Director of the Colonial Division in the Foreign
Office, was likely to replace him as Chancellor if he failed to obtain a
majority for the proposal. The Kaiser had set his heart on the project
and was prepared to intimidate Bülow into forcing it through by
threatening to remove him from office.[15] For the Chancellor, therefore,
motives of genuine *raison d'etat* became intertwined with personal
self-interest.

The reason why a majority of the budget committee rejected the
proposal to establish an independent office for colonial affairs had
little to do with the intrinsic merits of the idea. Few disagreed that
there were solid reasons why such a reform should be introduced. But
the candidate lined up for the post of Secretary of State in the new
office was profoundly antipathetic to a large number of Centre Party
members of the budget committee. He was 'sharply Protestant',[16]
and in his capacity as a leading member of the Evangelical League he
had conducted himself in a manner offensive to Catholics on a number
of occasions. In spite of the fact that he was a former Director of the
Colonial League, few claimed that he possessed much in the way of
professional knowledge or expertise to qualify him for the projected
post. Moreover, it was widely felt, not only in the ranks of the Centre
Party, that he lacked the qualities of strength and determination
necessary to undertake the thoroughgoing reform of the colonial
administration in Berlin, and in the colonies themselves, which the
recent series of scandalous revelations made a pressing necessity, and
over which, of course, Hohenlohe had been presiding in his capacity as
Colonial Director.[17] Added to these doubts about his abilities, and to
dislike of his religious prejudices, was the fact that he was a Prince
and a known favourite of the Kaiser. For the more democratically-

minded members of the budget committee this disqualified him even further for the post.[18] For these reasons the majority of the budget committee of the Reichstag rejected the proposal.

This did not put an end to the matter, however. It was open to the plenary session of the Reichstag to reincorporate this provision in the Bill at its second reading, which was due to take place on 28 March. This opening led Bülow to engage far more energetically than hitherto in a campaign to push the Bill through. The Kaiser was putting pressure on him to succeed in establishing the new office, and the Chancellor was well aware of the dangers to his own position if he failed. He was thus galvanised into action; and so were the Centre Party leaders. If they had been upset and alienated by the duelling controversy in January, they nevertheless regarded it as wholly in their interests to do all they could to preserve as Chancellor a man with whom they had had such a productive understanding in the past. The current rumours concerning the vulnerability of Bülow's position alarmed them all the more in view of the fact that their arch-enemy Hohenlohe was being tipped as his probable successor. That Hohenlohe's position should be made more powerful by his installation as head of an independent colonial office was distasteful to them; but the thought of his being appointed Reich Chancellor was infinitely worse. At all events, after the defeat of the provision by the budget committee, Bülow began operating with the high degree of resourcefulness which he could always muster when his own position was threatened, and Spahn and the other Centre Party leaders abandoned the equivocal posture they had hitherto adopted on this particular colonial question. Bülow and his old Centre Party allies were determined to achieve the success in the Reichstag which had eluded the government in the budget committee. This involved the leaders of the party in a campaign to defeat the wishes of a substantial section of the party's membership, but the bitterness within the party was now beginning to make such considerations irrelevant.[19]

On 22 March, immediately after the vote in the budget committee had been announced, Bülow summoned Count Lerchenfeld, the Bavarian envoy to Berlin, to ask him whether he could bring his influence to bear on Bavarian members of the Centre Party to persuade them to vote in favour of the controversial proposal in the forthcoming Reichstag debate.[20] When Lerchenfeld reminded Bülow that they would not be arriving in Berlin until just before the debate, the Chancellor asked whether the Bavarian Minister-President Podewils might be prevailed upon to do something to this effect in Munich before the deputies travelled northwards. Lerchenfeld communicated and commended this request, and Podewils indicated his readiness to do whatever he could in conjunction with the Bavarian Centre Party leader Oerterer.[21] A further meeting took place on 23 March, this time between Bülow, Lerchenfeld and Spahn. Spahn argued that the only way to secure a majority for the Bill would be if the Social Democrats abstained and only a small number of Centre Party deputies attended the debate. The Conservative and National Liberal parties would then be able to outvote the Centre, most of whose members would still feel compelled by reason of conscience to oppose the Bill. In the light of Spahn's analysis, Lerchenfeld again wrote to Podewils, in a tone of mounting impatience, explaining that the strategy now desired was not to convert the Bavarian Centre Party deputies to support the Bill, but to persuade them to stay away from Berlin altogether.[22] We see here again the lengths to which the establishment of the party was willing to go to avoid a further deterioration in its relations with the government and weakening of the position of the Chancellor. As it turned out, these manoeuvres proved successful. On 28 March the Bill did pass through the Reichstag on the second reading by 127 to 110 votes. This slender victory for the government was achieved because an overwhelming majority of the Centre Party deputies were indeed absent, including almost all the Bavarians, and also because the radical liberals, who had voted against the main proposal in the budget committee, now voted in favour of it in the Reichstag, a conversion which reflected the longer-term transformation being wrought at this time within the three Left-Liberal parties.[23]

This seeming victory for Bülow and the government was to be not only slender but also short-lived. The third reading of the Bill took place on 26 May. In the intervening period the Erzberger group had reinforced their case against the colonial administration, and in the debate the extent of the financial mismanagement and other more unsavoury features of the administration became more apparent. This in itself was probably enough to tilt the balance against the Bill. But also in this intervening period Bülow had been out of action, convalescing in his holiday home on the North Sea island of Nordeney after his collapse in the Reichstag on 5 April, an important personal reverse which will be referred to below. The manoeuvres of March could therefore not be repeated in May because of the incapacitation of the central participant. The result was that the Bill was defeated at its third reading by 142 to 119 votes.[24]

For the Chancellor this was a critical defeat. He knew that his dramatic collapse in the Reichstag had set the Kaiser and some of his intimates wondering about his fitness to continue in office. He knew that the recent humiliating outcome of the Moroccan crisis had damaged his reputation, even though he was convinced that this outcome was primarily the consequence of the Kaiser's indiscretions. Just a few days before the Reichstag debate he had assured the Kaiser of his loyalty in the following terms: 'It is my greatest joy to carry out Your Majesty's intentions and to clear a path for Your Majesty's great enterprises.'[25] But now the outcome of the debate had demonstrated to the Kaiser that his Chancellor was unable to carry out his intentions even in this matter which had become dear to his heart. The Kaiser was 'outraged' at the intransigence of the Centre Party.[26] He telegraphed Bülow on 28 May asserting that the Centre Party was 'arm in arm' with the Social Democrats.[27] He attempted to defy the vote in the Reichstag by ordering that the construction of the railway from Kubub to Keetmanshoop, funds for which had also been refused on 28 May, should go ahead by using the military budget and military personnel.[28] His anger with the Centre Party was such that he ordered the Prussian Minister of Justice Beseler to make it clear to Spahn that in the current circumstances he would not be allowed to retain his appointment as president of the *Oberlandesgericht* in Kiel unless he laid down his Reichstag mandate.[29] He again sent a telegram to Bülow informing him that the army was 'incensed' at the 'unpatriotic attitude' of the Centre Party.[30] And with each day that passed, the tone of the Imperial messages to Bülow became sharper: 'Are we then powerless to shield our civil service and officer corps from this habitual backstairs plotter, calumniator and slanderer Erzberger?'[31] It was clear that the Kaiser considered that Bülow was either unable or unwilling to take appropriately energetic measures against those whom he held responsible for wrecking one of his great enterprises.

In response to this series of increasingly impassioned communications from the Kaiser, Bülow wrote at some length on 17 July:

I entirely share Your Majesty's indignation over the unbelievable slanders and insinuations of the opponents of our colonial policies, and I have issued strict instructions that prosecutions should be initiated against those responsible for unproven imputations and exemplary sentences should be sought. Erzberger's conduct is intolerable, and it is disapproved of by his political friends. Apparently he gets his material from civil servants who have been dismissed from the colonial division, perhaps too from some who are still there. But I have also taken drastic measures against unpardonable actions which have taken place in the past in the colonial division. . . The present situation does not offer us any chance of attacking the Centre party as such because Erzberger is more intimate with some liberals than he is with the Centre party leaders. The latter have long been jealous of him, and he is troublesome to them. . . It is urgently necessary to introduce fundamental changes into the personnel of the colonial division so that order is established there and Erni Hohenlohe is given proper support.[32]

Whereas the Kaiser blamed the intransigence and unpatriotic obstructionism of the Centre Party as a whole for the failure to estabish an independent Reich office for colonial affairs — and Bülow's inability to overcome their opposition — the Chancellor was clearly trying to awaken a more discriminating attitude in him. Bülow had by this time good cause to know that the Centre Party was by no means ideologically monolithic or strategically united. A report had recently appeared in the *Kölnische Volkszeitung* which succinctly analysed the nature of the division within the party. The various confrontations which had taken place between Spahn and Erzberger, the report claimed, were simply the personal eruptions of an underlying difference of attitude. The two groups were easily distinguishable:

> On the one side we have the diplomatic group whose appetite has been whetted by the success of the Centre Party as a government party, a group which is willing to make many concessions and compromises for the sake of the sweet sensation of having a direct influence on the course of the Reich's development, concessions and compromises without which such influence would be impossible. . . On the other side we have the group of wild radicals, whose attentions are directed more downwards than up.[33]

By delivering private and public denunciations of the Centre Party as a whole, by hounding Spahn as well as Erzberger, the Kaiser was in danger of healing this breach in the party by converting them all into 'wild radicals'.

Bülow was desperately anxious to avoid alienating the moderate wing of the party because without their support he could hardly hope to go on governing. He sought to deter the Kaiser from giving further public expression of his indignation. And in an attempt to bring about an improvement, or at least a clarification, of his relations with the party, he invited a number of the moderate Centre Party leaders to visit him in Nordeney in September.[34] But these manoeuvres were taking place against a most unpromising background. The Kaiser felt that Bülow had not recovered his strength after his collapse in April. He wanted a Chancellor who would subdue the Centre Party, not negotiate compromises with them, and when he read in the *Korrespondenz Wedekind*, a news digest, of the confidential discussions that Bülow was conducting with the Centre Party leaders and other political figures, he ordered the Chancellor to break them off.[35] He was thus preventing the development of a new strategy by which the government could govern. This prompted Bülow to write to the Kaiser in the following month:

> Government and parliament must remain two separate camps with clearly delineated functions. It is the government's duty to resist the desire of parliaments to extend their influence and encroachment. Similarly I have always been very cautious in my intercourse with deputies, not only in the choice of personalities but also in my disclosures. But it is impossible to dispense with such personal contact entirely. For instance I must now take Spahn to task and make it clear to him that these attempted incursions by individual Centre party deputies into the affairs of the colonial service and the misuse of misappropriated official documents must absolutely stop.[36]

Bülow's carefully worded letter was a further attempt to educate the Kaiser in the realities of government. It was also a tactful expression of his growing frustration that the difficulties posed by the split in the Centre Party were being needlessly exacerbated by the Kaiser's blustering response to the failure of the colonial Bill. By his conduct the Kaiser was rendering the task of government immeasurably more difficult.

IV

The Kaiser's involvement in Germany's foreign policy provided similar problems for the Chancellor. The previous year had witnessed two major diplomatic policies being undermined by the Kaiser's impulsive interference. In June 1905 he had assured a French delegation that he wished to arrive at an understanding with France over the Moroccan question, and that he in no way contemplated the use of force to resolve this or any other issue between the two countries.[37] This assurance meant that the French no longer needed to offer what would in effect be unnecessary concessions over Morocco, and after June their resolve stiffened perceptibly. By his indiscretion the Kaiser had rendered ineffective the policy of firmness which Bülow and the powerful Foreign Office official Friedrich von Holstein had been pursuing in their attempt to drive a wedge between France and Britain and raise the diplomatic prestige of Germany. In July of the same year the Kaiser met Nicholas II of Russia in the latter's yacht in the Bay of Björkö in Finland. In the enthusiasm of conducting high policy with his cousin and fellow autocrat, the Kaiser changed a carefully prepared draft treaty between the two countries in such a way as to make it worthless for Germany.[38] When Bülow learned of this he was so angry that he submitted his resignation.[39] This threw the Kaiser into a panic. He was 'deeply aggrieved' at Bülow's wish to resign, and it was anyway incomprehensible to him as Bülow enjoyed his full confidence.[40] Bülow explained the situation in a memorandum to the Foreign Office recounting what he had told the Kaiser:

> I had not asked to be allowed to resign because of a temporary surge of emotion, nor out of obstinacy and certainly not out of a wounded sense of pride. I had done so because I was responsible before the German people for the course of our foreign policy. I could not carry this responsibility if His Majesty, without seeking my advice, were to introduce changes. . . in so decisive a text as the draft treaty had been. I would remain in office only as long as I could serve the country. If this were made impossible for me, I would go. I would make a final decision only after I had had a personal interview with the Kaiser.[41]

The Kaiser was on this occasion intimidated by Bülow's threat to resign. He agreed to seek a revision of the treaty in the sense favoured by Bülow, and relations between Kaiser and Chancellor were temporarily patched up. But the Kaiser soon sought to regain the initiative in foreign policy.

In September and October he was at his hunting retreat at Rominten. There he received the Russian Foreign Minister Count Witte and, on the basis of discussions with him, he issued instructions through Bülow concerning the conduct of German diplomats in Paris who were engaged in drawing up the agenda for the Algeciras Conference, the international gathering which had been called to resolve the Moroccan problem. In acting in this way, the Kaiser could not be said to be breaching his constitutional obligations as such, but he was certainly placing a provocative interpretation upon them.[42] And the Chancellor's suspicions were further aroused by the role played by Prince Philipp Eulenburg in these Rominten negotiations. Eulenburg had long been on intimate social terms with the Kaiser, he had been amongst the closest of his unofficial advisers on all diplomatic and political matters, but he had resigned from the diplomatic service in 1902 and therefore the Kaiser's relationship with him was purely informal. In spite of this Eulenburg was clearly playing a crucial role. Witte wrote in his memoirs that 'most of the time he [the Kaiser] sat on the arm of the chair occupied by Count Eulenburg, embracing him, as it were, with his right arm'.[43] When Witte left Rominten, the Kaiser suggested that he keep in contact by writing to Eulenburg, thus by-passing regular diplomatic channels. 'Writing to him is the same as writing to me, and his replies are my replies', the Kaiser told Witte.[44] The Kaiser did inform Bülow of this remarkable arrangement. In a letter from Liebenberg, Eulenburg's castle, where he had gone after his stay in Rominten, the Kaiser enclosed the first report received from Witte through these channels, and added: 'When you have read the enclosed, please send it back to Phili'.[45]

At the end of the Algeciras Conference in March 1906, the Kaiser strengthened the impression that Eulenburg had been playing a prominent role in the formation of German policy, though one of which the Chancellor was only dimly aware, by conferring on him the Order of the Black Eagle. He also conferred this honour on the chief official delegate to the conference, Radowitz, but the Chancellor was clearly indignant that the Kaiser should not only place reliance on the advice and diplomatic activity of a man who was constitutionally entitled to offer neither, but that he should also signal that he had done so by conferring upon this man the highest honour he had to bestow.

Eulenburg's unofficial entrance on the German diplomatic scene did nothing to improve the performance. Germany's handling of the Moroccan crisis was almost universally agreed to have been disastrous. A policy which had been conceived by Bülow and Holstein to raise Germany's international prestige and reverse the trend towards the diplomatic encirclement of the country had in fact resulted in humiliation and a strengthening of the ties binding Germany's enemies. Bülow held the Kaiser primarily responsible for the ruin of his foreign policy, but it fell to the Chancellor to muster some sort of defence in the Reichstag debate on 5 April. He ended his speech with the words:

It was a rather difficult hill that we have had to climb. Many traverses were not without danger. A time of trouble and unrest lies behind us. I believe we can now look to the future with a greater sense of ease. The Algeciras Conference has, I believe, concluded in a manner equally acceptable to Germany and France and useful for all civilized nations.[46]

It was during exchanges after Bülow had concluded his speech, when the government's record was being lambasted by the Social Democrat leader Bebel, that Bülow collapsed. Exhaustion, demoralisation and perhaps the strain of recognising the gap between the rhetoric of his speech and the reality of Germany's international position, had taken their toll.[47]

The Centre Party deputy Carl Bachem had an interesting encounter in the Reichstag immediately after this dramatic event:

> Immediately after Bülow had fallen unconscious I met Undersecretary of State (in the Foreign Office) von Mühlberg in the Reichstag restaurant. I told him straight to his face that I thought the restless Kaiser bore a large share of the responsibility for Bülow's exhaustion because he made so many demands on him. Then Mühlberg blurted out: 'You're absolutely right! Every day one and a half to two hours. And if you only knew of the plans he dreams up! And then added to this the endless reports and communications whenever His Majesty is away. It has become utterly intolerable here. The whole business in the Foreign Office cannot continue like this. It must be organized differently, otherwise everything will collapse'. I replied: 'How do you envisage this reorganization then? The main cause of the Chief's exhaustion remains indefinitely, and that's the Kaiser'. Mühlberg did not reply.[48]

V

In order to recover from his collapse in the Reichstag in April, Bülow left Berlin in May to spend the summer in Nordeney, his holiday retreat. He did not return to Berlin until October, and this prolonged absence provided his opponents with an ideal opportunity to intrigue against him.[49] From the moment of his departure rumours abounded concerning his disagreements with the Kaiser, the damage done to his prestige by the miserable outcome of the Moroccan crisis, the impasse he must shortly face in the Reichstag, and now was added uncertainty about his health.[50] An article in the *Kölnische Volkszeitung* on 22 May 1906 speculated on a list of possible successors should the Chancellor be forced into resignation. These included Hohenlohe-Langenburg, against whose name Bülow wrote 'Rubbish!' when he read the report, and, much more ominously, Philipp Eulenburg, to which his reaction was 'Aha!'.[51] Friedrich von Holstein, now in retirement but retaining close links with political developments, thought that Bülow's chances of remaining in office were slight,[52] and he evidently felt that he was not making a sufficiently determined stand. In a letter to his cousin in June, he complained that what Germany needed was 'a strong hand, an energetic Reich Chancellor', and he went on: 'and this is what the Kaiser will never have, at least not voluntarily. This is the danger'.[53]

The tactical disadvantage in which Bülow found himself persuaded him that it would be prudent to mount a holding operation until he could return to Berlin to take up the cudgels in earnest. In July he wrote to the Kaiser explaining his views on European historical developments over the previous century. He found that 'earthly things develop not in a straight line but in oscillations, or like the ebb and flood of the tide'.[54] He illustrated this principle by tracing the alternation of autocratic and democratic tendencies in modern European history, and he concluded that, after the great events of 1866 and 1870, 'the opinion was widespread that a strong monarch and a skilled minister were more valuable than liberal institutions, democratic tendencies and parliamentary trivialities'.[55] It is not difficult to understand why, in the vulnerable situation in which he found himself in the summer of 1906, Bülow should have deemed it expedient to reassure the Kaiser of his belief in the value of a strong monarchy, nor miss the opportunity of reminding him that a skilled minister was likewise not without his worth.

In the same month a scandal erupted in Berlin which seemed relatively trivial at first, but which developed into yet another battle between the Kaiser and Bülow. An official in charge of the Imperial Commissary Department, Major Fischer, was arrested and accused of accepting bribes from the firm of Tippelskirch, which provided the bulk of the supplies for the German troops stationed in South-West Africa. A press campaign suggested that the Prussian Minister of Agriculture Viktor von Podbielski was implicated in this corruption because he had helped organise the firm before his ministerial appointment, and on taking up office he had transferred his financial interests in the firm to his wife.[56] By early September this campaign had reached a peak, and Bülow decided that, as so many doubts had been cast upon the minister's integrity, there was no alternative for him but to resign. The Kaiser, on the other hand, responded differently. He was determined that no minister should be hounded out of office as a result of press or public pressure, and though he was not enamoured of what he knew of Podbielski's business methods and connections, he insisted that police investigations alone must be allowed to decide whether the minister had committed any offence.[57] When these investigations were complete, the Kaiser decided that there were in fact no grounds for demanding Podbielski's resignation, though he did order him to sever all his links with Tippelskirch immediately.[58]

In spite of the Kaiser's decision, Bülow remained firmly convinced that it was impossible for Podbielski to remain in office,[59] a reaction which led the Kaiser to insist categorically that he should. The issue was further complicated for the Chancellor by the fact that Podbielski, who had always had strong links with the agrarians, was at this time seeking an increase in the price of meat, a move which was inevitably popular with the producers.[60] This meant that Bülow was upsetting many sections of Conservative opinion in the Reichstag and Prussian Landtag by seeking to precipitate the minister's resignation. The Bavarian envoy Lerchenfeld reported on 9 November that the Kaiser's determination to appoint and dismiss his ministers independent of any interference from whatever quarter was well known, as was his small regard for public opinion and parliamentary considerations. He went on:

> His Majesty is deeply offended that the Chancellor has interfered in his Imperial prerogatives, and even if Herr von Podbielski is allowed to go — because he must go — the Chancellor's position in regard to His Majesty has suffered badly because of it. If the Chancellor had not been indisposed during the Summer, he would no doubt have been in a better position to arrange the affair more favourably. But because he was indisposed he has seen little of the Kaiser, and what is more, and this should not be underestimated, the Chancellor's illness appears to have provided certain circles with the opportunity they desired to work against him.[61]

Lerchenfeld then considered the support which Podbielski enjoyed from the Conservatives and concluded that this was a disadvantage to Bülow, but one which he would probably be able to overcome:

> The real and dangerous opponents of Prince Bülow [he continued] are to be sought in other, non-parliamentary circles. One can guess who these persons are, but one cannot name them. As long as the Chancellor stood in untroubled favour with His Majesty, they held back; now they advance on His Majesty. . . . At present I believe I can report as certain the fact that the relationship between His

Majesty the Kaiser and the Reich Chancellor has suffered a heavy blow. One can hope that when the Podbielski crisis has been resolved by the minister's resignation, these relations will regain their equilibrium, but they will almost certainly never become as intimate as they were until this Summer because His Majesty does not easily forget encroachments on his prerogatives.[62]

In making his determined stand against the Kaiser over the Podbielski affair, Bülow was reasserting the authority of his office. It was indeed the Kaiser's constitutional prerogative to appoint and dismiss his ministers at will, but the Chancellor's standing was inevitably diminished if the Kaiser refused to remove from office a minister whose continued presence in the government would be damaging. Bülow was unwilling to bow to the Kaiser's pressure. And in this he was not alone. As the Prussian Minister of War assured the Baden envoy Berkheim, it had become a question of 'Podbielski or the whole of the rest of the Prussian Ministry of State'.[63]

Podbielski did in fact resign from office immediately after Lerchenfeld had written his report, but far from this bringing about a return of equilibrium in relations between Bülow and the Kaiser, in these early days of November they reached their nadir.

VI

The renewed crisis in November concerned the related issues of the Kaiser's personal rule and the camarilla of unofficial advisers who surrounded him, it seemed to some, like a dense cloud. Numerous press reports referred to the fact that the Kaiser was making a further visit to Eulenburg's castle from 7 to 10 November. Plans were afoot here, it was claimed, to bring about radical changes in the upper echelons of the government. A Vice-Chancellor was to be appointed who would remove the heavy burden of work from the reportedly still ailing Bülow, and Bülow would then be gradually eased out of office. Thereafter the Kaiser himself would take over the conduct of foreign policy with the assistance of Tschirschky, and the new Chancellor would set about an energetic campaign of repression on the domestic front. The candidate for this new-style Chancellorship was the Chief of the General Staff Helmuth von Moltke.[64]

The circumstances in which this plot was being hatched were particularly alarming to Bülow. The long-standing intimacy between the Kaiser and Eulenburg had been dangerously manifested in the latter stages of the Moroccan crisis, as we have already seen. Now the

Liebenberg circle, which on this occasion included Kuno Moltke, Freiherr von Varnbüler, General von Leszczynski and an official of the French Embassy, Raymond Lecomte, seemed intent on recasting the Imperial government.[65] That these plans were not merely press rumours is confirmed by Berkheim and Lerchenfeld, both of whom were invariably well-informed.[66] It was clear that Bülow's Chancellorship was heading for an inglorious end unless he could quickly mount an effective counter-attack against these intrigues.

A central motive in Eulenburg's orchestration of this plot was financial. As German Ambassador to Vienna until 1902 he had run up substantial debts, and his fondness for fine living had done nothing to diminish these debts since. An interlude of financial tranquillity had been achieved when he managed to marry off his eldest son to the daughter of a rich Austrian industrialist two years previously. He had managed to pay off his debts, but now the financial advantages of the marriage were accruing exclusively to his son, and Eulenburg was in difficulties again.[67] In order to overcome these financial embarrassments he desperately wanted to be appointed *Statthalter* in Alsace-Lorraine, a post which happily combined prestige with a very substantial income. But Bülow was adamant that Eulenburg should never again hold any official post, so the fulfilment of Eulenburg's ambitions depended upon the removal of the Chancellor.[68]

The reasons why Bülow was determined to frustrate Eulenburg's ambitions are not difficult to unravel. First, as self-styled leader of the camarilla, he represented a most formidable threat to the continuation of Bülow's Chancellorship. Even if the current intrigues were to fail, it would probably only be a matter of time before they were resumed. Second, by inspiring or reinforcing the Kaiser's adherence to certain positions and doctrines, notably in the realm of foreign policy, Eulenburg was rendering the task of responsible government ever more difficult. The camarilla's involvement in the campaign to advance Hohenlohe-Langenburg and retain Podbielski had also run counter to the wishes of the Chancellor. Third, rumours had long been circulating about the homosexual activities of Eulenburg and other members of the camarilla. The scandal which would have been provoked if Eulenburg had returned to the service of the State would have added a new dimension to Bülow's problems, and he was willing to forestall this prospect by feeding damaging material about Eulenburg to Maximilian Harden, the campaigning editor of *Die Zukunft*. Harden launched what was to become a protracted press and legal assault on Eulenburg and the camarilla.[69] By exposing Eulenburg to the glare of unfavourable publicity, Bülow hoped to force him to abandon his ambitions by seeking refuge in obscurity.[70] In December, sensing the lengths to which Harden was willing to go to destroy his political influence, Eulenburg negotiated with Harden through an intermediary. He agreed to go into temporary exile and left for Territet on Lake Geneva. This exile was in fact to prove short-lived because Eulenburg returned to Berlin in January to attend a Chapter of the Black Eagle, an action which provoked Harden into a resumption of his attacks.[71]

In spite of the fact that the dangers posed by Eulenburg's influence over the Kaiser had not been wholly eradicated, Bülow could rest reasonably secure in the knowledge that Harden's campaign had the camarilla decidedly on the run. The Kaiser as yet remained in ignorance of the scandals swirling around the heads of his chosen intimates, but they themselves recognised the dangers well enough. Lecomte was sent back to Paris, Eulenburg, Kuno Moltke and the others retreated. It seemed as if for a while at least Bülow's position would not be assailed from this particular quarter.

The real danger of the camarilla had consisted in its influence over the Kaiser. While he remained determined to extend and consolidate the realm of his personal rule, the threat of camarilla politics could never be far distant, the position of the Chancellor and other ministers could never be secure, and the task of responsible government would remain extremely difficult. Bülow now therefore turned his attention to this central aspect of his problem, and while he had been content to operate against the camarilla behind the scenes, the focus of his attack now shifted. On 14 November, the day after the Reichstag reconvened after the long summer recess, Bülow made his first parliamentary appearance since his collapse in April. As if to underline the vigorous state of his health, he made a speech lasting over two hours at the end of which he turned to a topic which had been raised by many of the earlier speakers in the debate. What he had to say is worth quoting at some length:

> I once said in this House that a conscientious Reich Chancellor who is aware of his moral responsibilities will not remain in office if he is unable to prevent things happening which, according to his dutiful estimation, are seriously and permanently damaging to the welfare of the Reich. Had such things occurred, you would no longer see me in this place, for whatever you may think, I do not wish to cling to office – of that you may be sure. . . . Here in Germany ministers are not the organs of parliament and its majority at any one time;

they are rather the representatives of the Crown. Government
directives are not the directives of a minister independent of the
Monarch and dependent on a majority in parliament, they are rather
the government directives of the Monarch. The corrective in these
circumstances, and the guarantee of the constitutional conduct of
affairs, consists in the fact that these government directives of the
Monarch are only effective in so far as he is able to find a minister
willing to carry them out on his own responsibility, a minister who
can refuse to carry them out, who can explain to the Monarch that
if he wants to do or say something or other, then he — the minister —
can no longer remain in office. How far, Gentlemen, a minister
should defend the personal participation, and expressions of opinion
and feeling, on the part of the Monarch with his own responsibility is
a matter for his political judgement, for his sense of obligation towards
Crown and nation, and this belongs in the realm of political impon-
derabilia. I can very well imagine that a minister might find that the
exaggerated personal participation of a sovereign, that an over-
stressed monarchical subjectivism, that too frequent an appearance
of a Monarch without the cloak of ministerial responsibility. . . is
not compatible with monarchical interests. . .   and that he cannot
carry this responsibility before the Crown, the nation and history. . .
The German people do not want a shadow-Kaiser, they want a
Kaiser of flesh and blood. The participation and personal expression
of a strong personality, which our Kaiser is, as even his opponents
will admit, does not mean that the constitution is being breached.
Name me a single case where our Kaiser has set himself against the
constitution! I believe you cannot name me such a case now, nor
will you ever be able to, for I am convinced that our Kaiser will
always conscientiously observe the constitution, as is his duty. . . .
And finally, Gentlemen, Deputy Wiemer also spoke of camarilla.
Camarilla is no German word. Camarilla: that means an ugly, alien,
poisonous plant, and no one has ever planted it in Germany without
causing great harm to the people. . . . But our Kaiser is much too
straight a character, and he has much too clear a head, to wish to
seek advice on political affairs other than from within his own
sense of duty and from the circle of his authorized advisers.[72]

The Kaiser's political antennae were sensitive enought to pick up the
true message of Bülow's remarks, which amounted to a public warning to
him and to the camarilla. He was predictably furious when he read press
reports of the Chancellor's speech. On a copy of the *Frankfurter Zeitung*

he wrote: 'That was wrong and imprudent', and on a copy of the
National-Zeitung: 'That was incautious and not right' and 'Would have
been better left unsaid because it will be wrongly interpreted and people
will make political capital out of it'.[73] In his memoirs Bülow recalls that
he answered these 'irritable and mistrustful marginal notes' by telling
the Kaiser that

> for weeks I had had to make myself a breakwater against much
> criticism and numerous attacks on the throne, that I had turned these
> attacks against myself, and had certainly succeeded in improving the
> state of public opinion. I added that I would continue to do my
> duty, would shield the throne, and endeavour, to the best of my
> abilities, to ward off everything which might seem painful or harmful
> to His Majesty.
>
> 'As to the present discontent', I added, 'whatever Your Majesty
> may think, the best-contrived press campaign would never have been
> able to produce it had there not been something there to build on.
> The great majority of the German people is monarchist. But on the
> other hand our people are very sensitive to anything that savours
> of absolutism. . . . I beg you to believe that my speeches and
> suggestions are dictated by my deep solicitude and watchful care for
> Your Majesty.' In the margin of this the Kaiser wrote: 'Agreed.
> Thanks very much. But I don't intend to change, so they'll have to
> go on abusing me'.[74]

No doubt Bülow would have been dispirited by the continued intransigence exhibited by the Kaiser, but the fact remained that a storm of
indignation had been whipped up — with Bülow's help — in the press,
the Reichstag and the country about the camarilla and the autocratic
tendencies of the Kaiser. Any further manifestations of irresponsible
influence would have further inflamed public opinion to an extent that
even the Kaiser would not have wished to contemplate, so for the meantime Bülow's position had been further secured. How long this would
last was debatable. On 17 November, just a few days after Bülow's
Reichstag speech, Holstein wrote: 'As an onlooker I am following the
present quarrel in the Reichstag with much interest. I doubt whether
Bülow will be around much longer. The Kaiser will not forgive him
for removing Podbielski.'[75]

VII

The advantage which the Chancellor had so far gained was purely tactical. The fact that it had become temporarily impossible for reasons of political expediency for the Kaiser to dismiss him was useful; but this left most of the real problems of government untouched. Most important of all from Bülow's point of view, the recent crisis and the way it had been resolved had done nothing to bring about a solution to the problem of the drift of the Centre Party into opposition. In this respect the government had yet to find an effective basis for governing. Vitally important pieces of legislation were due to be presented to the Reichstag, and majorities would have to be found for them. Above all the Reich's financial position had become critical. This had been impressed upon the Chancellor in September,[76] and he was well aware that a major reform in this area was now urgent. There was no reason for Bülow to suppose that he would be able to attract sufficient numbers from within the Centre Party to ensure the passage of so controversial a piece of legislation. The Erzberger faction remained in the ascendant, and they showed no signs of modifying their hostility to the government. It was probably because he realised that there was little chance of regaining their support that Bülow now decided to take the formidable risk of seeking a premature dissolution of the Reichstag in the hope that a new majority alliance could be created on which the government would be able to rely.

A number of factors made this risk seem worthwhile. First, the Kaiser had long resented what he regarded as Bülow's over-reliance on the Centre Party. The Kaiser's congenital contempt for the whole idea of party politics had been sharpened in this case by suggestions made by members of the camarilla that Bülow's amicable relations with the Centre Party were not unconnected with the fact that his wife was Catholic. Since the Chancellor had anyway lost the Centre's support, he had little to lose and some political capital to gain by mounting an electoral assault upon the party. Second, a new wave of apprehension was breaking over the government and the ruling élite concerning the threat of Social Democracy. In January and February there had been street demonstrations in Berlin and some other cities in celebration of the first anniversary of the 1905 revolution in Russia. These demonstrations had become associated with demands for the reform of the plutocratic electoral system in Prussia, one of the most formidable bastions protecting entrenched conservative interests in the country.[77] In July the Chancellor had received an official report on the whole range of Social Democratic activity which, the report claimed, was becoming markedly more revolutionary.[78] In the same month the party won a by-election in the constituency of Altena-Iserlohn. This was the first parliamentary gain for the party since the Reichstag elections in 1903. The Chancellor, clearly disquieted by the moral boost which the Social Democrats had been given by their victory, ordered a careful analysis to be made of the by-election result.[79] This showed that in the run-off election, many liberal voters had either abstained or else voted for the Social Democrat, thus preventing the election of the Centre Party candidate whose victory, even with the current tensions between that party and the government, would have been much more acceptable.[80] The *National-Zeitung* reacted strongly to this result: 'This lack of middle-class solidarity is deeply regrettable and cannot be condemned strongly enough. The liberal voters of Altena-Iserlohn certainly did not have to regard it as a *pleasure* to help elect the Ultramontane this this time; but one might have expected them to regard it as a *duty*'.[81] In August the Prussian Ministry of State reviewed government policy towards Social Democracy. They discussed the possibility of some form of legislative initiative, though they recognised that they would have a problem passing any anti-Socialist legislation through the Reichstag as it was then composed.[82] On the same day Bülow reported to the Kaiser:

> In Spring of this year I made various suggestions to the Prussian Ministry of State concerning security measures against Social Democratic activities, especially in relation to the growing danger of the spread of Social Democratic philosophy in the army. It was felt that the revolutionary posture of the party, which has been remarked upon by the Social Democratic press especially since the last party congress, the anti-militarism movement, the repercussions here of the unrest in Russia which has been celebrated by Social Democrats, the franchise demonstrations in Dresden and the increase of Social Democracy in the army all make precautionary measures a pressing necessity.[83]

If, as the *National-Zeitung* had implied, middle-class solidarity in the face of the 'red menace' was beginning to disintegrate, the German political system was in deep trouble. This together with the other fears which Bülow had expressed made the idea of a Reichstag dissolution and a subsequent vigorous campaign against the Social Democrats seem particularly attractive. The government would be able to sound the alarm about the threat to national order which the Socialists represented, and this might clamp the middle classes more tightly into the status quo. If the Centre Party could be branded as the unpatriotic allies of the

Social Democrats, much as Bismarck had branded it a generation earlier, it too might be made to suffer a serious electoral reverse. The Chancellor could, moreover, confidently rely on the enthusiasm of the Kaiser for the idea of an electoral storming of the Social Democratic and Centrist barricades.

A further factor which made a Reichstag dissolution seem an acceptable risk was the changing political posture of the three left-wing liberal parties. While the prestigious and intractably radical Eugen Richter had reigned over them, they had been regarded as fundamentally opposition parties. But Richter had died in April, and there were now numerous indications that they wished to abandon their hostility to the government and instead enter into some form of partnership.[84] They were travelling the same road as the Centre Party, only in the opposite direction.

This welcome development was no doubt in Bülow's mind when he recommended the appointment of Bernhard Dernburg to succeed Hohenlohe-Langenburg, the latter having finally relinquished his post of Director of the Colonial Division of the Foreign Office in September. Dernburg's appointment was greeted with considerable surprise on all sides.[85] He was a prominent man of commerce holding a directorship of the Darmstadt Bank, he was half-Jewish and he was a member of the left-liberal *Freisinnige Volkspartei*. That a man with any of these attributes — leave alone a combination of all three — should have been appointed to this important office in succession to an aristocrat who had been a favourite of the Kaiser was a sensational turn of events. Even Dernburg's own amusing account of his appointment fails to shed much light on how Bülow managed to pull it off.[86] At all events Dernburg's energy and enthusiasm after taking up office impressed people on all sides, even those whose ideological commitments were at great variance with his.[87] Erzberger, for instance, expressed his pleasure when the new Director cancelled the contracts which had led to the Podbielski crisis earlier in the year,[88] and he responded by handing over to Dernburg material he had been collecting about colonial abuses which he had intended to use in his campaign against the government's colonial policy. But these early signs of friendly compromise proved misleading. On 3 December the Reichstag exploded into a violent confrontation between Erzberger and another Centre Party deputy Roeren on the one hand and Dernburg on the other over disciplinary cases pending against two officials of the Colonial Division who had been accused of leaking government secrets.[89] Many observers wondered why Dernburg had unnecessarily raised the temperature to such a high level over so relatively insignificant a matter. The logical explanation is that he had done so on

Bülow's orders, who by this time was clearly looking for a pretext to dissolve the Reichstag.[90]

Bülow recounts in his memoirs a conversation he claims to have had at this time with two of the Centre Party leaders, Spahn and Groeber. He warned them that he would not be trifled with on important national questions, a reference to the forthcoming Reichstag vote on the supplementary estimates which the government were seeking in connection with the suppression of the Herero rebellion in German South-West Africa. Bülow goes on:

> These two gentlemen assured me that they disapproved of the recent opposition and would do all they could to avoid any conflict with the government. Herr Spahn, with all the honest dignity of a magistrate, said to me: 'Erzberger is to blame for the whole thing. He is a stupid and pushing young arriviste whom our friend Groeber most unluckily got into parliament. He has an office at Lichterfeld where he writes parliamentary letters which make him the master of a good part of the Centrist press. My time is fully occupied by my duties as a magistrate at Kiel, but he has nothing to do, and so it isn't easy for me to settle with him'. The eloquent Groeber expressed to me his deep regret at ever having sponsored such a fellow: 'Certainly it would have been cleverer of me never to have brought that foul-mouthed Erzberger into the Reichstag. Now we must try to freeze him out again'. . . . On that occasion Spahn and Groeber left me with repeated promises that they would do all they could to prevent the Centre going into opposition on the forthcoming vote for supplementary estimates in South-West Africa.[91]

Considering the bitterness which had accumulated within the party and the angry indignation with which its leaders had witnessed Erzberger's success in transforming it into a party of opposition, the remarks which Bülow attributes to Spahn and Groeber have the ring of truth about them. But in spite of the fact that the Centre Party leaders had received this warning from the Chancellor — and another of their colleagues was convinced that it amounted to a threat to dissolve the Reichstag[92] — they were unable to swing the party behind them. The supplementary estimates were defeated by ten votes. On receiving news of this, Bülow immediately mounted the Reichstag podium and read out the Imperial Rescript of dissolution. He had found his pretext to attempt a reconstruction of his parliamentary base and, despite all the risks involved, he seized it with alacrity.

VIII

The crisis in Bülow's Chancellorship in the years 1905 and 1906 had a fugue-like quality. He was presented with interwoven problems of diplomacy, of parliamentary strategy, of ministerial personnel. These themes were played out against a background of industrial and political unrest which was threatening, at any rate in the minds of many members of the ruling élite, to bring about social discord in the towns and cities of the German Empire. The preservation of viable government in such circumstances represented an awesome task for the Chancellor. And while each of these problems had a character and history of its own, Bülow became increasingly convinced throughout 1906 that the common theme which ran through them was the conduct of the Kaiser and the camarilla. The crisis precipitated by the loss of the support of the Centre Party had been exacerbated by the Kaiser's public denunciations of the party, and a way out of that crisis had been blocked by his refusal to allow Bülow to engage in private negotiations with the party leaders. The Moroccan crisis had been at least partly brought about by the Kaiser's indiscreet remarks to the French delegation at Rominten, and the involvement of Philipp Eulenburg and other members of the camarilla in the preparation and conduct of the Algeciras conference had certainly done nothing to restore Germany's diplomatic prestige. The conflicts over Hohenlohe-Langenburg and Podbielski had derived from a stubborn determination on the part of the Kaiser to ignore the realities of press or public or Reichstag opinion. He had a bitter contempt for the very idea of constitutions, and he treated with scorn expressions of opinion on such matters as ministerial appointments from whatever quarter they might come. In this he was encouraged by the irresponsible sycophants with whom he chose to surround himself.

It was not so easy for the Chancellor to ignore the constitution or the mood of public or Reichstag opinion. He had to govern, and to do so effectively involved him in a continuous quadrille of compromise. This was the only way of avoiding the political paralysis which so frequently threatened to reduce the Second Reich to ungovernability. By November 1906 he had become convinced that, in the interests both of political stability and his own continuation in office, the influence of the camarilla had to be broken and the autocratic tendencies of the Kaiser had to be curbed. By reducing the political weight of the camarilla and the Kaiser, he was doing something to restore the constitutional equilibrium on which the stability of the Reich depended. A further tilt to the balance would be provided — or so the Chancellor hoped — by the Reichstag dissolution. If he could succeed in establishing a reasonably stable and permanent coalition in the Reichstag committed to supporting the government's programme of legislation, the urgent problems facing the Reich, especially those of a financial nature, would be much nearer solution. Such a Reichstag coalition would facilitate a much more coherent and forward-looking development of government policy than was possible in a situation where *ad hoc* majorities had to be found for each separate piece of legislation. It would also provide a powerful base from which Bülow would be able to beat off any further attacks on his own personal position or attempts to undermine the authority of the responsible government. Such a strategy — what was to become the Bülow-Block — depended upon the outcome of the 1907 election and the subsequent ability of the parties composing the Block to sink their differences, at any rate to an extent which would allow them to engage in positive cooperation with the government. The Reichstag dissolution of December 1906 was therefore the beginning of Bülow's campaign to place the government of Germany on a new footing.

This is not the place to recount the successes and the ultimate failure of Bülow's campaign.[93] What can be said in conclusion is that his response to the various crises of 1905 and 1906 shows him to have been far more weighty and courageous a statesman than his historical reputation would allow. Entangled in the web of Wilhelmine politics, his cosmopolitan sympathies enabled him to respond more effectively than Caprivi or Hohenlohe had to the problems of government. If he was ultimately unsuccessful in resolving these problems, the failure derived more from the inner conflicts of German society than from his own inability or lack of determination. His replacement by the narrow and fatalistic Bethmann Hollweg in the summer of 1909 marked the end of any chance that Germany might resolve these inner conflicts peacefully. Whatever one might think of Bülow's methods, his objectives must command respect.

Notes

1. Einem was Prussian Minister of War; Nieberding State Secretary of the Imperial Justice Office; Posadowsky State Secretary of the Imperial Office of the Interior. The presence on the committee of members of the military cabinet ensured an airing of the Kaiser's views of the matter.
2. HA Köln: Bachem Papers 235, Memorandum dated 26 January 1906.
3. Schulthess, *Europäischer Geschichtskalender,* 1906, xlvii, p. 8.
4. HA Köln: Bachem Papers 235, Memorandum dated 17 January 1906.
5. HA Köln: Bachem Papers 228, Memorandum dated 15 February 1906.

6. HA Köln: Bachem Papers 235, Memorandum dated 26 January 1906.
7. HA Köln: Bachem Papers 235, Memorandum dated 26 January 1906.
8. On Erzberger's rise to prominence, see K. Epstein, *Matthias Erzberger and the Dilemma of German Democracy* (Princeton, 1959), *passim.*
9. *Reichstag Debates*, ccxvi, p. 2049, 15 March 1906.
10. HA Köln: Bachem Papers 241, Memorandum dated 16 March 1906.
11. HA Köln: Bachem Papers 238, Memorandum dated 21 March 1906. See also Bachem Papers 241, Memorandum dated 30 April 1906.
12. See Epstein, *Erzberger*, pp. 52–3.
13. Colonial affairs had hitherto been handled by the Colonial Division of the Foreign Office, headed by a Director responsible to the Secretary of State.
14. GStA München: B4 MA III 2684, Lerchenfeld to Podewils, 22 March 1906.
15. HA Köln: Bachem Papers 238, Memorandum dated 21 March 1906.
16. GStA München: B4 MA III 2684, Lerchenfeld to Podewils, 22 March 1906.
17. Ibid. See also HA Köln: Bachem Papers 244, Memorandum dated 21 March 1906.
18. GStA München: B4 MA III 2684, Lerchenfeld to Podewils, 22 March 1906.
19. On Spahn and the other Centre Party leaders, see Epstein, *Erzberger*, pp. 38–46.
20. Lerchenfeld was in the Chancellor's confidence and frequently performed such missions.
21. GStA München: B4 MA III 2684, Lerchenfeld to Podewils, 22 March 1906; HA Köln: Bachem Papers 244, Memorandum of 21 March 1906.
22. GStA München: B4 MA III 2684, Lerchenfeld to Podewils, 24 March 1906; HA Köln: Bachem Papers 238, Memorandum dated 21 March 1906; ZSA Merseburg: Rep. 90a B III 2b Nr. 6, Bd.152.78–89, Minutes of the Prussian Ministry of State Meeting, 12 February 1906.
23. HA Köln: Bachem Papers 244, Memorandum dated 30 March 1906; see also O. Hammann, *Um den Kaiser, Erinnerungen aus den Jahren 1906/1909* (Berlin, 1919), pp. 9–10.
24. HA Köln: Bachem Papers 242, Memorandum dated 27 May 1906.
25. ZSA Merseburg: Rep. 53J, Hausarchiv, Wilhelm II, Lit.B, Nr.16a, Bd.3.17, Bülow to Kaiser, 20 May 1906.
26. GStA München: B4 MA III 2684, Lerchenfeld's Report, Nr.359, 27 June 1906.
27. BA Koblenz: Bülow Papers 153.10, Kaiser to Bülow, 28 May 1906.
28. GStA München: B4 MA III 2684; Lerchenfeld's Report, Nr.259, 27 June 1906; the Kaiser felt that the lives of German troops were being imperilled because of the lack of this railway.
29. Ibid.
30. BA Koblenz: Bülow Papers 153.5, Kaiser to Bülow, 30 June 1906.
31. BA Koblenz: Bülow Papers 153.14, Kaiser to Bülow, 2 July 1906.
32. ZSA Merseburg: Rep. 53J, Hausarchiv, Wilhelm II, Lit.B, Nr.16a, Bd.III.7–8, Bülow to Kaiser, 17 July 1906.
33. *Kölnische Volkszeitung*, 2 April 1906.
34. PA Bonn: Deutschland 122, Nr.13, Bd.11.
35. Hammann, *Um den Kaiser*, pp. 15–16.
36. ZSA Merseburg: Rep.2.2.1, Geheimes Zivilkabinett, Nr.3577.116.
37. R.v. Zedlitz-Trützschler, *Zwölf Jahre am Deutschen Kaiserhof* (Stuttgart, Berlin u. Leipzig, 1923), p. 74; Bernhard Fürst von Bülow, *Denkwürdigkeiten*, 4 vols., (Berlin 1930–31), vol. II, p. 193; N. Rich, *Friedrich von Holstein*, 2 Vols. (Cambridge, 1965), vol. II, pp. 699–710.
38. *Grosse Politik*, vol. XIX ii, p. 452.
39. Bülow, *Denkwürdigkeiten* II, pp. 140–5.
40. *Deutschland und die Mächte vor dem Krieg in amtlichen Schriften des Fürsten*

Bernhard von Bülow (ohne seine Mitwirkung herausgegeben von einem Ungenannten), (Dresden 1929), vol. II, p. 9.

41. Ibid.

42. Rich, *Holstein* II, pp. 726–7; *Grosse Politik* XIX ii, pp. 508–11; also *Grosse Politik* XX ii, pp. 590–1.

43. Sergei Witte, *The Memoirs of Count Witte*, ed. A. Yarmolinsky, (New York, 1921), p. 423.

44. Ibid.

45. Kaiser to Bülow, 17 October 1905, printed in *Letters of Prince Bülow*, trans. F. Whyte, (London, n.d.); see also J. Haller, *Aus dem Leben des Fürsten Philipp zu Eulenburg-Hertefeld* (Berlin 1924), pp. 310–11.

46. *Fürst Bülows Reden*, vol. II, p. 303ff.

47. See Bülow's amusing account of this episode: Bülow, *Denkwürdigkeiten* II, pp. 212–13.

48. HA Köln: Bachem Papers 244, Memorandum dated 7 April 1906.

49. GLA Karlsruhe: 233.34811, Berkheim's Report, Nr.24, 8 November 1906.

50. These rumours were constantly reflected in the press; see *Hannoversche Kurier, Neue Gesellschaftliche Korrespondenz, Berliner Tageblatt*, etc.

51. HA Köln: Bachem Papers 244, copy of Bülow's comments by (?) Mühlberg.

52. H. Rogge, *Friedrich von Holstein. Lebensbekenntnis in Briefen an eine Frau* (Berlin, 1932), p. 265, Holstein to Ida von Stülpnagel, 10 October 1906.

53. Rogge, *Friedrich von Holstein*, pp. 256–7, Holstein to Ida von Stülpnagel, 7 June 1906.

54. ZSA Merseburg: Rep. 53J, Hausarchiv, Wilhelm II, Lit.B, Nr.16a, Bd.III.6, Bülow to Kaiser, 17 July 1906.

55. Ibid.

56. GStA München: B4 MA III 2684, Lerchenfeld's Report, Nr. 531, 9 November 1906; ZSA Potsdam: Hammann Papers 12, Bülow to Hammann, 25 August 1906.

57. ZSA Merseburg: Rep. 90a BIII 2b, Nr.6, Bd. 153.135, Minutes of the Meeting of the Prussian Ministry of State, 20 November 1906.

58. GStA München: B4 MA III 2684, Lerchenfeld's Report, Nr.531, 9 November 1906; *The Holstein Papers*, ed. N. Rich and M.H. Fisher, 4 vols. (Cambridge, 1963), Vol. IV, pp. 437–8, Harden to Holstein, 3 September 1906.

59. ZSA Potsdam: Hammann Papers 72.4–8.

60. GLA Karlsruhe: 233.34811, Berkheim's Report, Nr.19, 13 October 1906; Rogge, *Friedrich von Holstein*, pp. 266–7, Holstein to Ida von Stülpnagel, 6 November 1906; Peter-Christian Witt, *Die Finanzpolitik des Deutschen Reiches von 1903 bis 1913*, (Lubeck und Hamburg, 1970), pp. 168–9.

61. GStA München: B4 MA III 2684, Lerchenfeld's Report, Nr.531, 9 November 1906.

62. Ibid.

63. GLA Karlsruhe: 233.34811, Berkheim's Report, Nr.24, 8 November 1906.

64. GLA Karlsruhe: 233.34811, Berkheim's Report, Nr.24, 8 November 1906; GStA München: B4 MA III 2684, Lerchenfeld's Report, Nr.531, 9 November 1906; see also *Neue Gesellschaftliche Korrespondenz*, 6 November 1906; H. Rogge, *Holstein und Harden* (Munich, 1959), pp. 99–103; Paul von Schwabach, *Aus Meinen Akten* (Berlin, 1927), p. 112.

65. Kuno Moltke was Commander of the Berlin Garrison; Varnbüler was Württemberg Envoy to Berlin; Leszczynski had retired from the army in 1891 but was a frequent member of the Kaiser's entourage.

66. See note 64 above.

67. GLA Karlsruhe: 233.34811, Berkheim's Report, Nr.24, 8 November 1906.

68. Ibid.

69. His first article, 'Präludium', appeared in *Die Zukunft*, vol. 57, 17. November 1906.
70. *Holstein Papers* IV, pp. 448–9, Holstein to Pascal David, 19 November 1906.
71. H. Rogge, *Holstein und Harden*, p. 108; see also Haller, *Eulenburg*, p. 326, Eulenburg to Bülow, 10 December 1906; *Holstein Papers* IV, p. 452, Harden to Holstein, 17 January 1907.
72. *Reichstag Debates*, vol. XI, 1905/6, Bd.5, pp. 3648–3650.
73. BA Koblenz: Bülow Papers 153.99.
74. Bülow, *Denkwürdigkeiten* II, p. 265.
75. Rogge, *Friedrich von Holstein*, pp. 268–9, Holstein to Ida von Stulpnagel, 17 November 1906.
76. ZSA Potsdam: Reichskanzlei 241.18–19, Stengel to Bülow, 12 September 1906; ZSA Potsdam: Reichskanzlei 241.33, Loebell to Bülow, 18 September 1906.
77. GStA. München: B4 MA III 2683, Lerchenfeld's Report, Nr.42, 21 January 1906.
78. ZSA Potsdam: Reichsamt des Innern 13689.72–76, 7 July 1906.
79. ZSA Potsdam: Reichskanzlei 1793.29, Below to Günther, 13 July 1906.
80. ZSA Potsdam: Reichskanzlei 1793.30–31, Günther to Below, 14 July 1906.
81. *National-Zeitung*, 11 July 1906.
82. ZSA Merseburg: Rep. 90a BIII 2b Nr.6, Bd.153.16–27, Minutes of the Prussian Ministry of State Meeting, 31 August 1906.
83. ZSA Merseburg: Rep. 2.2.1. Geheimes Zivilkabinett, Nr.3584.47, Bülow to Kaiser, 31 August 1906.
84. ZSA Potsdam: Fortschrittliche Volkspartei 36–37, Minutes of the Management Committee, 8 October 1906; see also D. Stegmann, *Die Erben Bismarcks* (Köln, 1970), pp. 143–6; B. Heckart, *From Bassermann to Bebel* (New Haven and London, 1974), pp. 49–54.
85. GStA München: B4 MA III 2684, Lerchenfeld's Report, Nr.458, 5 September 1906.
86. Dernburg's account is contained in an article in the *National-Zeitung* of 2 May 1929.
87. ZSA Potsdam: Hutten-Czapski Papers 33.97, Hutten-Czapski to Bülow, 9 September 1906; GLA Karlsruhe: 233.34811, Berkheim's Report, Nr.29, 30 November 1906.
88. Epstein, *Erzberger*, pp. 56–7.
89. *Reichstag Debates*, vol. ccxvii, December 3 1906, pp. 4084–4118.
90. BA Koblenz: Bülow Papers 153.172.
91. Bülow, *Denkwürdigkeiten* II, pp. 268–9.
92. HA Köln: Bachem Papers 259, Bachem to Spahn, 10 December 1906.
93. The present author hopes to publish the results of his research into the Bülow Block in the near future. In the foregoing paper, all translations are by the author. He would like to acknowledge his debt of gratitude to Dr. John Röhl of the University of Sussex for first suggesting this theme and then providing generous and patient supervisory guidance.

3 MILITARY-INDUSTRIAL RELATIONS: KRUPP AND THE IMPERIAL NAVY OFFICE

Richard Owen

I

In the plethora of works which deal with the socio-political and economic structure of Wilhelmine Germany the name of Krupp is never far distant. It is a name which conjures up different images to different people and one which more than most has suffered from partisan scholarship. During the First World War and indeed well into the Thirties, the belief persisted that industry, and especially the armament industry and its chief representative Krupp, had wielded a nebulous and malevolent power over governmental policy in the pre-war years.[1] In its most extreme form the firm of Krupp and the German Kaiser were charged with a diabolical conspiracy to destroy civilisation: 'Cannot we figure to ourselves', wrote a wartime commentator in *Littel's Living Age*, 'Krupp and the Kaiser, partners both in a business which flourished upon the destruction of mankind, coming to the conclusion that the day had dawned and the hour had struck when Essen required, in order that it should pile up blood money beyond computation, and win for them both countless wealth, that the world should run red with blood?'[2] In Germany itself another popular view, also held by those in informed circles, saw Krupp as the villain of the piece and the *Reichsleitung*, personified in the State Secretary for the Navy, von Tirpitz, as the gullible 'tool of the industrialists'.[3] Although expressed in such simplistic terms the suggestions were absurd, the theory that capitalist pressure on government led to war gained considerable currency.

With hindsight it is perhaps not difficult to see why such explanations became so fashionable. Like secret diplomacy, the greater part of governmental relations with industry was conducted behind closed doors, causing much suspicion and distrust. Confronted with a dearth of hard fact, rumour and speculation as to the real nature of the relationship abounded. That the armament industry exercised considerable influence as a lobby in government circles was no secret but the tangible evidence was missing: as a perspective observer of the internal workings of government, *Hofmarschall* (Marshal of the Imperial Court) Count Robert Zedlitz-Trützschler, wrote, 'The power of the steel barons weighs heavily and their concern for their business and their desire to see their shares

71

rise on the Stock Market has often been served up to us as a matter of national importance'. He concluded: 'along with the known enthusiasts [for the fleet] there are also all sorts of influential people who are against any limitations in armament spending: it would be very interesting to find out the many relationships which exist between the pro-fleet fanatics and those who actually build the fleet'.[4] In the case of Krupp this relationship had a long and interesting history.

Since the 1870s construction technology in shipbuilding, as in other fields, had made considerable advances.[5] The technological revolution in engineering, chemical and electrical processes had transformed the traditional defence industries into modern scientific establishments into which heavy industry, which had hitherto played a minor supply role, was inextricably drawn by the prospect of orders and profit. In Germany this process had been slow and heavy industry's involvement in the defence market had been unenthusiastic. To Admiral Stosch, the first Secretary for the Navy after the Franco-Prussian war, it was self-evident that the fleet should be built, for military and economic reasons, by domestic industry, and during his period of office Stosch implemented a policy of wooing heavy industry to the task.[6] As a result of this involvement industry had experienced 'a remarkable increase'[7] in both domestic and foreign orders. Although not completely won over to the cause (for the rate of building left much to be desired) industry was duly impressed and showed its appreciation.[8]

The decision of the German government to build a navy of world class is generally associated with the arrival of Vice-Admiral Tirpitz at the Imperial Navy Office (INO) in June 1897. Until that time the efforts of the INO under Tirpitz's predecessor, Admiral Hollmann, had been continually frustrated by the doubts of a suspicious Reichstag, the uninformed indifference of public opinion, and, not least, the indecision and aimlessness of the INO itself. Tirpitz brought with him personal qualities of determination, an acute organisational and political sense and above all a strategic plan, the lack of which, as the historian Eckart Kehr pointed out in his study of naval policy, had been the most important single factor that had hindered the development of the navy and that had contributed to maintain the Reichstag in its belief that as far as the Navy was concerned 'both the aim and the will were missing'.[9] Although Tirpitz's new Navy Bill was by no means assured of success in the 1897—8 winter session, the purposeful unity of the naval authorities was an important advance upon the internecine 'cruiser versus battleship' squabbles of the Hollmann administration: 'boundless plans', as the leading Left-Liberal Reichstag deputy Eugen

Richter was to describe them, were better than no plans at all.

As the new State Secretary was readily to prove, the nostrum of his mentor, Admiral Stosch, had not been lost on him. Before the more grandiose aims of *Weltpolitik* could even be entertained an efficient and sophisticated defence industry was essential: 'Without a German ship-building industry a German Navy is inconceivable'.[10] In the ensuing mobilisation of public opinion in favour of the Navy Law Tirpitz focused special attention upon two powerful and influencial sectors of the economy, commerce and heavy industry. That commerce would benefit indirectly from the Navy in its defence and encouragement of trade was clear, and once these interests had been reassured that they would not be required to foot the bill, as had been suggested by some groups of agrarians, they were easily persuaded to support the new Law. With heavy industry, however, Tirpitz was on more difficult ground and proceeded with caution. Urged on by the Kaiser and by his own departmental heads 'to get Krupp to involve the industrialists in the [naval] question',[11] Tirpitz wrote in September 1897 to Fritz Krupp, the owner of the Essen concern, and so opened negotiations 'to discuss various points which concern my intended strategy in the fleet question'.[12] Krupp's reply, in which he announced his intention to place himself at the State Secretary's disposal,[13] was followed by a meeting of the two men in Berlin on 1 October 1897 which proved of considerable importance to the content and direction of the consolidated strategy of the INO and industry. At the meeting Tirpitz outlined his plan for 'a great agitation on the part of commerce and industry'[14] which would demonstrate the solidarity of these sectors of the economy in a vindication of the navalist theories as expounded by the INO. Although Krupp assured Tirpitz of his full support, it was not without important tactical reservations. On 14 October 1897, after the meeting, he wrote to his Managing Director, Jencke:

> To Tirpitz's great amazement, I refused to become personally involved in the affair because any indiscretion in the direction could miscarry. Krupp cannot be associated with this matter either through me or through you. I did, however, offer to nominate someone from whom the first initiatives would come. This was Schweinburg. After Tirpitz had declared himself prepared to work with Schweinburg. . . . I withdrew completely from the matter.[15]

The reasons behind Krupp's determination to remain out of the public eye in the navy question are not hard to explain. More surprising perhaps is the apparent naïveté of the State Secretary in his expectation that the industrialist, whose name was a synonym for armament interests, should wish to do otherwise. Krupp's fears, which as he explained were primarily political, went further, however. The naval issue was too important to risk being jeopardised by early mistakes: Jencke, himself in a difficult position because of his activities on the Executive of the Central Union of German Industrialists, was urged to take special care. In the same letter Krupp wrote:

> As you see from the above, I am fully resolved to this course of action which cannot fail to make a certain impression and which will give the government some confidence. However, as I have already said, I can in no way participate personally and, as under no circumstances can the name of Krupp be linked with the matter, I should like to urge you strongly to confine your activity to that of an   advisor — *as much as possible behind the scenes.*

Thus whilst both Krupp's influence and considerable resources were mobilized,[16] the firm and its owner were to remain discreetly out of the public eye. It was the beginning of a relationship which was to continue, though not without its many attendant problems, until the collapse of the Empire.

Tirpitz's choice of Krupp as the most influential and powerful representative of west German industry was clearly a sound one. The Essen cannon king had always stood close to the navy;[17] would, after the passing of the bill, play an even bigger role; and had excellent connections with practically all the major industrial organisations, *Verbände*, trusts, syndicates and banks. He had, moreover, unrestricted access to the Court and was a good personal friend of the Kaiser, Admiral Hollmann, Tirpitz's predecessor at the INO, Lucanus, the Head of the Kaiser's Civil Cabinet,[18] and Gossler, the Prussian Minister of War. Furthermore, through his firm's shipbuilding, armour-plate and ship-steel interests, Krupp stood to gain more directly from the expansion of the fleet than any of his industrialist colleagues. The firm's dealing with the navy, although not stretching as far back as those with the army, did not begin with the founding of the armour-plating works in 1890. It had been suggested to Alfred Krupp as early as 1865 that the firm should develop vertically and break into shipbuilding.[19] The idea was again raised in 1873 and with it the more profitable undertaking to produce armour-plate, only, however, 'when orders from the state for armour ships were guaranteed'.[20] Although there is no evidence to suggest that such a guarantee was given, it is clear that by 1890 or slightly earlier the prospect of a growing fleet had convinced Essen of the profitability of expanding its industrial base.

Armour-plating had in the meantime become more and more sophisticated and costly. Until 1890, when Krupp was invited by the Navy to take up the production of armour-plate, the navy's requirements had been supplied by a rival firm, the Dillinger Hütte.[21] Hoping that it could in this way broaden the basis of its suppliers, the INO was to be sorely disappointed, for in the same year Essen and Dillingen joined forces to present a unified front.[22] Despite the Navy's protests, the two firms decided upon a policy of price collaboration, with Krupp undertaking all research and development projects.[23]

The firm's decision to concentrate more and more on its — at that time relatively limited[24] — domestic market was not made entirely of its own choice. In 1885 the French Chamber of Deputies, under pressure from its own armament industries, lifted the ban on the export of war materials and there followed what can only be described as a massive French export offensive in which both the industry and the French Foreign Ministry played a significant part.[25] The success of the French in this export campaign 'struck a desperate blow at the Krupp monopoly'[26] overseas. Having established a quasi-monopoly position for its armour-plate in the domestic market through its agreement with Dillingen, Krupp endeavoured to consolidate and safeguard this position, and at the same time bolster its weakened foreign standing by taking over its only serious rival, the Magdeburg Works of Gruson.[27] This limited company, which until 1886 had been privately owned by Hermann Gruson, had been in a strong financial position until 1889 when it suffered a dramatic setback on the Stock Exchange, its shares dropping from 288 points in 1888, to 180 in 1889, 152 in 1890 and finally to 139 at the end of 1891.[28] Offering the shareholders a guaranteed 9 per cent dividend for 25 years, Krupp bought out the firm in April 1893 and along with it a total monopoly in the export of armour-plate. Krupp commented at the time:

> The production of armour-plating was an absolute necessity for my works, but I knew at the same time that the world market could not accommodate two German firms in this field. I would have done the Fatherland a disservice if I had crippled this growing German firm with all its workers and officials with the overwhelming strength of my financial position.[29]

Although Krupp's patriotic altruism may be questioned, the effect of
the take-over cannot: the firm's overwhelming financial strength, which
along with its dynastic connections, was its most important asset, had
succeeded in eliminating competition where technical quality had
failed. A liberal newspaper, the *Vossische Zeitung*, commented with
prescience: 'an even bigger danger is the exploitation of the state
through high price-fixing. . . later they [Krupp] can dictate the
prices'.[30]

Finally, in order to supply not only the armour, artillery and
ordnance but also to be in a position to actually build the warships, the
firm had also been considering for some years an entry into shipbuilding. In 1874, Alfred Krupp had 'aired the question of building
the firm's own shipyard. . . if Prussia or other states assure us of
sufficient work'.[31] It is clear from this and other documents,[32] that
the firm saw in armour-plate and shipbuilding a logical avenue of
expansion for its war interests and that it was making concerted
attempts to control its production process from raw materials to finished
product. The acquisition of the Germania Shipyard in Kiel only
becomes meaningful if seen in this light. At the Germania's AGM on
26 September 1896, the Essen giant proposed a bid of 6,325,000
Marks, with a guaranteed 4 per cent dividend, and the option of buying
out the yard outright at a later date.[33] The bid was accepted and under
article six of the leasing contract the Germania yard became part of
the Krupp concern on 26 April 1902.[34] Whether the instigation for this
move came directly from the Kaiser is unclear. To suggest, as does
Fritz Krupp's son-in-law, Thilo von Wilmowski,[35] that the firm took
over Germania only because it was under pressure from the Kaiser, is
certainly too naive an interpretation, for it goes completely against
the direction of Krupp's industrial policy, namely, the rationalisation
of its naval armament interests with the intention of securing a substantial share of the forthcoming expansion. There can be little
doubt, however, that the firm's hurried, almost hectic, efforts at
vertical expansion during these years were based on more than
intuitive surmise and that the Kaiser was in some way involved. A
further attempt, made in April 1897, to amalgamate Germania with
another leading shipbuilding yard, the Vulkan, failed.[36]

By 1898 therefore, challenged overseas by the French, Krupp, though
still in a strong economic position, was being obliged more and more to
think in terms of the domestic German market. The Navy Bill of that
year, with its constitutionally laid down programme of naval expansion
(which was effectively doubled in the 1900 Supplementary Law),

offered the armament industry the incalculable advantages of continuity and stability[37] and with it an attractive solution to the Essen
dilemma.

II

Thus on entering the INO as State Secretary in June 1897, Tirpitz was
confronted with what he described as a Krupp 'business monopoly with
very high prices'.[38] From the technical evidence available to the Navy
Office, however, it was clear that Krupp produced the best steel and
armour-plate, so that although the INO confessed to misgivings about
the high level of concentration in the steel industry and, specifically,
'that Krupp absorbs everything',[39] its conscientious striving after a
qualitatively superior fleet gave it little or no choice but to remain, *faute
de mieux*, with its established suppliers. The State Secretary personally
favoured dealing with a large private concern and showed a definite
antipathy to smaller limited companies.[40] Further, he hoped that he
would be able to persuade industry, and Krupp especially, to lower its
prices.[41] During his first two years of office the State Secretary
adopted consequently a friendly attitude towards the armament
producers.[42] The INO carefully encouraged 'social contacts with Krupp
and Stumm'[43] and Tirpitz took it upon himself personally to represent
sympathetically the views of the two cannon kings in both the
Reichstag and the Budget Committee.

The honeymoon, however, was not to last. During the autumn of
1899 the clamourings of the German Navy League, which had been
nurtured and partially financed by Krupp donations, began to reflect
increasingly the aspirations of its paymasters for even greater expansion
and to confuse what for Tirpitz were interests of State with the blatant
money interests of the great industrialists.[44] By deliberately leaking
information about Krupp to the press, the INO was able to stir up
public opinion against the allegedly monstrous profits of the Essen
concern. Tripitz's reasons for doing this were twofold. Firstly, he was
angry at the Navy League's rapacious lobbying which threatened to
remove from the INO its power to control the rate and speed of
expansion, and he hoped that by publicly embarrassing the firm he
could place it at a strong psychological disadvantage when the time
came for the firm's contract to be renegotiated. Secondly, and equally
important to Tirpitz's calculations, was the reaction of the Reichstag
to the forthcoming 1900 Supplementary Law, and particularly the
reaction of the Catholic Centre Party which invariably displayed a
hyper-sensitivity when naval debates touched on the issue of fleet

finance.

If the ensuing public outcry against Krupp in both the press and the Reichstag meant that the INO had won the first round of the conflict, a total victory was far from assured. Furious at the State Secretary's tactics in publicising the firm's dealings with the INO, Krupp requested an audience with the Kaiser in which he declared his intention of 'opening His Majesty's eyes'.[45] The audience, which took place on 8 May 1900, is worth examining in some detail because it raises fundamental issues in the relationship between the two parties. During the first half of the audience, Krupp vigorously defended the actions and integrity of his concern and refuted the allegations which had been made in the press and in the Reichstag.[46] The firm, Krupp rightly claimed, had not begun the production of armour-plating on its own initiative but rather at the express invitation of the INO, and that even then its compliance with the Navy's request had been made 'very unwillingly',[47] a statement which was less than true. Having built its armour-plate rolling mill, however, the firm found that it had never been able to work to its full capacity and that some years it had indeed made a loss.[48] In the nine years since its establishment, the industrialist continued, the mill's overall domestic production had averaged 1,215 tons per annum or, as he testily pointed out, sufficient armour-plating 'for roughly half a ship'.[49] For the pragmatic industrialist such a 'modest annual quota' presented for the manufacturer a considerable financial risk, a risk which was further exacerbated 'as a result of a continuing rise of wages and materials.'[50] If such financial considerations were not enough to convince the Kaiser of the firm's integrity, Krupp went on to emphasise the costly nature of the firm's research and development projects which were always necessary to maintain the concern's pre-eminent technological position. The change-over from compound to nickel-steel plating which the firm had pioneered in the early 1890s was, Krupp submitted, an excellent sample of invisible capital outlay. It was, moreover, this expensive outlay which had later led to an improvement in quality and efficiency, and thus, paradoxically to a reduction in prices.[51]

Changing his line of argument from the purely business and economic aspects Krupp proceeded to outline the importance of his concern in the military-economic structure of the Empire. 'In the past', he told the Kaiser, 'this country was proud of the achievements of the firm of Krupp. Both the Army and the Navy were grateful for the firm's co-operation and were happy that it allowed them to be independent of foreign producers. Now we have a complete volte-face. The squalid attacks (on the firm) are not opposed but received with true satisfaction. It is nothing but *Schadenfreude*'.[52] For the firm the issue was clear: 'the feeling in naval circles is bent on opposing Krupp as much as possible because the firm exploits the Navy'.[53] Krupp contended that Tirpitz was particularly hostile though the latter had done nothing to inform himself of the problems which faced the firm.[54] Finally, however, Krupp reached the sting in his argument. He complained that Ehrhardt, another leading armament manufacturer, had experienced none of the troubles with which he was continually beset; but then, Krupp mused ruefully, Ehrhardt was a public company. He concluded:

> The administration of the firm and the demands of competition lay claim to so much of my energy that I am not also in a position to struggle against the malevolent authorities. . . In view of these facts I must inform Your Majesty in all seriousness that I am considering the question of turning the factory into a limited company.[55]

Although it was most unlikely that he intended to go through with his threat, as it went against the whole ethos of the Krupp concern, the industrialist's dialogue with Admiral Senden, the Head of the Kaiser's Naval Cabinet, after the Kaiser had retired, showed the latter's obvious concern at Krupp's threat and the extent of Krupp's determination to rid himself of Tirpitz's interference. In his notes of the audience Krupp gave the following account of his exchange:

> Senden: His Majesty leaves me no peace. Can the factory in fact go public without the consent of the Kaiser?
> I (Krupp): Oh yes.
> Senden: Tirpitz will not want that.
> I (Krupp): If this business with T(irpitz) continues as it is, then I am firmly resolved.
> Senden: I will speak to (Admiral) Sack in order to arrive at a *modus vivendi*.[56]

The audience with the Kaiser and the conversation with Senden is revealing for a number of reasons. Firstly, it throws some light on the nature of the relationship which existed between Krupp and the Kaiser; for although it would be erroneous to over-personalise the liaison between the firm of Krupp and the government, this personal aspect, in a political system in which all major decisions were made by a small number of men, cannot be ignored. Thus whether the Kaiser's signs of approbation during the audience signified a genuine siding with Krupp is problematic: it is clear, however, that the Kaiser was throughout most anxious to soothe the aggrieved industrialist and to minimise the number of bones of contention which existed between the warring parties. Certainly the Kaiser appeared to accept that the Navy's promises[57] had not been adequately fulfilled and 'that the armour-plate works [had] not been kept sufficiently busy', but added, with a reference to the forthcoming Supplementary Naval Law, that 'things will now be different'.[58] More importantly, though, the 1900 contretemps demonstrates the extent of the firm's power and the inability of the INO to successfully intimidate it. Senden's *modus vivendi* involved a compromise settlement which gave the INO slightly more favourable prices and Krupp freedom of action beyond the reach of the naval authorities. Thus although three other major anti-Krupp campaigns were launched in 1905, 1909–10 and 1913, these were waged by members of the Reichstag and elements of the press without the support or even the agreement of the INO, which found them as embarrassing as did the firm itself. The press attacks were for the most part transitory in nature, a few weeks of virulent anti-Krupp polemic which were soon forgotten. As for the Reichstag, the Social Democrats, always implacable in their opposition to Krupp, were supported as often as not by both the Left-Liberals and the Centre, but the fundamental constitutional weakness of the House meant that these parties' occasional advantage could not be translated into effective action.

If both in the Reichstag and in the Budget Committee Tirpitz quite openly accepted the existence of Krupp's monopoly position, the INO tried to placate criticism by making a number of attempts to find or create alternative suppliers of armour-plate. Three possibilities were entertained by the State Secretary: the building of works financed and run by the State, the possibility of contracting abroad and the encouragement of private domestic competition. The first two of these three alternatives were non-starters either for financial or for military-strategic reasons.[59] the INO was, however, more serious in pursuing its third alternative, and it made a number of attempts to interest the giant Thyssen concern to undertake the production of armour-plate. Yet the dilatoriness of these approaches suggests that the INO was all too aware of the stringent conditions and guarantees which Thyssen was sure to, and did, demand. In the end the latter declined because of the high capital costs and inherent risks involved in the venture.[60] To Krupp the issue was more straightforward: he rejected the monopoly charge, stating that there existed 'free access

for any manufacturer to compete'.[61] Although true in a strict sense, this
missed the point. As Tirpitz's son Wolfgang pointed out in his doctoral
thesis,[62] 'the reason for Krupp and Dillingen's unshakeable monopoly
position lay in the strength of its capital. He [Krupp] was always in a
position to outbid the tenders of other younger competitors from his
secret reserves and to force them to co-operate, unless, of course, they
prefered bankruptcy'. The result for Tirpitz was perhaps the desired
one. The INO could claim with truth that its efforts to broaden the range
of its suppliers had been frustrated by the monopoly-capitalist structure
of the economy and yet, at the same time, remain in a position which its
State Secretary privately prefered, namely, that of doing business with a
private concern with which he indubitably felt more at ease.[63]

In other respects too, the position of Krupp was equally formidable.
Unlike many other large industrial concerns in Imperial Germany, the
Krupp empire was controlled and owned by a sole proprietor.[64] Krupp
was, like the Kaiser, 'master in his own House', and both the firm and
the Empire were based on similar ideological premises. In practice this
meant that Krupp 'was. . . in his kingdom the successful representative
of a socio-political system',[65] and his factories served as 'a bastion
against the infiltration of social revolutionary ideas'.[66] This identity
of socio-political interests were further reinforced by the fact that Krupp
'represented an institution which [was] so closely connected with the
political and military greatness of Germany that it formed an integral
part of the Empire'.[67] Politically a Free Conservative, Krupp embraced
an ideology which Stumm's mouthpiece in the press, the ultra-right
newspaper *Die Post*, described as an 'industrial constitutionalism' of the
Prusso-German type which at the same time recognised the power and
influence of the new economic order.

'The first citizen of the German Empire',[68] 'the foremost industrialist
in the world'[69] stood at the head of a national institution which had
grown with the young Empire of which it was in many respects a
microcosm.[70] Writing to Bertha Krupp on the death of her father Fritz
in 1902, the Kaiser described the position of the Krupps in the
structure of the Empire. The work of the Krupp family, he wrote, was
'God given'.[71] Even allowing for Wilhelm II's incorrigible tendency to
overstate, the letter is a superlative exposition of a socio-political nostrum
which the twentieth century was fast eroding. He continued: 'it is your
duty willingly to take over this great task, without fear, because it has
been decreed and because it must be so. . . . The worker should and
must know that he is dependent upon Fraülein B. Krupp and not upon
a Board of Directors or managing body'. The privileges of such an

exalted position, however, also implicitly involved reciprocal responsibilities and 'were the Krupps ever tempted to forget this fact, the
Emperor would have been the first to remind them of it'.[72]

III

Although the *modus vivendi* of 1900 did not signify an end to Krupp-
INO disagreement on questions of price, delivery dates and so on, it
did nevertheless help to define the limits of the two sides' respective
spheres of interest and laid the foundation for the firm's relationship
with the Navy until the First World War. In the terms of this unwritten
understanding, Krupp enjoyed what can only be described as a special
relationship with the Imperial government and its naval officials who,
in their turn, acknowledged the firm's outstanding contribution to the
Navy's development. Thus the Head of the INO's Armament
Department, Paul Koch, wrote that in his opinion 'Krupp and the
Navy belonged together. . . . I am convinced that never was a customer
so fairly served as the naval administration by the firm of Krupp. . . .
The Navy was able to save itself the capital outlay involved in the
establishment of artillery works: the fact that no competition existed
is proof of the tremendously difficult demands posed by the INO'.[73]
And although, perhaps naturally, Tirpitz did not fully share this view,
he readily accepted the Navy's debt to the firm. In 1913 he wrote to
Krupp von Bohlen, Fritz Krupp's son-in-law, that 'Krupp and the
Navy belong historically together. Without Krupp the present development of our Navy would have hardly been conceivable'.[74]

There is more than a little truth in the State Secretary's statement,
for it is clear that as the First World War approached the firm of Krupp
became more and more closely involved in, and consequently identified
with, the armaments policy of the Empire. The reasons behind this
development were numerous. Thus the firm's (partly involuntary)
decision in the early 1890s to concentrate upon domestic contracts
was by no means unwelcome to the Navy, which like the Krupp
concern itself, realised that future armament production required the
solid financial backing which only heavy industry could supply. Krupp
was unique in Germany in that although it was primarily a manufacturer
of heavy industrial products, it also expanded vertically into shipbuilding. This move was important, for integrated firms were nearly
always more efficient because of their position of virtual independence
from the market fluctuations which plagued non-integrated firms.
Further, the firm's step in this direction was perfectly timed and left
it in a pivotal position when the big naval increases came in 1898 and

1900. Thus although Krupp's business with the Army was by no means inconsiderable, it was the Navy which was to assume a position progressively more and more important, until in the financial year 1912–13, Krupp's share of naval orders amounted to a staggering 53,000,000 Marks or 12 per cent of total Krupp production.[75]

This strengthening of ties between the Navy and heavy industry undoubtedly began with the era of aggressive and positive navalism pursued by Tirpitz. Yet the large quantitative and qualitative escalation in armament spending, and the increased demands of a new customer with heavy industrial requirements which resulted from it, were not the only reason which brought industry into the vortex of political or quasi-political activity. That navy-industry relations should come to play a more important role was equally the result of Tirpitz's own conscious and deliberate policy of politicising those sectors of the private economy which he believed would serve as his natural allies in furthering the Empire's armament policy. If for industry the reasons for cooperating in this scheme were different, they were no less attractive. Although after about 1895 the *Schlechtwetterzeit* (depression) was over, the effects of the 1870s and of the Great Depression had bequeathed to German industry a heritage of psychological insecurity and a 'fear of relapse',[76] which despite a growing prosperity continued to haunt industry until 1914. In such a business climate the presence of a skilfully manipulated armament programme could be useful in two important ways. Firstly, it could serve to stabilise and reassure an otherwise nervous market, and, secondly, in times of recession, it could supply the boost necessary for a recovery of confidence. Thus although until 1897 or so the potential of manipulating the economy as a direct result of armament spending was not fully appreciated, the greater demands of the 1898 Bill and the 1900 Supplementary Law brought the economic implications more clearly into perspective.

For these reasons Krupp and the INO evolved for their own mutual advantage a symbiotic relationship *par excellence*, a relationship in which the former needed and came to depend upon lucrative naval orders[77] and in which the Navy was dependent upon a concern which supplied much of its growing armament requirements. Yet in any such relationship the two parties cannot be completely equal and their motives, interests and aims are rarely identical or even similar. The resulting divergence of interest is the cause of an inherent conflict which, reduced to its crudest level, is about who uses whom. In the study of business-government relations this question is perhaps the most crucial and, at the same time, the most difficult to answer satisfactorily.

To the contemporary of the Wilhelmine business-political scene the problem, though not entirely new, was a recent one. From 1870 to 1914 the state came to play a more direct role in the economic sphere as a result of its ever-growing defence and social needs. Through the exercise of economic patronage government departments were to acquire considerable responsibility and power; yet at the same time this power posed hitherto unencountered difficulties of business and administrative practice.[78] As by far the greater part of public expenditure was handled through the War and Navy Offices, the bureaucracies of these departments were more than usually vulnerable to the attentions of the defence industries. In the case of the Navy, the new genre of businessmen which the Empire had produced were not unnaturally superior in business know-how to the traditionally trained bureaucrats of the INO. Yet the prevalence of malpractice is difficult to ascertain because of the very fine delineation which lay between legitimate lobbying and corruption. For the armament industry, the perhaps inevitable public conflict came in April 1913 when the Social Democrat Karl Liebknecht accused the firm of Krupp of bribery and improper practice in its dealings with the Artillery Commission.[79] The 'Brandt Affair', and the ensuing court case, which convicted a handful of Krupp employees including a member of the Krupp Board, caused a great public outcry in Germany and abroad. In business circles, however, the reaction was rather one of mild disapprobation that the case had been taken to court in the first place, combined with a reluctance to acknowledge that anything seriously unethical had taken place. In a significant passage, Richard Witting, the Chairman of the Board of the National Bank for Germany wrote:

> In this whole discussion people have tended to make the same basic error, namely to confuse the two roles of the State, firstly as the representative of sovereign rights and secondly as public entrepreneur. Legally it might be possible for the bureaucracy to cut itself off from the outside world but in its practical day-to-day functions this is out of the question. How should the Empire, state, province or district dig, build or produce without the emergence of some sort of symbiosis between the administration on one hand and on the other the entrepreneur who naturally regards himself as an equal partner?
>
> Since, therefore, the Empire, state and district are the biggest employers in Germany, thousands of business connections will be

formed: as long as they are as innocent as those between Brandt [the Krupp employee involved in the case] and the officers of the Artillery Commission, this can only be to the benefit of our State.[80]

Although the court did not share this attitude, Witting's comments are symptomatic of an indulgence in commercial and governmental life which firms like Krupp were able to exploit to the full. The firm's private relationship with the INO was never a particularly easy one and was throughout characterised by tactical manoeuverings on both sides. 'An indifferent man of business',[81] Tirpitz pursued after about 1900 a policy of non-interference in the firm's affairs. As a contemporary naval colleague of the State Secretary wrote in his diary, 'one says of T[irpitz] that he was the tool of the industrialists. . . . T[irpitz] went perhaps too often to Krupp, Thyssen, Ballin. They do not do anything for nothing'.[82]

Notes

1. Thus Crown Prince Rupprecht of Bavaria wrote to Count Hertling on 19 July 1917: 'In the last twenty years the entire foreign policy of the Empire has been the servant of the heavy industrialists. The profits which the consortiums made, or hoped to make, were the pertinent factors and not the interests of Germany as a whole'. Crown Prince Rupprecht, *Mein Kriegstagebuch* (Berlin, 1929), Vol. 3, p. 17.
2. From an unattributed article in *Littel's Living Age* of 4 May 1918.
3. BA-MA (Freiburg): Nachlass Behncke, Vol. 2, 27: Diary entry of 30 September 1918.
4. R. Zedlitz-Trützschler, *Zwölf Jahre am deutschen Kaiserhof* (Stuttgart-Berlin-Leipzig, 1924), p. 227.
5. See P. Padfield, *The Battleship Era* (London, 1973), p. 103: 'The decade of the 1880's began with ironclads and ended with battleships'. Also D. Pollock, *The Shipbuilding Industry* (London, 1905), p. 117: 'We are in a period of transition, even as regards guns and shipbuilding'.
6. U.v. Hassell, *Tirpitz: sein Leben und Wirken mit Berücksichtigung seiner Beziehungen zu A.von Stosch* (Stuttgart, 1920), p. 27–8.
7. GHH Archiv Nr. 300106/0: 'Ehrung des Generals von Stosch', 1883 and 1895.
8. Ibid. As a token of appreciation Stosch was given a present to the value of 34,900 Marks.
9. E. Kehr, *Schlachtflottenbau und Parteipolitik 1894–1901: Versuch eines Querschnitts durch die innenpolitischen Voraussetzungen des deutschen Imperialismus* (Berlin, 1930), p. 93.
10. U.v. Hassel, *Tirpitz*, p.46.
11. BA-MA, RMA: Nachlass Tirpitz, Vol. 4: Letter of Heeringen to Capelle of 13 August 1897. The Kaiser had urged a similar course of action to Knorr and Hollmann on 28 May 1896. In a Cabinet Order of that date he wrote: 'I should . . . like to recommend to you the strongest participation in favour of the fleet by that part of private industry which profits directly from it'.

Quoted in Kehr, *Schlachtflottenbau*, p. 100.

12. Historisches Archiv der Firma Fried. Krupp (hereafter 'Krupp') FAH III B 231, Privatbureau F.A. Krupp: Privatkorrespondenz von Tirpitz: Tirpitz to Krupp, St Blasien, 12 September 1897.
13. FAH III B 231: Krupp to Tirpitz, Scheveningen, 15 September 1897.
14. Ibid. Briefwechsel Krupp-Jencke betr. Action zu Gunsten der Marine Vorlage 1897: Krupp to Jencke, Baden-Baden, 14 October 1897.
15. Ibid. Schweinburg went on to found the Navy League in April 1898.
16. Shortage of space does not permit a more detailed account of the manoeuvrings and negotiations between the INO, Krupp, CDI, Deutscher Handelstag and prominent industrial and commercial figures which followed the 1 October meeting. Similarly even before Tirpitz had begun corresponding with Krupp, the latter, through his private secretary Dr Korn, had taken steps to rally support for the proposed Bill. See in this context G. Eley's unpublished Ph.D. thesis, 'The German Navy League in German Politics 1898–1914' (Ph.D., University of Sussex, 1974), and E. Böhm, *Überseehandel und Schlachtflottenbau. Hanseatische Kaufmannschaft und deutsche Seerüstung 1879–1902* (Düsseldorf, 1972). Another development which may be partly the result of Krupp's decision to support the Bill was the firm's acquisition, along with Henckel von Donnersmark and van der Zypen, of the *Berliner Neueste Nachrichten*, a daily newspaper which since its beginnings in 1880 had been associated with Bismarck and heavy industrial interests. See WA IV 2807, and GHH 3001073/3 and 300106/5 Betr. *Berliner Neueste Nachrichten*.
17. See the article 'Die ersten Beziehungen der Marine zu Krupp' in the *Marine Rundschau* of July 1912.
18. Fritz Krupp was a long-standing friend of Hollmann who often accompanied the Krupp family on their summer cruises. Another trusted confidant of Essen was Lucanus. The transfer of nearly 7,000 Marks 'vertraulich an den Chef des Civil Kabinetts Dr. von Lucanus, zu senden und auf sein Privatkonto zu buchen' from Krupp, and Lucanus' receipts of 5 October 1901 and 12 October 1901 respectively, even suggests that the relationship was a pecuniary one. See FAH IIIC 4, p. 142–7.
19. FAH II B 329: Hermann Orges to Alfred Krupp, 17 February 1865.
20. Ibid: Alfred Krupp to the Prokura, 20 July 1873. See also WA XVI 40 and WA IXa 172.
21. H. von Ham's Festschrift *250 Jahre Dillinger Hütte* (Koblenz, 1935). Until 1876 the Navy had been supplied by English firms.
22. W. von Tirpitz, 'Wie hat sich der Staatsbetrieb beim Aufbau der Flotte bewährt?' (Ph.D., Leipzig, 1929), p. 33. The cooperation between the two firms 'went so far that the replies of both firms to the INO resembled each other word for word'.
23. Von Ham's Festschrift suggests that each firm was given a half of the Navy's requirements (*250 Jahre Dillinger Hütte*, p. 190). Although this was at first the case, Krupp was later to receive the lion's share.
24. The production figures (war materials) of the firm show a dramatic decline after 1885:

Financial Year	Domestic	%	Foreign	%
1885–6	3,841,505 Mks	15.4	21,128,235 Mks	84.6
1890–1	2,114,275 Mks	13.6	13,442,760 Mks	86.4

W. Boelcke, *Krupp und die Hohenzollern in Dokumenten: Krupp-Korrespondenz mit Kabinettschef und Ministern 1850–1918* (Frankfurt a/M, 1970), Appendix. See also the Festschift, *Friedrich Krupp AG 1812–1912* (Essen, 1912).
25. The French onslaught was particularly successful in Russia, South America and Japan, all of which were, up until that time, good Krupp markets.

26. J.T. Walton Newbold, *How Europe armed for War* (London, 1916), p. 30. Krupp also had technical troubles at this time: see H. von Perbrandt's pamphlet, 'Ist die Monopolstellung Krupps berechtigt?' (Date and place of publication unknown), p. 9.

27. For the extent of Gruson's other shipbuilding interests, see G. Lemann-Felskowski, *Deutschlands Schiffbauindustrie* (Berlin, 1903), p. 51.

28. WA XIV 199: Uebergang des Grusonwerkes in Kruppschen Besitz.

29. J. Meisbach, *Friedrich A. Krupp wie er lebte und starb* (Cologne, 1903). Commemoration speech of Julius von Schüss, 7 December 1902.

30. *Vossische Zeitung*, No. 16 of 10 January 1893. See also *Rheinische-Westfälische Zeitung*, 2 May 1893.

31. XVIr 40, Betr. Schiff- und Maschinbau AG Germania Berlin u. Kiel: Abschrift einer eigenhändigen Niederschrift Alfred Krupps aus 1875. See also, WA IXa 172, pp. 9–10.

32. WA II 9, p. 763: Carl Meyer to Krupp of 8 May 1882 and the letters of Krupp to Graening, WA III 21, of 28 February 1883 to 1 August 1885.

33. WA XIV 199: Uebergang der Germaniawerft in Kruppschen Besitz. See also the *Frankfurter Zeitung* of 3 September 1896.

34. FAH III B 178: Erwerbung der Werft Germania.

35. T. von Wilmowski, *Rückblickend mochte ich sagen.... An der Schwelle des 150 jährigen Krupp-Jubiläums* (Oldenburg and Hamburg, 1961), p. 163.

36. FAH III B 179: Fusion der Germaniawerft mit Vulkan.

37. FAH IVc 90: Sitzungen des Directoriums 1909–1939. Ehrensberger's report to the Board of Directors on 3 December 1910, in which he stressed the dependability of arms orders, come boom or recession. He compared it unfavourably to the demand for peace materials which, though reasonable, was 'however, very unstable'.

38. BA-MA, RMA: Nachlass Tirpitz, 20: Notizen Tirpitz betr. Krupp. 1900.

39. Cited in V.R. Berghahn, *Rüstung und Machtpolitik* (Düsseldorf, 1973), p. 55.

40. A. von Tirpitz, *Erinnerungen* (Leipzig, 1920), p. 37: 'a limited company which has a monopoly easily pays too much attention to its annual dividends and not enough to the development of the product'.

41. BA-MA, RMA: Nachlass Tirpitz, 20: Notizen betr. Krupp.

42. V.R. Berghahn *Rüstung und Machtpolitik*, p. 55.

43. BA-MA, RMA: Nachlass Tirpitz 20: Notizen betr. Krupp.

44. E. Kehr, *Schlachtflottenbau und Parteipolitik*, p. 175.

45. WA III B 36: Krupp to Jencke, date uncertain but presumably early May 1900.

46. WA III B 36: Promemoria für den Kaiser, written by Jencke on 6 May 1900. The account of the audience is taken from Krupp's own notes of the meeting which are to be found in the same file.

47. Ibid.: Krupp's notes of the audience.

48. Ibid.

49. Ibid.

50. Ibid.

51. Ibid. Thus taking the battleship 'Wörth' as his example, Krupp showed that the greater resistance of the new nickel-steel armour permitted a 50 per cent reduction in weight, or, in other words, the quantity of armour required. Therefore, although the nickel-plate was more expensive at 2,320 Marks a ton, compared to the 1,521 Marks a ton paid for the old compound armour-plate, a considerable saving was made by the INO.

52. Ibid.

53. Ibid.

54. Ibid.

55. Ibid.
56. Ibid.
57. FAH B 39: Jencke to Krupp, 11 June 1898. Relating to Krupp a conversation he had had with Tirpitz, Jencke wrote that Tirpitz expressed 'the urgent necessity for the factory to increase its efficiency in the production of armour and warship artillery'.
58. WA III B 36: Krupp's notes of his audience with the Kaiser.
59. W. von Tirpitz, *Staatsbetrieb*, p. 34: 'with the chronic shortness of money in the Navy, it was an inconceivable thought [for the Navy to build its own works]'. With regard to contracting abroad, the INO did enter a correspondence with the Midvale Steel Company: the fact, however, that this would have left the Navy partly dependent upon an American firm suggests strongly that the idea was not seriously entertained.
60. BA-MA, RMA: 7631/Vol. 3: Verhandlungen mit Thyssen über Aufnahme der Panzerplatten Herstellung.
61. WA III B 36: Krupp's notes of his audience with the Kaiser.
62. W. von Tirpitz, *Staatsbetrieb*, p. 34.
63. In a significant speech before the *Reichstag's* Budget Committee, Tirpitz stated: 'That we have come so far with Krupp is due only to the fact that we are dealing not with a limited company but with a single entrepreneur who was open to our ideas'. Reported in *Kölnische Zeitung*, 6 March 1910.
64. Although the firm became officially a limited company ('AG') after Fritz Krupp's death in 1902, its shares were not quoted on any exchange nor did the company make public its annual reports. All the shares remained in the hands of the Krupp family. The notion that the Kaiser held some financial interest in the firm was an old one which was referred to in a speech made in the Reichstag by the Social Democrat member, Südekum, in 1908. An undated work, *Krupp in Essen* by Hermann Haase, further claimed that the imperial House had loaned the firm a substantial amount during an unspecified crisis. It is, however, a statement which appears to have no factual foundation and one which this author considers to be apocryphal. See WA XIV 235: Berdrow to Dr Pigrim of 25 November 1915, Betr. das Gerucht: Beteiligung des Kaiserhauses an der Firma Krupp. See also in the same file the Krupp-Eulenburg correspondence on the subject of 25 and 31 May 1908. For an opposing viewpoint, see B. Menne, *Krupp – Deutschlands Kannonenkönige* (Zürich, 1936), p. 183ff.
65. *Kölnische Zeitung*, 28 October 1902.
66. From a speech given by Jencke to the General Meeting of the CDI in Cologne on 17 March 1902.
67. A. von Schwering, *The Berlin Court under William II*, p. 215.
68. *F.A. Krupp: Eine Gedächtnissschrift* (Essen, 1903), No author.
69. Ibid.
70. Thus Krupp 'cared for his thousands of workpeople in a fatherly manner; but he was very severe with them. He would issue commands like an Emperor, which had to be obeyed to the letter.' Baroness H. Deichmann, *Impressions and Memories* (London, 1926), p. 238.
71. FAH IV E 782: William II to Frl. Bertha Krupp of 12 December 1902.
72. A. von Schwering, *The Berlin Court under William II*, p. 215.
73. P. Koch, *Krupp und die Marine* (published by its author, 1929).
74. BA-MA, RMA: Nachlass Tirpitz 17: Tirpitz to Krupp von Bohlen of 5 October 1913.
75. BA-MA, RMA: F7631, Nachlass Dähnhardt, iv: Marineanteil am Umsturz und Gewinn der Firma Krupp.
76. H.-U. Wehler, *Bismarck und der Imperialismus* (Cologne, 1969), p. 64.

77. Thus Krupp profits on armour-plating between 1897—8 and 1904—5 ranged from 57 per cent to 62 per cent, except for the financial year 1901—2 when they fell to 54 per cent. The detailed figures are to be found in WA IV 1768: Geschäftsberichte.
78. For a general exposition of public policy towards the business community, see W. Treue, 'Wirtschaft- und Sozialgeschichte Deutschlands in 19. Jahrhundert', p. 384ff, in *Handbuch der deutschen Geschichte*, edited by Gebhardt (Stuttgart, 1962).
79. F. Zimmermann, *Prozess Brandt und Genossen. Der soganannte Krupp-Prozess* (Berlin, 1914).
80. Ibid., p. 395.
81. Ministry of Defence, London: Admiralty Library, CA 2053, Germany No. 24: Hugh Watson (Naval Attaché, Berlin), to Goschen, 12 April 1912.
82. BA-MA, RMA: Nachlass Behncke: Vol. 2, 27: Diary entry of 30 September 1918.

4 POLITICS AND CULTURE: THE STATE AND THE AVANT-GARDE IN MUNICH 1886–1914

Robin Lenman

I

The years between the death of the Bavarian King Ludwig II in 1886 and the outbreak of the First World War were a period of great importance in Bavarian history. In marked contrast to the situation in Prussia, new forces created by social and economic change had a visible effect on the political system, so that by 1914 the balance of power between the Wittelsbach governing bureaucracy and Parliament had shifted appreciably in favour of the latter.[1] At the same time, the Bavarian capital experienced an upsurge of cultural activity which was perhaps unique in its modern history. The present study endeavours to relate politics to culture by examining how far political change affected the behaviour of the state towards the Munich artistic community, and especially towards those of its members who rejected traditional aesthetic ideas, and whose work and life-style (epitomised for contemporaries by the single word 'Schwabing',[2] though not all of Munich's intellectuals lived in that northern suburb) challenged prevailing orthodoxies. It will be argued that, although the institutional diversity of Imperial Germany gave certain important advantages to intellectuals residing in Bavaria, their freedom was also bound up with the survival of the 'ministerial republic' of the Regency period; and that after 1912 certain sections of the Munich *avant-garde* were directly threatened by the emergence of a new élite which owed its rise to power at least partly to pressure from below.

II

There were two principal ways in which the state could make its presence felt among Munich writers and artists. On the positive side, at least as far as painting and sculpture were concerned, it could offer material encouragement by buying or commissioning works of art. But it also had at its disposal a battery of legal and administrative sanctions which could be used (subject to certain restrictions) to set limits to artistic and literary experiment. It is necessary to discover how both patronage and repression worked in practice.

Like their colleagues in Vienna, Munich intellectuals often complained about popular indifference and meanness towards the arts. Artists, they felt, were regarded at best as an asset to the local economy to be piously but platonically admired, and at worst quite simply as a colony of resident buffoons.[3] But at the turn of the century Munich was only just over a quarter of the size of Vienna (the contrast with Berlin was even greater), and conspicuously lacked the Austrian capital's stratum of very rich and enlightened private patrons.[4] This meant that the Crown and the state had a particularly important cultural role; indeed, Munich's position as a nineteenth-century art centre could never have been achieved without the generosity and initiative of the Wittelsbachs. As far as the Regency is concerned, it is necessary to distinguish between two types of patronage 'from above': purchases and commissions paid for by Prince Regent Luitpold out of his own pocket (the Crown itself was still burdened with Ludwig II's vast debts); and acquisitions of modern works for the state collections which required the Regent's approval but were mainly financed by a parliamentary grant of (from 1890 onwards) 90,000 Marks per year.[5]

Between the early 1850s and his death in 1912, Prince Luitpold spent almost 900,000 Marks on paintings and sculptures, the majority of them by Munich artists;[6] and after becoming Regent he clearly prided himself on continuing the dynastic tradition. But his taste was essentially conservative and he showed little interest in contemporary trends, so that his personal impact on the Munich art world was probably more important in other ways. He was a close friend of several prominent figures and was warmly sympathetic towards artists in general. He did not interfere with Government patronage policy, and refrained absolutely from All-Highest pronouncements on taste and aesthetics of the kind familiar further North. His presence in the background can probably be seen as a substantial safeguard for Munich's artistic freedom.[7]

Responsibility for buying works of art for the state collections lay with the Minister for Church and School Affairs, who was advised by a Purchasing Committee consisting partly of practising artists and partly of gallery officials and various local experts.[8] Much of the State's money in this period seems to have gone to a fairly restricted group of established local painters: men usually distinguished by their prominence either in the Artists' Guild (*Künstlergenossenschaft*) or in the rival but not greatly dissimilar Society of Munich Artists (*Verein bildender Künstler Münchens*) — the Secession — founded in 1892, by membership of the influential artists' club *Allotria*, and frequently also by possession of a variety of titles and decorations. Notable examples were Friedrich August von Kaulbach, Director of the Munich Academy between 1886 and 1891 and a close friend and hunting-companion of the Regent; Franz von Defregger, famous for his scenes from peasant life and history; and accomplished society painters like Leo Samberger and Albert von Keller. Most outstanding was Franz von Lenbach, international portraitist and 'painter-prince', President of both the Guild and the *Allotria*, and from the late 1880s until his death in 1904 the virtual dictator of the Munich art establishment.[9] By 1902 he had no less than nine pictures in the *Neue Pinakothek*, where the cream of the state's collection was housed.

This policy naturally antagonised the *avant-garde* and invited complaints that the Ministry was paying large sums of money to those who least needed support. Otto Julius Bierbaum described Kaulbach's *Burial of Christ*, bought by the state for 20,000 Marks in 1892,[10] as 'an *Oberammergauerei* of the dreariest, most conventional and most inartistic kind';[11] while the Naturalist writer and critic Michael Georg Conrad wrote that in the same year more than 5,000 oil-paintings had had to be compulsorily auctioned in the city, nearly all of them by the artists themselves.[12] Of course, given the number of painters and sculptors living in Munich (in 1907 there were 1,882, compared with only 1,475 in Berlin[13]) and the amount of public money available, even a radical change of official policy would hardly have made much difference to the city's artistic proletariat as a whole. But it was certainly true that in the 1890s some highly original and talented individuals were passed over. Lovis Corinth, one of the most outstanding painters working in Munich, did not have a single picture bought by the state; and this may have been one reason why he left for Berlin at the turn of the century, writing to a friend 'I really can't stand Munich any longer'.[14]

On the other hand, although its taste was sometimes questionable, the Government was not afraid to buy unorthodox or controversial work. The impressionist and 'poverty-painter' Fritz von Uhde, for instance, offended many Catholics by his naturalistic treatment of religious themes (which tended, according to his critics to 'reduce the Christian idea to the level of ordinary existence'[15]). Yet both the state and the Regent paid large sums for his pictures, and ministers defended him against angry attacks in Parliament.[16] A much more sensational example was Franz Stuck, who had risen by his mid-thirties from the humblest of peasant origins to extraordinary fame and affluence. Whether or not one accepts the current psycho-analytical interpretations of his work,[17] there can be no doubt about its uninhibited erotic hedonism, and it was this which made Stuck the darling of the *Jugendstil*[18] *avant-garde*: 'There was no morality in Paradise', wrote Bierbaum in one of the first monographs on the painter, 'and art is Paradise regained'.[19] Nevertheless, the Bavarian Government not only paid 25,000 Marks for his symbolic painting *War* in 1894,[20] but the following year accepted as a gift for the *Neue Pinakothek* a version of *Sin*, one of the most blatantly erotic (and also celebrated) pictures of the decade.[21] Like some of his canvases, Stuck's reputation had decayed considerably by his death in 1928. But at the turn of the century he possessed all the trappings of an outstanding successful artistic career: not only a princely income, a palatial residence and a flourishing school (its pupils included at various times Kandinsky, Klee and Weisgerber), but also personal nobility, *entrée* to the court, and a royal Bavarian professorship conferred at the exceptionally early age of thirty. Finally, there was the case of Max Slevogt, also strongly attracted by erotic themes but in importance, style and concern for sometimes provocative realism much closer to Corinth than to Stuck. Like Stuck, however, and regardless of the fact that he was an early contributor to the satirical paper *Simplicissimus*, Slevogt soon received the official accolade: a professorship at 33 and the purchase of his work (including the subtly erotic *Leisure Hour* for the *Neue Pinakothek*) by both Luitpold and the government.[22]

Unfortunately, at least as far as paintings were concerned (purchases for the State's graphic collections showed a fairly lively awareness of contemporary trends), official interest in unusual work seems to have flagged after 1900. There were probably two main reasons for this. One was the healthy disintegration of the Munich artistic community after the turn of the century and the appearance of numerous small groups outside the orbit of the Artists' Guild and the Secession which made it harder to plot new developments. The other was the combination of growing financial stringency with the fundamental re-orientation of Bavarian purchasing policy which took place in the years before the war.

The long-standing custom, strongly supported by both Parliament and local artists, of spending most of the government's money at the annual exhibitions put on by the Guild and the Secession had inevitably allowed serious gaps to develop in the State collections. Not a single French Impressionist was represented in the *Neue Pinakothek* until shortly before the First World War, and even major Bavarian painters had been badly neglected: Leibl's important *Portrait of Frau Gedon*, for example, which had been praised by Courbet in 1869, was not acquired until 1913.[23] Yet although this state of affairs had been causing concern for a long time,[24] it was not until the appointment of Hugo von Tschudi (who had resigned from the Berlin National Gallery after friction with Wilhelm II) as Director of the Bavarian State Galleries in 1909 that decades of parochial buying began to be made good. The task of a modern state gallery, wrote Tschudi in 1911, was to provide local artists with inspiration rather than cash; and he also had hard words for the system of purchase by committee.[25] But while many of the outstanding pictures now acquired (among them Manet's *Luncheon in the Studio*, Van Gogh's *View of Arles* and others of similar quality[26]) were donated or bought by Tschudi's rich acquaintances, the rest had to be paid for out of the State's limited resources: for example Géricault's *Horse Artillery* (35,000 Marks), Courbet's *Lock in the Optevoz Valley* (10,000 Francs), Monet's *Bridge at Argenteuil* (15,000 Marks) and Leibl's *The Painter Schuch* and *Frau Gedon*.(30,000 and 130,000 Marks respectively).[27] At the same time, the government seems to have been unable either to obtain more funds from Parliament or to escape from its obligation to buy at least some traditional work from local artists at the annual exhibitions. Shortage of money may therefore have been one reason why paintings by Kandinsky, Marc, Jawlensky and other members of Munich's last pre-war *avant-garde* had not found their way into the Bavarian state collections by the time buying was suspended in 1914; although the growth of clerical power and the appointment of the conservative von Knilling as Minister in 1912 were probably factors of at least equal importance.

III

If official patronage tended for the most part to affect established or conventional figures, the opposite was true of the state's repressive powers. The paragraphs of the Criminal Code dealing with *lèse-majesté* (99-101), incitement (130), blasphemy (166), the distribution of obscene material (184), and so-called 'gross mischief' (360/11 — increasingly used as a weapon against the press in the 1890s), though hardly a threat to novelists like Ludwig Ganghofer or to Munich's battalion of *genre* and landscape painters, created dangerous pitfalls for the Naturalist *avant-garde*, for the new satire of the late 1890s and for the pioneers of *Jugendstil* illustration and design. In the first decade of Wilhelm II's reign there was also strong pressure to intensify some of these measures, and the Bavarian Government did little to resist it.[28] Between 1889 and 1900 it supported a series of repressive proposals, including the so-called

Lex Heinze, which was aimed initially at urban vice but gradually broadened to include a very flexible extension of the law on obscenity.[29] Indeed, the suggested new Paragraph 184a, which greatly alarmed artists and writers, may possibly have owed its origin to the inability of the Munich authorities to deal effectively with certain productions of the local *avant-garde*.[30] The best that can be said for Bavarian ministers on this issue is that by March 1900, when the controversy was at its height, they were evidently having second thoughts about the Bill, less perhaps because of the noisy public debate than because of protests from the Munich Academy[31] and probably also pressure from the Regent. But the episode as a whole seems to have had a chastening effect, so that it was several years before a majority of ministers were prepared to contemplate even minor legislative proposals which might be construed as an attack on the arts.

It is hard to decide how repressive a climate prevailed in Munich during the 1890s. Without doubt, some intellectuals lived in fear of the law: in February 1891, for example, Michael Georg Conrad wrote specially to the Police Director to deny press allegations that he was an atheist and a revolutionary;[32] and the disintegration of the Modern Life Society (*Gesellschaft für modernes Leben*), of which Conrad was the figurehead, seems to have been hastened by the danger of prosecution.[33] In August 1891, Hanns von Gumppenberg was sent to a fortress for having recited a poem by Karl Henckell which was interpreted as a libel of the Emperor;[34] and in April 1895 Oskar Panizza was gaoled for a year for blasphemy because of his 'heavenly tragedy' *The Council of Love* (*Das Liebeskonzil*).[35] But the state's oppressiveness should not be exaggerated. On several occasions, attempts to prosecute members of the *avant-garde* were blocked by the courts or ended in discharge; and it would certainly be unwise to generalise from the Panizza case. The theme of *The Council of Love* (described by one of Panizza's own colleagues, the dramatist Joesph Ruederer, as 'filth'[36]) was the origin of syphilis as divine retribution for debauchery at the court of Pope Alexander VI, and was handled in a highly provocative way. Panizza, who later went mad (he claimed in 1903 that Karl May was really Wilhelm II[37]), seems in fact to have had an exhibitionistic desire for confrontation, and in court practically demolished his own case: 'I never saw a person defend himself in a crazier fashion' wrote Conrad to the Socialist leader Georg von Vollmar after the trial.[38] In normal circumstances, both Paragraphs 166 and 184 were interpreted fairly narrowly by the courts, hence the desire of the prosecuting authorities, at least as far as obscenity was concerned, for a

broader formulation of the law. But the *avant-garde* was also protected
against wholesale persecution by a feature of the German federal system
which will presently be discussed in more detail: the rule in Bavaria
(and in certain other states, but not Prussia or Saxony) that offences
committed by means of the press — defined to include books and
most process work, even photography — had to be tried by jury. This
was a crucial safeguard; and it probably explains why, even in the year
of the Panizza trial, a man like Conrad was prepared to write a glowing
panegyric on Munich's tolerance and cultural vitality.[39]

After 1900, until the last months before the war, conditions not
only did not deteriorate but may even have improved. From the turn
of the century onwards, the State's task was complicated by the fact
that *avant-garde* art and literature had to be dealt with alongside a
growing flood of pornography, some of it produced for various reasons
by genuine artists and men of letters: as Franz Blei wrote in 1903,
commenting on the fact that a literary magazine had been financed by
a highly profitable edition of Aretino, '2 such pieces of high-class
pornography a year and you can survive'.[40] It was often far from easy
to draw the line between art and superior exploitation material, and
in court the most dubious productions were sometimes saved by
massive recruitment of 'expert' witnesses by the defence. Some convictions were obtained during the pre-war period: in 1911, for example,
a set of Beardsleyesque illustrations depicting 'masturbation, pederasty,
sodomy, lesbian love and sadism'[41] by the Austrian Marquis von Bayros
was condemned (Bayros himself had wisely fled abroad; his collaborator,
Dr Semerau, went to prison for eight months).[42] Like Panizza, however,
Bayros would hardly have fared better anywhere else, and cases like his
were offset by others with a different outcome: Ludwig Thoma and
Olaf Gulbransson were acquitted of obscenity for their broadsheet *Away
with Love!!* (*Fort mit der Liebe!!*) in 1906;[43] a year later, Willi Geiger
escaped punishment for his highly erotic album *The Common Pursuit*
(*Das gemeinsame Ziel*);[44] and in 1912 the State failed to convict Georg
Queri for his dictionary of peasant sexual and scatological expressions,
Kraftbayrisch, even though the police maintained that the 'shameless
smut and obscenities' it contained had little to do with peasant life.[45]
Not surprisingly, cases like these provoked Munich's leading morality
campaigner into describing the city as a 'haven for pornographers'.[46]
Matters were made still more difficult for the authorities by the appear-
ance of literary movements more esoteric than Naturalism, and this
was strikingly illustrated by the case of the Expressionist paper *Die
Revolution* in 1913. Among other provocative items, the first number

included a poem entitled *The Hangman* by Hugo Ball which, in conjunction with confused references to the Virgin Mary, described an executioner's voluptuous feelings on dispatching a beautiful woman. But although charges were brought under Paragraphs 166 and 184, Ball and his accomplices eventually had to be discharged on the grounds that the poem was 'so obscure and incomprehensible that it leaves room for every possible interpretation';[47] and in the end the Reich Appeal Court even rejected an application for the confiscated copies of *Die Revolution* to be destroyed.[48]

After 1900, just as before, the Munich *avant-garde*'s most valuable shield against state interference was the Bavarian press 'privilege' of trial by jury. It was this institutional safeguard, created in 1848, rather than Munich's supposedly more tolerant atmosphere, which made the Bavarian capital a safer place to say daring things in print or caricature than cities like Dresden or Berlin, where press offences were dealt with by tribunals of professional judges. Although Munich jurymen often appear to have been artisans or peasants (during the Bayros trial, the foreman passed a note to the judge asking why, if there were such strict laws against spreading cattle disease, the law against moral contamination was so lax[49]), the system nevertheless made convictions much harder to obtain and often deterred the authorities from starting proceedings in the first place.[50] In 1870, the Munich Police Director himself had described trial by jury as 'the highest palladium of press freedom',[51] and intellectuals reacted with understandable vehemence to right-wing demands for its abolition. For most of the pre-1914 period there was little real likelihood that this method of dealing with press offenders would be interfered with. But as Bavaria had the right to abandon it unilaterally if she so wished,[52] the considerable growth of clerical influence on the eve of the war eventually made such action a definite possibility.

The protection afforded by the jury system was most strikingly demonstrated by the career of *Simplicissimus*.[53] Although its quality was declining by 1914, Albert Langen's creation was undoubtedly one of the most brilliant satirical papers in Europe and, like Georg Hirth's *Jugend* (*Youth*), was closely linked with the Munich *avant-garde*, for which it also served as an appreciable source of income.[54] Many of *Simplicissimus*'s regular collaborators — for example Thomas Theodor Heine, Bruno Paul and Ignatius Taschner — were also distinguished illustrators and designers (in 1908 it was suggested that examples of their work should be bought by the state[55]); Thomas Mann and Frank Wedekind were closely associated with it in its early years; and the

Simplicissimus 'circle' was one of the liveliest of the many Munich intellectual coteries.

Compared, for example, with the very similar *Assiette au Beurre* in France which satirised domestic politics practically with impunity,[56] *Simplicissimus* clashed with the law fairly frequently. On two occasions at least, members of its staff received prison sentences: Heine and Wedekind in Leipzig in 1898 for libelling the Emperor; and the editor, Ludwig Thoma, in 1906 in Stuttgart for insulting some morality campaigners. The former case was much the more serious and led the paper's management to abandon its Saxon printer and find a new one, as a suitable firm could not be found in Munich, in Stuttgart, where press cases were also tried by jury. 'As long as we stay in Leipzig', wrote the acting editor, Korfiz Holm, a few months before the move, 'we always face the danger of being destroyed . . . it would not be difficult to lock us all up, one after the other'.[57] In general, however, in spite of the fanatical hatred it aroused in clerical and conservative circles, *Simplicissimus* suffered remarkably little damage. One reason for this was a protracted wrangle between Bavaria and Württemberg as to whether the authorities in Munich or Stuttgart should have the thankless task of dealing with it, and between 1906 and 1910 the paper's practical immunity to interference increased considerably as a result.[58] It was also extremely difficult to carry out effective confiscation when charges were actually brought: one of several discouraging examples was the attempted seizure of the notorious 'Ambassador's Education' number (which accused Bülow in the crudest terms of obsequiousness towards foreign governments) in May 1903 which yielded only 1,341 copies out of a total edition of 80,000.[59] Above all, however, *Simplicissimus* was protected by the extreme reluctance of the authorities to risk trials which were almost bound to end in acquittal by a jury, and which Thoma and his legal advisers, most notably Conrad Haussmann, skilfully exploited to increase circulation. Even the administrative sanction, used eventually in 1909, of banning the paper from sale on State railway stations probably did it less harm in the long run than the loss of several outstanding collaborators and the general effects of middle age.[60] Only wartime conditions finally gave the authorities the power to snuff out *Simplicissimus* altogether. But in August 1914 the paper became so chauvinistic (it had always been anti-Russian and often anti-British) that its value to the German war effort soon had to be recognised.[61]

Paradoxically, although the Bavarian Government's ability to interfere with literature and satire was limited, the institutional untidiness of Unification had left it with one formidable weapon against artistic freedom: practically unrestricted power to censor the stage.[62] The machinery here was not only quite different from that governing the press (it is interesting to compare the freedom enjoyed by *Simplicissimus* with the close supervision of its stage counterpart, the Eleven Executioners cabaret[63]), since it was entirely administrative and operated mainly by the police, but was considerably more arbitrary than theatre censorship in Prussia, where local bans could be and in some important cases were overturned by a Higher Administrative Court.[64] The Bavarian system was absolutist in conception and at all levels, from the serious theatre down to the music-hall and eventually also the cinema, often heavy-handed and petty in application. But in spite of constant criticism this relic of the traditional police state remained fundamentally un-altered until the abolition of all German stage censorship in November 1918.

The rigour of this system was only slightly mitigated by the creation in 1908 of a Censorship Advisory Council (*Zensurbeirat*) to help the police in assessing serious plays.[65] This body had no decision-making powers; and although it included some writers and critics (among them Max Halbe and Thomas Mann, both of whom eventually resigned), they were outnumbered by an assortment of more or less conservative school-masters and academics, with an expert on venereal disease and the world-famous psychiatrist Emil Kraepelin added for good measure. One of the Council's first actions was in fact to persuade the police to allow a heavily-cut version of Wedekind's great play about adolescence, *Spring Awakening* (*Frühlings Erwachen*), to be publicly performed in Munich in 1908. But the problems connected with *Lulu* and several of Wedekind's other works proved to be so divisive that by 1914 the Council was in considerable disarray; and it certainly failed to fulfil its main purpose, which seems to have been to make censorship a politically less sensitive issue.

On the other hand, however, the censor's power over the public stage was partly offset by the apparently tolerant attitude of the police towards Munich's numerous private dramatic societies. One of the most important of these was the University Dramatic Society (*Akademisch-Dramatischer Verein*), which was run by students but supported by many artists and writers and able (with the help of actors lent by the Court Theatre – in Munich there were many bridges between the *avant-garde* and the cultural establishment) to mount productions comparable to those of the Berlin Free Stage (*Freie Bühne*).[66] Although dissolved by the University in 1903 after a controversial performance of part of Schnitzler's *Ein Reigen* (*La Ronde*), the group was immediately reconstituted as the New Society (*Neue Verein*) and remained very active until the outbreak of war. Its records indicate that 'closed' performances often had large audiences: in February 1907, for example, *Spring Awakening* was put on in the Playhouse (*Schauspielhaus*), which seated 730 people, and seven times as many tickets were issued as there were members of the Society.[67] In practice, therefore, provided that certain formalities were observed, controversial plays were accessible to any adult with a serious interest in drama, a fact underlined by court orders and letters from theatrical agents concerned about their authors' rights. But by 1914, although the New Society's own immediate problems stemmed from the quarrelsomeness endemic among Munich intellectuals,[68] the political climate was becoming increasingly unfavourable to un-censored productions, the Court Theatre was less willing to cooperate, and the future was clouded with uncertainty.

IV

From what has been said so far, it seems that for most of the period the cultural record of the Wittelsbach State was by no means bad. In the 1890s, it is true, the Bavarian Government sought wider powers against supposed threats to the social order, but so did governments elsewhere. Munich theatre censorship was often oppressive, but not necessarily more so than the English system; and in Nuremberg the censor was particularly tolerant.[69] Patronage policy could have been more imaginative, yet the appointment of Hugo von Tschudi and the acceptance of his ideas was a sign of considerable open-mindedness. Bavarian ministers and other high officials seem to have been cultivated men with a genuine and active concern for Munich's position as an art centre. Indeed, in 1901 fear that this might be undermined even led the Government to object to Reich financial support for a major exhibition of German painting in Berlin.[70] Ministers also had many contacts with the intellectual community: via organisations like the local Journalists' and Writers' Association and as guests at the innumerable social functions involving painters and men of letters; through discreet discussions about honours and patronage; and as private individuals with 'dear, honoured and highly-esteemed friends'[71] in the art world. Above all, although officials looked askance at the antics of Schwabing celebrities like Frank Wedekind, kept a close watch on the 'gentleman-anarchist' Erich Mühsam and other suspicious elements,[72] and probably ground their teeth at the embarrass-ment caused by *Simplicissimus*, they regarded the State's task in relation to the *avant-garde* as an essentially limited one: to protect the citizen, as far as the law permitted, against moral or religious outrage, but not to impose particular aesthetic doctrines.

It was becoming increasingly uncertain, however, how long this would continue to be the case.[73] From the late 1880s onwards, the liberal-conservative ministerial bureaucracy and its mainly Protestant, urban and unitarian supporters in the Chamber of Deputies (the lower house of Parliament) faced growing pressure from the Bavarian Centre Party, which represented the Catholic, rural and particularist majority of the population. The electoral decline of liberalism, the emergence of new political forces (in 1893 the first five Social Democrats entered the Chamber, while agricultural crisis was already provoking an upsurge of radicalism in the countryside), and the Centre's aggressive use of the Chamber's budgetary powers made it difficult for the Government to maintain its independent position 'above the parties'; and gradually compelled it to adopt a more conciliatory attitude towards moderate elements in the opposition. Partly because of the ascendancy of a radical section of the Centre Party led by Georg Heim, this new course was interrupted by serious conflict around the turn of the century which culminated in the resignation of Prime Minister Crailsheim in February 1903. But events soon led to its resumption: 1906 brought the long-awaited reform of the Bavarian franchise which strengthened the Centre and further weakened the Liberals; and this approximately coincided with the subjugation of the Heim faction by the Centre's conservative wing, led by ecclesiastics like Franz Seraph Pichler and senior officials like Dr Georg Ritter von Örterer. Although Crailsheim's successor, Count Clemens von Podewils-Dürnitz, was prepared to some extent to seek the cooperation of the Social Democrats, these developments appear to have confirmed the Regent's closest advisers in the belief that the constitutional status quo could best be preserved by drawing close to men like Pichler and Orterer who seemed more concerned to improve their own political and social position than to press for fundamental change.

Whatever the political merits of this strategy, it had grave implications for Munich's cultural life. For the objective of broadening and thus stabilising the Bavarian establishment could only be achieved at the expense of some of its existing members and beneficiaries: liberal press barons like Georg Hirth, owner of Munich's largest daily newspaper, the *Münchener Neuesten Nachrichten*, as well as *Jugend*; major art-publishing firms like Bruckmann and Hanfstaengl, whose reproductions were frequently attacked by morality campaigners; and all those intellectuals who had cause to fear the growth of clerical influence on government.

Between the Bavarian elections of 1907 and the outbreak of war, culture
was a particularly inflammable political issue, and for important reasons.
Hostility to modern art and literature, and to 'urban decadence' in
general, seems to have been common to all sections of the Centre Party
and (together with longstanding confessional and educational grievances)
probably had a useful integrating function in an organisation which had
been bedevilled by internal strife throughout its history. Visible concessions by the Government in this area were therefore likely to be part
of the Centre leadership's price for 'responsible' use of its parliamentary
power, as a sop for the now frustrated Party radicals. On the other side,
those with a vested interest in resisting the Centre's advance clearly
found it expedient to revive the *Kulturkampf* slogan of 'Catholic
barbarism' whenever ministers seemed to be giving way to the majority
in the Chamber; and the political situation was defined largely in terms
of a conflict between liberal culture and the philistinism of priests and
Catholic peasants. This was certainly the line taken by *Simplicissimus*,
above all in Ludwig Thoma's brilliant 'Correspondence of a Bavarian
Deputy', which began to appear in the paper in November 1907.
'Painting is certainly an art', writes Thoma's protagonist Josef Filser,
who was intended to represent the more rustic type of Centre
parliamentarian, 'but only down to the navel. Below the navel it's
filth, because there it's sexual'. Significantly, Filser's outrage at the
nudity on display in Munich's great galleries makes him ask 'Why do
we have to vote money for new pictures when the old ones are even
worse?' [74]

Grotesque though such satires were, the fears they expressed were
real enough. The Centre Party was not only tight-fisted on cultural
matters, but insisted in a militantly repressive way that the purpose
of art was 'not simply to make life beautiful and pleasant but also to
ennoble it'.[75] It had enthusiastically supported the Lex Heinze in its
most extreme form, and after 1900 continued to demand strong
measures against pornography, satire (*Simplicissimus* and *Jugend* were
among its particular *bêtes noires*), the cabarets and contemporary
drama, as well as the 'excesses' of the Carnival and all the other 'ulcers'
of the city's 'Simplicissified' society.[76] One of the Party's most
energetic allies was a Catholic journalist from the Rhineland called
Dr Armin Kausen, a man of inflexible moral purpose and narrow
outlook who had made his Munich début in 1891 by violently
denouncing the Modern Life Society.[77] In 1904, Kausen founded the
Allgemeine Rundschau (General Review), a Centrist weekly which set
out with some success to expose anyone suspected of spreading moral

corruption. One of its victims was a well-known cabaret manager, Josef Vallé, who eventually lost his licence and had to leave the city.[78] Another was Karl Schüler, a main supplier of books to the *avant-garde*, distributor of tickets for the leading dramatic societies and former opponent of the Lex Heinze, who between 1909 and 1911 was dragged into a long and damaging series of libel suits connected with certain items in his catalogue.[79] In 1906, Kausen also helped to found the Munich Men's Association for Combating Public Immorality (*Münchener Männerverein zur Bekämpfung der öffentlichen Unsittlichkeit*), which aimed to put pressure on the Government to take more energetic repressive action.[80]

The background to this agitation, of course, as the Police Direction's annual reports show,[81] was Munich's development from a rather sleepy royal capital into a modern city. Between the late 1880s and 1914 its population approximately doubled; industry expanded; and a large influx of tourists encouraged the growth of vice and exploitation. Yet Kausen and his associates were not just interested in the suppression of prostitution, clip-joints (*Nepp-Lokale*), book-stall pornography and the tango, although they devoted much energy to these problems. They took the much more dramatic view that Munich was a hotbed of subversion which threatened all accepted values, and, as Archbishop Faulhaber was to put it in 1917, 'the headquarters and invasion-gate for the whole of Bavaria of guerillas hostile to both religion and the Church'.[82] The Schwabing *avant-garde* was therefore one of their principal targets: not simply on account of its artistic and literary products, but because of its links with anarchism, free thought and Russian student politics, its '*Simplicissimus* festivals' and carnival exuberance, and what was supposed to be its general attitude towards morality and life. Although intellectuals ridiculed the '*General Pornographic Review*'[83] and Kausen's collection of specimen erotica ('über Dausend Scheisslikeiden' according to Josef Filser[84]), the vendetta was pursued with hatred on both sides; and in November 1914 a contributor to the *Allgemeine Rundschau* exulted at the war's ruinous effect on the Schwabing community. He wrote:

One thing was common to them all: complete lack of discipline and constant resistance to order and morality. Leading a cat-and-dog life among themselves, they were ready at every moment to demonstrate in favour of public shamelessness, debauchery and unbelief under the cloak of artistic and scientific freedom, and to complain to the world about Bavarian backwardness.

Now, the writer concluded, they were scattered to the winds, and the 'literary and artistic Bohemianism (*Schlawinertum*) signified by the word Schwabing must be eliminated for ever. German discipline is more important than anything else!'[85]

Kausen himself could not share this triumph as he had died in March 1913, the news of his death having been celebrated North of the *Siegestor* with orgiastic glee.[86] 'Armin Kausen's voice is stilled', wrote Mühsam, 'and with it the telephone-bell of the vice squad'.[87] Yet by this time the cause of the Men's Association was clearly prospering. Whereas at first its relations with the authorities had been cool (ministers had been put off not only by its attitude to the arts but also by its evident determination to attack Munich's freethinkers[88]), its position had been much strengthened by political developments. The sharp polarisation of Bavarian politics, and the Centre Party's militant anti-Socialism, had made Count Podewils' strategy of balancing between the parties increasingly problematical, since concessions to either left or right provoked fierce attacks from the other side. So it was that, in the autumn of 1911, the Centre's anger at the Government's mild attitude towards the Socialist railwaymen's union led to parliamentary deadlock, which was followed by the dissolution of the Chamber and a furious election campaign.[89] In spite of a combined onslaught by most of the other parties, the Centre retained its overall majority; Podewils and all his colleagues had resigned on polling-day, 5 February 1912, before the results became known; and after complicated negotiations behind the scenes Count Georg von Hertling, chairman of the German Centre Party's Reichstag fraction since 1909, was invited to form a ministry.

The difficult question of whether this change amounted to the establishment of 'parliamentary' government in Bavaria[90] is here less important than the consequences for the arts in Munich. Hertling's own personality and previous record hardly justified the more hysterical reactions to his appointment.[91] His relations with most Bavarian Centrist leaders had not been close, and in 1905 he had warned against the danger that the Centre as a whole might become too much a party for the 'little man', neglecting, among other things, the interests of art and learning.[92] Yet his choice of colleagues in February 1912 was not reassuring. Out of seven ministers, only two were Protestants; and although five were, as usual, officers or career officials, two of these were known to have strong leanings towards the Centre. Especially ominous, however, was the selection of Count Maximilian von Soden-Fraunhofen as the new Minister of the Interior. Von Soden was a conservative landowner and Centrist who regarded Social Democracy as a 'disease',[93] was a prominent member of the Men's Association (as were Hertling and the new Minister of Transport, von Seidlein[94]), and had caused a stir in 1906 by publicly attacking the Bavarian press 'privilege' of trial by jury.[95] On 13 February, a senior civil servant named Gottlieb Krais wrote to his friend Joseph Ruederer predicting that the 'Soden administration', as he called the new Government, would be both inept and repressive. Von Soden himself, he claimed, though in-experienced, intended to fight not only Socialism but also immorality in all areas of public life, and in general to intensify the activity of the police. 'You're in a real mess' he told Ruederer. 'The only thing to do is to emigrate from the bloody country'.[96] Krais' language, like the *Simplicissimus* cartoons showing searchlights mounted on the *Frauenkirche*,[97] may well have been over-dramatic, and no doubt reflected the resentment of the career official against a 'political' out-sider. But during the next eighteen months more rigorous theatre censorship, more interference in Munich's night-life and the Carnival, and a general increase in political tension showed that his pessimism was not unjustified.[98]

V

Certain significant conclusions emerge from this study. In the first place, it is clearly dangerous to make sweeping generalisations about the degree of freedom enjoyed by intellectuals in Imperial Germany. Indeed, it is even difficult to draw clear-cut distinctions between individual German states, since conditions differed considerably from one field of activity to another: the treatment accorded to Ludwig Thoma's satires on the one hand and Frank Wedekind's plays on the other proves this point decisively. Much depended on the wording of sometimes obscure procedural rules and, in areas where administrative discretion remained an important factor, on the attitude of the local authorities. As far as theatre censorship was concerned, practice varied not only from state to state (all efforts before 1918 to obtain a Reich Theatre Law proved fruitless), but in Bavaria even from town to town, and the Munich police made little headway in their attempts to create a centrally coordinated system.[99]

Secondly, Munich's decline from its position as Germany's leading art centre in the mid-nineteenth century to rather secondary importance in the 1920s was a gradual process. It was due in large measure to the growth of other cities, which for various reasons became increasingly attractive to mature artists in search of a market. Munich not only lacked wealth on the scale of Berlin and Vienna but also perhaps, less tangibly, the 'neurotic' atmosphere of the great metropolises.[100] Despite its growth by 1914, the Bavarian capital was still far from being the limitless expanse of brick and asphalt which seems to have appealed to the new *avant-garde* of the pre-war years. Nevertheless, certain events stand out as milestones on the city's downward path. The outbreak of war in 1914 destroyed at one stroke the exceptionally cosmopolitan nature of Munich's artistic community, took many of its members away on active service (from which Franz Marc, Albert Weisgerber and others never returned), and ushered in a period of gloom and foreboding for those who stayed behind. The future gives me the horrors', Wedekind told Mühsam in the summer of 1915. 'They'll sit there and talk about their heroic deeds, and when people like us want to give their opinions on questions of art or religion, they'll shout us down: "You weren't there, how can you expect to have a say?" ' [101] The suppression of the Soviet Republic in the spring of 1919 brought the victory of political reaction in its crudest form, further discredited Bohemianism and foreign participation in Munich's intellectual life, and intensified the anti-Semitism which had been present in the city for many years. But even before the war and the revolution, the events of February 1912 had marked the end of the 'liberal era' in Bavarian politics and foreshadowed the ascendancy of ultraconservative forces under the Republic.

Although not prodigiously libertarian, the system of ' "liberal-conservative" late absolutism'[102] by which Bavaria was governed until shortly before the First World War undoubtedly provided a framework within which art and literature were able to flourish. However desirable it may have been in general terms for this apparatus to be dismantled, the growth of parliamentary influence on government presented an unmistakable threat to Munich's cultural life. Not all the groups pressing for political change were hostile to *avant-garde* ideas: both the left-wing Liberals associated with Ernst Müller-Meiningen and the Bavarian Social Democrats led by Georg von Vollmar were exemplary in their defence of artistic freedom.[103] But Munich was an island in a sea of peasants. As long as more than half the Bavarian population lived in communities of fewer than 2,000 inhabitants, and 70 per cent of it was Roman Catholic,[104] every step towards more representative government was bound to add extra political weight to the cultural prejudices of seminaries and market towns.

Finally, the nature of these prejudices was also significant for the future. Of course, clerical-conservative and later National Socialist views on art did not exactly coincide, any more than did their political ideologies (conversely, the Centre Party's Liberal opponents at times betrayed some markedly illiberal attitudes): 'Nazi culture' incorporated elements — for example, the cult of heroic nudity and various forms of paganism — which would hardly have been acceptable to Bavarian clericalism. Yet the latter's denunciations of Naturalism, *Jugendstil* and Expressionist 'negro art' certainly anticipated later propaganda campaigns; while repressive idealism, provincial narrow-mindedness and hostility to urban civilisation were woven into the whole cultural fabric of the Third Reich.

Notes

I am grateful to the British Academy and the University of Warwick for grants which enabled me to carry out additional research for this study in Munich in 1976. The primary sources on which it is based are drawn mainly from the files of the Bavarian Foreign Ministry (MA) in the *Geheimes Staatsarchiv* (GStA); the Ministries of the Interior (MInn), Church and School Affairs (MK) and Justice (MJu) in the *Bayerisches Hauptstaatsarchiv, Allgemeine Abteilung* (AStAM); the Munich Police Direction (Pol.Dir.), the *Regierung von Oberbayern* (RA) and the *Staatsanwaltschaft München I* (St.Anw.) in the *Staatsarchiv München* (StAM); and from private papers in the *Monacensia-Abteilung* of the Munich City Library (Stadtbibliothek, Munchen).

1. See especially Willy Albrecht, *Landtag und Regierung in Bayern am Vorabend der Revolution von 1918: Studien zur gesellschaftlichen und staatlichen Entwicklung Deutschlands von 1912–1918* (Berlin, 1968); Dieter Albrecht, 'Von der Reichsgründung bis zum Ende des Ersten Weltkrieges (1871–1918)', in Max Spindler (ed.), *Handbuch der bayerischen Geschichte*, Vol. IV, No. I (Munich, 1974), pp. 283–386; and Karl Möckl, *Die Prinzregentenzeit. Gesellschaft und Politik während der Aera des Prinzregenten Luitpold in Bayern* (Munich, 1972).
2. See for example Gerdi Huber, *Das klassische Schwabing: München als Zentrum der intellektuellen Zeit- und Gesellschaftskritik um 1900. Miscellanea Bavarica Monacensia*, 37 (Munich, 1973).
3. See in particular Joseph Ruederer, *München* (Stuttgart and Munich, 1907).
4. See Peter Vergo, *Art in Vienna, 1898–1918. Klimt, Kokoschka, Schiele and their Contemporaries* (London, 1975).
5. The state also had the income from a capital grant of 450,000 M., and from two other funds totalling 80,000 M. Before the late 1880s, parliamentary contributions for artistic purposes were very small.
6. Erwin Pixis, *Verzeichnis der von Weiland Seiner Königlichen Hoheit dem Prinzregenten Luitpold von Bayern aus privaten Mitteln erworbenen Werken der bildenden Kunst* (Munich, 1913).
7. See for example R.J.V. Lenman, 'Art, society and the law in Wilhelmine Germany: The Lex Heinze', *Oxford German Studies*, VIII (1973), p. 106.
8. Details of its organisation in AStAM, MK 14 250.
9. See Siegfried Wichmann, *Franz von Lenbach und seine Zeit* (Cologne, 1973).
10. AStAM, MK 14 280: MK von Müller to Kaulbach (draft), 26 February 1892.
11. *Die Freie Bühne*, Vol. III, No. 3 (1892), p. 751. The allusion was to the increasingly commercialised Oberammergau Passion Play.

12. *Die Gesellschaft*, Vol. 9, No. I (1893), p. 230.
13. *Statistik des Deutschen Reichs*, Bd. 209 (1910), pp. 47, 442.
14. Stadtbibliothek München, *Nachlass* Ruederer Br.e.74.8: Corinth to Ruederer, 27 January 1901.
15. Balthasar von Daller on Uhde's *Ascension:* minutes of Finance Committee of Chamber of Deputies, 18 March 1898, in AStAM, MK 14 280.
16. See for example Baron Crailsheim, *Stenographische Berichte über die Verhandlungen der bayerischen Kammer der Abgeordneten (VdKdAbg)*, 1889/ 1890, Bd. V, 28 March 1890, p. 603.
17. See especially Heinrich Voss, *Franz von Stuck 1863–1928. Werkkatalog der Gemälde mit einer Einführung in seinen Symbolismus* (Munich, 1973).
18. *Art Nouveau*, named in Germany after the Munich periodical *Jugend* (*Youth*).
19. O.J. Bierbaum, *Stuck* (Bielefeld and Leipzig, 1899), p. 79.
20. See documents of June and July 1894 in AStAM, MK 14 280 and MK 14 302.
21. J.A. Schmoll, 'Franz von Stuck im Spiegel der zeitgenössischen Literatur' in H. Kreuzer and K. Hamburger (eds.), *Gestaltungsgeschichte und Gesellschaftsgeschichte: literatur-, kunst- und musikwissenschaftliche Studien* (Stuttgart, 1969), pp. 439–44.
22. See AStAM, MK 14 225, MK von Landmann to Gen. Adjutant von Lerchenfeld (draft), 20 October 1898, for recognition of Slevogt's talent.
23. AStAM, MK 14 284: MK von Knilling to Prince Regent Ludwig, 1 February 1913.
24. See material in AStAM, MK 14 278.
25. AStAM, MK 14 284: Tschudi to MK, 1 March 1911.
26. The items in the '*Tschudi-Spende*' are listed in AStAM, MK 14 284.
27. Details of purchase in AStAM, MK 14 284.
28. See for example the material in GStA München: MA 76 531, and MA 76 537 ('Umsturz-Vorlage').
29. For details, see Lenman.
30. See StAM, Pol.Dir. 520: Pol.Dir. to *Reg. von Oberbayern* (draft), 16 September 1891.
31. GStA München: MA 76 787: Academy to MK von Landmann, 9 March 1900.
32. StAM, RA 3795/57851: Conrad to Pol.Director von Welser, 3 February 1891.
33. See letters from Julius Schaumberger to Max Halbe in 1891, in Stadtbibl., Halbe Archive; and material in StAM, Pol.Dir. 520.
34. Hanns von Gumppenberg, *Lebenserinnerungen: Aus dem Nachlass des Dichters* (Berlin and Zurich, 1929), pp. 173–5; *Moderne Blätter*, Vol. I, No. 23 (5 September 1891), pp. 1–3.
35. See Ludwig Leiss, *Kunst im Konflikt. Kunst und Künstler im Widerstreit mit der 'Obrigkeit'* (Berlin, 1971), pp. 138–139; and R.J.V. Lenman, 'Censorship and Society in Munich, 1890–1914, with special reference to *Simplicissimus* and the plays of Frank Wedekind', Oxford D. Phil. thesis, 1975, pp. 25–8.
36. Stadtbibliothek München: *Nachlass* Ruederer Br.a.25.II: Ruederer to Carl Graeser, 9 December 1894.
37. W. Kosch, *Deutsches Literatur-Lexikon* (2nd edn., Bern, 1956), III, 1976.
38. International Institute of Social History, Amsterdam, Vollmar Papers 405: Conrad to Vollmar, 4 May 1895.
39. 'Münchener Frühlings-Wunder', *Die Freie Buhne*, VI (1895/1), pp. 503–7.
40. Stadtbibliothek München: *Nachlass* Bierbaum 465/74: Blei to Bierbaum, 10 January 1903.
41. Stadtbibliothek, München: *Nachlass* Kerschensteiner AKM 227: draft *Gutachten* (1911).
42. Leiss, *Kunst im Konflikt*, pp. 171–4; Lenman, 'Censorship and Society', pp. 122–4.

43. Lenman, 'Censorship and Society', pp. 116–22.
44. Leiss, *Kunst im Konflikt*, pp. 194–7.
45. StAM, RA 3830/58113: Pol. Dir. to *Reg. von Oberbayern*, 12 March 1913, pp. 99–100.
46. Otto von Erlbach (Armin Kausen), *Ein Asyl für Pornographen? Zur Frage der Zuständigkeit der Schwurgerichte* (Munich, 1911).
47. AStAM, MJu XII/25: Deputy Prosecutor Federschmidt to *Oberstaatsanwalt*, 3 December 1913.
48. Ruling of 6 April 1914 in StAM, St. Anw. 1735; and see also Leiss, *Kunst im Konflikt*, pp. 232–6, and Lenman, 'Censorship and Society', pp. 200–2.
49. *Münchener Neueste Nachrichten,* 8 July 1911, nr. 315.
50. Lenman, 'Censorship and Society', pp. 7–10.
51. AStAM, MInn 65 592: Pol. Director von Burchtorff to Ludwig II, 3 March 1870.
52. *Die Strafprozessordnung für das Deutsche Reich mit Kommentar*, ed. Löwe-Hellweg (12th edn., Berlin, 1907), p. 9.
53. For a detailed account, see Lenman, 'Censorship and Society', chaps. 3 and 4. See also E. Koch, *Albert Langen: Ein Verleger in München* (Munich, 1969); Richard Christ (ed.), *Simplicissimus 1896–1914* (E. Berlin, 1972); and Gerhard Benecke, 'The politics of outrage: social satire in the cartoons of *Simplicissimus* 1896–1914', *Twentieth Century Studies*, Vol. 13, No. 14 (December 1975), pp. 92–108.
54. See for example the correspondence in Stadtbibliothek München, *Nachlass* Bierbaum, Box III.
55. *VdKdAbg* 1908, Bd. V, 19 June 1908, p. 467.
56. E. and M. Dixmier, *L'Assiette au Beurre: revue satirique illustrée* (Paris, 1974), pp. 219–24.
57. Stadtbibliothek München: *Nachlass* Holm: Holm to Langen, 22 March 1899 (copy).
58. See the large quantity of material in AStAM, MJu XII/22 and MInn 65 710.
59. AStAM, MJu XII/22: Prosecutor von Sartor to Oberreichsanwalt (draft), 17 June 1904. The number was *Simpl.* VIII/6 (5 May 1903).
60. See the auditors' reports in Stadtbibl., *Nachlass* Thoma.
61. AStAM, MJu XII/23: MInn von Soden, circular of 14 September 1914.
62. For a detailed discussion of the Bavarian censorship system, see Lenman, 'Censorship and Society', chap. 4.
63. Documents in StAM, Pol. Dir. 2057/1–3.
64. For example, in cases involving Hartleben's *Hanna Jagert*, Hauptmann's *Die Weber* and Wedekind's *Frühlings Erwachen*. For details, see H.H. Houben, *Die verbotene Literatur von der klassischen Zeit bis zur Gegenwart* (Bremen, 1925, 1928), I, 255–70, 337–49; and Günter Seehaus, *Frank Wedekind und das Theater* (Munich, 1964), pp. 95–7.
65. For details, see Lenman, 'Censorship and Society', chaps. 7 and 8; Leiss, *Kunst im Konflikt,* pp. 267–82; and H. Lehnert and W. Segebrecht, 'Thomas Mann im Münchener Zensurbeirat (1912/13). Ein Beitrag zum Verhältnis Thomas Manns zu Frank Wedekind', *Jahrbuch der deutschen Schillergesellschaft*, VII (1963), pp. 190–200.
66. See Lenman, 'Censorship and Society', pp. 228–38.
67. Stadtbibliothek München, *Sammlung* Rosenthal: Pol. Director von der Heydte to Rosenthal, 5 February 1907.
68. See Kurt Martens, *Schonungslose Lebenschronik, 1901–1923* (Vienna, Berlin &c., 1924), pp. 169–71.
69. Seehaus, *Wedekind und das Theater*, p. 201.
70. AStAM, MK 14 163: MK von Landmann to Ambassador von Lerchenfeld, 13

January 1901.
71. MJu von Leonrod, *VdKdAbg* 1899/1900, Bd. IV, 20 April 1900, p. 34.
72. See the essays by U. Linse and L. Schneider in K. Bosl (ed.), *Bayern im Umbruch* (Munich, 1969).
73. The following account is based on Möckl, *Prinzregentenzeit;* Dieter Albrecht; and R. Kessler, *Heinrich Held als Parlamentarier. Eine Teilbiographie 1868–1924* (Berlin, 1971).
74. Ludwig Thoma, *Gesammelte Werke in sechs Bänden* (Munich, 1968), IV, pp. 457–8.
75. Party programme of April 1887, printed in Möckl, *Prinzregentenzeit*, p. 221.
76. Franz Schädler, *VdKdAbg* 1903/1904, Bd. XI, 20 October 1903, p. 231.
77. See cuttings from *Münchener Fremdenblatt* in StAM, Pol. Dir. 520.
78. Lenman, 'Censorship and Society', pp. 191f.
79. Ibid., p. 202f.
80. See material in AStAM, MInn 73 589.
81. StAM, Pol. Dir. 4124–4126; and RA 3830/58113.
82. Quoted in Leonhard Lenk, 'Katholizismus und Liberalismus. Zur Auseinandersetzung mit dem Zeitgeist in München 1848–1918', in *Der Mönch in Wappen. Geschichte und Gegenwart des katholischen München* (Munich, 1960).
83. See Erich Mühsam's articles in *Kain. Zeitschrift für Menschlichkeit.*
84. Literally 'over a thousand dreadful things'. *Simpl.*, Vol. XII, No. 52 (23 March 1908).
85. Franz Rainer, 'Schwabings Untergang', *Allg. Rundschau,* Vol. XI, No. 46 (14 November 1914).
86. Erich Mühsam, *Namen und Menschen. Unpolitische Erinnerungen* (Leipzig, 1949), p. 196.
87. 'Abschied vom Kausen', *Kain*, Vol. III, No. I (April 1913), p. 11.
88. AStAM, MK 19 101: draft memo. of 11 June 1906.
89. See Willy Albrecht, *Landtag und Regierung in Bayern*, pp. 20–6.
90. See J. Reimann, *Ernst Müller-Meiningen senior und der Linksliberalismus seiner Zeit. Miscellanea Bavarica Monacensia,* II (Munich, 1968), pp. 134–7.
91. For example Hirth's leading article 'In letzter Stunde', *Münch. Neueste Nachrichten,* 10 February 1912, nr. 71, cited in W. Albrecht, *Landtag und Regierung,* p. 43.
92. Georg von Hertling, 'Politische Parteibildung und soziale Schichtung', *Hochland,* Vol. II, No. 2 (April 1905), pp. 55–6.
93. W. Albrecht, *Landtag und Regierung,* p. 47.
94. See membership list in AStAM, MInn 73 589.
95. *Münch. Neueste Nachrichten*, 2 February 1906, nrs. 53, 54; and *Verhandlungen der Kammer der Reichsräte* 1905/1906, Bd. I, 23 February 1906, pp. 117–118.
96. Stadtbibliothek München, *Nachlass* Ruederer Br.e.262.15: Krais to Ruederer, 13 February 1912.
97. *Simpl.*, Vol. XVIII, No. I (31 March 1913). The Cathedral of Our Lady, in the Old City, is Munich's most famous landmark.
98. Lenman, 'Censorship and Society', pp. 192–3, 307–11; W. Albrecht, *Landtag und Regierung,* pp. 71–3.
99. See material in StAM, Pol. Dir. 4342/II.
100. For an interesting later parallel, see B. Rosenberg and N.E. Fliegel, 'The vanguard artist in New York', *Social Research,* 32 (1965), II, pp. 141–162.
101. Mühsam, *Namen und Menschen,* p. 225.
102. Möckl, *Prinzregentenzeit,* p. 30.
103. See Reinhard Jansen, *Georg von Vollmar: Eine politische Biographie*

(Düsseldorf, 1958).

104. Figures for 1910 in *Statistisches Jahrbuch für das Deutsche Reich*, 35 (1914), pp. 4–5, 9.

5 THE WILHELMINE RIGHT: HOW IT CHANGED

Geoff Eley

I

Discussion of the past century of German history is still dominated by
the events of 1933—45. Knowledge of National Socialism and the desire
to explain its victory continue to shape the main trends of German
historiography: they help select the subjects of most interest and inform
the kind of questions that get asked. This is obviously true of the
Weimar Republic, but it has affected discussion of the nineteenth
century as well. It appears to be equally true of the academic specialist
and of the various categories of interested lay-people, whether teachers,
journalists, students, book-club subscribers or public library users. All
tend to be attracted by the dramatic quality of the Nazi period, drawn
by a mixture of concern and excited morbidity, rather like the crowds
at the scene of an unpleasant catastrophe, such as an explosion or an
air-crash. This is probably inevitable. If we are honest most historical
interests — in a period, a country, a topic — are motivated to some
extent by extraneous considerations. The effect is clearest where a
national history is dominated by a bout of convulsive change as in the
French and Russian Revolutions. On a more modest scale the decline of
the Liberal Party, the General Strike, the origins of the Welfare State
and the Irish troubles are all instances of British history in which an
important development has been allowed to structure the preceding
history of the respective fields. But to recognise the source of one's
interest is easy: it is far more difficult to stop this distorting one's
perspective on it. In the past nationalist historians were notoriously
guilty of prejudging complicated processes of historical development,
and more recently many radical historians have been finding that the
mere celebration of popular struggles is a poor guide to the substance of
popular achievement.[1] But the problem is seldom as close to the surface
as this. More often it results from a submerged teleological view of the
past which reduces historical processes to their known results. In this
case a chain of causation can easily be constructed which owes far too
much to the vantage-point of the historian.

The recent history of the *Kaiserreich* has fallen into this trap. As
suggested above, it is fairly easy to regard 1933 as a terminal point in
Germany's historical development and this tendency has been

112

magnified since the early 1960s by the lasting effects of the Fischer Controversy: whereas earlier the older generation had regarded Nazism as an irrational aberration which diverted German history from its true course, their successors have now gone to an opposite extreme by seeing it as the end-product of a continuous authoritarian and manipulative tradition of the German right since Bismarck; in both cases the history of the *Kaiserreich* is pressed into the service of a larger view of the German past focused on the events of 1933.[2] This has unfortunate implications for our understanding of Nazism, still more of the political movements which preceded it. There is an increasing tendency to interpret the years between the 1860s and 1914 — and the Great Depression in particular — as a crucial founding period which broadly determined the fascist possibilities of the 1920s and 30s. It is based on a particular analysis of the state and of the ruling coalition which sustained it which is then linked to the problem of Nazism by a rather simple notion of continuity. Underlying this are some important assumptions about the origins and nature of fascism which do justice neither to the phenomenon of Nazism nor to the real character of the Wilhelmine right, still less to the complex processes of change which enabled one to emerge from the other. My aim in this essay is to subject existing ideas about the long-term origins of National Socialism to some critical scrutiny and in the process to clarify our understanding of Wilhelmine conservatism. This will involve some consideration of existing interpretations and their weaknesses, together with a brief indication of how the latter might be rectified. I will conclude with some suggestions for an alternative chronology of the right between the early-nineteenth and mid-twentieth centuries.

II

There are two main ways of linking Nazism to an earlier nineteenth-century tradition. The first, which gained currency in the Anglo-Saxon West during and after the Second World War, concentrates on the discovery of intellectual pedigrees, the uncovering of a German tradition of authoritarian thinking through which the appeal of Nazi ideology could be made more readily intelligible.[3] The procedure has normally involved the selection of a number of nineteenth-century intellectuals whose ideas and values are then made to exemplify a set of attributed cultural dispositions; these are then held to be dominant amongst the educated classes and to be proto-Nazi in tendency. Classically this has meant reconstructing the intellectual pursuits of an earlier epoch in the image of Nazi ideology and its familiar terminology. Thus we find

Rohan Butler, in *The Roots of National Socialism* published in 1941,
arguing that Nazism was merely the political climax of a dominant
indigenous tradition. His method is to ransack the German past for
any idea with the remotest resemblance to those of the Nazis. He does
this for 'the exaltation of the heroic leader', 'the racial myth', anti-
Semitism, 'the concept of the all-significant totalitarian state', 'the
community of the folk', 'the full programme of economic autarky', 'the
tradition of militarism', the idea of 'the dynamic originality of German
culture in contrast to the superficial civilisation of the West', 'the
polemic against reason', 'the supernatural mission of German culture',
'living-space', 'Pan-Germanism', 'law as folk-law', and finally for the
'abasement of the individual before the state'.[4] All these ideas are
described as in some way distinctively German and all are traced back
to the eighteenth century as aspects of an unbroken linear continuity.
The following quotation is typical of the method: 'The Nazis say that
might is right; Spengler said it; Bernhardi said it; Nietzsche said it;
Treitschke had said as much; so had Haller before him; so had Novalis'.[5]

   This is surely a fruitless exercise, the worst kind of traditional intellectual history, which makes its connections by lifting ideas from their
proper context. The original impetus was provided by the Second World
War, when the Allies had a pressing interest in finding historical
justifications for their hostilities with Germany. The Cold War then
tended to harden this into a habit of mind, which characterised 'the
West' as a sort of historic zone of freedom and the German past as an
equally historic revolt against it, dating from the romantic-nationalist
reaction to the French Revolution. German exiles, often of Jewish
extraction and preoccupied with the 'German Mind', have tended to be
the architects of this view, and the most considerable achivement of
the transplanted Central European culture, the Institute of Social
Research, whilst avoiding the uncritical identification of enlightenment
with the territorial extent of NATO and substituting the notion of
the 'authoritarian personality' for that of the 'German Mind', has also
mirrored these concerns. So has the work of A.J.P. Taylor, though it
sometimes masquerades as a geopolitical argument about Germany's
strategic position in the centre of Europe. So too have the more
popular works best represented by the UNESCO collection of 1955,
The Third Reich, and William Shirer's *The Rise and Fall of the Third
Reich* — perhaps the single most influential work of German history since
Treitschke.[6] This is not a totally barren tradition of explanation. In its
more sophisticated versions it has produced important studies of a
particular social-cultural milieu, that of the 'non-political German', the

nationalist bourgeois who preferred a romantic and illiberal anti-
modernism – so-called – to the values of Western liberal democracy.[7]
But its basic weaknesses as an approach to the origins of Nazism and
the problem of continuity in German history cannot be reiterated too
strongly: the connections are made predominantly, even exclusively, in
the realms of ideology and consciousness, the roots of Nazism are
seen to lie in a particular frame of mind.

The second conventional method of placing Hitler in longer historical
context is in no way incompatible with this approach, but has rather
tried to underpin it with an analysis of the German social formation.
This second approach concentrates on what Bracher has called a continuity of 'authoritarian and anti-democratic structures in state and
society', which obstructed any liberal evolution towards parliamentary
forms before 1918, paralysed the Weimar constitution after 1918, and
facilitated the Nazi success in conditions of crisis after 1930.[8] It has
been most influential inside Germany itself and has made most headway since the early 1960s when the liberating effects of the Fischer
Controversy made historians more receptive to a conceptual framework
devised principally by sociologists and political scientists.[9] As already
suggested, this and the other approach to a great extent complement
each other. They both diminish the importance of the conventional
chronology of political events and they both stress an underlying continuity of authoritarianism which sets Germany apart from the liberal
'West'. One sees this mainly as an intellectual tradition, the other
stresses material interests and structures of rule. The first finds
Hitler's precursors in the romantic anti-modernists who allegedly
inhabited the Pan-German movement and created a cultural disposition
towards authoritarianism in the middle class. The second sees
them in the coalition of heavy industrialists and big landowners
which pulled the strings of government, it is claimed, more or less
continuously after 1878–9. In a further sense both approaches share
the intellectual patrimony of Talcott Parsons, whose 1942 essay on
fascism has left an indelible imprint on subsequent non-Marxist
thinking about National Socialism.[10]

I want to argue that both these dominant approaches are deficient
and that together they represent an over-simplified view of the continuity problem which so exercises German historians at the moment.
To illustrate this two of their central ideas may be isolated for critical
comment, both of which have become part of the conventional wisdom
of modern German history. The first is that of 'cultural despair' with
its connotations of anti-modernism and romantic opposition to the

new urban and industrial civilisation.[11] A number of weaknesses con-
spire to reduce the value of the social-cultural stereotype associated
with this idea. On one count, the real anti-modernists — agrarians,
artisans and traditional small businessmen with a grievance against
progress — were motivated much less by an intellectual cultural
pessimism than by the prospects of *economic* decline. By contrast,
the urban middle class with whom the mood of cultural pessimism is
normally associated seem readily to have grasped the benefits of the
new society with all the buoyancy and self-confidence which was so
natural in a prosperous and rapidly growing economy. In general they
confined their hostility only to certain features of 'modernity',
principally those arising from the social and political situation of the
new industrial masses and the threats this appeared to contain. Moreover, the idea of cultural despair exaggerates the political impact of a
few maverick thinkers (most notably Lagarde, Langbehn and Möller
van der Bruck, to name the three chosen by Stern), rests on a selective
reading of their work, and ignores the complexity and contradictions
of the intellectual climate which gave them meaning.'Above all: by
concentrating on this social-cultural milieu with its suspicion of conventional politics, it distracts from those organisations in Wilhelmine
society which *were* politically more influential and which produced an
ideology which was genuinely proto-fascist. In other words, the
'cultural despair' approach tends to focus on the wrong areas of
German society.

The second key concept is that of *Sammlungspolitik*. Literally, 'the
politics of cohesion' or 'rallying-together', this meant the attempt to
unite all anti-Socialist forces in a common front against democratic
reform, the political expression of a protectionist pact between heavy
industry and big agriculture. It has been claimed that this idea supplies
the interpretative key to German politics in the entire period between
the 1870s and 1933. It denoted a force far stronger than the challenge
raised by the reforming left before 1918 and provided the crucial
foundations for the right-wing counter-attack against the Weimar
Republic.[12] Yet whatever its positive merits, and these have been considerable, the ultimate effect is again reductionist, for this simplifies
the development of the conservative tradition between Bismarck and
Hitler and elides the successive problems of readjustment to changed
conditions which faced the right in this longer period. Moreover, by
stressing the manipulative abilities of the ruling class and the stability
of its power-base, it underestimates the extent to which its survival
depended on a responsiveness to certain kinds of pressure *from below*.

Consequently this second concept also suffers from failing to focus on a special area of political life which is particularly crucial to this problem, namely that of the forms of petty-bourgeois mobilisation. In their respective ways both of the influential approaches outlined above tend to divert our attention from the real foundations of later developments: the *first* by fixing on intellectual currents whose typicality is assumed rather than demonstrated and whose political implications are misinterpreted by referring them forward to Nazism rather than to their own proper and very different contemporary context; the *second* by stressing the manipulative achievement of the 'ruling strata' in equipping themselves with popular support in the new conditions of mass politics, and by neglecting the extent to which this 'modernisation' was determined by novel pressures from social groups which had previously been marginal to the political system.

The rest of this essay will consider the problem of petty-bourgeois mobilisation by looking at those areas of the political culture where *masses* of people were set into motion. It is only by this means that we can avoid the tendentious generalisations critised above, for the diagnosis of an alleged cultural disposition or state of mind in an entire society surely requires the investigation of a sufficiently large collectivity. Thus Fritz Stern's work has always been vitiated by his narrow biographical perspective: the wider influence of the intellectuals he has studied is only ever illustrated by finding formal traces of their ideas elsewhere; there is rarely any sense of the determinate social context which might influence their reception. To rectify this is the first aim of what follows. The second is to question the tendency of recent historians to draw straight lines of continuity between Bismarck and Hitler and to contest the view that Wilhelmine conservatism and Nazism are just different variations on a single theme of authoritarianism, reflecting the same constellation of industrial-agrarian interests, and distinguished only by the types and levels of political manipulation required by these so-called 'ruling strata' to guarantee their interests.[13] The gist of the argument is this: that we cannot understand the conditions enabling the rise of a German fascism without recognising the existence of a profound metamorphosis in the character of the German right between the 1870s and the 1920s, involving a massive expansion of its social base and a drastic radicalisation of its ideology and general political style; and we cannot understand the nature of that radicalisation without appraising the novel impact of the petty-bourgeoisie on the Wilhelmine political system between the early 1890s and the First World War.

III

By the petty-bourgeoisie I mean two groupings of people in a capitalist society: the old or traditional petty-bourgeoisie of small-scale producers and owners (artisans, carters, shopkeepers, farmers and other small businessmen) whom in Germany came to be known as the *Mittelstand*; and the newer petty-bourgeoisie of salaried employees and white-collar workers (lower-grade civil servants, junior managerial and technical personnel, teachers, clerical workers and certain strata of the professions) known in Germany as the 'new *Mittelstand*'. Though occupying different economic positions these two groupings exhibited enough common characteristics to enable them to regard each other − and to be so regarded − as members of a larger collectivity. These derived from a process of negative self-definition, for each occupied an intermediate position between the bourgeois and the proletarian which easily induced a profound suspicion of both major classes. The traditional small businessman was strung between self-ownership in the means of production and increasing real dependence on the power of big capital: separated from the working class by the social ideals of small property and independence, yet prevented from joining the ranks of the bourgeoisie proper by poor resources and the rising pressures of technological change and large-scale production. In the same fashion the salaried employee was caught between economic dependence and the self-sealing ideology of white-collar respectability with its status compensations, both resentful of the boss and superior to the uncultured worker. There is room here for only the barest of remarks concerning the place of the petty-bourgeoisie in the class structure, and as they stand these twin categories are clearly abstractions with limited historical value. There is no doubt, for instance, that in Germany both groupings were in a state of massive flux at the turn of the century as the pace of industrialisation imposed new patterns of mobility, recruitment and depletion onto the old petty-bourgeoisie, whilst ensuring a huge expansion of the new. Moreover, precisely because of this flux it is extremely difficult to generalise about the petty-bourgeoisie's political affiliations, for at any one time before 1914 it was likely to consist of large numbers who were *en route* for somewhere else − upwards to join the ranks of the more successful businessmen, downwards into the working class, or sideways between different fractions of itself. There were also serious internal divisions which set old against new, artisan against retailer, small employer against employee, and which seriously inhibited the ideological identity of the petty-bourgeoisie as a whole class. This made its political reactions extremely unpredictable and in view of its numerical importance gave it a key role when parties began to compete for mass support.[14] Whilst conceding each of these complexities and acknowledging both the theoretical and empirical difficulties of generalising about the petty-bourgeoisie as a class, particularly in this period, therefore, I want to offer some comments about its impact on the right in the years before 1914 by considering the forms of its political mobilisation. I will do this by looking at three different categories of organisation.[15]

The first of these categories is that of a rural and small-town protest movement, encompassing the independent and semi-independent peasantry and the so-called *Mittelstand* of shopkeepers, carters, independent craftsmen and petty entrepreneurs. This took the form of defensive sectional organisation at a time of rapid industrial and commercial concentration and declining agricultural prices. Small producers and traders started to band together in a series of interest groups of both an occupational and regional character. Artisans, fortified by traditions of guild organisation and assisted by some half-hearted protective legislation between 1881 and 1897, found this easier than most: a first national body was launched in 1873, passing into the General League of German Artisans in 1882, and as a result of successive legislation this was paralleled by the Central Committee of the United Guilds in 1884 and the standing Conference of the Chambers of Handicrafts and Trade in 1900.[16] Small tradesmen were less successful. An abortive Association of Traders formed in Berlin in 1878 was followed a decade later by the Central Association for Commerce and Trade, which grew from an initiative in Leipzig into a loose umbrella for other regional groups. In both sectors, of course, individual trades retained and expanded their occupational associations, and these were further supplemented by purchasing co-operatives, credit, savings and discount associations, and local defensive unions of artisans and tradesmen.[17] The new national bodies were clearly intended to represent their members' interests at the level of government and their activities registered the first moves towards overt and coordinated political commitment. This embraced affiliation with a number of right-wing parties, but not as yet the foundation of an independent *Mittelstand* party as such.[18] The anti-Semitic parties which emerged in the 1880s came closest to providing such a new departure,[19] but the proliferating organs of agrarian protest in the 1890s generally succeeded in subsuming *Mittelstand* grievances beneath the rubric of their protectionist and anti-plutocratic programmes. These included the Agrarian League in 1893 and the Catholic Peasants'

Associations, most of which were founded in the 1880s. But they also encompassed a wider variety of political initiatives, ranging from the anti-Semitic groups of Central Germany and the regional foundations of the Centre Party in the South to the final exclusion of Adolf Stöcker's Christian-Social Party from the official Conservative Party and the concurrent launching of the National-Social Association in 1896, itself a break-away from the Christian-Socials.[20]

The 1890s must be regarded as the great period of agrarian organisation, when the countryside was incorporated into the national political arena and all parties, including the SPD, made systematic efforts to penetrate the rural electorate. This was reflected in the organisational proliferation just mentioned, in the increased participation of rural voters at the polls, and in the greater number of highly contested constituencies in the countryside. In the elections of 1893 and 1898, for instance, the SPD was incomparably more active in rural areas and by 1898 was able to contest all 397 seats but one, though in a number of others it failed to register a single recorded vote.[21] In 1898, moreover, whilst the party experienced serious setbacks in West Prussia, Posen and parts of Pomerania, in the Catholic regions of Prussia and in Bavaria as a whole, it nonetheless managed an impressive advance in three rural areas: in the seven Mecklenburg seats where almost ten per cent more votes were polled than in 1893, pushing the Socialist share up to over 40 per cent of the total; in the Province of East Prussia excluding Königsberg, where the party's total vote rose from 12,000 to some 33,000, and in the seats of Rastenburg, Ragnit and Heiligenbeil from between one and five to between seventeen and twenty-three per cent;[22] and finally in Hesse, where the party competed fairly successfully with the anti-Semites for the votes of small producers. This was a time of tremendous political ferment in the countryside, producing a considerable fluidity of allegiance in which the simple correlations of rural discontent with unambiguously authoritarian or right-wing politics are not easily made.[23] In some constituencies of Hesse, for instance, the electorate displayed an extraordinary fluidity of allegiance, and anti-Semitic particularist, Left-Liberal National-Social, Centre and SPD were distinguished by little more than varying shades of anti-Prussian populist radicalism.[24]

The new volatility of the rural electorate and the unprecedented truculence of German conservatism's natural supporters created big problems for the right-wing parties at the very time when they most needed fresh reserves of popular support against the SPD. Paradoxically, the myth of the *Mittelstand* as the strongest pillar in the social order gained in popularity amongst Conservatives just at the point where small producers and owners were starting to repudiate old traditions of deference.[25] This led to new modalities of public life in country areas and helped disintegrate the old informal style of politics in the very areas where it seemed most destined to survive. The Conservative Party bore the first brunt of this in the Protestant areas of the rural North, for having deflected the rebukes of the Christian-Socials and anti-Semites in the 1880s it found itself newly threatened from within in the 1890s by the Trojan horse of the Agrarian League. Then by the 1898 elections the right-wing National Liberal Party found its traditional rural preserves in Hanover, Schleswig-Holstein and the Palatinate under severe attack from the Agrarian League's independent nominees: sitting National Liberals survived the onslaught only by formally committing themselves to the Agrarian League's programme. In the same way the Catholic Centre Party found it hard to keep its peasant supporters without a clear affirmation of protectionist intent: this could be seen in the tensions between the party leaders and the Catholic Peasants' Associations, in the foundation of the Bavarian Peasants' League in 1893 and in the ongoing threat of a Bavarian secession from the national Centre. In general the 1890s were a period when the groundwork of agrarian organisation and agitation proceeded largely outside the effective surveillance of those political parties under whose banner it was officially proclaimed. As yet there was no comparable upsurge of activity by the *Mittelstand* as such. There were faltering attempts at national and regional organisation, such as the abortive announcement of a *Mittelstand* Party in Thuringia in 1895, but on the whole artisans and small businessmen had to be content with the Chambers of Handicrafts and Trade established in 1897, their guild organisations and the existing political parties. It was not until later — in 1904 with the short-lived German *Mittelstand* Association and then in 1911 with the more substantial Imperial-German *Mittelstand* League — that the national organisation of the *Mittelstand* took place.[26]

The second category of organisation to be mentioned concerns the white-collar fractions of the petty-bourgeoisie, the so-called 'new *Mittelstand*' which was so much a product of the growing bureaucratisation of economic life after 1890. The comments which follow are necessarily fairly brief, for we know far less about this area than about the traditional petty-bourgeoisie, and far less progress has been made in understanding what to all accounts was a highly complex and politically ambiguous phenomenon. By the census of 1907 there were about two million 'private' white-collar workers and something like one and a half

million in the employ of the state. One in three of the former were
already members of an occupational association. By 1913 the 53 white-
collar organisations ranged from the combative trade union to the non-
combative social association, and politically from the Socialist Central
Association of Commercial Assistants with 24,000 members to the right-
wing and anti-Semitic German-National Commercial Assistants'
Association with some 148,000. It has been claimed that distinctively
German traditions of status and deference separated white-collar workers
'much more emphatically and unequivocally' from manual workers than
elsewhere, and that the German term 'Privatbeamter' or 'Angesteller'
carried a much stronger social charge than the English 'white-collar'
or the French 'employé salarié'.[27] But even if this was true, which seems
unlikely, it would still be a long step to concluding that these strata
were somehow easier meat for right-wing predators than in say Britain.
On the contrary, this was in many ways the contested zone of German
politics: the 'new *Mittelstand*' was by no means uniformly right-wing in its
political loyalties. Many of its members joined the liberal Hanse-Union,
an anti-agrarian umbrella launched in 1909, for instance, and with its
102,000 members in 1913 the more liberal Association of German
Commercial Assistants managed to run its German-National counterpart
reasonably close. The Union of Technical-Industrial Officials (23,000
members in 1913) was militantly critical of employers and embraced
the strike weapon, whilst even the civil servants' 'Union of the Salaried'
embraced progressive demands for heavier taxation of higher incomes,
reform of the Prussian three-class franchise and more representative
government at all levels. This was perhaps the liberal parties' natural constituency, for as business circles shifted rightwards and the Agrarian
League usurped the traditional primacy of the liberals in the northern
and central German countryside, the latter were thrown increasingly
back on these strata for their votes. But against all this must be set the
success of the radical-rightist German-National Commercial Assistants'
Association and the attempts to float white-collar equivalents of the
company unions between 1911 and 1918. Less obtrusively there was
also the apolitical inertia of the older professional organisations: the
Association for Commercial Clerks of 1858 (127,000 members in
1913), the German Foremen's Association (62,000, founded 1884), and
the Association of German Technicians (30,000, also founded 1884).
At all events these groupings displayed the typical diversity of the petty-
bourgeoisie's politico-ideological reactions. The main political division
of German society ran through the class rather than to the left of it.
By the early years of the Weimar Republic white-collar workers were

roughly polarised between the Socialist AFA with 690,000 members
and the right-wing Gedag with 463,000.[28]

The third category of organisations I want to consider is rather
different, in that it arose not from the defensive needs of occupational
or sectional groupings, but from the affirmation of a powerful nationalist
commitment of an imperialist, militarist or cultural kind. These
organisations qualify for consideration with the other two categories
because by and large they recruited their active membership from
precisely the same strata of the old and new petty-bourgeoisie. They
were the so-called *nationale Verbände*, the nationalist pressure groups,
those organisations with the official object of attracting popular backing
for the notion of exclusive national priorities, normally from an
overtly anti-Socialist and anti-liberal perspective. The first was the
Colonial Society, formed in 1887 from the coalescence of two earlier
organisations. It was followed by the Pan-German League in 1891, the
Society for the Eastern Marches in 1894, the Navy League in 1898 and
the Defence League in 1912. These were the classic representatives of
the milieu. To them must be added cultural organisations with a less
aggressive public persona – the Society for Germandom Abroad, the
Patriotic Book League, the Christian Book League and the German-
Union are all examples – and a range of organisations whose primary
responsibility lay elsewhere, but who consciously situated themselves
within the same nationalist tradition. The latter included the veterans'
associations, the Young Germany Union sponsored by the state in 1911,
and the gamut of anti-Socialist labour organisations, from the
Evangelical Workers' Associations to the company unions and the
Imperial League Against Social Democracy launched in 1904. The
direct political influence of these groups can easily be over-estimated.
Many historians have been misled by their large paper membership
and impressive propagandist output into making excessive claims for
their political importance. In reality membership tended to mean very
little in terms of time, energy and commitment, and supporters were
normally required to do little more than read the literature which their
subscriptions helped to produce. In this way the *nationale Verbände*
had a less formative impact on the consciousness of their ordinary
members than did the occupational groups or the economic defence
leagues. But on the other hand, they did provide a political platform for
a sizable minority who recoiled from involvement in the conventional
political parties and their 'cattle-trading' in the Reichstag, and who
sought a practical surrogate in the untainted moral crusades of nationalist
education. The Pan-Germans and the naval enthusiasts were bitterly

resented by the established party politicians, particularly as they legitimated their agitation from an angry critique of the latter's inadequacy. The nationalist pressure groups were a noisy and disruptive presence in German politics after the turn of the century, and played no small part in radicalising the general tone of right-wing politics. In this their contribution rivals that of the Agrarian League and its allies.[29]

The point is this: that together these three sets of organisations, most of them founded in a crucial period between the 1880s and the turn of the century, registered a profound seismic shift at the base of German society, which sent heavy tremors of social aspiration upwards to the political surface of the new German nation-state. This was a period of unprecedented social change — of astonishing urban growth, massive migration and pervasive cultural dislocation, in which men who had previously led sheltered lives in small enclosed communities were forced either to defend their accustomed way of life or to adapt rapidly and resourcefully to a new environment. We are now very familiar with the efforts of a particular tendency of the German working class — that organised in the SPD — to cope with these problems, and there are many studies of the so-called Social Democratic 'sub-culture' in which the Socialist worker was provided, it is claimed, with a self-contained and self-sufficient social and cultural world of trade unions, cooperatives, friendly societies, educational and recreational institutions, including everything from the Socialist cycling club to the Socialist public house. The great absence in German social history at the present time is any comparable attempt to extend the same degree of imaginative and analytical sympathy to the world of the peasantry, the urban petty-bourgeoisie and the *Mittelstand*. As it is, these groups tend to be seen only as the voting fodder manipulated at will to the polls by the political managers of the big businessman and the Junker. The point I want to stress, therefore, is that the organisations enumerated above were more often than not the autonomous achievements of social strata which had previously been dormant politically, which were now impelled into motion by the desire to protect a traditional way of life in the case of the *Mittelstand* and peasantry, or to affirm their confidence in the new modernity of the industrial nation-state, in that of the clerical, professional and managerial strata in the towns, and finally whose entry into politics was at first deeply resented by the closed establishment which dominated the existing non-Socialist parties.

The critical problem of German history between the 1870s and the First World War was thus in many ways that of how the old governing establishment was to absorb this new mobilisation. This is the full

meaning of terms like 'mass politics' and 'mass society' if they are to
have any use at all. They mean not simply the new conditions of
universal manhood suffrage and mass literacy, nor just the efforts of
manipulative politicians like Bismarck, Bülow or Tirpitz to equip themselves with pliant popular support. It also and even primarily meant that
'the masses have come of age (through elementary education, mass conscription, universal suffrage and the cheap oil-lamp)', and were consequently demanding that their voices be heard.[30] To capture the real
changes at work in German society, in other words, the notion of mass
politics has to imply not only manipulation from above, but also
militant pressure from below. This is precisely where the currently
influential ideas of *Sammlungspolitik*, 'secondary integration',
'caesarism' and 'social imperialism' reveal their limitations. For they all
advance the idea of a successful manipulation of popular emotions
from above by entrenched élites: this is made into the unifying theme
of the entire period between the 1860s and the 1930s, and Nazism
becomes merely the most extreme manifestation of the same
authoritarian syndrome. But if instead of regarding the pressure groups
as the transparent fronts of traditional ruling interests and the ciphers
of an unchanging authoritarian tradition, we try to see them as the
organic expressions of a powerful and variegated movement of popular
protest, with their own distinctive styles of propaganda and agitation,
their own aggressive ideologies and their own vigorous corporate
identities, and if we try to regard these organisations as the vehicles
through which the new techniques of mass agitation were reluctantly
and painfully assimilated by establishment politicians, *then*, it seems to
me, we have a more satisfactory means of understanding that radicalisation of conservative politics which made possible the rise of a German
fascism. If we wish to identify the sources of change in the forms of
conservative politics, therefore, it is at the points of friction between
the political parties and the pressure groups, the real mass organisations
of Wilhelmine Germany, that we must look.[31]

IV

Looking back from the vantage-point of 1933, but bearing in mind the
above remarks, therefore, it is possible to regard Nazism as merely the
most recent in a succession of conservative redefinitions, each more
advanced than its predecessor in its achievement of a broader social
appeal and the appropriation of methods and tactics which corresponded
more tightly to the current historical moment. It is fatally misleading to
use a term like conservatism as a conceptual monolith to be shifted

around the whole century before Hitler at will and with a perfectly autonomous explanatory power all of its own. Between the start of the nineteenth century and 1945 German conservatism underwent some profound changes in its sociological, organisational and ideological character, which together constituted an important political metamorphosis. It is possible to see Nazism as one of a series of dissolutions and regroupings at a higher level and on an enlarged basis, through which the German right developed in three sorts of ways: *convulsively*, through a series of protracted crises; *progressively*, by adjusting to changed conditions; and *laterally*, as a result of the convergence of new social and political forces from different directions. Building upon the achievements of recent work, therefore, I want to suggest a broad chronological framework within which Nazism can be successfully located without incurring the distortions of historical perspective mentioned at the beginning of this essay. Basically, it is possible to distinguish six broad phases in an overall reorientation of German conservatism since the start of the last century.

The *first* of these spans the two key periods of nineteenth-century legal and constitutional experiment in Germany, that of 1807–1812 and that of 1862–79. This was the period of resistance to the new bourgeois civilisation, in which the landowning class, whose institutional equivalents were the monarchy, the army and the bureaucracy, attempted to defend its political predominance by warding off demands for unification, constitutional reform and economic rationalisation. This general reactionary stance precluded neither the limited progressive role of the State bureaucracies nor the detachment of significant sectors of the landowning class and their realignment with the progressive forces, in areas like Hanover, certain parts of eastern and western Prussia and South Germany. Moreover, the territorial fragmentation of Germany as well as its social and economic diversity made for a high degree of uneven development in this respect.[32]

The *second* period extended from 1879 to 1909. This was a phase of significant reorientation away from an entrenched counter-revolutionary stance and of political-ideological consolidation within new positions. It involved a series of compromises with the formerly antagonistic bourgeois coalition, in which conservatives in Bavaria and Prussia came to terms with the newly constituted nation-state, acquiesced in the new constitutional arrangements and recognised the need for political alliance with the new industrial bourgeoisie. There resulted a gradual fusion of social forces into a new hybrid ruling class, a process which was accelerated by the inter-penetration of industrial and agrarian capital in the boom years ending in 1873. The political consummation of this process was the Bismarckian settlement of 1878–9, when the twin compulsions of economic crisis and revolutionary anathema culminated in a new decisive configuration of protectionism and repressive anti-Socialism: *Sammlungspolitik*. This naturally entailed a radical transformation of the social base of German conservatism, if we define this to mean the political defence of an existing system of social, economic and political power, as distinct from Conservatism with a capital 'C', which implies a more specific political tradition. But although we may detect the formation of a new dominant bloc at the centre of German society, denoted by its own ideological forms and made sharply visible in the crisis years of 1878–9, the very speed of the realignment – which took a matter of decades rather than centuries as in Britain – produced a high degree of political, that is organisational, fragmentation. In other words, the new socio-economic bloc did not yet find its organisational equivalent in a new united party of the right. The old independent parties – Conservative, Free Conservative, National Liberal and Centre – remained as the monuments to important sectional interests and loyalties.

The crucial problem of the German right, for which this organisational fragmentation became a decisive impediment, was the achievement of the necessary political strength to meet the rising threat of the working class. This general problem broke down into three particular ones: the ideological adjustment to conditions of parliamentary democracy and the development of an appropriate scepticism towards proposals for a violent suppression of political debate; the transcendence of sectional divisions within the dominant conservative bloc and an ultimate organisational reconstruction of the right on a unitary basis; and finally, the winning of mass popular support in order to compete effectively under conditions of parliamentary rule. The last of these three problems proved especially difficult, for the established right-wing parties proved unable to readjust their newly consolidated practice (from the 1860s and 70s) by paying lip service to the principles of democracy and by mobilising fresh strata to their banner. Their resistance to the demands of new popular forces for recognition – the petty-bourgeoisie in town and country, the peasantry, the professional and administrative strata – led to a process of political fermentation beginning in the 1880s and continuing throughout the period, with a phase of accelerating organising activity in the 1890s. This produced a string of economic interest groups, agitational pressure groups behind nationalist issues like the Navy, the colonies, the defence of the German language and culture, and so on, and a number of minor political parties – all standing broadly on the right, but in opposition to the established conservative parties. In general the older parties found it difficult to assimilate these new forces or to accommodate them in political alliances – the Catholic Centre Party managed this better than most – and the period was stamped by great political tension between old and new groups. The period was characterised by a general failure of the conservative parties to meet the challenge of popular mobilisation: their popular base was a diminishing one, and the electoral success of 1907 was only a temporary diversion from this problem. These were the years of the rise of the petty-bourgeoisie, which established its own organisations and forged its own distinctive ideologies, whose common characteristic was a militant populist nationalism, and whose point of negative definition was the political exclusiveness of the established party-political oligarchies.[33]

The *third* phase ran from 1909 to 1918, years in which conservatism engineered a further feat of self-orientation no less far-reaching than the earlier one of 1878–9. It was characterised by a further ideological compromise, this time with the freshly mobilised petty-bourgeoisie, and by the decisive acquisition of a genuine popular base. Several factors assisted this development. One was the temporary resolution of the tax question in 1913, which removed a principal bone of contention between industry and agriculture and restored the cohesion of their alliance.[34] Another was the faltering emergence of a new reformist coalition seeking the basis of cooperation with the labour movement, which also helped to drive the conservative forces closer together. A third factor was the deterioration of German capitalism's position in the world market, especially after 1911, and a fourth was the renewed pressure of the working class after the SPD landslide in the 1912 elections. The nationalist panacea supplied the ideological fixative which aided the integration of previously discordant forces. This complex of factors forced a coalescence of the right of great novelty. The protectionist and anti-Socialist motifs remained constant, but to them were now added a new seriousness in the conciliation of the *Mittelstand* and the seduction of the expanding white-collar interest. This marked the arrival of the petty-bourgeoisie in the magic circle of conservative politics after the angry and divisive altercations of the preceding decades. The circumstances under which the new conservative regrouping was announced to the world symbolised this important development: the so-called 'Cartel of the Productive Estates' was officially proclaimed at the third annual congress of the Imperial-German *Mittelstand* League at Leipzig in August 1913.[35] It was also registered by the growing importance of the

Pan-Germans in the counsels of the right.[36] Politically it resulted in calls
for a more aggressive foreign policy and a more strident denunciation of
parliamentary forms. Its manifestations included an unprecedented
willingness to criticise the Kaiser, the ideological recourse to the *Volk*
as an alternative focus of political legitimacy, a pronounced interest in
corporative as opposed to representative institutions of government,
and the revival of plans for a *Staatsstreich* or *coup d'état.*

Although clarification of these issues was interrupted by the outbreak of war in 1914, the domestic wrangles concerning the nature of
Germany's war aims and the spectre of post-war reconstruction soon
gave the changes fresh impetus. Things were clearly tending towards an
organisational reconstitution of the right on a unitary footing. Strong
evidence was provided by the continuing drift of heavy industry from
the National Liberals to the Conservatives.[37] Moreover, by now the latter
had been completely reshaped in the image of the Agrarian League and
the tone of conservative politics was set almost entirely by people with
strong connections in the respective organisations of the petty-
bourgeoisie. This was certainly true of the Fatherland-Party launched in
1917, the prototype of a future united party of the right. Yet even this
was forced to coexist in parallel with the existing parties by maintaining
an official restriction of its activities to the field of foreign affairs. It
required the trauma of defeat and revolution in the autumn of 1918
before the organisational reconstruction which had been implicit since
the 1890s could finally be precipitated. This initiated a *fourth* major
phase of development, in which the German-National People's Party
emerged from the fusion of five older parties (Conservatives, Free
Conservatives, Christian-Socials and the two main anti-Semitic remnants)
to form the unitary organ of the right.[38] This also marked the definitive
victory of populist and pseudo-democratic notions of political activity
in conservative ranks, manifest in the very title of the new party.
Although the uncertainties of the revolutionary ferment which lasted
until the autumn of 1923 gave some scope for fresh contradictions of
a moderate-radical nature inside the rightist bloc, the dissenting currents
were largely confined to the periphery of the new State, as in the Munich
Putsch of 1923,[39] and by the Weimar Republic's period of relative
stability between 1924 and 1928 the new party had also consolidated its
own legitimacy with some success.

Given the Wilhelmine emphasis of this essay, the *fifth* and *sixth* phases
in the chronology of the right require comparatively little description.
The former began with the crash of 1929 and the protracted crisis this
inaugurated. This first fractured the unity and self-confidence of the

dominant conservative organ, the German-National People's Party, already under pressure from an independent process of internal factionalism, and then enabled the Nazis to constitute themselves as the largest popular force on the right. The result was a fresh synthesis, on broader social foundations than ever before and on an incomparably more radical basis. The central role of the petty-bourgeoisie in the Nazi movement is well-attested, though its precise relationship to the State apparatus established after 1933 remains the subject of involved debate. Moreover, the collaboration of big business and the residual aristocracy with the Nazis, despite certain evident uneasiness and the desperation of the July Plot in 1944, extended across the entire life of the Third Reich, though again its precise forms remain to be established. It was not until the defeat of 1945 and the imposition of a new political settlement by the Western Allies that the final and most recent phase began, namely that of adjustment to conditions of parliamentary rule.[40]

V

The overall argument of this essay may be briefly recapitulated as follows. It is first premised on the belief that the conditions of petty-bourgeois mobilisation are crucial to our understanding of fascism and of National Socialism in particular. There will be exceptions, but on the whole most commentators are agreed on the importance of the petty-bourgeoisie in the structure of fascist movements: this is true of the most perceptive contemporary observers like Trotsky, Thalheimer, Gramsci and Bloch, it is also true of subsequent theorists like Parsons and Lipset or Poulantzas, and of recent historical studies like those of Allen, Noakes or Pridham. If we want to pin down those conditions which *specified* fascism in Germany, which favoured its success there but which were absent in say Britain, then there are some grounds for looking closely at the terms under which the petty-bourgeoisie was admitted — or compelled its own admittance — to the political system. Secondly, arising from this, I feel that previous historians of the Wilhelmine period have not given this problem sufficient critical attention and have rather smoothed over many of the complexities it presents. Thirdly, I have tried to indicate some of the ways in which these complexities might be dealt with. This is naturally a partial view of Nazism's prehistory, but my aim has been principally to redress the balance by identifying a problem and proposing a framework within which it might be tackled.

The central point deserves one further reiteration. Of course there were manipulative elements at work in the organisations of the petty-bourgeoisie, both at their initial foundation and in their subsequent

history; of course traditional politicians saw the pressure groups as a
vehicle for some much-needed popular support against the Socialists; of
course the size and vitality of the autonomous popular movement can
easily be exaggerated, whether in the case of the Agrarian League or in
that of the *nationale Verbände*; of course the populist complexion of
petty-bourgeois ideology must be kept carefully in proper perspective;
and of course the petty-bourgeoisie ended up in large numbers in the
camp of the Nazis. But we will not understand the routes which were
travelled to that conclusion, nor the nature of the right-wing
radicalisation which provided some of the necessary preconditions for a
German fascism, unless we also appreciate the strength of the popular
aspirations and resentments to which the old-style conservative parties
were subjected between the 1890s and 1914. In 1900 the Pan-Germans
were dismissed as 'beer-bench politicians', the radical peasants of
Central Germany were scorned as 'gutter-antisemites', and the extremist
agrarian agitators attacked as 'irresponsible meddlers'. By 1913 the
Agrarian League had reshaped the Conservative Party in its own image,
the anti-Semites had been successfully assimilated to it, a new national
Mittelstand organisation had given its annual congress for the announcement of a new right-wing front, and the Pan-Germans had become important intermediaries between industrialists and agrarians. Something
had clearly happened in the meantime. In 1900 the established
politicians saw the petty-bourgeoisie as something to be manipulated;
by 1913 they had given its organic spokesmen a voice of their own. The
phenomenon I have been trying to highlight is the interaction of
manipulative intentions from above with the formulation of demands
from below. Because it was only from this *friction* that the forms of
a proto-fascist ideology and political practice were born.

Notes

1. For an excellent discussion of these matters see A.S. Kraditor, 'American
   Radical Historians on their Heritage', *Past and Present*, 56 (August 1972),
   pp. 136–53.
2. The three best discussions of the Fischer Controversy are all in German:
   A. Sywottek, 'Die Fischer-Kontroverse', in I. Geiss and B.J. Wendt (eds.),
   Deutschland in der Weltpolitik des 19. u. 20. Jahrhunderts (2nd edn.,
   Düsseldorf, 1974), pp. 19–47; I. Geiss, 'Die Fischer-Kontroverse', in *Studien
   über Geschichte und Geschichtswissenschaft* (Frankfurt, 1972), pp. 108–98;
   W. Schieder, 'Ergebnisse und Möglichkeiten der Diskussion über den Ersten
   Weltkrieg', in W. Schnieder (ed.), *Erster Weltkrieg. Ursachen, Entstehung und
   Kriegsziele* (Cologne, 1969), pp. 11–26. But see also J. A. Moses, *The Politics
   of Illusion* (London, 1975).

3. For a useful critique of this approach, see G. Barraclough's three articles in *New York Review of Books*, 'Mandarins and Nazis' (19 October 1972), 'The Liberals and German History' (2 November 1972), and 'A New View of German History' (16 November 1972).
4. R. D'O. Butler, *The Roots of National Socialism* (London, 1941), pp. 277f.
5. Ibid.
6. For a sample of works following this approach: H. Kohn, *The Mind of Germany* (London, 1966); F. Stern, *The Politics of Cultural Despair* (Berkeley, 1961); G.L. Mosse, *The Crisis of German Ideology* (London, 1966); A.J.P. Taylor, *The Course of German History* (London, 1945); UNESCO, *The Third Reich* (London, 1955); W. Shirer, *The Rise and Fall of the Third Reich* (New York, 1960). For the work of the Institute of Social Research (the so-called Frankfurt School: Marcuse, Adorno, Horkheimer, Neumann, Kirchheimer, etc.), see M. Jay, *The Dialectical Imagination* (London, 1973), especially pp. 113–72.
7. See Stern, *Politics of Cultural Despair*, and the edition of his essays, *The Failure of Illiberalism* (London, 1972). By far the most sensitive discussion of these themes to date is R. Pascal, *From Naturalism to Expressionism. German Literature and Society 1880–1918* (London, 1973), especially pp. 16–66, 277–314.
8. K.D. Bracher, 'The Nazi Takeover', *History of the 20th Century*, XXXXVIII (1969), p. 1339.
9. The works of Bracher and Dahrendorf are most familiar to an English-speaking audience, but lesser-known figures in this country have been equally important for West German historians. See for instance, M.R. Lepsius, 'Parteiensystem und Sozialstruktur: zum Problem der Demokratisierung der deutschen Gesellschaft', in W. Abel *et al.* (eds.), *Wirtschaft, Geschichte und Wirtschaftsgeschichte* (Stuttgart, 1966), pp. 371–93.
10. T. Parsons, *Essays in Sociological Theory* (Glencoe, 1964), pp. 104–41. For a useful critique: M. Clemenz, *Gesellschaftliche Ursprünge des Faschismus* (Frankfurt, 1972), pp. 96–118.
11. The term has been enshrined for posterity in the title of Fritz Stern's highly influential book.
12. I have discussed the idea of *Sammlungspolitik* in an earlier essay: Eley, '*Sammlungspolitik*, Social Imperialism and the Navy Law of 1898', *Militärgeschichtliche Mitteilungen*, XI, 1 (1974), pp. 29–63. For a summary statement of the conventional usage: H.-U. Wehler, *Das Deutsche Kaiserreich 1871–1918* (Göttingen, 1973), pp. 100–5, 48–59.
13. The emphasis on continuity between Bismarck and Hitler implies a definite understanding of Nazism (and of fascism) which has never been properly explicated or theorised as such in the work of the recent Wilhelmine historians. A useful object for future discussion (for which there is no space here) would be to reconstruct that understanding from the often invisible web of theoretical assumptions which holds their argument about continuity together. This may be clarified by the fact that a number of the authors who began work on the Wilhelmine period have now moved on to the Weimar Republic.
14. On the most recent estimate we are probably dealing with upwards of 1.5 million artisans, 0.5 million small traders and 5.0 million small farmers (i.e. those owning less than 20 hectares or 50 acres of land) in 1907. To them must be added some 3.5 million white-collar workers in private and state employment. See J. Kocka, *Klassengesellschaft im Krieg* (Göttingen, 1973), pp. 65ff., and G. Hohorst, J. Kocka, G.A. Ritter, *Sozialgeschichtliches Arbeitsbuch* (Munich, 1975), pp. 66–77. See also H. Handtke, 'Einige Probleme der inneren Struktur der herrschenden Klasse in Deutschland vom

Ende des 19 Jahrhunderts bis zum ersten Weltkrieg', in F. Klein (ed.), *Studien zum deutschen Imperialismus vor 1914* (Berlin, 1976), pp. 85–114.

15. Again: it is worth stressing that these comments are concerned mainly with right-wing tendencies in the petty-bourgeoisie. They do not present an exhaustive survey of its political mobilisation and are not meant to suggest that Left-Liberals and Social Democrats made no appeal to these groups of people, for they clearly did. The main point is that during the 1880s and 1890s a political fermentation began which affected the practice of all parties in Germany: in this particular essay I am concerned with the impact of this on just one group of parties, those of the right.

16. For the details of legislation, see the entry under 'Gewerbegesetzgebung' in *Handwörterbuch der Staatswissenschaften*, IV (3rd edn., Berlin, 1910). See also H.A. Winkler, 'From Social Protectionism to National Socialism: The German Small-Business Movement in Comparative Perspective', *Journal of Modern History*, 48:(March, 1976), 1–7; Winkler, *Mittelstand, Demokratie und Nationalsozialismus* (Cologne, 1972), pp. 26–64.

17. See R. Gellately, *The Politics of Economic Despair. Shopkeepers and German Politics 1890–1914* (London, 1974), pp. 83–111. In south-west Germany until the turn of the century the 'Trade Associations' organised into an umbrella federation in 1891 performed a common function for artisans, traders and small manufacturers. See Winkler, 'Der rückversicherte Mittelstand: Die Interessenverbände von Handwerk und Kleinhandel im deutschen Kaiserreich', in W. Ruegg, O. Neuloh (eds.), *Zur soziologischen Theorie und Analyse des 19. Jahrhunderts* (Göttingen, 1971), p. 166.

18. A '*Mittelstand* Party' was formed abortively in Halle in 1895. See Gellately, *Politics of Economic Despair*, pp. 150f.

19. The best guide to the confusing universe of the anti-Semitic parties is still P.W. Massing, *Rehearsal for Destruction* (New York, 1949), but see also P. Pulzer, *The Rise of Political Antisemitism in Germany and Austria* (London, 1964), and R.S. Levy, *The Downfall of the Antisemitic Political Parties in Imperial Germany* (London, 1975).

20. See the indispensable handbook, D. Fricke *et al.* (eds.), *Die bürgerlichen Parteien in Deutschland*, 2 Vols. (Leipzig, 1968–1970), which contains individual entries on each organisation. See also H.-J. Puhle, 'Parlament, Parteien und Interessenverbände 1890–1914', in M. Stürmer (ed.), *Das kaiserliche Deutschland. Politik und Gesellschaft 1870–1918* (Düsseldorf, 1970), pp. 340–77.

21. This was true in twelve constituencies altogether: in six of the ten in Posen, two each in Bromberg and Minden, and one each in Liegnitz and Arnsberg. These were all in Prussia, and all lay in either the Junker or the Centre heartlands.

22. Königsberg itself was already held by the SPD and in both 1893 and 1898 the vote held steady there at around 13,000.

23. The guiding assumption of most work on the agrarian and *Mittelstand* movements before 1914 is that they provided the seed-bed of authoritarianism: they represented the casualties of 'modernisation' and stood in direct lineage with the Nazis. There is some truth in this received wisdom, but as it stands the explanation cuts too many corners. Two points may be briefly made. First: unless we pay meticulous attention to the egalitarian and radical components in the make-up of these protest movements in the Wilhelmine period, we will not adequately understand the ambiguous strength of the Nazis' populist appeal later. Second: petty-bourgeois radicalism was perfectly capable of propelling its exponents in either political direction, left or right, and in the Wilhelmine period when masses of traditional small

owners were being proletarianised the SPD and liberals benefited as much as the far right. For a sensitive discussion of the *Mittelstand* in its actual Wilhelmine context, see D. Blackbourn, 'The *Mittelstand* in German Society and Politics 1871–1914', *Social History*, 4 (1977), pp. 409–33.

24. This was particularly marked in Marburg, where in 1898 seven parties fought the election and polled between 995 (SPD) and 2,886 (anti-Semite) on the first ballot; for the run-off, which the anti-Semite won against the Conservative (the odd man out amongst the other six radicals!) by 5,417 to 4,937, it is anybody's guess how the spare votes were distributed. In 1903, in a similarly confused fight, the anti-Semite lost the seat to a National-Social, Helmuth von Gerlach, who later became a liberal democrat and pronounced pacifist!

25. See Blackbourn, 'The *Mittelstand* in German Society and Politics', for further discussion of this point.

26. See Gellately, *Politics of Economic Despair*, pp. 148–96.

27. Kocka, *Klassengesellschaft im Krieg*, p. 66.

28. Ibid., pp. 65–71; Hohorst, Kocka, Ritter, *Arbeitsbuch*, p. 138.

29. For lack of space these comments may appear unnecessarily elliptical. I have treated the problem of radicalisation in more detail in my unpublished thesis, 'The German Navy League in German Politics, 1898–1914' (Sussex DPhil., 1974), chaps. 5 and 6.

30. Rassow to Tirpitz, 12 April, 1898, in Bundesarchiv-Militärarchiv Freiburg, 2223, 94943. Hermann Rassow, a *Gymnasium* headmaster, was one of the most important naval propagandists of the period.

31. This argument should be considered together with those of two earlier articles: '*Sammlungspolitik*, Social Imperialism and the Navy Law of 1898', *Militärgeschichtliche Mitteilungen*, XI, 1 (1974), pp. 29–63; and 'Defining Social Imperialism: Use and Abuse of an Idea', *Social History*, 3 (1976), pp. 265–90.

32. H. Mottek, *Wirtschaftsgeschichte Deutschlands. Ein Grundriss*. II. *Von der Zeit der Französischen Revolution bis zur Zeit der Bismarckschen Reichsgründung* (Berlin, 1969); W. Conze (ed.), *Staat und Gesellschaft im deutschen Vormärz 1815 bis 1848* (2nd edn., Stuttgart, 1970); L. Krieger, *The German Idea of Freedom* (Boston, 1957); J. Kocka, 'Preussischer Staat und Modernisierung im Vormärz', in H.-U. Wehler (ed.), *Sozialgeschichte Heute* (Göttingen, 1974), pp. 211–27.

33. This motif is generally neglected in the recent monograph literature. For the best survey of the period, which brings together the findings of the latter, see H.-U. Wehler, *Das Deutsche Kaiserreich 1871–1918* (Göttingen, 1973).

34. For an exhaustive analysis of the tax question, see P.-Ch. Witt, *Die Finanzpolitik des Deutschen Reiches von 1903–1913* (Lübeck, 1970).

35. The 'Cartel' was supported by the Central Union of German Industrialists, the Agrarian League and the Imperial-German *Mittelstand* League; there was a looser connection with the Catholic Peasants' Associations, and the various nationalist pressure groups were also represented at the Leipzig Congress, as was the Imperial League Against Social Democracy. For the details: D. Stegmann, *Die Erben Bismarcks* (Cologne, 1970), pp. 342–408; F. Fischer, *War of Illusions* (London, 1974), pp. 272–90; V.R. Berghahn, *Germany and the Approach of War in 1914* (London, 1973), pp. 145–65.

36. See Stegmann, *Erben Bismarcks*, pp. 293–305, 356, 396f, 449ff, 480f, 489ff.

37. Ibid.

38. A. Thimme, *Flucht in den Mythos. Die Deutschnationale Volkspartei und die Niederlage von 1918* (Göttingen, 1969); L. Hertzmann, *DNVP – Right Wing*

Opposition in the Weimar Republic 1918–1924 (Lincoln, Nebr., 1963);
G.A. Ritter, 'Kontinuität und Unformung des deutschen Parteiensystems 1918
bis 1920', in G.A. Ritter, (ed.), *Entstehung und Wandel der modernen
Gesellschaft* (Berlin, 1970), pp. 342–84.

39. The major exception was the Kapp Putsch in 1920. For the best study of the
radical right in this period, see U. Lohalm, *Völkischer Radikalismus* (Hamburg,
1970).

40. The literature on Nazism and fascism is obviously vast. The most useful are
probably the following: M. Kitchen, *Fascism* (London, 1976); N. Poulantzas,
Fascism and Dictatorship (London, 1974); T. Mason, 'The Primacy of
Politics – Politics and Economics in National Socialist Germany', in S.J.
Woolf (ed.), *The Nature of Fascism* (London, 1968), pp. 165–95; Clemenz,
Gesellschaftliche Ursprünge des Faschismus; E. Hennig, *Thesen zur deutschen
Sozial- und Wirtschaftspolitik 1933 bis 1938* (Frankfurt, 1973); *Gesellschaft.
Beiträge zur Marxschen Theorie 6* (Frankfurt, 1976).

6 POPULISM IN THE COUNTRYSIDE: THE PEASANT LEAGUES IN BAVARIA IN THE 1890s

Ian Farr

I

The last decade of the nineteenth century witnessed a remarkable proliferation of peasant and farmers' political associations in Europe, as the traditional role of agriculture in economy and society confronted the increasing pressures of industrialisation and overseas or Russian competition. The spread of urban culture gave the peasantry new potential for communication and political consolidation, while simultaneously reducing the significance of the countryside within the national economy. In Imperial Germany this process was marked by the emergence of new agrarian movements which added fuel to an intense political debate about the degree of protection which home-grown agricultural produce and the farmer's income should be afforded. Historical attention has largely been concentrated on the activities and influence of the powerful Junker-dominated Agrarian League (BdL) in shaping the outcome of this crucial issue, and this has tended to obscure the appearance of a more radical rural consciousness across southern Germany. This reflects the persistent indifference among historians to the evolution of rural society in Germany in the more recent past. The neglect shown towards recent and fruitful exchanges among social scientists about the characteristics of peasant protest[1] has ensured the perseverance of older images of a conservative peasantry.[2] A study of Bavaria in the mid 1890s shows how misleading it may be to dismiss the small farmer as suspicious, ignorant, or, above all, submissive to traditional patterns of authority and political manipulation. Indeed, the very first and stormy meetings of the Lower Bavarian Peasant League (*Niederbayerischer Bauernbund*) in the spring of 1893 showed the determination of the local farmers to dispense with their former reliance on priests, nobles or officials.[3] It might well accord with the more dated and romanticised conceptions of peasant political mentality to interpret the expansion of agrarian agitation in Bavaria merely as evidence of the BdL's ability to exploit the peasantry for its own political objectives. But local examination shows that the various peasant leagues, which were at the heart of a political radicalisation in the Bavarian countryside, cannot be seen as some monolithic appendage of the BdL. While

the founding of a dynamic agrarian movement in northern Germany undoubtedly gave an impetus to rural politicisation in Bavaria, the sheer
variety of peasant movements illustrates how local grievances, contrasting patterns of farming and existing political or confessional
loyalties were influential in determining the nature of political commitment.[4]

II

Given the importance of the small farmer in the social and economic
structure of Bavaria, it comes as some surprise to find so little effective
or independent representation of his interests in the years before 1893.
A brief study of the few organisations which did make some small headway in this area soon shows why they were unable to achieve any permanent mobilisation of the peasantry into a cohesive political force,
and gives us a useful clue as to how the *Bauernbund* movement
captured the imagination of rural voters in the 1890s.

The rural body with the largest membership and the least political
muscle was the *Landwirtschaftlicher Verein* (Agricultural Association).
Founded in 1810 under government encouragement, it remained for
some decades the preserve of more prosperous landowners and a large
number of non-farmers, interested in the practical education of the
Bavarian peasant. The association had long been regarded with distrust
by the great bulk of the rural population. The statutes were successively
revised and annual subscriptions lowered in attempts to establish a
wider basis of popular support. Although a substantial increase in
membership was achieved in the second half of the century, it remained
essentially a bureaucratic mechanism for effecting legislative decisions
and technical improvements at the local level.[5] There seems little doubt
that these preoccupations aroused considerable antipathy among the
ordinary farmers towards the visible trappings of 'official' agriculture,
such as winter courses, peripatetic instructors and exhibitions. Lectures,
at which everyone, including the capitalist farmers and the officials,
were gradually lulled into slumber by Latin names and complicated
chemical formulae naturally became the object of ridicule.[6] The activities
of the *Landwirtschaftlicher Verein* may well have provided occasional
opportunities for the more articulate peasant to voice his grievances,
and to gain some experience of conducting meetings and associational
affairs, but the distrust of local officialdom which the association
generated was probably more decisive in the long run.

An indication of the difficulty of maintaining any relatively sizable
and coherent rural movement is revealed by the fluctuating fortunes of

the patriotic peasant associations (*Patriotische Bauernvereine*). They were formed in 1868–9 under the banner of 'God, King and Fatherland' to harness the spontaneous upsurge of agrarian resentment against the imminent Prussian threats to Bavarian and papal sovereignties and to Catholic freedom of worship, and were decisive in the success of the Patriotic Party.[7] Their aggressive Catholicism and anti-liberalism effectively restricted their activities to south-east Bavaria, but that did not diminish their unattractiveness in the eyes of the bureaucracy. As long as the Catholic church remained the object of discrimination during the *Kulturkampf*, these patriotic associations were assured of some support. The healthy survival of the church and the clear irrevocability of unification were thus to rob these associations of much of their rationale. By 1872 meetings had become poorly attended and the sympathy of the clergy and the larger landowners had been lost.[8] The occasional successful gathering could not disguise the inability of the peasant groups to achieve some concrete benefits for a rapidly diminishing following. The numbers in the Deggendorf association slumped from 8,604 in 1870 to a nadir in 1882, when the annual meeting attracted only six participants.[9] The other surviving group, based in Tuntenhausen, and with a membership of some 2,000, managed to preserve a nominal independence over subsequent years, continuing to survive on past traditions long after its political potential had been outstripped by the growth of more formidable Catholic peasant associations in the 1890s.

Nevertheless, the *Patriotische Bauernvereine* had helped to develop a political programme which appealed to a group of influential agitators, who were determined to curtail the influence of older aristocratic elements in the Catholic political movement. Certain individuals, who were at the forefront of the radical Catholic wing in the years before 1890, later became closely involved in the initiatives for the *Bauernbund* movement. Dr Johann Sigl, editor of the widely-read polemical newspaper, *Das bayerische Vaterland*, was just one who found his mixture of particularist anti-Prussianism, anti-liberalism and contempt of militarism well suited to the more receptive climate of the 1890s. Another was Georg Ratzinger, a well-known clerical publicist, who promoted a wide-ranging programme of agrarian reform under the auspices of the patriotic association. His criticism of facilities for cheap rural credit and vituperations against the evils of capitalist latifundia, stock market cliques and factory labour reflected a long career peddling anti-Semitic tracts, but other demands — increased tariff levels, the reintroduction of restrictions on mobility and employment, economies in military expenditure — established clear guidelines for later agitation in the *Bauernbund.*[10]

Similar lines of continuity are discernible in other parts of Bavaria. The years after 1882 saw several attempts to establish a viable peasant party in Franconia and Bavarian Swabia. These were due almost entirely to the initiative of Baron von Thüngen-Rossbach, member of a large noble family with widespread estates in Lower Franconia, who had first come to public prominence in the protectionist Union of Tax and Economic Reformers in 1878–9.[11] After the success of his agitation in helping to secure Bismarck's conversion to protection, he continued his propaganda in Bavaria by forming a Franconian Peasant Association in September, 1882.[12] Subsequent attempts to extend the orbit of the association met with mixed fortunes; further groups were established in Swabia, and, after some delay, in Central Franconia, but there was little success in neighbouring Upper Franconia.[13] Again it is a picture of the occasional well-attended meetings, interspersed with long intervals of non-activity when the associations lost their committed political backing. Thüngen extended his zeal for agitation to a wide range of fiscal issues, and continued to use his associations for condemnations of the gold-standard, usury and the 'princes of the stock-market'.[14] His supporters exploited similar themes, though the impact of bimetallist arguments on rural audiences was probably minimal. While the particular emphasis on currency questions bore the hallmarks of Thüngen's substantial influence, there is no overlooking the fact that many of his basic demands paralleled those of the radical Catholics on points such as taxation, tariffs, and the unacceptable face of liberal capitalism.[15] However no attempt was made to achieve closer cooperation, because the Swabian and Franconian Associations were little more than electoral pressure-groups for those conservative politicians who commanded some affiliation in the Protestant enclaves of Bavaria. Like the patriotic agrarian movement, it failed to offer any realistic economic assistance to the peasantry. However these groups did establish and consolidate the liberal and conservative position in rural areas, especially those inhabited by Protestants. It was on this basis that the Agrarian League was able to build with some success, in stark contrast to its hostile reception in the predominantly Catholic regions.[16]

III

The two decades after unification thus saw the evolution in Bavaria of a reasonably coherent programme of reform, appealing primarily to the peasant and the small independent tradesman. It was a mixture of economic conservatism, social egalitarianism, radical politics and lightly-veiled anti-Semitism which was to play a decisive part in the politics of the German *Mittelstand* in the years to come. But despite the range and even the occasional ambiguity of its demands, and the existence of some determined agitators working on its behalf, the programme failed to inspire any unified movement capable of overcoming the difficulties inherent in rural political organisation. The level of political conflict, and hence participation, in many rural areas was minimal. Elections aroused little interest, because there was no effective challenge to the mono-poly of the Centre and the Liberal parties. Though official reports of clerical control over the Catholic electorate were probably exaggerated, there is little doubt that the clergy were active in shepherding men to the polling stations and preventing them from voting for any other party but the Centre. To disobey would mean to incur the wrath of the priest and, so it was threatened, of higher authorities as well![17] This pattern was broken in the elections of 1893, as the Peasant Leagues made sub-stantial inroads in some former Centre Party strongholds. Of 39 Reichstag constituencies contested by the Centre, only 9 managed to retain the levels of support gained at the preceding election. In all parts of Lower Bavaria the Centre suffered considerable voting losses; setbacks elsewhere were not as severe, but still clear in their message,[18] as Centre candidates faced strenuous rural opposition for the first time. The exertions of the Reichstag campaign tended to diminish interest in the Landtag elections later in the same year, but that did not prevent the peasant parties from amassing a sizable 9 to 10 per cent of the total vote, and securing the election of nine delegates of varying political shades. The most notable successes were again in Lower Bavaria, where the Peasant League gained nearly 40 per cent of the intermediate electors under the indirect voting system, while a reconstituted peasant association in Central Franconia made a noticeable advance. From this point onwards, the *Bauernbund*, in its different manifestations, was to play a significant part in mobilising rural politics. Although its direct influence in terms of election success and parliamentary power waned after the turn of the century, the repercussions of the Peasant League's advance during and after 1893 belied its immediate numerical strength.[19]

It is therefore necessary to account for the ability of a new rural movement to make such significant inroads into the existing political structure, while relying to a large extent on known agitators and ideological attitudes. Why were the seeds of agrarian radicalism suddenly flourishing where previously they had fallen on stony ground? A number of factors can be identified, but none would have been significant but for the fundamental economic problems facing Bavarian agriculture.

There seems no reason to question the view, widely held by many contemporaries, that an appreciable deterioration had occurred in the levels of prosperity of many peasants and farmers. Already during the 1880s high land prices, occasioned by the favourable years up to 1873, heavy mortgage and interest payments and rising wage-levels for agricultural labourers were leading to acute shortages of working capital.[20] There were considerable difficulties in the more northerly parts of Bavaria, where holdings were smaller and less well blessed by physical conditions, and where many peasants earned a living from produce, such as hops, wine or fruit, which was vulnerable to harvest fluctuations and heavy market pressures.[21] Response to official encouragement to rely more on cooperatives and credit unions for additional capital was favourable, but slow. A very perfunctory survey of rural conditions in the 1880s suggests considerable local and seasonal variations, through which the peasants on marginal properties and the larger landowners with high overheads may have survived less well than others. In contrast, the period after 1890 saw a more widespread and deep-rooted crisis in the countryside. The substantial decline in prices in the wake of Caprivi's 'new course' compounded the low levels of profitability in many enterprises. Common problems recurred over much of Bavaria – shortages of surplus or working capital; inadequate mechanisation,[22] animal husbandry, rational fertilising and education, and so on.[23] Improvements in all these areas presumed the ready availability of credit at low rates of interest, and many peasants still preferred to meet urgent needs by borrowing money from friends or relatives. In Bavaria very little land was leased to tenants; two-thirds of all holdings and 95 per cent of the land were farmed by the owners.[24] A large number of peasants on medium-sized farms were thus badly hit by the growing indebtedness, and their heirs were compelled to assume sizable debts when returns were declining. Indebtedness was generally higher on the larger consolidated farms of the South-east than in the rest of Bavaria, where there were more opportunities for secondary employment. Involuntary alienations of property and the breaking-up of estates, which both increased to a peak in 1898, indicate the difficulties confronting the owners of more sizable farms, particularly on the occasion of inheritance.[25] Clearly, the picture was not as black as some contemporaries painted it, and some areas were more badly hit than others. Nevertheless, a feeling of crisis is just as potent as the actuality, and there is no doubting that a crisis mentality did pervade much of the Bavarian countryside in the years before 1900.

The rapid appearance of the Peasant Leagues can be seen in part, therefore, as a response to a long-term structural crisis in certain essential sectors of Bavarian agriculture. Equally, short-term difficulties may have helped to accelerate their expansion. In 1893 southern Germany was afflicted by a particularly severe drought. The adverse conditions drastically reduced stocks of fodder and potatoes; in Augsburg and Bayreuth the hay yield was only one third of normal expectations.[26] The government dispensed large interest-free loans to tide farmers over the worst effects of the fodder shortage. Huge quantities of foodstuffs were purchased to ensure that farmers would not have to sell off their animals at depressed and uneconomic prices. The problems created by the drought were felt over much of Franconia, Swabia and the Upper Palatinate. They were a cause of considerable official consternation and helped to generate a mood of pessimism among those peasants who were less directly disadvantaged by falling prices.[27]

This climate of uncertainty, plus the general squeeze on rural incomes, does much to explain the degree of sympathy for those parts of the populist propaganda calling for an immediate reduction in the peasant's financial commitments. Excess taxation for 'luxury' military expenditure was bitterly attacked on both economic and strategic grounds. This issue divided some of the Peasant Leagues from the militarist expansionism of the BdL. The financial burdens on farmers incurred by the contributions to the recently established social insurance schemes also aroused considerable resentment. Agitation against this legislation had been initiated in 1888 by the Social Democrats in Nuremberg. It was revived in 1892 and quickly accumulated support in many rural districts of southern Bavaria;[28] calls to revoke some parts of the legislation then became absorbed into the agrarian programme. Antipathy towards the financial privileges enjoyed by the aristocracy and by commercial wealth led to regular and comprehensible suggestions for reform of the Bavarian taxation system. Progressive income and property taxes were deemed essential by the peasant parties to end what they saw as excessive tax discrimination against peasant farmers and small businessmen. Fiscal reform was to be combined with severe budgetary restraint on all forms of national, regional and communal expenditure. Most vociferous of all the demands propagated by the Peasant Leagues was that calling for the abolition of *Bodenzinse*. These were fixed annual payments at 4 per cent interest, contracted by large numbers of peasants in 1848 to replace their outstanding feudal obligations. The costs of feudalism had borne much more heavily on the peasantry in Bavaria than in the rest of southern Germany, and it is clear that rural Bavarians continued to pay for their emancipation long after their fellow southern Germans.[29] Legislation in 1872 had improved the position in Franconia, but considerable anomalies and inequalities remained elsewhere. The complex network of redemption procedures was eventually only rationalised in 1898, after sustained pressure from the *Bauernbund* had attracted sufficient support from the other parties to leave the government no choice but to legislate.[30] Further elements of the peasant campaign became beacons for the future navigation of government policy. Many were limited in their scope, but did constitute a sensible response to some of the economic problems of the entire Bavarian *Mittelstand*. In themselves, suggested measures like greater governmental regulation of insurance and credit facilities or wholesale distribution were not dramatic, but the initial pressure from the rural radical movement galvanised the authorities into implementing reforms on these lines, all of which were of some immediate practical benefit. Like much agrarian propaganda, the broad programme of the Peasant Leagues contained much that was opposed to the 'predatory' forces of industrial modernisation. However, these should not obscure the large number of genuinely radical causes and enlightened economic proposals which underlay the more rhetorical appeals to the solidarity of the peasantry in its struggle against the competition of the capitalist economy.[31] It is precisely the existence of such apparent contradictions which renders a simple categorisation of Peasant League ideology into 'right' or 'left' virtually impossible. In this context it is reasonable to talk of a style of peasant *populism*, capable of accommodating a wide range of political, social and economic viewpoints, which themselves corresponded to both economic grievances as well as to a desire to reassert certain normative values. Only when removed from their immediate environment do the various strands of populist propaganda appear contradictory. Thus demands for the abolition of all aristocratic prerogatives could accompany a fairly explicit anti-Semitism because of the prevailing mistrust of all forms of vested interest and privilege, conspiring, so it seemed, to subvert the prosperity of the small producer. A campaign for greater governmental involvement to curb the worst abuses of the liberal capitalist economy can be either forward-looking or backward-looking, depending upon the ideological position of the observer. Therein lies much of the difficulty of the term populism, unless one accepts its very ambivalence as both inevitable and essential.[32]

IV

If the prevailing economic climate in Bavaria can be taken as the essential
spur to a more widespread rural agitation, other factors and traditions con-
ditioned the intensity, the success and the degree of radicalism of the
peasant movements. The varying relationships between the Agrarian League
and the Bavarian Peasant Leagues are a good indication of this. In Catholic
southern Bavaria, the BdL's attempts to secure a foothold remained
almost entirely fruitless. As will be seen, there was considerable
sympathy, especially in Lower Bavaria, for some of the Junker demands,
but this should not be confused with organisational control by the BdL.
In particular, the two Upper Bavarian Peasant Leagues (one being a
relatively insignificant association geared to the interests of the mountain
and forest farmers) made no secret of their animosity towards the BdL.
Equally reprehensible were those personalities within Bavaria who had
reached a close accommodation with the militarist Prussian Junkers —
together Junkers and Jews were the greatest barriers to the prosperity
of the Bavarian peasantry.[33] Peasant meetings showed the continuing
strength of particularism as a mobilising force, and the Prussian BdL
was an obvious target. Eventually the Agrarian League was forced to
rely on Ludwig Wenng, one of the foremost anti-Semitic agitators in
southern Bavaria, to organise the occasional meeting, at which discussion of agrarian issues merged into virulent condemnations of Jewish
capitalism.[34]

The hostility towards the BdL in southern Bavaria was in considerable contrast to attitudes elsewhere in the country. Among the
delegates to the Tivoli meeting, which led directly to the creation of
the BdL, were Thüngen and Friedrich Lutz, a Conservative agrarian from
Central Franconia. This was symptomatic of later developments when
some compromise was achieved between the BdL and the new Franconian
and Swabian peasant movements which had been established independently
of any initiative from Berlin. In northern Swabia, Lutz was one of those
instrumental in integrating the recently formed Farmers' Club into the
Agrarian League in the Spring of 1893.[35] Lutz was also active in trying
to win members for the BdL in the Upper Palatinate. After some initial
success, the BdL was forced to concede ground to the Peasant League
and the new Catholic associations. Renewed agitation at the turn of
the century likewise yielded few rewards.[36] A similar competition for
rural support among the variety of agrarian organisations occurred in
Upper Franconia. Occasional arrangements were reached between
Thüngen and the BdL, allowing the former to concentrate his attentions
on the exclusively Catholic districts in Lower Franconia, and the latter to

infiltrate into Upper Franconia. Agitation among some local large land-owners in 1892–3 was channelled by Lutz and others into activity on behalf of the demagogic BdL, which attained a membership here of some 3,000 by the end of 1895. Periodic and well-orchestrated campaigns marked out Upper Franconia as the heart of the BdL's independent thrust into Bavaria. The League chose an Austrian to spearhead its attack, rather than a representative from Berlin. But at no time was the BdL able to establish that degree of control which it exercised, for example, in Württemberg, and this led to the adoption of an increasingly moderate line at the turn of the century.[37] This brought a renewal of electoral cooperation with the National Liberals and some important but isolated victories in 1907 and 1912. The fortunes of the BdL in Upper Franconia reflected its ambivalent relationship with the peasant movements under Thüngen, but, above all, its failure to win any support from Catholics. This drawback also limited the BdL's development in other parts of Franconia and Swabia. Its more explicit anti-Semitism coincided with that of the most influential agitators in the Peasant Leagues in these areas, but ultimately confessional differences were the single most important factor shaping the relative experiences of the BdL. The apparent paradox of small peasants and farmers giving their support to the Junker-controlled BdL has led to an undue concentration on the manipulative potential and capabilities of this organisation, rather than to the localised conditions favouring a welcome response to the techniques employed by the BdL. In Bavaria we can see that peasant support for Conservative and BdL candidates in the elections of the 1890s merely represented their continued affiliation to the Protestant agrarian tradition established during the previous decade. Apart from this infiltration into Protestant areas of Franconia, the BdL was unable to achieve any widespread or independent organisational success, as it was increasingly squeezed between the various Peasant Leagues and the Catholic *Bauernvereine*. It is small wonder that the President of the BdL used the occasion of a meeting in Bayreuth to express his exasperation with particularist and local tendencies operating within the agrarian movement in Bavaria.[38]

This process of diversification was due largely to the rapid growth in the popularity of the vociferous radicalism forwarded by the Lower Bavarian Peasant League. The final impulse for the foundation of the organisation was given by the news from Berlin of the Tivoli meeting, but its initial advances were due almost entirely to other factors. One essential ingredient was the increasing hostility in peasant circles to the existing authorities, in response to the prevailing pessimism about the future of Bavarian agriculture. Sharp attacks on the bureaucracy at both state and local level were very popular across much of Bavaria. Memories of the malignant influence of officialdom during the eighteenth century [39] merged with the growing animosity towards bureaucratic ignorance of basic rural problems. More explicit resentment was provoked by proposals to improve the salaries and financial security within the bureaucracy. These suggestions were symbolic of the growing alienation of the bourgeois-aristocratic bureaucracy from the mass of ordinary people[40] and probably compounded the legacy of suspicion bequeathed by the *Kulturkampf*. The view of Eisenberger, leader of the Upper Bavarian Peasant League, that 'officials know as much about farming as donkeys do about taking notes in shorthand' was undoubtedly shared by many.[41] The later government refutations of agrarian accusations that nothing had been done to improve the conditions of the rural population were belied by the conspicuous growth in legislation after 1893.

Indignation over the inadequate consideration of peasant interests was vividly mirrored in the wave of anti-clericalism which pervaded the *Bauernbund* movement, especially in the South-east. This represented a significant departure from previous political behaviour, because the persecution of the Catholic church during the *Kulturkampf* had created an apparently solid base in the countryside for the supremacy of the Centre Party. The shock of the Centre's eclipse in a by-election in Stadtamhof (Upper Palatinate) in 1882[42] was evidence of the strength of its assumption that confessional ties would be transferred automatically into political loyalty. It is difficult to assess how far this new mistrust of the Centre's monopoly of rural Catholic politics was either spontaneous or artificially manufactured. Certainly the growing accord between the Bavarian Centre Party and the State bureaucracy had angered old radical and 'social' Catholics like Sigl and Ratzinger. An anti-clerical campaign was already under way before 1893, when potential agrarian discontent offered a new tactical option. Furthermore, some of the more extreme leaders of the Lower Bavarian Peasant League were known to have indulged in previous attacks on clerical domination of local affairs.[43] It is unlikely, however, that such campaigns could have prospered if the Centre Party had not already temporarily lost the confidence of many rural inhabitants. Priests and Centre parliamentarians who tried to defend the record of their party in the large and stormy *Bauernbund* meetings were often jeered into silence.

The fundamental cause for this disillusion was the knowledge that many Centrists had given their support to the series of trade treaties introduced by Chancellor Caprivi. This reorientation of German commercial policy had led to a substantial fall in grain prices and became the primary mobilising force behind agrarian protest throughout Germany. The fact that the new policies had won the approval of the Centre Party added to the disaffection of the Bavarian peasantry. The declining price levels for agricultural produce were a serious blow to many Bavarian peasants and farmers, and their impact was particularly deleterious on the larger grain-growing holdings in South-east Bavaria. The *Bauernbund* achieved much of its most solid commitment in those parts of Lower and Upper Bavaria where the combination of impartible inheritance, large peasant farms and extremely favourable environmental factors had encouraged a heavy reliance on wheat, rye and oats, and where now growing indebtedness and falling income presented major problems. It is thus little surprise that such farmers rallied to a spontaneous cry for higher protective tariffs. Protectionist sentiment was not, however, restricted to this particular section of the peasant community; the call for the reintroduction of tariffs against foreign competition became the essential plank of all agrarian agitation in Bavaria. The strength of protectionism in southern Germany has never been adequately explained, with the result that historians have perhaps laid undue emphasis on the malevolent sectional interests of the Junker agrarian class in the vital debate on tariffs.[44] Recent studies suggest that relatively large numbers of peasants benefited from protection and from the rigorous controls on livestock imports[45] – certainly more than is frequently implied. Only more detailed investigations of individual peasant economies can resolve the question of how far protection accorded with rational economic considerations. A crude indication can, however, be given by the results of the official Bavarian investigation into 24 representative rural communities. Reports on eight of the villages give precise details on the number of peasants either buying or selling bread-grains. Of the 1,072 farms in question, 634 (59 per cent) produced surplus grain for sale on the market; a further 214 attained subsistence levels, and only 224 of the enterprises regularly purchased grain.[46] It is also worth emphasising that in the subjective cognition of even the smallest peasant, prices may have ranked as a more valuable index of prosperity than those which historians can apply with suitable retrospective rationality.[47] Whatever the fundamental reasons, there is no denying the widespread disaffection in rural Bavaria with the policies of Caprivi, and their repercussions on agricultural prosperity until the turn of the century.

In the long run, there is no doubt that protection, as afforded by the revised tariff levels of 1902, kept land prices artificially high, thereby increasing rural indebtedness,[48] and delayed the rationalisation of German agriculture. Government efforts to persuade more farmers to switch from less competitive grain-growing to animal husbandry and market-gardening were largely unsuccessful. For many farmers the 'limited good' provided by profit from grain was probably preferable to the risks involved in a complete change of course, for which both adequate cheap credit and technical expertise were lacking.[49] It was a sounder policy for the Bavarian peasant to join the campaign for higher protective tariffs, or alternatively to combine with other peasants in cooperatives to ensure a higher return from their joint surplus. That this was an option for many farmers was shown by the hostility of the more extreme Peasant League agitators to practical forms of assistance. Credit unions, collective marketing arrangements and similar institutions were all likely to divert peasant frustrations away from essentially political solutions, and the radical agrarians were not slow to berate those of their colleagues who endorsed the value of self-help.

V

The manifest radicalism of the Peasant Leagues, especially those in the South-east, was to have substantial repercussions in two important areas. In the first place, the movement clearly caused considerable consternation in government circles. Bureaucratic paranoia about the growing threat of Social Democracy in the cities was suddenly compounded by a similar menace to political stability from the least expected quarter, the countryside. Meetings of the Peasant League were subjected to the same rigorous police regulation which still circumscribed all socialist activities.[50] This brought a ready sympathy in *Bauernbund* circles for the problems endured by the Social Democrats, followed by consistent demands for the abolition of all constraints on freedom of speech and assembly. While careful observation of agrarian meetings by leading local officials tried to assess the popular mood, official enquiries were hastily organised into the state of Bavarian agriculture. The statutes of the Agricultural Association were again changed, and its responsibilities were widened so that local groups could implement the reforms suggested by these surveys. In Lower Bavaria particular stress was laid on the need to increase the competitiveness of the local grain producers. The emphasis on practical forms of self-help often placed local officials in a difficult position because of the prevailing strong animosity towards the bureaucracy. Their only consolation against the vicious personal abuse occasionally heaped upon them was that their enthusiastic efforts were deemed an essential contribution to the solution of 'this most important social question'.[51] Under such circumstances it was inevitable that many officials would blame the activities of the Peasant League for preventing local farmers from engaging in the various self-help schemes proposed by government. Nevertheless, steady progress in this direction was achieved and it helped to ensure the survival of many peasant farms. In response to this activity, the Agricultural Association continued to expand in size to over 100,000 members, while simultaneously undertaking more operations. But the association lacked a fully democratic internal structure; this enabled it to withstand infiltration by influential agrarian politicians, but it also guaranteed the continuing role of many non-farmers within the organisation. In the years preceding the outbreak of war, the government attempted to introduce a new form of association which could be truly representative of all agricultural producers, as well as more capable of initiating suitable legislation. But the fear that, in a freely elected body, radical or politically disruptive elements from the Peasant Leagues would come to the fore brought strong resistance from many sections of the Agricultural Association, many of which were still controlled by local clergy, officials and big landowning aristocrats. Though this attempt foundered, it was illustrative of how the initial successes of the Peasant Leagues had stimulated a growing official awareness of the problems and requirements of the rural economy, and of the need for a more adequate 'official' organisation to serve the Bavarian peasantry.

A similar change of attitude was evident in another important political institution, the Catholic Centre Party. The Peasant Leagues did more than anything else to stir the Bavarian Centre Party from its previous indifference towards the struggles and aspirations of its rural electorate, itself one of the foundations of the Centre's pre-eminence in national politics. 'The sparks from the incendiary torch of the Peasant League'[52] ignited sufficient fires among Bavarian Catholics to put in some jeopardy and essential security given by the Centre Party's position in Bavaria. The propaganda of the Centre was later to bristle with sanctimonious self-congratulation about its contributions to the restoration of agricultural prosperity, but these had been generated in the first intance by the potential loss of vital rural votes. In areas like the Upper Palatinate the clergy's stronger hold over local attitudes prevented the Peasant League from establishing anything but a tenuous grip on the districts bordering Lower Bavaria.[53] Elsewhere, however, the danger was rather more imminent, and those Centre politicians who were more in tune with the grievances of the peasantry than the conservative and aristocratic sections of the party began to inspire organisations capable of rivalling the Peasant Leagues. These Catholic Peasant Associations (*Katholische Bauernvereine*) had already begun to appear by the end of 1893 and within a short space of time a well-organised regional and State hierarchy had been erected. What needs to be emphasised here is that, in their exertions to restore the credibility of the Centre Party, the Catholic Peasant Associations relied almost exclusively on the populist programmes of the rival Peasant Leagues. The chances of any fundamentally different policies attracting the necessary support were probably never considered; the *Bauernbund* was to be fought on its own territory to a large extent. Bimetallist arguments joined calls for an end to the activities of cattle-traders and the practice of entail by large landowners, for reform of the *Bodenzinse* and rural taxation, and for the repeal of the social insurance legislation.[54] Opposition to militarism and, above all, demands for the reinstitution of adequate levels of protection all served to reinforce the ideological resemblance to the Peasant Leagues.

The direct antagonism between the two agrarian movements became an essential feature of rural politics in much of Bavaria during the 1890s. The increasing success of the Catholic Peasant Associations effectively limited the potential for growth of the Peasant Leagues. At the same time the extension of these associations was instrumental in effecting a reorientation within the Centre Party in favour of the more radical and democratic wing. The localised competition between the two peasant movements – often providing the ideal source of rural entertainment in the slack winter months[55] – thus had a number of far-reaching ramifications.

In this contest for rural support the Catholic associations ultimately came to hold most of the trump cards; in the mid 1890s the Peasant League had succeeded by playing the joker of surprise, but thereafter a number of inter-related factors began to strengthen the Catholic movement at the expense of its adversary. In the first instance, the Catholic associations were welcomed by the government as a conservative counter to the influence of the extremists in the Peasant Leagues. The natural bureaucratic hostility towards Catholic organisations and excessive clerical influence was diluted by the abuse which both officials and priests had to endure from the *Bauernbund* agitators. Despite the mood of anti-clericalism which had erupted in some parts of Bavaria, the rural clergy remained one of the few social organisations through which the government could hope to encourage the urgent stabilisation of agrarian sentiment. Official sanction, if not active assistance for the Catholic *Bauernvereine* also seemed appropriate because of their more constructive attitude to practical reform. Unlike the more radical Peasant Leagues, the Centrist movement made a much more sustained contribution towards establishing cooperative enterprises, as a complement to their political strategy. In time they came to embrace a wider variety of financial and legal services designed to liberate the farmer from the clutches of Jewish usurers — such was the normal way of attracting support for these facilities. The mixture of anti-Semitism, doctrinaire anti-liberalism, agrarian populism and large-scale institutional aid for the peasant farmer, which characterised much of the activity of the Catholic associations, was closely associated with the name of Georg Heim.[56] Politically Heim was to symbolise the popular-based antipathy towards the clerical aristocracy within the Bavarian Centre Party, while, on the more economic level, his initiative and enormous energy was vital to the success of the self-help methods directed by the Catholic agrarian movement. The turnover of the Central Co-operative run by Heim increased almost tenfold within the years 1899–1904,[57] and indicated the growing appeal of pragmatic assistance. Once the Centre Party had regained some respectability, by embracing the broad lines of Peasant League populist propaganda, its ability to offer additional forms of relief was ultimately to prove extremely valuable.

The career of Heim as an organiser and initiator also pointed to another fundamental weakness of the Peasant Leagues, their lack of skilful individual or collective leadership. Factional disputes between the various leaders of the *Bauernbund* were probably inevitable in a movement whose diversity reflected considerable political, social and confessional differentiations, but they became an easy target for Centre Party pamphleteers.[58] The Catholic associations had the inestimable advantage of a well-established sub-culture, and the ready basis for sophisticated organisation, in the church. On the other hand, the Peasant Leagues were faced with the customary problems of all new rural political organisations, those of establishing a successful and coherent administrative structure capable of raising sufficient revenue to maintain a committed following. The inability of the various Peasant Leaguers to submerge their personal and ideological differences for any sustained period played into the hands of the Catholic groupings. This was shown by the varying reactions within the Peasant Leagues to Kanitz proposals for a state monopoly in imported grain.[59] Agitation on behalf of the Kanitz plan was supported vigorously by the Lower

Bavarian Peasant League, because of its identification with the big grain-farmers of the region, as well as by Thüngen, on the basis of his political sympathies with the BdL. But, unlike more general protectionism, the envisaged control of grain distribution under the Kanitz design was not really in the interests of many peasants. This led to divisions within the Peasant League which were fully exploited by the Catholic movement; it was able to portray the *Bauernbund* as a Prussian import, a mere puppet of the evil northern Junkers. In contrast, the Catholic Peasant Associations presented a more unified front, partly because their range of enemies was much wider. They opposed equally Prussian Conservatism, the BdL, the Peasant Leagues, Social Democracy and Liberalism, the last being condemned by one Catholic priest as a 'Satanic abortion'.[60] The willingness of the Catholic groups to undertake much of the campaign against the growth of the Social Democrats meant that there was little room in Bavaria for the anti-socialist People's Association for Catholic Germany,[61] with the result that the Catholic Peasant Associations became one of the largest social and political groupings in pre-war Bavaria.[62]

The increasing success of the Catholic associations, especially after the turn of the century, forced the *Bauernbund*, with its meagre organisational resources and ailing leadership, to concentrate almost all its activism on electoral propaganda. The Peasant Leagues continued to make some advances in the various by-elections which followed the campaigns of 1893, and in the Reichstag election of 1898 they attained 18 per cent of the popular vote, almost identical to the support amassed by the Social Democrats. Thereafter, the gradually improving economic situation and the inability to counter the continuing expansion of the Catholic groups made even the tactical emphasis on election-eering an increasing liability. The lack of an extensive administrative machinery forced the Peasant Leagues to make large numbers of local compromises, and these reduced their credibility in the eyes of the electorate. In some areas the *Bauernbund* employed intimidatory techniques such as the boycott to make up ground on the other parties.[63] But even this could not break the grip which the younger members of the clergy (dubbed by some officials as the '*ecclesia militans*'[64]) were trying to exert over the rural voter. In the succeeding Reichstag elections the *Bauernbund*'s share of the vote declined steadily until 1912, when it was overtaken by the BdL. Despite the continued allegiance of some areas to the Peasant League, the trend in the elections for the Bavarian Landtag was also a steadily downward one after the important reverses suffered in 1899.

VI

To conclude by stressing the declining fortunes of the *Bauernbund* would, however, seriously undervalue its impact on both Bavarian and German political life in the Wilhelmine period. It might seem that the Peasant Leagues suffered from the very impermanence which had characterised previous peasant movements, but that disguises their long-term legacy. They were certainly bedevilled from the outset by differences over approach and leadership, themselves symptomatic of the divisions in Bavarian rural society created by contrasting political traditions, varying types of farming and confessional loyalties. Such a stress on the internal problems of the Peasant Leagues tends, however, to obscure their catalytic effect on agrarian politics. Sparked off themselves by economic distress and by frustration with the clerical and bureaucratic establishment, the Peasant Leagues forced significant changes in both. Despite pressure from various municipal and commercial pressure-groups, the Bavarian government was compelled to take greater heed of the demands of the rural majority. At all levels, the bureaucracy committed itself much more fully to the needs of agriculture, including the issue of greater protection for the peasant producer. Those parts of agrarian propaganda which stressed that higher protection, by raising the income and thus the purchasing power of the peasantry, would have beneficial consequences on the domestic demand for industrial products, was fully integrated into government thinking.[65] Official attitudes could not fail to have been swayed by the unanimity shown during the great peasant rally in Regensburg in October 1901, when all the agrarian associations in Bavaria combined for the first and only time in a common call for higher tariffs on all basic agricultural produce.[66]

Similarly, it has been shown how the serious threat which the *Bauernbund* posed to Centrist dominance in rural Catholic areas brought a swift response from the radical figures within the Centre Party. Where-ever the Peasant Leagues confronted the Catholic *Bauernvereine*, electoral participation and the general level of political awareness of the rural population rose markedly. Certainly many voters still preferred farm-labour to the ballot-box on polling day, which was usually in mid-summer, but nothing can conceal the growing involvement of the majority of the peasantry in the exercise of some political responsibility. Parallel to the stimulus given to urban politics by the Social Democrats, as well as by the radicalisation of the petit-bourgeoisie analysed above by Geoff Eley, the *Bauernbund* benefited from, and also helped to accelerate the political mobilisation of the Bavarian countryside.[67] The widespread adoption of populist objectives among the agrarian movements in Bavaria was indicative of the more egalitarian tendencies introduced by the *Bauernbund* into rural areas. The Peasant Leagues had from an early stage campaigned for a much more democratic franchise to restore what were seen as the essential rights of the individual. When after 1900 the Peasant Leagues decided to oppose the suggested revision towards a direct voting system on purely tactical grounds,[68] they were bitterly attacked by the Catholic Peasant Associations for reneging on their previous populist commitment to more democratic elections and parliaments. While corporatist, anti-Semitic and anti-capitalist tendencies were often prominent in peasant agitation, they should not be seen as inconsistent with the willingness of the Peasant League to embrace a number of radical and democratic tendencies, which it could share quite equably with the Social Democrats. This raises considerable question marks against the widely held view of the peasantry, as manifested through its political outlook, as a social group helping to preserve certain pre-modern attitudes — resisting rather than adapting to the process of economic modernisation in Germany. The further implication, that the triumph of Nazism can be attributed to the survival of pre-modern structures or values from the mid-nineteenth century onwards, clearly conflicts with what we know of those groups naively categorised as pre-industrial, or of the Nazi movement itself.[69]

Ultimately, the success of the Peasant Leagues was hindered by their devotion to purely political issues[70] and the weaknesses resulting from their lack of sufficient financial and administrative resources. But, if nothing else, they had served to galvanise a previously lethargic Centre Party into more sustained activity at both the practical and the political level. Any future indifference to the fate of the Catholic peasantry raised the spectre of a radical revival in favour of the Peasant Leagues. There seems little reason to doubt that such pressure, emanating from the local level on a vital question such as protection, did much to condition the Centre's disposition in the national political debate. Much of the contemporary analysis of the tariff reform of 1902 conveniently ignores the key role of the Centre Party in carrying this legislation through the Reichstag. No alliance of big agrarians and big industrialists — itself not a true reflection of the true state of affairs[71] — could have won the day but for the decision of the Centre Party to respect the long-felt needs of its indispensable rural electorate. The influence of the Peasant Leagues may well have forced the Catholic Peasant Associations in Bavaria to become more radical than some of their counterparts,[72] and they certainly helped to forge a new solidarity between the church and the Bavarian peasant.

Further, more general observations can be made on the basis of this study. Historians should heed the warning of Barrington Moore, and not treat the peasant as a mere object of history, a form of social existence immune to historical changes, and contributing nothing to them.[73] The populism implanted by the *Bauernbund* and assumed by other peasant political groupings in the Catholic parts of Bavaria was parallel to the radical mobilisation of the petit-bourgeoisie in Protestant Germany. To see this rural politicisation as the result of integrative or manipulative strategies on the part of an élite is clearly misguided. This can be seen most clearly in peasant resistance to all symbols of financial profligacy such as the navy or military expansionism. Interpretations of national policy in terms of social imperialism[74] clearly take little heed of both the political awareness, and the immediate economic problems of the peasantry. For the peasant on his farm, militarism was despised for its obvious association with higher taxation and for the iniquities of forced billeting on army manoeuvres, a source of antagonism rather than legitimation. Similarly, the Catholic peasantry was, in contrast to the urban *Mittelstand*, to prove relatively immune to the appeals of Nazism in Bavaria. This was clearly not because of any backwardness of peasant mentality or political sophistication. In the Protestant parts of Franconia, the peasantry voted in much greater numbers for the Nazi party, whereas in Catholic Bavaria the previous innoculation with a populist experience could well have helped to immunise the peasant against further radicalism.[75] That, in itself, indicates the problems created by studying the processes of German modernisation with models which are based almost exclusively on Prussian developments, and which thereby relegate southern Germany and a great number of its inhabitants to that historical insignificance from which they have suffered for far too long.

Notes

1. H.A. Landsberger, 'Peasant Unrest: Themes and Variations', in H.A. Landsberger (ed.), *Rural Protest: Peasant Movements and Social Change* (London, 1974), pp. 1–64. Teodor Shanin, 'Peasantry as a Political Factor', in Teodor Shanin (ed.), *Peasants and Peasant Societies* (Harmondsworth, 1971), pp. 238–63.
2. For some criticism of these older images see Wilhelm Wehland, 'Werthaltungen und Ideologien im Entwicklungsprozess der deutschen Landwirtschaft', *Sociologia Ruralis*, Vol. 12, 3/4 (1972), pp. 410–11.
3. StAL, 168/5, 1071. *Augsburger Allgemeine Zeitung*, 22.3.1893.
4. It is perhaps misleading to talk of *a Bauernbund* in Bavaria. A variety of peasant groups are subsumed in this nomenclature, but the term is retained

here for convenience. The early years of the *Bauernbund* were characterised by a continuous shifting of personalities and regional alliances; the resultant conflicts are unsympathetically discussed in Alois Hundhammer, *Geschichte des bayerischen Bauernbundes* (Munich, 1924), which remains the basis for all subsequent interpretations. See also D. Fricke, *Die bürgerlichen Parteien in Deutschland* (Leipzig, 1968), Vol. 1, pp. 66–78; S.R. Tirrell, *German Agrarian Politics after Bismarck's Fall* (New York, 1951), especially pp. 194ff. Hans-Jürgen Puhle, *Politische Agrarbewegungen in kapitalistischen Industriegesellschaften* (Göttingen, 1975), pp. 62–3 offers no new viewpoints. A good introduction to the role of the Peasant Leagues in Bavarian politics can be found in the indispensable study by Karl Möckl, *Die Prinzregentenzeit* (Munich, 1972), pp. 446ff.

5. StAM, Polizeidirektion 4689; also, *Satzungen des landwirtschaftlichen Vereins in Bayern*, 1895. A steady rise in membership from under 10,000 to 56,467 in 1888 reduced the preponderance of bureaucrats and other non-peasants, but the majority of district and county committees remained in the hands of officials. See the details in *Die Landwirtschaft in Bayern. Denkschrift, nach amtlichen Quellen bearbeitet* (Munich, 1890), pp. 782–7; Alois Schögl, *Bayerische Agrargeschichte* (Munich, 1954), pp. 559–60; A. Hundhammer, *Die landwirtschaftliche Berufsvertretung in Bayern* (Munich, 1926), pp. 11ff.

6. *Illustrierte bayerische Bauernzeitung*, 1.2.1880.

7. George Windell, *The Catholics and German Unity 1866–1871* (Minneapolis, 1954), pp. 182ff.

8. StAAG, Reg., K.d.I. (1949), 13869.

9. See the reports in StAM, R.A., 57826; AStAM, M. Inn., 38982, 38983, 38989, 66316, 73483; StAL, 168/5, 1072.

10. Georg Ratzinger, *Die Erhaltung des Bauernstandes* (Freiburg, 1883).

11. Karl W. Hardach, *Die Bedeutung wirtschaftlicher Faktoren bei der Wiedereinführung der Eisen- und Getreidezölle in Deutschland 1879* (Berlin, 1967), pp. 130–6, 162; Helmut Böhme, *Deutschlands Weg zur Grossmacht* (Cologne, 1966), pp. 555–6.

12. AStAM, M. Inn., 38982, 66316; StAWg, Regierungsabgabe 1943/45, 486.

13. AStAM, M. Inn., 38983, 38984; StAN, Reg., K.d.I. (1968/II), 182–4; StABg, K 3 (Regierung von Oberfranken; Präsidial-Registratur), 850.

14. Karl Frhr. von Thüngen-Rossbach, *Die Nachteile der Goldwährung* (Wurzburg, 1886).

15. A copy of the programme is in StANg, R.A. 9618.

16. Hans-Jürgen Puhle, *Agrarische Interessenpolitik und preussischer Konservatismus im wilhelminischen Reich, 1893–1914* (Hanover, 1966), pp. 67–8.

17. AStAM, M. Inn., 47329; StAWg, 1943/45, 9141.

18. Dietrich Thränhardt, *Wahlen und politische Strukturen in Bayern 1848–1953* (Düsseldorf, 1973), p. 107.

19. *Handbuch der bayerischen Geschichte*, Ed. M. Spindler, Vol. 4/I (Munich, 1974), pp. 314–5.

20. *Schriften des Vereins für Sozialpolitik*, Vol. 24 (Leipzig, 1883), pp. 115ff.; Vol. 35 (Leipzig, 1887), pp. 85–6.

21. For the problems faced by hop farmers, see AStAM, M. Inn., 38986, 46131; StAN, Reg., K.d.I. (1968/II), 182.

22. Bavarian agriculture was no less mechanised than the rest of Germany, but substantial improvements were essential. *Die Landwirschaft in Bayern*, pp. 189ff.

23. *Untersuchung der wirtschaftlichen Verhältnisse in 24 Gemeinden des Königreichs Bayern* (Munich, 1895).

24. *Beiträge zur Statistik des Königreichs Bayern (BzSdKB)*, 81 (Munich, 1910), pp. 38–48.
25. *BzSdKB*, 66 (Munich, 1906), pp. 363ff., 499ff. Eugen Jäger, *Denkschrift über die Lage und die Organisation des Bauernstandes* (1894).
26. SAA, Akten des 19. Jhs.; Abgabe 1930/I, 3601; StABg, K3, 748. See also StAWg, 1943/45, 142 and 3093; StAAg, Reg., K.d.I. (1949), 4018/1.
27. AStAM, M. Inn., 66322; GStAM, M.A., 99792.
28. StAN, Reg., K.d.I. (1968/II), 184; AStAM, M. Arb., 1239. Axel Schnorbus, *Arbeit und Sozialordnung in Bayern vor dem ersten Weltkrieg* (Munich, 1969), p. 10.
29. Friedrich Lütge, *Geschichte der deutschen Agrarverfassung* (Stuttgart, 1963), pp. 164, 211ff. Sebastian Hausmann, *Die Grundentlastung in Bayern* (Strasbourg, 1892).
30. Eugen Jäger, *Kurze Geschichte des bayerischen Bauernstandes mit besonderer Rücksicht auf die Grundentlastung in Bayern* (Speyer, 1898), pp. 46–58.
31. Details of the various programmes in StAM, R.A., 57824, 57825; StAL, 168/5, 1071. A. Hundhammer, *Geschichte*, pp. 218ff. Contrast with agrarian programmes in the south-west of Germany, James C. Hunt, *The People's Party in Württemberg and Southern Germany, 1890–1914* (Stuttgart, 1975), pp. 89–110.
32. H.-J. Puhle, *Politische Agrarbewegungen*, pp. 34, 55–6, 62 indicates the more democratic and populist nature of the *Bauernbund*. There has been a vigorous debate among American historians about the real nature of populism, generated by the ambiguities of the populist response to capitalism. See ibid., pp. 142–7, 358–9. Those who stress the progressive features of populism still rely on the seminal John D. Hicks, *The Populist Revolt* (1931; 2nd. ed. Lincoln, 1961); for an important contrary view, see Richard Hofstadter, *The Age of Reform* (London, 1962). A useful introduction into this bitter controversy is Sheldon Hackney (ed.), *Populism: The Critical Issues* (Boston, 1971).
33. StAM, R.A., 57824.
34. StAM, R.A., 57825. See also StAM, Polizeidirektion 480, 613, 633 and 667 for Wenng's more explicit anti-Semitic activities; also H-J. Puhle, *Agrarische Interessenpolitik*, p. 134.
35. StANg, R.A., 9622, 9623; SAA, Akten des 19. Jhs.; Abgabe 1926, 22.
36. StAAg, Reg. K.d.I. (1949), 13883, 14112, 13753.
37. StABg, K 3, 831xi – 831xiii/a. See also J.C. Hunt, 'The "Egalitarianism" of the Right: The Agrarian League in Southwest Germany', 1893–1914', *Journal of Contemporary History*, Vol. 10, 3 (1975), pp. 514–19.
38. StABg, K 3, 831xii.
39. F. Lütge, *Die bayerische Grundherrschaft* (Stuttgart, 1949), p. 17.
40. K. Möckl, *Die Prinzregentenzeit*, pp. 439ff.
41. StAM, R.A., 57824.
42. AStAM, M. Inn., 38981, 47328.
43. AStAM, M. Inn., 73455 gives some biographical information on a number of Peasant League agitators.
44. Alexander Gerschenkron, *Bread and Democracy in Germany* (New York, 1966, 2nd. edn.), pp. 18–80. Hans-Ulrich Wehler, *Des deutsche Kaiserreich* (Göttingen, 1973), p. 55.
45. J.C. Hunt, 'Peasants, Grain Tariffs and Meat Quotas: Imperial German Protectionism Re-examined', *Central European History*, Vol. 7, 4 (1974), pp. 311–31.
46. *Untersuchung der wirtschaftlichen Verhältnisse*, passim. Only one of the 24 communities studied was totally reliant on the purchase of grain.

47. H-J. Puhle, 'Aspekte der Agrarpolitik im "Organisierten Kapitalismus". Fragen und Probleme vergleichender Forschung', in H-U. Wehler (ed.), *Sozialgeschichte Heute* (Göttingen, 1974), p. 554, rightly stresses the need for more systematic studies of the subjective attitudes of the smaller landholders towards their position.

48. *Schriften des Vereins für Sozialpolitik*, Vol. 148 (Berlin, 1914).

49. George M. Foster, 'Peasant Society and the Image of Limited Good', *American Anthropologist*, Vol. 67, 2 (1965), pp. 293–315, suggests cogent reasons for the inhibitions on economic progress in peasant communities.

50. StAL, 168/5, 557.

51. StAL, 168/5, 965. See also StAAg, Reg., K.d.I. (1949), 5644; StAM, R.A., 61428; StABg, K 3 F Va. 128, 165.

52. *Allgemeine Zeitung*, No. 28, 4.6.1910.

53. StAAg, Reg., K.d.I. (1949), 5087.

54. StAL, 168/5, 828:

55. See e.g., StAAg, Reg., K.d.I. (1949), 13750.

56. Full details of Heim's career can be found in the otherwise sycophantic biography of Hermann Renner, *Georg Heim. Der Bauerndoktor* (Munich 1960).

57. *Der Fränkische Bauer*, No. 13, 1.4.1905.

58. An example is Xaver Wahrmund, *Bauernbund gegen Bauernbund. Aktenmässige Urteilen von Bauernbundsführern über den Bauernbund und seine Führer* (Neumarkt, 1898). Countless examples can be seen in the Catholic agrarian press.

59. Further discussion is in H-J. Puhle, *Agrarische Interessenpolitik*, pp. 230ff.

60. The same priest in Ochsenfurt would brand any Catholic who did not vote for the Centre as a Judas: AStAM, M. Inn., 47335.

61. Emil Ritter, *Die katholisch-soziale Bewegung und der Volksverein* (Cologne, 1954), pp. 183, 231.

62. In 1897 the combined membership was just over 22,000 (*Der Bauernfreund*, No. 41, 13.10.1897); by 1907 it had reached 121,000, divided among more than 3,000 local groups, with Upper Bavaria and Lower Franconia showing the greatest strength (*Der Fränkische Bauer*, No. 44, 2.11.1907), The circulation of the most popular Catholic agrarian newspaper rose from 4,500 copies per weekly edition to 14,500 in 1902 and more than 34,000 in 1907 (*Der Fränkische Bauer*, No. 4, 22.1.1897; No. 42, 18.10.1902; No. 3, 19.1.1907). See also G. Heim (ed.), *Der bayerische Bauernverein in Vergangenheit, Gegenwart und Zukunft* (Ansbach, 1906).

63. AStAM, M. Inn., 47335.

64. AStAM, M. Inn., 47342.

65. AStAM, M. H., 11707.

66. AStAM, M. Inn., 73728.

67. The number of registered political associations in Bavaria rose from 208 in 1884 to 300 in 1890 and to 704 by the end of 1898: AStAM, M. Inn., 38986, 66320–22. See also David Blackbourn, 'The Mittelstand in German Society and Politics, 1871–1914', *Social History*, No. 4 (January, 1977), pp. 409–433.

68. The Peasant Leagues argued that the proposed electoral reform would discriminate excessively in favour of urban over rural areas. It was eventually ratified for subsequent Landtag elections in 1906 through the combined action of the Centre Party and the Social Democrats. For a fuller discussion, see K. Möckl, *Die Prinzregentenzeit*, pp. 491–534.

69. See especially M.R. Lepsius, 'Parteiensystem und Sozialstruktur: zum Problem der Demokratisierung der deutschen Gesellschaft', in W. Abel *et al.* (eds.),

Wirtschaft, Geschichte und Wirtschaftsgeschichte (Stuttgart, 1966), pp. 371–93; Ralf Dahrendorf, *Gesellschaft und Demokratie in Deutschland* (Munich, 1968). For a criticism of this viewpoint, see the comments above by Geoff Eley; also, Tim Mason, 'Zur Entstehung des Gesetzes zur Ordnung der nationalen Arbeit vom 20. Januar 1934: ein Versuch über das Verhältnis "archaischer" und "moderner" Momente in der neuesten deutschen Geschichte', in H. Mommsen, *et al.* (eds.), *Industrielles System und politische Entwicklung in der Weimarer Republik* (Düsseldorf, 1974), pp. 322–8.

70. Wilhelm Mattes, *Die bayerischen Bauernräte* (Stuttgart, 1921), pp. 30–7. In his fine study of agrarian-democratic movements in Canada, Lipset indicates the tendency of populist farmers to attack visible, transitory evils, to show a genius for protest, not performance or endurance: Seymour M. Lipset, *Agrarian Socialism: The Co-operative Commonwealth Federation in Saskatchewan* (2nd. edn., Berkeley, 1959), p. 9.

71. A useful critique of the agrarian-industrial front suggested by Eckart Kehr with respect to the issues of 1902 can be found in H-J. Puhle, *Agrarische Interessenpolitik*, pp. 158–9.

72. Compare with the activities of the Centre Party in the more industrialised Rhineland, Klaus Müller, 'Zentrumspartei und agrarische Bewegung im Rheinland, 1882–1903', in K. Repgen and S. Skalweit (eds.), *Spiegel der Geschichte; Festgabe für Max Braubach* (Münster, 1964), pp. 828–57.

73. Barrington Moore, *Social Origins of Dictatorship and Democracy* (Harmondsworth, 1969), p. 453.

74. For further discussion of this theme, see the introduction to this volume.

75. For details of the impact of Nazism on Bavaria, see Geoffrey Pridham, *Hitler's Rise to Power: The Nazi Movement in Bavaria 1923–33* (London, 1973), especially pp. 188, 224ff.; D. Thranhardt, *Wahlen*, pp. 136.ff; Charles P. Loomis and J.A. Beegle, 'The Spread of German Nazism in Rural Areas', *American Sociological Review*, Vol. 11, 6 (1946), pp. 724–34.

7 THE PROBLEM OF DEMOCRATISATION: GERMAN CATHOLICS AND THE ROLE OF THE CENTRE PARTY

David Blackbourn

I

Wilhelmine Germany's economic dynamism contrasted strongly with its inability to develop a mature political and constitutional system.[1] This failure at the political level has attracted a wide variety of explanations, ranging at their most general from the peculiar power of the Prussian army to the peculiar flaw in the 'German Mind'.[2] At a more directly political level, explanation has centred on the fateful displacement of reformist political energies: into business, into chauvinism, and into cultural life (the civic quietism of the 'unpolitical German'). In recent years the effects on German political life of Bismarck's manipulation from above have been emphasised. Reinforced by a new attention to the economic arrangements of the *Kaiserreich*, this approach has been responsible for establishing a number of important generalisations about the weakness of the German political system.[3] These can be fairly quickly enumerated. First, the forced pace of national unification created a series of overlapping struggles – national, constitutional, religious, economic. The legacy of this was a chronic segmentation of both German society and the political parties.[4] Secondly, Bismarck's manipulation emasculated the parties, rendering them capable only of a negative role. Liberalism, especially, was split into a left wing, purist but impotent, and a right wing (the National Liberals) whose cutting edge had been lost along with its political principles. Thirdly, and related to this, the parties degenerated into vehicles of economic interests, and this too weakened their challenge to the status quo. The Conservatives defended their sectional agrarian interests; the National Liberals, alarmed by the working-class threat, contracted the infamous 'marriage of iron and rye' with the estate-owning Conservatives; and the Social Democrats (SPD) were confined in the isolation of their proletarian sub-culture. These features of German political life were palpable impediments to democratisation before 1914.

The party which has usually proved too awkward to fit into this framework is the Centre, the party of German Catholics. While other parties have been examined against a backdrop of economic and social interests, the Centre still appears historiographically as a disembodied political phenomenon. Characteristic is Eckart Kehr's classic formulation, from which so much recent work has proceeded, of the political dealings which accompanied the passage of the first Navy Law in 1898. According to Kehr, National Liberals and Conservatives were reconciled on the basis of an economic trade-off: the National Liberals received the battle fleet for heavy industry, the Conservatives a promise of higher protective tariffs for agriculture. The Centre, by contrast, was won over solely by the offer of the political hegemony.[5] This idea of the Centre as a narrowly political and opportunist party has persisted. So, too, has its corollary — first expressed by contemporaries like Hans Delbrück and Friedrich Naumann — that the political opportunism of the Centre was motivated by sectarian or clerical considerations. This attenuated view of the Centre is all the more unfortunate, given the decisive political position of the party prior to 1914.[6] The Centre had originally established its position during the *Kulturkampf*, Bismarck's assault on the Catholic Church, in the 1870s. As the State asserted its right to control over education, introduced compulsory civil marriage, expelled the Jesuits and imprisoned priests, the Centre became the spokesman for a Church under siege. At the same time Centre attacks on discrimination against ordinary Catholics — the dismissal of officials, the non-ratification by the Prussian government of elected politicians, trade boycotts of Catholic businesses — helped to attract over four out of five voting Catholics to the party. It was in the 1870s that the Centre achieved the position of strength it was to retain until 1914, holding about 100 out of 397 Reichstag seats. In the circumstances, however, the Centre naturally tended to be a party of opposition, a stance epitomised by the regular parliamentary hostilities between the party leader, Ludwig Windthorst, and Bismarck. Despite Centre support for the reintroduction of tariffs in 1879 and for much of Bismarck's social legislation in the 1880s, it largely remained a political pariah until 1890.

From 1890, however, with the numerical decline of the National Liberals and Conservatives who had previously made up Bismarck's Reichstag majority, the Centre's 100 votes became decisive, and in subsequent years the party used its pivotal position to become the parliamentary mainstay of successive chancellors — Caprivi, Hohenlohe, Bülow and Bethmann.[7] The one major governmental attempt after 1890 to create a working majority without the Centre — that of Bülow between 1906 and 1909 — failed. Members of the party filled important honorary posts in the Reichstag, while Centre leaders like Ernst Lieber, Peter Spahn and Karl Trimborn built up close relations with state secretaries in the imperial government. Above all, the Centre gave parliamentary support to most of the major legislative measures of the Wilhelmine period — the trade treaties of 1892—4, the financial reforms of 1896 (the 'Lex Lieber'), the German Civil Code of the same year, the Navy Laws of 1898 and 1900, the military law of 1899, the tariffs of 1902, the commercial courts law of 1904, the finance laws of 1904 and 1906, the 1905 military law, the finance reforms of 1909, and the increased spending on armaments in the years up to 1914. The development of the Centre into a pro-governmental party clearly requires some explanation.

Any explanation, however, needs to take into account the Centre's relations with the other parties. The parliamentary balance which made the Centre decisive for the government's majority also made it decisive for any putative coalition in the Reichstag, of either the left or right. The Centre could choose which way to lean, a choice which steadily assumed more importance in the Wilhelmine years, as the Reich became more unitary and the Reichstag emerged as the real powerhouse of German politics.[8] It is true that the Centre generally found allies of any political persuasion hard to come by: it was widely distrusted, even reviled, as a party which had elevated opportunism into a political creed. There was, nevertheless, a pattern to the Centre's alignment. It normally supported the parties of the Right, especially the Conservatives; and it eschewed in the Wilhelmine years that alliance with Left-Liberals and SPD which was to pass the Erzberger Peace Resolution in 1917, and later form the basis of the Centre-Left Weimar coalition.[9] In a situation where the forces of political liberalism were incapable of wresting a measure of parliamentary control from the government, the unwilling- ness of the Centre to fill this 'liberal lacuna'[10] took on added importance.

The anti-left alignment of the Centre, like its support for the govern- ment, deserves more consideration than it has usually received. The ex- planation most commonly offered, of sectarian opportunism on the part of Centre leaders, has two real drawbacks. In the first place, it is difficult to reconcile with the fact that it was precisely in the period that it became more pro-governmental that the Centre also became markedly less clerical. This was clear in the hostility the party in- creasingly showed towards the attempts of Rome and the German bishops to influence policy. Tension between party and ecclesiastical hierarchy had already been evident during the final phase of the *Kulturkampf*, when Bismarck chose to negotiate directly with Rome, hoping thereby to undercut and weaken the position of the Centre.[11]

Relations between the Centre and the Vatican never completely recovered from this, and in the late 1880s and 1890s party leaders disregarded the wishes of Rome and influential German bishops over a number of important issues. In 1893, for example, the Centre angrily rejected pressure from these sources to support Caprivi's 'big' military bill, and the conservatives in the party who wished to follow the clerical lead were isolated.[12] Three years later the party similarly overrode clerical objections in supporting the new Civil Code containing provisions for compulsory civil marriage.[13]

In later years this de-clericalisation of the Centre became even more pronounced. When, in 1906, Julius Bachem published his famous article 'Wir müssen aus dem Turm heraus' (We must Leave the Tower), calling for a final abandonment of the Centre's confessional character, he already had the majority of the party behind him.[14] There were geographical pockets within the Centre where the advocates of a clerical party had a power-base, notably in Trier, the Saar and Silesia; but in general the intemperate allegations of 'deism' and heresy' thrown at Centre leaders were a measure of the impotent frustration to which the sectarian diehards had been reduced.[15] The Centre, of course, continued to have a special interest in legislation which affected the Church, and was happy to receive concessions to the Church as a reward for its support of government policy – the return of impounded ecclesiastical property, for example, and permission for the banned Redemptorist order to return to the Reich. But these were not the issues which determined the policy of the Wilhelmine Centre Party; nor were they the issues which divided it from the left. After 1890 matters concerning the Church were dwarfed by Centre involvement in legislation on economic, social, fiscal and military matters. To understand why the Centre took up the position it did on these issues it is necessary to overcome the second major limitation of current interpretations: their narrow focus on the game of high politics in Berlin.[16] This is, in fact, a particularly inappropriate focus in the case of the Centre, for the party was – like the SPD – the political embodiment of an entire sub-culture within Wilhelmine Germany.[17] It is significant, for example, that the Centre had no annual party conference of its own: its place was taken by the annual Assembly of German Catholics (*Katholikentag*). The Centre was, moreover, rivalled only by the SPD among political parties in the extensiveness of its auxiliary mass organisations, including the People's Association for Catholic Germany (*Volksverein für das katholische Deutschland*) with over 800,000 members by 1914,[18] and an enormous number of associations for

Catholic peasants, artisans, apprentices, workers, shopkeepers, shop-assistants, businessmen and other social groups.

The policies pursued by the Centre were inseparable from the grievances and aspirations nurtured within this sub-culture. And, in this respect, one fact stood out prominently: the economic and social 'backwardness' of German Catholics. It was the effect of the various policies through which the Centre Party addressed itself to this problem which drove the party into the arms of the government, and divided it from the left.

II

The generation of Centre leaders which emerged in the 1890s had very different perspectives from those of the party's leaders in the previous two decades. The earlier generation had formulated their policies at a time when unification by the sword was still a fresh memory, and when flesh and blood still had to be given to the bare bones of the Reich constitution. In those decades the *Kulturkampf* and the Anti-Socialist Law (1878–90) treated major parts of the newly-unified population – Catholics and the labour movement – as overt enemies of the State, almost as occupied powers under siege. The earlier preoccupation of the Centre with attacks on a Church whose priests were being imprisoned was a natural result of the position in which German Catholics found themselves in the uncertain first decades of the Reich's existence. The new men, by contrast, reflected the changed conditions of German politics after the internal consolidation of the Reich. Their emphasis was not so much on the security of the Church and Catholic worship within a still loosely-bound Reich, but on the economic, social and political equality of Catholic citizens within the consolidated German state. While the 1880s saw the repeal of the more crass forms of discrimination against Catholic religious observance, inequality remained apparent in most other spheres. Catholics, for example, were under-represented in the ranks of business owners and salaried managers and officials. On the other hand, they were over-represented in traditional branches of the economy, particularly agriculture. Corresponding to this, there were more Catholics in the poorer countryside and small towns, and fewer in the better-off cities, than was appropriate to their share of the overall population.[19] This was clearly reflected in the statistics of personal wealth. In 1908, for example, Catholics in Prussia still paid less than a sixth of all income tax, although they made up a third of the population. The picture of relative Catholic poverty was similar in every state.[20]

This evidence of backwardness, seized upon by the Evangelical League and others for anti-Catholic propaganda, was not restricted to income. In Baden only 36 per cent of students were Catholic in a state where they comprised 60 per cent of the population; in Prussia the figures were 25 per cent and 36 per cent respectively. Among academics the disparity was even more pronounced. In 1896–7 Catholic provided only 11.75 per cent of the *Dozenten* in the non-theological faculties of Prussian universities, and only 8.75 per cent of the *Privatdozenten*. In Bavaria at the same time, only 43 per cent of all professorial chairs (including those in theology) were held by Catholics in a state where 71 per cent of the population was of that confession.[21] This discrimination was felt above all in civil service appointments, especially in Prussia. Silesia (56 per cent Catholic) and Trier (80 per cent Catholic) had no Catholic *Regierungsrat* in the lifetime of the Reich; Alsace-Lorraine (80 per cent Catholic) had only one Catholic *Statthalter* (the later chancellor, Hohenlohe). The same situation prevailed at lower administrative levels. In Posen there were only two Catholic *Landräte* out of twenty-seven in 1911, although twenty-six of the twenty-seven corresponding administrative districts had a Catholic majority: in all, Catholics provided only 14 per cent of the Reich's 487 *Landräte* at that time.[22] Discrimination extended down to municipal level. In towns where Catholics made up a majority or a large minority of the population, professional employees in the municipal gas and electricity works, abattoir, hospital and architect's department were commonly non-Catholic.

Both discrimination and the perception of it were, of course, circumstances which German Catholics shared with the German labour movement, and as we have seen Catholic Germany constituted in many respects a sub-culture analogous to that of the Social Democrats. The response to discrimination in each case, however, yielded very different results. One of the most important differences concerned the roles played by the SPD and the Centre Party as the vehicles of economic interests. This assumed an increasing significance in the Centre with the dismantling of *Kulturkampf* legislation and the removal of proscriptions on Catholic worship. These eroded the party's traditional source of appeal: by the 1890s to be a Catholic was still a necessary but by no means a sufficient condition for voting Centre.[23] Among party leaders there was a clear and growing realisation that the residual religious bond within the Centre needed to be supplemented by a greater attention to the material interests of Catholics. This was a matter, partly, of Catholic workers, although their interests continued to be relatively neglected by the party. It meant, much more, the interests of primary producers and those in traditional branches of production and distribution,

interests which predominated in about three-quarters of the constituencies won by the Centre.[24]

In the years before 1914, often under pressure from agrarian and
petty-bourgeois grassroots feeling which threatened the unity of the
party, the Centre became a spokesman for the grievances of these groups
against the industrial capitalist system. The result was Centre support for
(and initiation of) a wide range of economically 'protectionist' or
'restorationist' measures: tariffs, meat import quotas and anti-margarine
legislation for the peasantry; the partial reintroduction of guilds and
changes in the tender system for artisans; restrictions on consumer
cooperatives, special taxes on department stores and other measures
to curb 'unfair competition' for shopkeepers.[25]

These policies did not conflict with those of Wilhelmine governments,
which in theory at least were committed to the preservation of the
peasantry and of an independent lower-middle class on the grounds of
social conservatism.[26] But Centre policies did alienate the party from
the left. It was not merely the Left-Liberals, historically the advocates
of *laissez-faire* capitalism, and mindful of their important following
among white-collar consumers, who rejected Centre economic policy.
The SPD too opposed measures which tended to raise prices for the
working class. The roots of its opposition went deeper, though. The SPD,
like the Centre, maintained that the part of the German nation it
represented was exploited economically. The SPD argued, however,
that this could never be ended by ineffectual sniping at the industrial
capitalist system or by attempts to turn the clock back. True
emancipation would be achieved only when capitalism had reached its
most fully developed stage and was in turn succeeded by socialism.
Until that time the system was to be helped in bringing about its own
demise, not arbitrarily shackled. The SPD, for example, explicitly cited
trusts as a progressive form of economic organisation which had shown
their superiority over small concerns; and the party similarly scorned
Centre efforts to trim the wings of department stores. On such issues
the Centre and SPD might agree on a diagnosis; they could seldom agree
on a cure.[27]

The fundamental differences between the Centre and the SPD over
economic policy reflected accurately the very different sets of values
within the two sub-cultures. Social Democracy was an urban movement:
its supporters were workers concerned with seeking a better life within
modern industrial society — securer employment, better work conditions
and higher wages (through trade unions), cheaper consumer goods
(through cooperatives), better housing (through municipal land reform,

advocated by the SPD). The mass support of the Centre was in the small Catholic towns and villages, where the social problem was perceived rather differently. As we have seen, the material objectives of Centre supporters were frequently at odds with those of urban workers. Moreover, class feeling in Centre strongholds was usually of a more traditional kind, though none the less sharp or volatile. These communities were concerned particularly with the role of 'outsiders': bankers, grain dealers on the exchanges and other 'speculative' capitalists who were blamed for economic exploitation; and more directly identifiable figures like the railway administrator or commercial traveller, who in the second half of the nineteenth century replaced the landlord's agent and the itinerant pedlar as the characteristic objects of small town resentment. Antipathy of this sort was accompanied by a widespread distrust of the city, the symbol of wealth, political power, administrative caprice and immorality.[28]

These attitudes were apparent in the response of Catholics to the *Kulturkampf*; and in the years that followed they were the raw material of political exploitation, as rapid economic change, greater geographical and social mobility, the railway and the press exposed the small town to the penetration of new forces and ideas. In the years between the 1880s and 1914 'backward' Catholic Germany was in a state of flux, caught between parochialism and half-completed modernisation.[29] In response to this transformation of the countryside the Centre developed a distinct political style which was the inverted mirror-image of that developed by the SPD in response to the transformation in the towns. Like the SPD, the Centre did not simply take up the material grievances of its supporters. It also provided them with a morally satisfying world within a world, where Catholic self-esteem was confirmed by the identification of external enemies. The Centre created, in fact, a demonology to appeal to its supporters' apprehensions. This demonology was extensive. It included arrogant and 'over-educated' bureaucrats who were allegedly of little practical use to Catholic communities – like the 'veterinary surgeon with top hat and kid gloves' cited by one Centre leader in the south-west.[30] At the economic level it identified obvious targets like department store owners, grain dealers, bankers and the owners of mobile capital in general, as well as clamant urban workers selfishly ignorant of poverty on the land. Finally it took in a range of those – writers, academics, politicians and journalists – who were supposedly threatening to undermine settled family life and household economy by their support for female emancipation, contraception, 'degenerate' literature and other unwholesome manifestations of modernity.[31] At best, argued the Centre, they did nothing to help the neglect and material distress of Catholic communities; and at worst they actually exacerbated the situation by their subversive tendencies.

These arguments were, of course, not just for popular consumption. There was a genuine strain of anti-bureaucratic feeling among Centre leaders, just as there was a dislike of the 'war of all against all' unleashed by *laissez-faire* capitalism. Party leaders were also usually conservative on moral matters, viewing with alarm the questioning of traditional values. Evidence of this came in the 1890s, when the party in the Reichstag attempted to turn the 'revolution bill' (*Umsturzvorlage*) into an attack on 'freethinking professors' and the Lex Heinze into an attack on 'immorality' in the arts.[32] On the other hand, there were many examples of attitudes being struck by Centre men which were characterised more by demagogy than by jejune conservatism; and the closer one approaches the reality of provincial Centre life, the more apparent this becomes.

The Centre naturally ran the danger that it might be consumed by the very forces of social resentment which it was encouraging. The *Bayerischer Bauernbund*, for example, won over many Centre voters in rural Bavaria by stigmatising Centre leaders themselves as arrogant and manipulative outsiders.[33] There were instances in other states of tension arising when the Centre offended the parochial, petty-bourgeois sensibilities of its supporters. On the whole, though, party leaders proved adept at marrying their own lofty moral conservatism with the more inchoate antipathies of small town Centre voters. The success of this technique was particularly marked in the sphere of educational reform, consistently opposed by the Centre in all the German states. Non-denominational schools, raising the school leaving age, more teaching of modern languages, the introduction of 'ethical' as well as religious education: these and similar proposals were feared by many Centre leaders because of the likelihood that they would raise expectations and undermine traditional sources of authority. They were, at the same time, measures against which support could be readily mobilised among Catholic heads of families, concerned that their taxes would be raised, and (rightly) that their sons' and daughters' heads would be turned away from a lifetime on the farm or in the family workshop.[34]

The political implications of this Centre populism were by no means straightforward. The prominent anti-bureaucratic strain in the party frequently led to attacks on Reich and state governments; and as the example of the Lex Heinze and similar instances in the states showed, the Centre could often oppose and outflank Wilhelmine governments in its anti-immorality campaigns. There were, in addition, occasions when the Centre indicted the traditional ruling élite for immoral self-indulgence: characteristic was the party's hostility to duelling and horse-racing.[35] But Centre views on social morality divided it most sharply of all from the left. The Left-Liberals were the most obvious opponents of the Centre on these issues. It was they, in particular, who were branded the agents of 'alien' ideas; and Centre attitudes constituted a direct attack on their most cherished ideals of the free exchange of both goods and ideas. The SPD, again, followed the lead given by the Left-Liberals on moral and cultural issues. The party had major reservations, of course: there were many in the SPD who eschewed bourgeois liberal values and wanted the development of a specifically proletarian culture.[36] But there were also prominent Social Democrats who enjoyed close links with advanced liberal cultural circles, especially in the south and south-west — Georg von Vollmar, Bavarian SPD leader, was perhaps the most important.[37] Moreover, Social Democrats generally were aware of the difficulties which party journalists still regularly faced over censorship, and were determined to prevent the success of an obscurantist morality campaign led by the Centre. The SPD played a major role in defeating Centre proposals in the Lex Heinze for increased censorship; and in the state parliaments the party invariably joined forces with the Left-Liberals on issues concerned with artistic freedom, public morality and education. In these matters, as in economic ones, the Social Democratic and Catholic sub-cultures had little in common.

III

Centre policy received much of its cutting edge from the everyday reality of backwardness and neglect among its Catholic supporters. At the same time as the party became a vehicle for the grievances of the Catholic peasantry and lower-middle class, however, it also became a vehicle for the aspirations of middle-class Catholics. This, too, had the political effect of dividing the Centre from the left and drawing it closer to the government.

The 1890s constituted once again a crucial watershed, as middle-class Catholics began to demand a fairer and fuller share in various areas of German national life. One index of this was a more affirmative attitude among some Catholic businessmen, aware of the under-representation of Catholics in industry and commerce, and anxious that the shortfall be made good.[38] The mood was perhaps more pronounced, though, among the non-business middle classes. Catholic civil servants and academics (and would-be members of these professions) began to react more strongly to the discrimination which they encountered; particularly, in the case of academics, to the continuing widespread prejudice which asserted that Catholics could never discharge the disinterested service to scholarship required of their profession.[39] The tone adopted by Catholic intellectuals generally became brisker and less apologetic. This was clearly demonstrated in successive revised editions of the Görres *Staatslexikon*, as it adopted within German intellectual life a position at once more confident, more engaged and more outward-looking.[40] The appearance, finally, of newspaper articles and books written by Catholics and dealing with the problem of Catholic 'backwardness', its causes and possible solutions, was in itself evidence of a mounting awareness that the Catholic community should assert itself.

This movement for greater recognition added a new slogan to contemporary debate: the 'parity question' (*Paritätsfrage*). In its narrowest sense the phrase was applied to the prospects of Catholics seeking entry into, or promotion within, the civil service. More generally, it articulated a demand for the equality of Catholics as citizens within the State. First taken up seriously in 1891 at the annual Assembly of German Catholics, the issue was seldom absent from the agenda of subsequent Assemblies: it engaged the attention of a generation of middle-class Catholics.[41] The desire for a greater degree of acceptance and recognition achieved particularly powerful expression at the political level. It can be seen in the comment of a Centre agent in Siegen, writing to party leader Lieber about the political circumstances necessary locally for the Centre to 'come into its own'.[42] The growing consciousness of anti-Catholic electoral gerrymandering, and moves to end it in Baden, the Rhineland and elsewhere, were signs of a similar sentiment.[43] It was evident, above all, in the attitudes of the new generation of Centre leaders which emerged in the 1890s and guided the party on to its pro-government course.

The new generation was a perfect embodiment of those members of the Catholic middle class to whom the idea of parity was important. For, just as the 1890s saw a de-clericalisation of the Centre, so it was marked also by the emergence of a more bourgeois leadership. There was a noticeable decline in the political influence of aristocrats within the party. Formerly dominant figures like Franckenstein, Schorlemer and Löe died in these years; many others lost their seats in the 1893 Reichstag election, over the issue of the 'big' military bill;[44] and in the same year a number of important Silesian aristocrats, whose policy over the military bill had been rejected in the Centre, resigned their party posts.[45] Lieber's accession to the party leadership over the rival claims of the Silesian, von Huene, was a sign of the change which was taking place. So was the defection of highly-born Catholics to the Conservative parties.[46] The eclipse of aristocratic influence, while most marked in Bavaria, Westphalia and the Rhineland, was a general one; and it was often actually encouraged by the new leadership. Typical were the exclusion of the Rhineland aristocrat Count Oppersdorff from the important Augustinus Press Association, and the frustration of attempts to rehabilitate von Huene politically by means of a party 'directory' advising Centre leaders.[47]

On the other hand, this new bourgeois leadership had few roots in industry and commerce, a reflection, partly, of the continuing under-representation of Catholics in these areas of national life.[48] There were, of course, Catholic entrepreneurs who played an important part in local Centre politics: Cahensly in Limburg, Bell in Essen, Urfey in Krefeld. Others were the political confidants of major Centre leaders; this was true of Lieber's relationship with Cahensly, and with the Württemberg industrialist, Braun. And of the national leaders, Karl Trimborn had a considerable income from business interests, while Richard Müller, the Centre financial expert, was a textile magnate in Fulda.[49] The number of such men was limited, though, and fewer throughout the years 1890–1914 than in the National Liberal or Left-Liberal parties. The new leaders reflected bourgeois Catholic aspirations faithfully, in that they were men of the non-business middle classes; above all lawyers. Ernst Lieber was a lawyer; so were three of the four men who constituted the collegiate leadership of the Centre after Lieber's death in 1902 – Trimborn, Peter Spahn and Adolf Gröber (the fourth, Hertling, was an academic). In addition, a large number of the party's most outstanding Reichstag figures, who made up the transmission belts between Berlin and local Centre organisations, shared this profession: in the Rhineland and Westphalia, Fritzen, Würmeling, Julius and Karl Bachem; in Silesia, Porsch, Stephan and Nadbyl; in Hesse, Schmitt; in Württemberg, Alfred Rembold; and in Baden, von Buol, Fehrenbach, Marbe and Zehnter.[50]

Their specialist skills, both in drafting legislation in committee and debating it in plenary sessions, clearly helped to determine this con-centration of lawyers in the upper echelons of the Centre; and the indifferent quality of many members of successive intakes of Centre deputies to the Reichstag led to a further concentration of work-load and political initiative on to this group, which developed a discernible *esprit de corps*. Above all, the more rigorous demands of electioneering and parliamentary business in the 1890s and after, compared with the

1870s, made lawyers both more fitted and more willing than other groups like the clergy, aristocracy or entrepreneurs to conduct the party's affairs. Yet these advantages could also be weaknesses. Financially, for example, the new leaders were relatively isolated and exposed, as the episode of the Centre newspaper *Germania* revealed. In the 1890s powerful aristocratic supporters of the paper threatened to remove their backing on political grounds; but Lieber's confidant, Cahensly, had some difficulty arranging alternative support among the Catholic business community.[51] At a more fundamental level, the position of the lawyers who led the Centre made them more vulnerable to cooptation by the government of the day. As lawyers, their very freedom from the need to administer an economic concern meant that they lacked an independent basis of social power like that possessed by the Catholic aristocrats formerly active in the Centre, or the entrepreneurs active in other German parties.

What the Centre leaders did have was a solid block of 100 Reichstag seats, and these they showed every willingness to use. Centre votes were deployed partly to build up credit and goodwill with the government which could be drawn on in demanding specific legislative measures; more generally, to back their claims for 'parity' with a demonstration that the Centre, like the Catholics it represented, was not an 'enemy of the Reich' (*reichsfeindlich*). It might, in fact, be more accurate to describe those at the head of the Centre Party as political brokers rather than political leaders;[52] and as brokers they were concerned less with power than with influence and respectability. Lieber especially, the 'malcontent from Nassau' of earlier years, shed the prickliness he had sometimes shown towards those with political power, and assiduously cultivated his contacts with chancellors and state secretaries. There was in Lieber's behaviour an almost desperate desire to please: his ingratiating and conspiratorial arrangements to meet for discussions with Reich treasury secretary Posadowsky about a projected tobacco tax without alerting the 'sniffing pack of hounds' in the press;[53] his advice to State secretaries generally on the best way to circumvent parliamentary opposition to their measures; his suggestions to Chancellor Hohenlohe on how to time Reichstag business in 1899 to neutralise the intriguing of Prussian finance minister Miquel.[54] This pattern of arrogance combined with self-abasement was to find its apogee in the conduct of Lieber's successors in the years between 1902 and 1906.

Those who led the Wilhelmine Centre Party were determined to appear 'two hundred per cent German'. It was for this reason that the

sense of pique in Centre circles was so great on those occasions when
the party was faced with the loss of the government's ear. At the end
of the 1890s, for example, Miquel tried to reactivate the old Bismarckian
alliance of Conservatives and National Liberals — the so-called policy of
Sammlung.[55] And in 1906, after Centre attacks in the Reichstag on the
government's colonial administration, Bülow succeeded in forging a
majority out of these parties, together with the Left-Liberals.[56] On both
occasions the Centre saw itself faced with losing what it had seized in
the years after 1890: the intoxicating novelty of political influence
exercised to confirm its own respectability.

IV

The deft single-mindedness with which the Centre used its Reichstag
position, and the seemingly arrogant *hauteur* which accompanied its
parliamentary hegemony, antagonised all the other parties. But it
alienated the left especially. When the Left-Liberals were offered a place
as a partner of government — something which seemed a possibility
under Caprivi's New Course in the early 1890s, and was more substantially held out to them as a member of the Bülow Bloc — they
showed themselves eager to grasp the opportunity. Each Left-Liberal
leader could imagine himself playing Cobden to Caprivi's or Bülow's
Peel.[57] But the Left-Liberals were neither so large and stable, nor so
politically flexible, as the Centre, and their reaction to the successful
hegemonial position of the Centre was correspondingly embittered by
their own failure to achieve one like it.

　The SPD, too, was hostile to the way the Centre exercised its key
role; and this reflected the different responses of the German labour
movement and German Catholics to the experience of having
previously been the pariahs of German society. While the Centre led
German Catholics — middle-class Catholics particularly — in a bid to
transcend the ghetto mentality and second-class status which had
been inherited from the *Kulturkampf*, the SPD stood at the head of a
labour movement which remained self-consciously outside of 'respectable'
society. It is true that the sense of self-sufficiency and ideological purity
within the labour movement was breached by the political role assumed
by SPD reformists in Baden, Württemberg and Bavaria (as well as by
the 'revisionist' intellectuals). But the SPD group in the Reichstag
modelled its political tactics on those of its more repressed and intran-
sigent Prussian and Saxon branches, and was in accordance bitterly
critical of the Centre.[58] Whereas the Centre was prepared, by means of
judicious amendments, to try to find a means of passing almost any

government bill, even one unpopular with many of its supporters (as the navy was with the peasantry), the SPD in the Reichstag took an attitude of principled opposition to measures which it could not completely support. Instead of finding the Centre an ally which, in line with its professed anti-militarism, opposed army and navy expenditure, the SPD found rather a party which customarily reserved its position on the first reading of such a measure, argued at the committee stage for a more equitable distribution of the additional tax burden, and voted for the government on the third reading.[59]

The hostility aroused on the left by the Centre's parliamentary methods was fully reciprocated. The Reichstag leadership élite of the Centre, legal draftsmen and apostles of procedural rectitude, had a scornful, professional impatience with everything they regarded as negative or obstructionist. This outlook was apparent even in their relations within the Centre Party. Lieber is a good example of this, a man lacking in patience towards those of his colleagues who made no positive contribution to the legislative process, and incontinently hostile to the Centre press, parts of which he viewed as enemies of his party's attempt to secure its position in Wilhelmine politics.[60] His attitude was shared by others. Richard Müller attacked the 'idiocy' of the agrarians' extreme demands;[61] Hertling lamented the lack of constructive parliamentary potential among his fellow deputies from Bavaria;[62] and Karl Bachem complained along the same lines about the 'nonentities' who owed their position in the Centre group to special interests rather than to their usefulness in contributing to the business of legislation.[63]

These Centre leaders, with their keenly developed sense of compromise, were quick to reproach other parties for irresponsibility. For all the demagogy employed by local Centre men in addressing their own rank and file, the leadership in Berlin remained more instinctively conservative than that of any other party. On a number of occasions the Centre responded with an attitude of pained propriety to the wild demands of the right. But this reaction directed itself mostly against the left, above all the SPD. Characteristic was the response of Peter Spahn and Karl Bachem to the filibustering speeches of Arthur Stadthagen, the SPD representative on the committee dealing with the Civil Code. The anger which Stadthagen's tactics induced in a man like Bachem symbolised the gulf that separated Centre and SPD: the former trying to demonstrate its devotion to the national cause, the latter reacting to its pariah status with hostility to the efforts of the bourgeois parties. It is a telling sign of this difference that while the work of

Centre representatives on the committee was singled out by the Kaiser for special praise, Stadthagen's obstructionist role was at least in part the result of a threatened gaol sentence for *lèse-majesté* which hung over him.[64]

The different attitudes of left and Centre towards cooperation and compromise in parliament assumed a particular importance in the years 1897–1902. In these years the political anchorage of the Centre was relatively uncertain. Despite its striving, the party had not by this time established the degree of close legislative collaboration with the government which was to characterise the years 1902–6. Indeed, the political events of 1897 thoroughly alarmed the Centre. A number of state secretaries favourable to the party were dropped, while the Prussian finance minister and new vice-president of the Prussian Ministry of State, Miquel, was attempting to construct an alliance of National Liberals and Conservatives in a policy of *Sammlung* which Centre leaders believed to be aimed against them. At the same time, the Centre feared that the right-wing policy of *Sammlungspolitik* might lead after the 1898 Reichstag elections to a *coup d'état*.[65] This situation might have pushed the party towards closer cooperation with the left. It certainly led to widespread support by the Centre for Left-Liberal candidates in the 1898 elections, and Richard Müller was sufficiently concerned to weaken the potential strength of the *Sammlung* parties that he advocated electoral collaboration with the SPD in certain states.[66]

In the event, however, the Centre turned away from a policy of confrontation with the government, despite the latter's turn to the right. The reasons for this were complex. Partly, the fear of *coup d'état* was itself double-edged: it cowed some Centre leaders into a conciliatory position.[67] Furthermore, the party could plausibly assume that it would continue to play a part in the government's calculations. Miquel himself, in fact, acknowledged the importance of the Centre (although Lieber remained deeply suspicious of Miquel's intentions). And Tirpitz's approaches over the first Navy Bill could certainly have left Centre leaders in no doubt about the role still expected of them. There was, though, another important consideration which hardened the Centre in its dislike of cooperation with the left; one which derived from the differences between Centre and left over the question of parliamentary propriety. This was the unprecedented level of the obstructionist tactics employed in the 1898–1903 Reichstag by the left, principally the SPD. Between December 1898 and April 1903, three SPD deputies alone — Bebel, Singer and Stadthagen — were called to order 70 times by the Reichstag President and reprimanded on 54 occasions.[68] The impact of this was heightened by the fact that most of the parliamentary turmoil was concentrated in the periods covered by two measures: the Lex Heinze and the 1902 tariffs. On 4 December 1902 Singer was called to order three times and refused to leave the chamber when formally expelled from the sitting. Ten days later, during the 19-hour final sitting on the tariff bill, the SPD deputy Antrick spoke for eight hours in an attempt to delay passage of the measure. The outrage that this behaviour evoked in the Centre was equal to the outrage felt by the left over the substantive aspects of the legislation. Bachem referred to the 'revolution in parliament', and likened obstruction to 'open war'. The reactions of Trimborn and Gröber were similar, and it was the latter who drafted a bill designed to limit speeches on procedural motions to five minutes.[69] In subsequent years the Centre remained a staunch supporter of measures aimed at preventing a recurrence of obstructionist tactics like those used in the parliament of 1898–1903.[70]

Centre and left were, as we have seen, bitterly divided over the substance of measures like the Lex Heinze and the tariffs of 1902. The procedural aspects of their mutual antagonism should not, however, be underestimated. In their different attitudes towards parliamentary rectitude, Centre and SPD represented two different reactions to what, in the early years of the Reich, had been a common fate as outsiders. The SPD, even after the turn of the century, remained outside German society in many important respects. The Centre, on the other hand, was concerned to demonstrate that Catholics and their political leaders were the equal of other Germans in national feeling, if only they were given a chance to show it.

V

In historical accounts of Wilhelmine Germany the Centre has commonly appeared to be a special case, a peculiarly opportunist party dedicated to pure politicking. It has been the intention of this essay to suggest that the Centre was, in fact, a characteristic political creature of the *Kaiserreich*; and, furthermore, that the motives behind its pro-governmental, anti-left stance in the years 1890–1914 can help to illuminate some of the more general springs of political action in Wilhelmine Germany.

One important respect in which the Centre was a characteristic Wilhelmine party was its role as a vehicle of economic interests. The part played by interest groups in the other political parties is well-known: agriculture in the case of the Conservatives, heavy industry in the National Liberals, commerce and light industry in the Left-Liberals, trade unions and consumer cooperatives in the SPD. This feature of the Centre has generally received less attention, although it was no less important. With the de-clericalisation of the Centre, and the decline of aristocratic notable (*Honoratioren*) leadership, interest groups under the aegis of the party played a vital part in cementing its popular support. The social structure of the Centre's natural constituency in Catholic Germany naturally helped to determine those groups to whose interests party leaders accorded priority: the independent lower-middle class, and — especially — the peasantry. The economic policies which the Centre, in turn, tended to favour were partly responsible for anchoring the party politically on the right and cutting it off from the left. Ideologically, neither the *laissez-faire* Left-Liberals nor the orthodox Marxist SPD had anything but contempt for what they regarded as futile, reactionary Centre attempts to preserve the independent peasant and small businessman. For both Left Liberals and the SPD, moreover, Centre policies were anathema for electoral reasons. Where efforts to prop up the peasant producer, craftsman and shopkeeper succeeded, they almost invariably led to higher prices: for the Left Liberals, with their white-collar and petty-professional following, and the SPD with its working-class support, such efforts were an attack on the living standards of the consumer.

The market-place element in the political conduct of the Centre, and of the other parties, should not, however, be exaggerated. The uncertain early years of the *Kaiserreich*, coupled with Bismarckian manipulation, had encouraged the rival party blocs — Conservatives, Liberals, Socialists, Catholics — to become the standard-bearers not only of interest groups, but of sharply divided sets of values within German society. The Wilhelmine political parties were actually, therefore, curious hybrids, combining crass material demands with a stubborn, almost ritual attachment to old ideological positions.[71] On the one hand they maintained their support through formal organisational ties and the promise of material concessions from the government; but on the other hand they maintained their identity and sense of separateness by giving voice to the aspirations of powerful communities of sentiment. The problem, viewed from the perspective of parliamentarisation through common action by the parties, was not simply the conflict of economic interests — that, after all, was the hard currency of political negotiation in all European legislatures. It was the fact that these broader aspirations were conflicting and competitive. In the case of German Catholics, two particular sets of aspirations tied men to the Centre. In the first place, Catholic peasants and members of the petty-bourgeoisie looked to the Centre for a reaffirmation of their social worth; a sense of self-respect to set against material neglect, administrative *hauteur* and a suspected urban contempt for 'the idiocy of rural life'. In the second place, the Centre offered middle-class Catholics a means of exerting political pressure to achieve professional equality and social respectability. Indeed, the political role of the Centre itself was an embodiment of Catholic middle-class aspirations to a domestic place in the sun.

This essay has sought to show how the translation of these aspirations into political practice tended to divide the Centre from the left and align it instead with successive governments. More generally, the case of German Catholics and the Centre Party suggests that arguments about the diversion or blunting of reformist energies in Wilhelmine Germany need to take account of many complicated cross-currents. Attitudes among the Catholic peasantry and petty-bourgeoisie, for example, differed considerably from the picture which is often presented for imperial Germany of a population being manipulated and mobilised behind the status quo. The rural parts of Catholic Germany seem to have been almost untouched by the blandishments of 'social imperialism'; there was little enthusiasm for the navy (or, in many cases, the army), and the membership of *nationale Verbände* like the Pan-German League and Navy League was very small.[72] There was, in fact, an instinctively radical temper in many of these communities, expressing itself at least in part against the idea of distant government and arrogant officialdom. The Centre was able to carry these supporters with it politically because the view of the world which it presented — in which the men of the left were equated with arrogant officials as 'outsiders' — was deftly attuned to the actual experience of small-town Catholics. The demagogy of the Centre was better equipped to channel the currents of petty-bourgeois and agrarian radicalism than the blunt instrument of a 'manipulative' social imperialism.

The case of middle-class Catholics similarly suggests that a refinement of some current ideas is in order. It is, for example, commonly argued that the German middle classes were diverted from the task of domestic reform by a belligerent foreign policy with which they identified; and that in time they became 'feudalised', adopting the manners and values of Junker aristocracy, bureaucracy and officer corps. This bourgeois type is best represented, perhaps, by Heinrich Mann's fictional figure, Diederich Hessling, with his duelling scars, reverence for the Kaiser and vicarious satisfaction taken in German arrogance abroad.[73] The blunting of reformist ambitions among the Catholic middle class is hardly consistent with this picture. They did not, as we have seen, share the ethos of the student duelling fraternities: Catholics had their own fraternities, within which a strong anti-duelling movement developed in the Wilhelmine years. Partly for this reason Catholics did not enjoy easy access to the officer corps. Catholics were also, as we have seen, consistently discriminated against in appointments of the bureaucracy, particularly the higher grades. There was, in fact, a quickly-awakened strain of resentment against bureaucratic high-handedness among middle-class as well as lower-class Catholics, finding expression in Centre leaders like Adolf Gröber. It seems clear that when middle-class Catholics indicated their desire for acceptance as equal German citizens, they did so as part of an emancipatory urge which made itself felt in spite of, rather than because of, the particular values associated with the Junker aristocracy, bureaucracy and officer corps.

This had its relevance, too, at a more directly political level. The Centre was, of course, highly conservative on moral and cultural matters. But it is significant that, this aside, it was not the Prussian-particularist and 'feudal' features of the political status quo, but the national and bourgeois ones, to which Centre leaders made their strongest commitment. Here the support for the Civil Code and navy may stand as examples. Both, by implication, were measures which looked beyond a society governed by arbitrary abuse of law and the values of the Prussian officer corps; a society, that is, in which Catholics were likely to be eternally consigned to second-class status. Centre policy, in fact, ran in parallel with that of the Left-Liberals, who supported *Weltpolitik* not because it reinforced 'feudal' values, but because they believed its domestic corollary – industrial expansion and social change – would erode such values.[74] It was not common attachment to an archaic status quo which dampened the pressure from the political parties for democratisation, so much as the rivalry and mutual recrimination as each party sought to secure its own ends. The result was division among the potential parties of reform, and stasis. The Left-Liberals, for example, harboured a residual distrust of the SPD, claiming that the latter put narrow class interest before the broader interest of an anti-reactionary bloc. At the same time, the Left-Liberals accused the Centre both of strengthening the SPD (by supporting 'dear food' policies), and of deserting the bourgeois forces of reform in favour of clerical selfishness. It was this sharp sense of betrayal which lent particular bitterness to the charges of clerical horse-trading made by men like Friedrich Naumann. The Centre, for its part, reacted with accusations which were a mirror-image of those levelled by the Left-Liberals. Advanced liberal ideas about the free play of ideas and social forces had, it was alleged, both disrupted the life of Catholic communities and hastened the rise of the SPD.

Nowhere was this rivalry and mutual recrimination more evident than in relations between the two great mass parties of Wilhelmine Germany, the Centre and SPD, which in the first decades of the *Kaiserreich* had shared the common role of defending pariah communities within German society. By the 1890s the SPD was echoing most of the Left-Liberal criticisms of the Centre: the party was reactionary in its economic and cultural policies; its leaders had been flattered into adopting a pro-governmental stance, and were prepared to sacrifice any principle in exchange for concessions to Catholic interests. The Centre, conversely, indicted the SPD for adopting the intolerant values of the Left-Liberals in religious, educational and cultural matters, and for threatening the rule of law by their irresponsible actions and verbally revolutionary goals. For sober middle-class Catholics who, in politics as in other areas of public life, were bent on achieving respectability, the latter charge was decisive. The policy of the SPD appeared to run directly counter to their own prim legalism.

There was, of course, a deep irony in this. Within the SPD itself the advent of revisionism signalled a serious ideological debate over the extent to which the status quo should be accepted. At the same time, Social Democrats in southern Germany were behaving politically as reformists. Moreover, even in orthodox leaders like Karl Kautsky a gap was steadily opening up between formal revolutionary rhetoric and actual revolutionary unpreparedness.[75] In the Wilhelmine period there were, therefore, already clear signs in the SPD of those changes which were to culminate in the party's vote for war credits in 1914 and its own consistent legalism in the 1920s. These changes, though, did not fully register with those on the outside, like the Centre. In this respect, as in others, the division of German society and the political parties into rival and hostile camps distorted the perception of real changes which were taking place. Instead, the impulse towards acceptance and respectability on the part of the Centre, and the outward resistance of the SPD to the same process, were sources of a crucial mutual antagonism.

Notes

Parts of this essay were delivered to seminars at the Institute for European History in Mainz, and at Yale University. I benefited from the discussion in both cases. I also wish to thank Richard Evans for his criticism of an earlier draft.

1.   A classic consideration of the connection between the two, first published in 1915, is Thorstein Veblen, *Imperial Germany and the Industrial Revolution*

(London, 1939). See, generally, R. Dahrendorf, *Gesellschaft und Demokratie in Deutschland* (Munich, 1968).

2. G. Craig, *The Politics of the Prussian Army, 1640–1945* (Oxford, 1955) is representative of the first approach; H. Kohn, *The Mind of Germany* (London, 1965) of the second.

3. The important works along these lines include H. Rosenberg, *Grosse Depression und Bismarckzeit* (Berlin, 1967); H.-U. Wehler, *Bismarck und der Imperialismus* (Cologne and Berlin, 1969); H.-U. Wehler, *Das Deutsche Kaiserreich 1871– 1918* (Göttingen, 1973); H.-U. Wehler (ed.), *Moderne deutsche Sozialgeschichte* (Cologne and Berlin, 1966); M. Stürmer (ed.), *Das kaiseriche Deutschland. Politik und Gesellschaft 1870–1918* (Düsseldorf, 1970). The new approach draws generally on the work of Eckart Kehr: *Schlachtflottenbau und Parteipolitik 1894–1901* (Berlin, 1930); and *Der Primat der Innenpolitik*, Kehr's collected essays edited by H.-U. Wehler (Berlin, 1965).

4. See, especially, the work of M. Rainer Lepsius. Representative is 'Parteiensystem und Sozialstruktur: zum Problem der Demokratisierung der deutschen Gesellschaft', in W. Abel *et al.* (eds.), *Wirtschaft, Geschichte und Wirtschaftsgeschichte. Festschrift zum 65. Geburtstag von Friedrich Lütge* (Stuttgart, 1966).

5. Kehr, *Schlachtflottenbau*, p. 205.

6. The standard work on the Centre remains K. Bachem, *Vorgeschichte, Geschichte und Politik der Deutschen Zentrumspartei*, 9 vols. (Cologne, 1927–32). The best summary is R. Morsey, 'Die deutschen Katholiken und der Nationalstaat zwischen Kulturkampf und dem ersten Weltkrieg', *Historisches Jahrbuch* (1970). There are two recent American works: John K. Zeender, *The German Center Party 1890–1906* (Philadelphia, 1976), and Ronald J. Ross, *Beleaguered Tower: The Dilemma of Political Catholicism in Wilhelmine Germany* (Notre Dame, Ind., 1976). The former is useful; the latter should be used with care.

7. Morsey, *Historisches Jahrbuch* (1970), pp. 40–59.

8. On this, see M. Rauh, *Föderalismus und Parlamentarismus im Wilhelminischen Reich* (Düsseldorf, 1973).

9. On the emergence of the Weimar Coalition, see R. Morsey, *Die Deutsche Zentrumspartei 1917–1923* (Düsseldorf, 1966); on the importance of such an alignment in the Wilhelmine years, A. Rosenberg, *Imperial Germany* (Oxford, 1931), esp. pp. 18–19.

10. Rauh, *Föderalismus*, pp. 349–50.

11. Morsey, *Historisches Jahrbuch* (1970), pp. 43–4; and the same author's article, 'Georg Kardinal Kopp, Fürstbischof von Breslau (1887–1914). Kirchenfürst oder "Staatsbischof"?', *Wichmann-Jahrbuch für Kirchengeschichte im Bistum Berlin* (1967–68), pp. 46 ff.

12. Historisches Archiv (HA) der Stadt Köln, Karl Bachem Papers, 56,66c: memoranda; Pfälzische Landesbibliothek (LB) Speyer, Ernst Lieber Papers, S. 195, Schaedler to Lieber, 20 June 1893. There is also relevant material in folder IX of the unpublished papers of Franz von Ballestrem, in private family possession. For earlier attempts at interference along the same lines (in 1880 and 1887), see Karl Bachem Papers, 55, 56,61: memoranda; E. Hüsgen, *Ludwig Windthorst* (Cologne, 1911), pp. 231–2; G. von Hertling, *Erinnerungen aus meinem Leben*, 2 vols. (Munich, 1919–20), II, pp. 64–6.

13. HA Köln, Karl Bachem Papers, 7: memoranda on the passing of the Civil Code.

14. J. Bachem, 'Wir müssen aus dem Turm heraus', *Historisch-politische Blätter* (1906), I, pp. 376–86. See also Morsey, *Zentrumspartei*, pp. 36–40; L. Bergsträsser, *Geschichte der politischen Parteien in Deutschland* (Munich 1960), pp. 175–7; J. Bachem, *Erinnerungen eines alten Publizisten und*

Politikers (Cologne, 1913), p. 180–1.

15. Ross, *Beleaguered Tower*, pp. 123–31.

16. An exception is the comprehensive work by Karl Möckl, *Die Prinzregentenzeit. Gesellschaft und Politik während der Ära des Prinzregenten Luitpold in Bayern* (Munich, 1972), which has much material on the Bavarian Centre.

17. On the Social Democratic sub-culture, see G.A. Ritter, *Die Arbeiterbewegung im Wilhelminischen Reich* (Berlin, 1957); G. Roth, *The Social Democrats in Imperial Germany* (Totowa, N.J., 1963); D. Groh, *Negative Integration und revolutionärer Attentismus* (Frankfurt/M and Berlin, 1973).

18. D. Fricke (ed.), *Die bürgerlichen Parteien in Deutschland 1830–1945*, 2 Vols. (Leipzig, 1968–70), II, p. 810.

19. On this, see generally J. Rost, *Die wirtschaftliche und kulturelle Lage der deutschen Katholiken* (Cologne, 1911); and A. Neher, *Die wirtschaftliche und soziale Lage der Katholiken im westlichen Deutschland* (Rottweil, 1927).

20. Rost, *Die wirtschaftliche und kulturelle Lage*, pp. 82–3.

21. Ibid., pp. 98–9.

22. Ibid., pp. 163–66; Neher, *Die wirtschaftliche und soziale Lage*, pp. 98–9; J.C.G. Röhl, 'Higher Civil Servants in Germany, 1890–1900', *Journal of Contemporary History* Vol. 2, No. 3 (1967), pp. 109–11; Ross, *Beleaguered Tower*, pp. 20–1.

23. By 1912 the Centre share of Catholic votes cast at Reichstag elections had fallen from 83% (1874) to 54.6%. J. Schauff, *Die deutschen Katholiken und die Zentrumspartei* (Cologne, 1928), p. 75.

24. H. Gabler, *Die Entwicklung der Parteien auf landwirtschaftlicher Grundlage von 1871–1912*, Dissertation (Berlin, 1934), p. 16, cited H. Gottwald, *Zentrum und Imperialismus*, Dissertation (Jena, 1966), p. 41. Also, Rost, *Die wirtschaftliche und kulturelle Lage*, p. 9ff; F. Naumann, *Demokratie und Kaisertum* (Berlin, 1900), p. 122.

25. For details, see ch. 1 of my unpublished thesis, 'The Centre Party in Wilhelmine Germany: the Example of Württemberg' (Cambridge Ph.D., 1976), pp. 29–49.

26. For the extent to which theory and practice actually coincided over the question of *Mittelstandspolitik*, see my article 'The *Mittelstand* in German Society and Politics, 1871–1914', *Social History*, 4 (1977), pp. 409–33.

27. I have already dealt in some detail with the conflict over economic policy in one particular state, in 'Class and Politics in Wilhelmine Germany: The Center Party and the Social Democrats in Württemberg', *Central European History* (1976), esp. pp. 241–7.

28. D. Blackbourn, 'The Centre Party in Wilhelmine Germany', esp. pp. 233–40.

29. See D. Blackbourn, *Social History* (1977), pp. 426–9, on this opening up of the countryside and small town.

30. Hans Kiene, in *Verhandlungen der Württembergischen Kammer der Abgeordneten auf dem 36 Landtag. Protokoll Band IV, p. 2483, 100. Sitzung, 14 June 1905.*

31. For the development by the agrarian *Bund der Landwirte* of a similar demonology, see H.J. Puhle, *Agrarische Interessenpolitik und preussischer Konservatismus im wilhelminischen Reich 1893–1914* (Hanover, 1966).

32. R.J.V. Lenman, 'Art, Society, and the Law in Wilhelmine Germany: the Lex Heinze', *Oxford German Studies*, 8 (1973–4), pp. 86–113.

33. Möckl, *Die Prinzregentenzeit*, pp. 451–3.

34. D. Blackbourn, 'The Political Alignment of the Centre Party in Wilhelmine Germany: A Study of the Party's Emergence in Nineteenth-Century Wurttemberg', *Historical Journal* (1975), IV, pp. 844–5; for more detail, see Blackbourn, 'The Centre Party in Wilhelmine Germany', pp. 195–8.

35. On duelling, see the editorial in the *Waldse'er Wochenblatt*, 15 January 1898

(reprinted from the *Augsburger Postzeitung*); Rost, *Die wirtschaftliche und kulturelle Lage*, writes (p. 6) that 'the anti-duel movement is supported principally by educated Catholics, and more than 20,000 academically educated Catholic men (i.e. members of Catholic fraternities) have no contact with the barbarism from the start'. For a characteristically hostile view of horse-racing from a Centre newspaper, see *Deutsches Volksblatt*,15 June, 1895.

36. See G. Fülberth, *Proletarische Partei und bürgerliche Literatur* (Neuwied and Berlin, 1972).
37. Lenman, *Oxford German Studies* (1973–4), pp. 103–4; Fülberth, *Proletarische Partei und bürgerliche Literatur*, p. 172, n. 294. The close links between liberal intellectuals and socialists in the south-west is attested in the autobiographies of two Social Democrats, Wilhelm Blos and Wilhelm Keil.
38. Gottwald, *Zentrum und Imperialismus*, pp. 25–30; Neher, *Die wirtschaftliche und soziale Lage*, p. 107.
39. On the most celebrated instance of such prejudice, the 'Spahn Affair', when the Catholic Martin Spahn was elevated to a chair of history at Strassburg in 1901, see *Schulthess' Europäischer Geschichtskalender, 1901* (Munich, 1902), pp. 145–7.
40. C. Bauer, *Deutscher Katholizismus. Entwicklungslinien und Profile* (Frankfurt/M., 1964), p. 54 ff.
41. HA Köln, Karl Bachem Papers, 92–96: material on the *Paritätsfrage*.
42. Pfälzische LB Speyer, Ernst Lieber Papers, B.10, G. Brust to Lieber, 26 July 1893.
43. On the situation in Baden, see J. Schofer, *Erinnerungen an Theodor Wacker* (Karlsruhe, 1921), pp. 15, 84–5. On the Rhineland: Pfälzische LB Speyer, Ernst Lieber Papers, T.20, Karl Trimborn to Lieber, 1 August 1899. Rhineland Centre leaders had been calling for electoral reform in 1898, as a *quid pro quo* for the party's support of the Navy Bill. It was made clear that if any particular demand was to be levelled in exchange for Centre support, they would prefer electoral reform to repeal of the anti-Jesuit law. On this, see also H. Cardauns, *Karl Trimborn* (M.-Gladbach, 1922), pp. 83–4; Zeender, *The German Center Party*, p. 70.
44. K. Bachem, *Zentrumspartei*, V, p. 294; J.A. Nichols, *Germany after Bismarck. The Caprivi Era 1890–1894* (Cambridge, Mass., 1958), p. 255.
45. An excellent account of the feelings of Franz von Ballestrem (who resigned as chairman of the Centre Reichstag group) and of his fellow-Silesians Huene, Letocha and Matuschka, is contained in folder IX of the Ballestrem Papers, esp. the diary entries from 27 April 1893 to 4 June 1893, and a long memorandum written in 'Autumn 1893'.
46. Thus, for example, Schorlemer-Lieser to the Conservatives, Prince Hatzfeld, the Duke of Ratibor and Prince Lichnowsky to the Free Conservatives. D. Stegmann, *Die Erben Bismarcks* (Cologne, 1970), p. 31.
47. See esp. Pfälzische LB Speyer, Ernst Lieber Papers, L. 243, Lieber to Gröber, 14 June 1894.
48. Rost, *Die wirtschaftliche und kulturelle Lage*, pp. 21–3, gives in tabular form a confessional break-down of ownership in the various branches of industry.
49. Gottwald, *Zentrum und Imperialismus*, pp. 25–30.
50. K. Bachem, *Zentrumspartei*, V, pp. 27–8.
51. Pfälzische LB Speyer, Ernst Lieber Papers, G. 24, Gröber to Lieber, 20 June 1894. See also Gottwald, *Zentrum und Imperialismus*, pp. 136–7; Zeender, *The German Center Party*, p. 36, n.4.
52. For some fruitful general observations on the modern political role of lawyers, see M. Weber, 'Politics as a Vocation', in H.H. Gerth and C. Wright Mills (eds.), *From Max Weber* (London, 1948) esp. pp. 94–5. To consider Centre leaders

in this light, as 'brokers', is, I think, a useful way of approaching two obvious features of the party in the Wilhelmine period: its role as a mediator of interest group demands, and its strikingly 'pure political' character, which so antagonised its opponents.

53. Pfälzische LB Speyer, Ernst Lieber Papers, L. 39, Lieber to Posadowsky, 10 July 1894. For similarly conspiratorial communications, see ibid., L.36, L.37, L.38, Lieber to Posadowsky, 24 June, 29 June and 3 July, 1894.
54. C.zu Hohenlohe, *Denkwürdigkeiten der Reichskanzlerzeit*, ed. K.A. von Müller (Stuttgart, 1931), p. 397, 523–4, 535, 545.
55. See above, p. 175.
56. On the background to this, see G.D. Crothers, *The German Elections of 1907* New York, 1941); and Zeender, *The German Center Party*, pp. 99–114; see also above, the essay by Terry Cole, pp. 40–70.
57. Th. Heuss, *Erinnerungen 1905–1933* (Tübingen, 1963), p. 53.
58. The literature on the SPD reformists in the south is considerable. One work dealing specifically with the problem of the reformists' influence is H. Schlemmer, *Die Rolle der Sozialdemokratie in den Landtagen Badens und Württembergs und ihr Einfluss auf die Entwicklung der Gesamtpartei zwischen 1890 und 1914*, Dissertation (Freiburg i.B., 1953).
59. For some shrewd, though hostile, comments on Centre practice, see Naumann, *Demokratie und Kaisertum*, p. 126.
60. See n. 53, above. A similar attitude of impatience and hostility towards the press, mixed with a strong sense of personal persecution, can be seen in Pfälzische LB Speyer, Ernst Lieber Papers, L.243, Lieber to Gröber, 14 June 1894.
61. Fricke, *Die bürgerlichen Parteien*, II, p. 896.
62. Pfälzische LB Speyer, Ernst Lieber Papers, H. 142, Hertling to Lieber, 26 March 1891.
63. Speech of Karl Bachem to Augustinus Press Association AGM, 2 September 1900. HA Köln, Karl Bachem Papers, 21, copy of *Augustinus-Blatt*, with speech.
64. See the numerous and comprehensive memoranda of Karl Bachem on the negotiations over the passage of the Civil Code: HA Köln, Karl Bachem Papers, 7.
65. On the background to 1897, *Sammlungspolitik* and the threat of *coup d'état*, see G. Eley, 'Sammlungspolitik, Social Imperialism and the Navy Law of 1898', *Militärgeschichtliche Mitteilungen*, 15 (1974); D. Stegmann, 'Wirtschaft und Politik nach Bismarcks Sturz. Zur Genesis der Miquelschen Sammlungspolitik 1890–1897', in I. Geiss and B.J. Wendt (eds.), *Deutschland in der Weltpolitik des 19. und 20. Jahrhunderts. Fritz Fischer zum 65. Geburtstag* (Düsseldorf, 1973); Röhl, *Germany without Bismarck*, pp. 246–51. On the Centre and these developments, see Zeender, *The German Center Party*, pp. 62–4, 71.
66. HA Köln, Karl Bachem Papers, 86c, 86d: extensive correspondence on the 1898 elections. The impression given by Zeender (pp. 63–4 and p. 72, n.77) concerning Centre electoral agreements is misleading.
67. HA Köln, Karl Bachem Papers, 88: memorandum, 24 June 1898. Empirical research to test the validity of argument about the supposedly 'permanent threat of *Staatsstreich*', and its effects on party leaders, is urgently needed.
68. Calculated from the lists of reprimands and calls to order in J. Seidenberger, *Der parlamentarische Anstand unter dem Reichstagspräsidium des Grafen von Ballestrem nebst parlamentarischem Lexikon* (Cologne, 1903), p. 69 ff.
69. On the obstruction during the tariff debates, and Centre reactions, see folder IX, Ballestrem Papers; Cardauns, *Trimborn*, p. 113; Seidenberger, *Der parlamentarische Anstand*, p. 9 ff.
70. Like the government attempt in 1906 to reduce the quorum of the Reichstag.

See K. Bachem, *Zentrumspartei*, VI, pp. 305–7.

71. On these sharply-divided blocs, see the work of M. Rainer Lepsius, 'Parteiensystem und Sozialstruktur: zum Problem der Demokratisierung der deutschen Gesellschaft', in W. Abel *et al.* (eds.), *Wirtschaft, Geschichte und Wirtschaftsgesichte*. Festschrift zum 65. Geburtstag von Friedrich Lütge (Stuttgart, 1966), pp. 371–93; G. Schmidt, 'Innenpolitische Blockbildungen am Vorabend des Ersten Weltkriegs', *Das Parlament*, 20 (1972), pp. 3–32. The real significance of these rival camps is that they were not simply the artificial by-products of manipulation from above, but had a powerful internal momentum. The respective characters of these 'worlds within worlds' has been studied in the Social Democratic case; and sub-cultures of liberalism, conservatism and Catholicism deserve more attention.

72. D. Blackbourn, 'The Centre Party in Wilhelmine Germany' shows how divorced local Centre politics in the south-west were from the currents of militarism, navalism and Pan-Germanism. Evidence from other parts of the Catholic south and west suggests a similar picture: Kehr, *Schlachtflottenbau*, p. 131 ff; Gottwald, *Zentrum und Imperialismus*, pp. 117–42, 189–202; Möckl, *Die Prinzregentenzeit*, esp. p. 350; K. Bachem, *Zentrumspartei*, V, p. 275 ff. See also G. Eley, 'Defining social imperialism: use and abuse of an idea', *Social History*, 3 (1976), esp. pp. 277–8.

73. Heinrich Mann, *Der Untertan* (first edition, 1918).

74. On this point, see Eley, *Militärgeschichtliche Mitteilungen* (1974).

75. See, particularly, Groh, *Negative Integration und revolutionärer Attentismus*.

8 LIBERALISM AND SOCIETY: THE FEMINIST MOVEMENT AND SOCIAL CHANGE

Richard J. Evans

I

The social history of Wilhelmine Germany is only just beginning to be written; but already the battle-lines between rival interpretations are being drawn. The most recent attempt to analyse Wilhelmine society as a totality, Hans-Ulrich Wehler's *Das deutsche Kaiserreich 1871—1918* (Göttingen, 1973) takes a pessimistic view. It portrays the social structure and political constitution of the German Empire under Bismarck and Wilhelm II as fundamentally illiberal and authoritarian in character. Germany was ruled by an anachronistic power élite composed of feudal aristocrats and big industrialists; their attempts to preserve the social and political *status quo* in the face of the growing demands of new social classes thrown up in the rapid expansion of Germany's industrial economy reduced the political system of the Empire to a state of permanent crisis. The means the élite used to retain power varied from the threat of a military *coup* and the perversion of justice to more subtle strategies such as 'secondary integration' (cementing the élite together by stigmatising groups such as Catholics or Social Democrats as dangerous enemies of state and society), 'social imperialism' (diverting the masses' demand for social emancipation and political reform into nationalist and imperialist enthusiasm), the provision of 'social insurance instead of social reform', and the employment of the Church, the educational system and other social institutions as means of indoctrinating the middle and lower classes into habits of deference and mistrust of democracy. These policies, claims Wehler, were by and large successful. The power élite remained in charge despite the disaster of its foreign policy, the Revolution of 1918 and the advent of the Weimar Republic, to continue its policy of political manipulation through the crisis of 1933, when it brought Hitler into power, up to its final breakdown in the Second World War, when it was finally destroyed after the failure of the July plot of 1944. Already by 1918, the adherence of the bourgeoisie and proletariat to emancipatory ideals and democratic beliefs had been fatally weakened by these strategies of political domination. In both these respects, the German Empire laid the foundations for the Nazi tyranny.[1]

This interpretation has not found universal acceptance. Two of Wehler's recent critics, Thomas Nipperdey and Hans-Günter Zmarzlik, have accused him of painting too black a picture. They argue that Wehler's model of continuity from Bismarck to Hitler is simplistic and one-dimensional. Not only does it ignore the major discontinuities that occurred within the period 1871–1933, it also neglects the alternative, positive continuities which made Wilhelmine Germany in particular something more than a historical one-way street leading straight to the Third Reich. The possibilities of reforming the social and political structure of Wilhelmine Germany, it is argued, are underestimated.[2] Wehler's account misses the significance of the growth and development of the Social Democrats or the liberal revival which took place after the turn of the century. A number of progressive social movements emerged at this period, at the same time as the right-wing pressure-groups on which Wehler concentrates, and, argues Zmarzlik in particular, they constituted a 'movement of renewal . . . which structured the pre-political area of society'. In the long run, according to Zmarzlik, these movements were far more significant than the more immediately successful associations of the far right; and the concept of continuity in German history, he suggests, should be extended beyond the attempt to locate the prehistory of Nazism in Wilhelmine society to embrace a longer-term view. Wilhelmine Germany should be seen as the decisive phase in the prehistory of the post-1945 Federal Republic and the Social Democratic-liberal coalition of the 1970s.[3] Only in this way can full justice be done to every aspect of the historical potentialities inherent in German society under Bismarck and, especially, under Wilhelm II.

It is obviously impossible within the brief compass of a short essay to discuss these arguments in their full range and complexity. What I want to do rather is to test some of them by looking at one aspect of social change that is given particular prominence by Zmarzlik in his critique of Wehler's views: the emancipation of women and the rise of feminism. According to Zmarzlik,

> It was in the *Kaiserreich* that women's position in society, accepted for millennia, became a critically formulated 'woman question' for the first time. Between 1890 and 1914 more than half a million women were organised — with socially important demands, which to some extent have still to be caught up with today. However limited and restricted by their own time the bulk of these women must appear to the retrospective observer, their emergence nevertheless marks a turning-point. . . Before 1870 the only public places

for women were in soup kitchens, charity bazaars and similar charitable positions on the margin of public life. It was in the *Kaiserreich* that women became for the first time an indispensable factor in industrial production and service industries, as workers. And for the 'young ladies' of the middle classes, the way was opened to the educational system, parts of the professions, and finally the party-political scene.[4]

Here is a phenomenon, it is suggested, which gives the lie to Wehler's portrait of Imperial Germany as an illiberal and restrictive society, undermines his contention that 'emancipatory urges' were diverted into imperialist enthusiasm and points forward to the democratisation of German society under the Social Democratic-liberal coalition of the 1970s.

Zmarzlik's citation of the women's movement and the emancipation of the female sex itself implies a considerable revision of our historical perspective on the *Kaiserreich*. For the great majority of German historians, if they pay any attention to the feminist movement at all, regard it as a marginal phenomenon in German history. There are many reasons for this. Most important perhaps has been the long confinement of German historiography to a narrow and exclusive concern with high politics. There has also been a persistent inability on the part of historians of all varieties to link feminist movements and changes in women's status in the past to their historical context. Instead, they have usually treated these subjects in isolation, dealing with them simply in terms of a crude, linear continuity of progress and improvement unrelated to other aspects of historical change (except, in a very general and unreflective way, industrialisation). Finally, knowledge of the radical and advanced nature of the early and middle phases of Wilhelmine feminism was suppressed by the conservative women who wrote the history of the German women's movement from the vantage-point of the Weimar Republic and whose works remained standard right into the 1970s. Despite all this, however, the feminist movement and the 'woman question' did not seem marginal to contemporaries before 1914. Women's emancipation was one of the great social issues of the day; the women's movement was bracketed with the youth movement and the labour movement as one of the major emancipatory trends of the era — or, by extreme conservatives, as one of the greatest and most dangerous threats to the civilisation and social order of their time. Politicians of all varieties, from August Bebel, the Social Democratic leader, whose book, *Woman and Socialism*, was by far the most widely read of all Social Democratic texts, to Kaiser

Wilhelm II himself, who devoted part of a speech delivered in 1910 to warning women to stay clear of feminism and remain at home far from all subversive movements of this kind, paid it far more than mere political lip-service. The prominence of the 'woman question' in all European countries forced politicians to take notice of it; the example of the English suffragettes showed just how explosive an issue it could become. In the longer run, too, the political significance of the feminist movement was indisputable. German women were given the vote in 1918, and throughout the Weimar Republic they constituted by a considerable margin the majority of the German electorate.[5] How the Protestant middle-class women who formed the overwhelming mass of the supporters and members of the women's movement used their voting power after 1918 was thus a matter of some importance; and they cannot but have been affected in their views on society and politics at least to some degree by the feminist movement, whether they belonged to it or not. For all these reasons, therefore, the feminist movement lends itself well as a yardstick for measuring the persuasiveness and utility of the rival theories of continuity advanced by Wehler and Zmarzlik.

II

There were a number of women's organisations in Germany in the 1870s and 1880s, chief of them the General German Women's Association (*Allgemeiner Deutscher Frauenverein*), numbering about 12,000 members. But all of them were mainly charitable in orientation, steered well clear of politics, and entered the public arena only to petition cautiously for the admission of women to the medical profession and the improvement of girls' education. Both these demands were based on the desire to defend the femininity of middle-class women, which (it was argued) was misunderstood by male physicians and distorted by male-oriented education.[6] In 1894, however, the women's movement took on a new lease of life, with the foundation of the Federation of German Women's Associations (*Bund Deutscher Frauenvereine*, or BDF). Initially, under the leadership of the General German Women's Association, the BDF aimed simply to coordinate women's welfare work, gathering under its aegis some 70,000 members and 137 associations by 1901, and claiming a total membership of half a million by 1914.[7] But after the death or retirement of the founding generation of BDF leaders around the turn of the century, a new generation, headed by Marie Stritt (1856–1928), perhaps the most important German feminist of the Wilhelmine period, took the BDF rapidly towards a more clearly defined feminist stance. In 1902 the BDF

officially endorsed the principle of votes for women, and (in a hotly
contested reversal of policies pursued since 1894) condemned the police
regulation of prostitutes, which international feminism had long opposed
as giving official sanction to sexual immorality on the part of men while
condemning and punishing it in women.[8] In 1907 the BDF, overcoming
the objections of its more conservative members, who thought that it
should not venture on to such controversial terrain, issued a lengthy
declaration of the 'principles and demands of the women's movement',
to which all member associations were supposed to subscribe. These
demands included full legal equality for women within marriage, the
reform of the bastardy law to include legal responsibility of the father
for the support of his illegitimate child and its mother, equal education
for girls, including full co-education at secondary level, equal pay for
equal work, equal status in all professions including the civil service and
the law, and the right to vote and stand for election for all representative
bodies up to and including the Reichstag.[9] Finally, at its General
Assembly in 1908, the BDF devoted most of its energies to debating a
proposal by its Legal Commission that it should campaign for the repeal
of paragraph 218 of the Criminal Law Code and for the legalisation of
abortion which this would entail.[10]

Up to this point, then, the development of the German feminist
movement seems to support Zmarzlik's view that it formed an example
of the beginning of a *progressive* continuity in German history. Yet this
is by no means the whole story. For after 1908 this process of
historical change went into reverse. The proposal to support the
legalisation of abortion was rejected by the BDF General Assembly in
1908, and the proponents of sexual liberation were effectively excluded
from the movement.[11] A series of behind-the-scenes manoeuvres within
the BDF's executive committee brought about the resignation of the
BDF President Marie Stritt, whom the bulk of committee members now
found 'one-sidedly radical', in 1910.[12] She was replaced by Gertrud
Bäumer (1873–1954), under whose leadership the movement abandoned
the idea of the equality of the sexes and adopted the view that women
were fundamentally different in character and abilities from men.
Rather than compete with men, it was now argued, women should simply
seek out the 'female sphere' in life and develop their 'specifically female
qualities' there. This doctrine, propounded on innumerable occasions by
BDF leaders after 1908, and ultimately enshrined in the organisation's
revised programme of 1919, registered the abandonment by the feminist
movement of any attempt to carve out new roles for the German woman
outside her traditional sphere of the home and its extension into public

life via social welfare activities. 'If she limits herself to house and family', wrote Gertrud Bäumer, 'she is under certain circumstances acting in this way more in accordance with the ideals of the women's movement than if she goes into any male profession.'[13] The movement's retreat from the emancipatory tenets of feminism was sealed by its adoption of an increasingly authoritarian Social Darwinist ideology, its commitment to 'racial hygiene' and 'population policy' (*Bevolkerungspolitik*), and its support of attempts to stop the decline in the German birth-rate, which it came to see as a danger to the long-term future of the German race.[14] Discussion of these matters was suppressed within the BDF; the General Assembly ceased to be a forum for democratic debate and became instead a passive audience for edifying speeches.[15] Finally, the radical wing of the feminist movement, which had made all the running in the years up to 1908, underwent a process of rapid decline and disintegration from 1908 to 1914. The female suffrage movement, which stood to the left of the left-wing Liberal political parties up to 1908, opposing for example their participation in the governmental Reichstag coalition known as the Bülow Block and lending their full support to the principle of universal suffrage at all levels of the constitution, was by 1914 split into three different factions, the two largest of which were associated with the Left-Liberal and National Liberal Parties and supported merely *equal* suffrage for women, thus accepting the existence of property franchises in Prussia and other German states.[16] A similar process of collapse occurred in the sexual liberation movement, the *Bund für Mutterschutz* in the period 1908–1914, as it broke up into mutually hostile groups, shifted ideologically away from liberal individualism and was abandoned by the most influential of its supporters, both within the women's movement and without.[17]

Here we have, then, a liberal movement of social emancipation which before 1908 certainly came close to advancing demands that are still controversial today, and which mobilised large numbers of previously politically inactive people and drew them into the political system, preparing them for the advent of democracy in the Weimar Republic. At the same time, it is clear that an assessment of the feminist movement — such as Zmarzlik's — which went no further than this would be very partial indeed, just as partial in fact as an account of Wilhelmine society — such as Wehler's — which ignored the emergence of liberal reform movements altogether. It is evident from the foregoing brief sketch that the feminist movement abandoned liberalism, at least in the generally understood sense of the word, after 1908. The search for the causes of this abandonment brings us to the heart of the current debate about the nature of Wilhelmine society. Many historians have tried to explain the weakness of liberalism among the German middle classes; and in the feminist movement's shift to the right we have an example of middle-class abandonment of an emancipatory ideology which may serve as a means of putting some of these historical generalisations to the test.

The most widely accepted of these explanations has been the theory of 'social imperialism', that is (in its current usage among German historians) the idea that German governments and conservative politicians diverted the reformist impulses of the middle classes into nationalist and imperialist enthusiasm. How far does the case of the feminist movement bear this out?[18] At first sight, it seems to provide an almost ideal illustration. The movement's swing to the right was accompanied by a growth of nationalist sentiment among its leaders and members. Gertrud Bäumer, who became BDF President in 1910, declared liberal opposition to imperialism 'outmoded' and argued that 'military power is . . . simply a necessity of national self-preservation'. Under her leadership the BDF supported the development of German 'national identity' (*Volkstum*), opposed what she called 'cosmopolitan aims and international policies' and became very reluctant to cooperate with the International Council of Women in its efforts to develop a common policy for the preservation of peace.[19] The 'radical' feminists who dominated the BDF up to 1908, including Bäumer's predecessor Marie Stritt, were by contrast, to a greater or lesser degree, supporters of the pacifist movement.[20] The adoption of Social Darwinist ideas by the feminist movement after 1908, and its growing obsession with 'racial purity' and the birth-rate, can be seen as further evidence of a conversion to the nationalist and imperialist creed. These ideas certainly played a role in persuading the BDF General Assembly to reject the legalisation of abortion. Finally, there was no shortage of anti-feminist propagandists on the far right to accuse the women's movement of being an internationalist, pacifist conspiracy to subvert the German family and thereby destroy the German race. Such accusations — raised by pan-Germans, *völkisch* nationalists and other right-wing extremists — undoubtedly had an effect on the feminist movement, forcing it to defend itself by asserting its commitment to family, nation and race.[21]

Yet the theory that the liberalism of the middle-class women who formed the feminist movement was the victim of a classic 'social imperialist' strategy, diverting its emancipatory impulses into nationalist enthusiasm, will not really stand up to close examination. In the first place, direct social imperialist pressure on the feminist movement did not really amount to very much until the formation of the German League for the Prevention of the Emancipation of Women (*Deutscher Bund zur Bekämpfung der Frauenemanzipation*) by right-wing nationalists (including August Keim, Dietrich Schäfer, Ludwig Schemann and Otto Schmidt-Gibichenfels) in 1912. By this time, the feminist movement was already firmly committed to nationalism and in full retreat from liberal values and liberal policies, a process that had begun some four years previously.[22] Secondly, though Social Darwinism certainly played a role in the movement's rejection of legal abortion and sexual emancipation, and encouraged a collectivist rather than an individualist attitude to politics, the main influence here was, in fact, religious, the main opposition from the German-evangelical Women's League and from women (such as Gertrud Bäumer) associated with the Evangelical-Social Congress. In any case, Social Darwinism itself, despite its ideas about the 'survival of the fittest' and the 'struggle for existence' could be a strongly reformist doctrine, encouraging the 'improvement of the race' through the provision of better housing, better medical care and better social welfare. In fact, nationalism was really given a place in the women's movement by disciples of the influential liberal politician and theorist Friedrich Naumann, who explicitly linked imperialism with social reform, arguing that the two were mutually interdependent, rather than offering Empire as an alternative to reform. Getrud Bäumer herself was a close collaborator of Naumann's and worked with him in the editorship of his magazine *Die Hilfe*. Nationalism as such, however, played no real part in the internal disputes of the women's movement until the First World War.[23] And most important of all, there were other significant, indeed decisive reasons for the movement's abandonment of liberalism which had nothing at all to do with social imperialism as it is conventionally understood by historians of Wilhelmine Gemany.

It was not by chance that 1908 formed the watershed between the liberal and illiberal phases of German feminism's historical development. For it was on 15 May of that year that the single most significant legislative improvement in the position of women to be enacted in Wilhelmine Germany came into force: the Imperial Law of Association (*Reichsvereinsgesetz*), which replaced a variety of local laws existing previously.[24] Under these local laws, women in most parts of Germany (including Prussia) were forbidden by law from joining political associations or attending political meetings. These laws, which were mainly used by the police as a pretext for dissolving Social Democratic

meetings where women were present, but were also on occasion used
against the feminist movement itself, acted as a powerful deterrent to
the great mass of law-abiding middle-class women from participating in
the less charitable and more political organisations of the women's
movement.[25] The principal sufferer was the women's suffrage movement,
which in 1908, six years after its foundation, still had less than 2,500
members;[26] but the BDF itself, whose 1907 programme was undeniably
political and whose General Assemblies from 1902 onwards always included debate on political subjects, was also affected; in early 1908 it
probably comprised little more than 100,000 women all told — a considerable number, but, as the next few years were to show, far below
the number of women the organisation was potentially capable of
reaching.[27] The new Imperial Law of Association changed all this. It
made female participation in politics possible all over the Empire, above
all in Prussia. Membership in women's associations no longer carried
the stigma of illegality. Consequently the floodgates were opened and
large numbers of more conservative women streamed in. The German-
evangelical Women's League, 8,000 strong in 1908, with close ties to
the Conservative Party, joined the BDF in September 1908. Its first
act was to use its massive voting strength (50 votes) to help defeat the
proposal to legalise abortion at the BDF General Assembly the
following month, and to frustrate a reorganisation of the BDF which
would have had the effect of giving the radical feminists more voting
power. Under its leader Paula Müller, who later sat in the Reichstag
during the Weimar Republic as a deputy for the right-wing German-
national People's Party (the DNVP), it opposed female suffrage outright and played a major part in weakening the BDF's commitment to
votes for women.[28] By 1914 the entry of many other right-wing groups
into the BDF, including the German Women's League (*Deutscher
Frauenbund*), which began life as the women's section of the Imperial
League Against Social Democracy,[29] had increased the BDF's size
enormously; from uniting perhaps 120,000 women in 1910 it grew so
fast that by 1914 its total female membership was probably not far
short of a quarter of a million.[30]

The female suffrage movement was also swollen to an unprecedented
size with the entry of more conservative women into its ranks after
1908; from a total membership of 2,500 in 1908 it grew to a membership of at least 14,000 in 1914.[31] Before 1908 the suffragists had been
on the extreme left of left-wing Liberalism. Many of their leaders were
associated with the Democratic Alliance (*Demokratische Vereinigung*), a
radical splinter-group which broke away from the Bülow Block liberals

in that year.[32] But by 1914 the bulk of the suffragists were associated
rather with the mainstream Left-Liberals (the Progressives), and not a few
owed their allegiance to the National Liberals, who were even further
to the right. The Progressives were lukewarm about women's suffrage;
the National Liberals indeed were actively hostile to the idea.[33] In this
case, then, as with that of the BDF as a whole, expansion of membership,
in the case of the BDF growth into a mass movement, was the major
development underlying the retreat of liberalism. The women's movement proved unable to combine liberal ideology with mass support. The
terms on which the great mass of the middle-class women who joined
the BDF in the Wilhelmine period entered the public arena thus had
little to do either with liberalism or with women's emancipation. They
had little to do either with what were to become the demands of the
Women's Liberation Movement in the 1960s and 1970s. Nor did they
relate in any obvious way to the real problems faced by women in post-
1945 Germany and the society presided over by the Social Democratic-
liberal coalition of 1969. The feminist ideas and demands of which
these statements could − at least to a limited degree − be made, had
ceased to be the creed of the women's movement in Germany by the
time that it came to have mass appeal.

The catalyst for the feminist movement's abandonment of liberalism
was thus provided not by the diversionary tactic of social imperialism,
but by the emancipatory reform of 1908, the Imperial Law of
Association, which allowed women to take part in politics without fear
of legal reprisal. Other reforms came to fruition in 1908 as well; in that
year in particular Prussia admitted women to its universities as full-
time students − the last of the German states to do so − and
promulgated an important educational reform establishing a system of
State secondary education for girls. Already by the turn of the century,
indeed, women had been admitted to the medical profession. And
since the mid-1890s, the feminist movement, previously ridiculed or
ignored, had found increasing acceptance in public life.[34] While this
series of reforms failed to bring the status of German women up to
that of women in America or the Scandinavian countries, where for
the most part reforms such as these had long since taken place, they
did mark a significant advance over the situation of German women
in the 1890s.[35] Moreover, political parties, which had previously
ignored the German feminist movement altogether, now felt increasingly
constrained to incorporate at least some of its demands into their
programmes. This was the case above all with the left-wing Liberals, but
other parties too felt obliged to voice their concern for women's

welfare, even if they explicitly rejected the majority of the feminists' demands.[36] By the mid-1900s, too, most newspapers in the centre and on the left of the political spectrum ran a regular column on the feminist movement and employed special women correspondents to write it. In 1901 the radical feminist leader Minna Cauer noted the changing attitude of the press with some satisfaction, if also with a certain amount of cynicism:

> A decade ago, every woman who supported the entry of women into the universities was 'emancipated' . . . About five years ago, even women who called themselves friends and acquaintances of the women's movement prophesied its downfall as middle-class women called popular assemblies in which statements were made on current affairs. Today, at least in the capital city, people are immediately dissatisfied and accuse the leaders of the women's movement of forgetting their duty if they do not take a public stand on notable events.[37]

The growing public acceptance of women's role in national life was marked not only by reforms such as that of the Law of Association in 1908 — which encountered virtually no opposition in this respect[38] — but also by the increasing concern even on the part of those who opposed female emancipation that women should enter public life on the right terms. It was for this reason that the Conservative Party tolerated the formation of an 'Alliance of Conservative Women' in 1911,[39] that right-wing groups including the *nationale Verbände* formed women's sections, some of them dating back to the early 1900s,[40] and finally that right-wing politicians joined in 1912 to form the German League for the Prevention of the Emancipation of Women in order to mobilise *women* against the feminist movement, to show that the female sex in Germany did not want to be emancipated.[41] Similarly, the conservative women who mobilised themselves and entered public life after the reform of the Law of Association in 1908 did so explicitly in order to counter the influence of radical feminists. As Paula Müller remarked, writing to the local branches of the German-evangelical Women's League on the advantages of joining the BDF in 1908, if the League did enter the BDF, 'we would, together with the moderate party, far outweigh the radical and progressive elements; indeed, we would have a great majority over them'.[42]

III

Changes such as those which took place within the feminist movement can in fact only be fully understood by looking at the changes which were taking place in the social position of the women of the middle classes who formed the movement's social constituency. For behind the numerical growth and political development of the feminist movement in the Wilhelmine period lay important changes in the social and economic position of middle-class women, changes which themselves reflected the transition of Germany to a mature industrial society in these years. The spread of girls' education in the 1870s and 1880s, the growth of an adequate system of secondary schools for girls from the 1890s and finally the opening of the universities to women as full-time matriculated students from 1902 (Baden) to 1908 (Prussia) — all this provided the basis for a rapidly expanding female petty-bourgeois intelligentsia, most of whom found employment in the teaching profession. In Prussia, for instance, the number of women teachers doubled between 1861 and 1896, rising from 7,366 to 14,600.[43] Women teachers' pay was much lower than that of their male colleagues doing the same work, the conditions of employment were highly restrictive (they had to remain single, for example, or resign on marriage), their numbers were limited by law, especially in the 'scientific' subjects, their qualifications did not have to come up to the standard required of male teachers, and the higher teaching posts were barred to them not only *de facto* but also *de jure*. In the Prussian reform of girls' education which came into effect in 1908, it was ruled that at least a third of the science teaching in girls' secondary schools had to be done by men, and no woman was to be appointed to the headship of a girls' school. Women teachers in boys' schools were unheard-of, and co-education was dismissed in Prussia as immoral. In general, too, women schoolteachers came from a higher social background than that of their male colleagues; for the daughters of academics, lawyers, officers and professionals, teaching was a means of maintaining social status without marrying; for the sons of artisans, shopkeepers, primary school teachers and white-collar employees it was a means of social advancement. This social gap gave an added sharpness to the conflict between male and female teachers. It was commonly agreed that a numerically significant body of support for the German League for the Prevention of the Emancipation of Women came from schoolteachers, above all *Oberlehrer*, fearful of female competition. It was not surprising, then, that women schoolteachers, intellectually aware, economically independent, but neither socially nor economically nor politically equal with their male colleagues, provided the largest, most vocal and most active body of support for feminism in Germany in the late 1890s and early 1900s.[44] Many leading feminists began as school-teachers or spent some of their time teaching in a variety of institutions. Contemporaries noted that women teachers formed the mainstay of active support for the feminist movement in Wilhelmine Germany. 'The most important and reliable troops in the federal army', remarked one anti-feminist tract in discussing the composition of the BDF, 'are the women teachers' associations'.[45]

This assessment can be supported by the evidence of a list of the 82 members of the German Union for Women's Suffrage, Hamburg branch, which was submitted in the second year of its existence (1904) to the police.[46] It shows that six of the members were men (one medical specialist, two factory owners, a pastor, a merchant and a stockbroker), 28 of the women were housewives (most probably married to men active in Left-Liberal politics) and 48 of the women were single. Of these latter, two lived off private incomes, four lived at home with their parents, and ten lived in the suburb of Altona, which came under Prussian jurisdiction, and so were not investigated. No less than thirteen were schoolteachers; four were accounts clerks, two were shopkeepers, and there was also a nurse, a painter, a receptionist, a dress-maker, a commercial student and a factory inspector's assistant. The predominance of schoolteachers among unmarried members is clear. Apart from the housewives and the schoolteachers, the main occupational group was drawn from the ranks of women white-collar workers, whose numbers were also expanding with unprecedented rapidity at this time. Like the schoolmistresses, the female salaried employees had formed their own professional association in 1889, and leading radical feminists such as Minna Cauer and Lida Gustava Heymann were active in organising it on both a local and a national scale. The problems of this group of women — unequal pay and prospects compared with those of male colleagues, poor working conditions, restricted opportunities — were similar to the schoolmistresses', and the feminist movement profited from this in a similar way.[47] These two petty-bourgeois groups formed the basis for the new wave of radical feminism which revivified the German women's movement from the mid-1890s until the passage of the Imperial Law of Association in 1908.

The expansion of German feminism into a mass movement which followed on the passage of this legislative enactment was achieved primarily through the recruitment of married women. While there was a high proportion of unmarried women in radical feminist organisations such as the German Union for Women's Suffrage, as we have seen, the picture in 'moderate' and conservative women's organisations was very different. Here the great majority of members and local officials tended to be married women, though the full-time leaders and organisers were generally not; obviously, running a household and family usually prevented married women from involving themselves in political and organisational life full-time. Moreover, after 1908 the social base of the feminist movement was diversified by the mobilisation of the wives of civil servants, naval officers, industrialists, academics and other local dignitaries. The women's movement ceased to be a movement of the unmarried female petty-bourgeois salaried employee and became a wider movement, embracing the consumer interests of housewives and the social and political aspirations and concerns of the middle and upper ranks of the industrial and professional bourgeoisie, even indeed on occasion the aristocracy, the armed forces and the bureaucracy.[48] Within the rather narrower confines of the female suffrage movement, the mobilisation of women from the industrial, commercial and managerial bourgeoisie of Silesia and the Rhineland — Germany's two major areas of heavy industry, where new groups were formed in 1909–11 — introduced a disruptive element, for it was precisely in these areas that opposition to universal suffrage within the female suffrage movement originated, and that the foundation of the right-wing breakaway German Alliance for Women's Suffrage (*Deutsche Vereinigung für Frauenstimmrecht*) was begun.[49]

The disintegrative effects of this were more than evident both in the break-up of the suffrage movement after 1908 and in the deep divisions and fierce controversies that threatened to split the BDF itself at the General Assembly of the same year. On numerous occasions after 1908, too, the German-evangelical Women's League, perhaps the most important of the new 'Establishment' groups that joined the BDF after the passage of the Imperial Law of Association, launched strong attacks on BDF policy, above all on its support for female suffrage; it came close to leaving the BDF altogether over this issue in 1912.[50] In these circumstances, unity could only be achieved — as it was in 1908 over the abortion issue, in 1912 over the suffrage question, and ultimately in 1911–16 within the female suffrage movement itself over the question of a property franchise — by a substantial shift to the right, masked by an increasing vagueness and fuzziness of aims and ideas and accompanied by the *de facto* abandonment of many of the movement's more radical goals. Already by 1912, the BDF had in practice declared its allegiance to the idea that became its official guiding principle in the subsequent revised programme of 1919: that women's task was to heal social divisions and unite the German nation in a national racial community (*Volksgemeinschaft*) above party and class. Clearly this was an attempt to bridge the social differences that were threatening to split the BDF. Equally clearly, however, it also marked a significant shift away from commitment to parliamentary and party-political means of regulating social conflict.

On a more general level, these developments also reflected the growing social antagonism between the bourgeoisie and the working classes. From a middle-class point of view, the problem with the demands advanced by the radical feminists was that the only political party to back them all was the SPD. Some of them, too, such as universal suffrage, equal pay for equal work, co-education or equal rights for women within marriage, were felt by more conservative middle-class women to be playing directly into the hands of the Social Democracy by spreading egalitarianism through society, removing property qualifications for the vote or undermining the stability of the authoritarian family.[51] Moreover, the Social Democrats themselves had a large, active and (also after 1908) rapidly growing women's movement of their own, which consistently refused to cooperate with the bourgeois feminists and showed itself unremittingly hostile to middle-class liberalism while supporting most of the radical feminists' own demands.[52] It was in fact often difficult for outsiders to distinguish between the Social Democratic and radical feminist line on a number of important aspects of the 'woman question', all the more so in the years (c.1896–1907) when the radical feminists were actively – though unsuccessfully – trying to recruit working-class women, issuing a stream of demands and petitions aimed at improving the lot of the woman factory worker, and giving active financial and moral support to strikes such as those of the women textile workers in Crimmitschau (1906).[53] As the SPD itself grew in size, and hostility to it on the right increased, middle-class women felt it increasingly important to distinguish their brand of feminism from the Social Democrats'. One opponent of universal suffrage within the German Union for Women's Suffrage remarked in 1912: 'What use is flirting with Social Democracy, what use is the fearful avoidance of an apparent "withdrawal" from the working-class women's movement, if this movement always declares that a deep gulf divides it from all bourgeois women?'.[54] More generally, they argued, it was dangerous for the feminists to align themselves with the Social Democrats in opposing the Wilhelmine State. Instead, they should seek integration in it, to stabilise it against the growing threat of social revolution which they perceived in the rise of Social Democracy and the spread of labour unrest.[55] Such integration appeared all the more profitable in view of the reforms granted by the State to women in the expansion of girls' secondary and tertiary education, the opening of the medical profession and the passing of the Law of Association.

By 1914, the women's movement had become integrated into the social and political fabric of Wilhelmine Germany in many ways. It was taking a full part in political life. Its Congresses and Assemblies were patronised by local mayors, officials and dignitaries. It contained many individuals, groups and organisations closely associated with the political and social Establishment. Most important of all, perhaps, it was being consulted by the government on questions of education and social welfare. Many of its members were active in local government institutions dealing with these subjects, and by 1914 the BDF was coming to be regarded by Imperial and local administration as the representative of these women. As Gertrud Bäumer remarked in 1913, 'the State has come nearer to women, has become more alive and comprehensible to them'.[56] This process culminated in the government's request to the BDF to organise welfare services for women on the outbreak of war in 1914.[57] Integration in this sense amounted to far more than a mere response to any deliberate or unconscious manipulative strategy on the part of the authorities. It formed part of a general process that had been at work in Wilhelmine politics since the early 1890s — the extension of the political nation from small elites of local notables (*Honoratioren*) to encompass the entire population — the entry of the masses on to the political scene.

One of the influences prompting this development — which in its widest sense was the consequence of Germany's transition to industrial maturity — was the increasing intervention of the State in the everyday life of the people. As far as women were concerned, this manifested itself in growing government and administrative regulation of labour opportunities and conditions, education, food, health and drug legislation, and many other government enactments through which the State, as it were, entered the home. This was a major influence in politicising women and bringing them into the public arena through their participation in local health economic, welfare and education boards, the formation of Housewives' Associations and the increased interest of all kinds of women's groups in questions of this sort. It also encouraged women to enter public life as defenders of the 'women's sphere' and representatives of specifically female interests, rather than as crusaders for individual freedoms and equal rights with men in every walk of life.[58] As the women's movement came to an increasing extent after 1908 to represent the interests of married women and housewives as well as those of unmarried women, teachers, white-collar workers and professionals, so it shifted away from demanding equal rights on the basis of the freedom of the individual woman and her equality with man, towards an acceptance of women's role in society and an attempt to defend the interests of women within the confines of this role. This development was hastened by the tendency of the professional associations of women white-collar workers and schoolteachers to take support away from radical feminist associations as they grew in size, became more effective in protecting their members' interests and adopted an increasingly 'unpolitical' and trade-union orientation which took them in the end right out of the feminist movement altogether. The General German Women Teachers' Association (*Allgemeiner Deutscher Lehrerinnenverein*), which had enjoyed the closest ties with the feminist movement in the 1890s and early 1900s, sharing in effect the same leadership, had by 1914 narrowed its horizons to encompass only questions directly affecting the position of women teachers; and in 1907 the Commercial Union of Female Salaried Employees (*Kaufmännischer Verband weiblicher Angestellten*), founded and controlled for many years by leading radical feminists such as Minna Cauer and Lida Gustava Heymann, voted to sever its ties with the women's movement and to adopt a purely trade-union orientation. This development was not unconnected with the growth of Social Democratic attempts to unionise women white-collar workers. It undermined the position of radical feminism within the women's movement as the social groups which had been the mainstay of its support began to see in professional and trade-union organisations a more effective means of representing their interests than the feminist movement had been able to provide.[59]

What the feminist movement was doing in the years 1908–14 was in essence adjusting its strategy for the defence of bourgeois social institutions which it had criticised in its radical phase. Radical feminism meant, for example, the criticism of existing family institutions. In 1896 the BDF had launched a massive campaign against the family law clauses of the Civil Code (*Bürgerliches Gesetzbuch*) then being debated in the Reichstag.[60] In 1902 by attacking the State regulation of prostitution it had aligned itself with Social Democratic allegations – above all, with those made by the SPD leader August Bebel in his widely-read book *Woman and Socialism* – that the bourgeois family was a hypocritical sham whose economic and contractual basis provided the major reason for the spread of prostitution in the late-nineteenth century.[61] In 1905–6 the ideas of the radical feminist Helene Stöcker gained increasing currency in the radical wing of the feminist movement; Stöcker supported equal rights for unmarried mothers and illegitimate children, argued against 'traditional clerical-ascetic moral teaching' and propounded a 'modern, individualist, scientific moral teaching' which she called the New Morality and which led her (among other things) to demand legal recognition of 'free marriages', the public distribution of contraceptives and the legalisation of abortion.[62] In a more general way, the feminists' concentration on demanding more opportunities for women in public and professional life implied that their role in the family was second-best to an active personal career. Women's emancipation meant to a considerable degree their emancipation from the family. After 1908 the BDF repudiated this individualist attack on the bourgeois family and affirmed its commitment to existing family institutions. It condemned extra-marital sexuality, opposed the legalisation of abortion and the public availability of contraceptives, and launched a fierce attack on the ideas of Stöcker and her associates. Similarly, as we have seen, after 1908 the suffrage movement withdrew from its alignment with the SPD in demanding universal suffrage and came round to the defence of existing property franchises.[63]

These changes did not signify a simple reversion to the acceptance of the status quo. On the contrary, the BDF continued to campaign for reforms. After 1908, the reforms it wanted no longer aimed at the legitimation of bourgeois social institutions through democratising them (as, for example, in Stöcker's plea that her ideas sought to create a 'higher form of marriage' in which husband and wife would be equal in every way).[64] They aimed instead at legitimising them by extending their existing functions, by enabling them to do more of the things they were doing already. Thus the bourgeois family was to produce more children, to receive more support from the State, to gain more moral authority (through the suppression of extra-marital sexuality), to have a wider appeal to women who at present stayed unmarried, and finally to have more 'racial value' through the barring of marriage to alcoholics, the mentally ill, the physically handicapped, the hereditarily diseased or the 'racially inferior'.[65] Similarly, the property franchise (which in many parts of Germany, above all in Prussia, was the main political institution preserving the parliamentary strength not only of Conservatives but also of liberal and middle-class parties and keeping the Social Democrats from power) was to be strengthened by extending it, not vertically, down the social scale, but laterally, across it, to the women of the propertied classes, thus further reducing the relative voting strength of the Social Democrats.[66] One implication of this, of course, was the reform of the Civil Code of 1900 to allow women to control their own property within marriage and so enable them to fulfil voting qualifications. The BDF, then, was still committed to the reform of the social and political institutions of Wilhelmine Germany. It did not accept the *status quo*. On the contrary, it was still dissatisfied with many aspects of Wilhelmine society — the declining birth-rate, the official sanctioning of immorality in the State regulation of prostitution, the legal barriers to married women's possession of property, and so on — as with many other features of the Wilhelmine social and political system, above all of course the restriction of voting rights to men. It was not least in the hope of securing reforms such as these that the BDF committed itself to full support of Germany's efforts in the First World War and to the organisation of welfare services under official auspices. When the opportunity eventually presented itself in 1917—18, the BDF was not slow in presenting its own demands for the 'political-social transformation' of Germany in the post-war era.[67] To what extent these demands were actually met is of course another matter; certainly, without the Revolution of 1918—19, it is unlikely that many of the BDF's demands would have been ful-filled, and altogether implausible to suppose that the most controversial of the women's movement's proposals, the enfranchisement of women, would have met with any more approval than it did up to the end of October 1918.[68]

IV

The example of the feminist movement, then, underlines the inadequacy of conventional interpretations of liberalism in Wilhelmine Germany. To approach liberal or middle-class groups in Wilhelmine society merely under the aspect of their contribution to a negative continuity leading to the triumph of Hitler in 1933, or a positive one leading to the advent of the Social Democratic and liberal coalition government in 1969, necessarily does major violence to the complex dynamics of their historical development. Both theories of continuity bring with them a selective approach which distorts the reality of Wilhelmine society. Above all, perhaps, they involve a simplistic theory of the relationship between politics and society which reads back social developments from political ones in an unreflective way, and infers general characteristics of social classes from the characteristics of political organisations which are assumed to represent them. Because the feminist movement (it is argued, for example) was progressive, therefore it arose out of social developments – the involvement of women in economic and public life – that were also progressive. Alternatively, because many right-wing extremist political groups drew their members from the *Mittelstand*, it is assumed that the *Mittelstand* – or the petty-bourgeoisie – possessed uniformly reactionary political views.[69] Yet as we have seen it was women's involvement in the petty-bourgeois occupations of primary school teaching and white-collar work that provided the social basis for the radicalisation of the feminist movement around the turn of the century.

The models of continuity advanced by Wehler and Zmarzlik in fact break down at several points when applied to the feminist movement. It is certainly clear that the feminists' move to the right after 1908 constituted a significant step along a road which would lead them to a qualified acceptance of Nazi rule in 1933.[70] But it was only a step. Other events, such as the Revolution of 1918, the inflation of 1923 and the economic and political crises of 1929–33, had to occur before the potential susceptibility to the appeal of fascism created after 1908 could be actualised.[71] Although the allegation that Hitler was carried to power by the votes of women is a myth,[72] it is undeniable that the feminist movement did nothing to educate the Protestant middle-class women who formed its constituency to support democracy and develop a critical attitude towards fascist ideology. By 1930 most of them were probably voting for the Nazis.[73] Yet to present this as the result of political seduction by manipulative pre-industrial élites is highly misleading.

Three distinct arguments are in fact involved here. The first of them concerns the idea of manipulation. Although it has been argued that the attention of the middle classes were diverted away from emancipation and reform by 'social imperialism' or repressed through the technique of 'negative integration' and other varieties of social control, this involves, as we have seen, an implied contradiction between eman-cipation and reform on the one hand, and social control, national enthusiasm and political integration on the other, which is simply not applicable in the case of the feminist movement. The major factor in precipitating the feminists' move to the right was a *reform*, the Law of Association of 1908, which was genuinely emancipatory and integrative. It admitted into the feminist movement the kind of 'Establishment' women who were opposed to female emancipation in every country, for the wives of military and naval officers, civil servants, and other notables, were no more likely to embrace the feminist cause in Britain or America than they were in Wihlemine Germany.[74] It was after the admittance of these women that the feminist movement became nationalistic, not before, a development which in no way stopped it agitating for political and social reform, though it changed the nature of the reforms for which it agitated and the reasons it gave for wanting them. In addition to this, as we have seen, there were social changes taking place both in the situation of housewives and in the position of middle-class working women which provided an additional impulse for the feminists' retreat from the radical ideas of the liberal individualists. Even if it were correct to see the development of the feminist movement in the Wilhelmine period in terms of a continuity leading directly to 1933, therefore, the continuity involved would not be one of political manipulation.

Secondly, the manipulative model of continuity also implies that the middle classes were potentially capable of espousing emancipatory ideologies, indeed that in the normal course of events they were almost bound to do so, had they not been diverted towards authoritarian ones instead. The problem here is to demonstrate the existence of such a 'normal course of events'. The usual solution has been to point to other industrialising countries – notably the United States – and show that in these countries the middle classes did espouse emancipatory ideologies. This is far from easy to establish in the case of women's emancipation however. In all countries, the feminists were a small minority even among the women of the educated middle classes; and the German women's movement, far from being insignificant by international standards, was by the outbreak of the First World War the third largest in the world, after Britain and America. Numerical contrasts appear only when we look at female suffrage movements. The German suffragists, 2,500 strong in 1908, rose to 14,000 in 1914, but by that time they were divided into three mutually hostile factions. By contrast, the National American Woman Suffrage Society, 17,000 strong in 1905, reached 75,000 by 1910 and 100,000 in 1915. However, it would be wrong to leap to the conclusion that these figures demonstrate that American women had in some way fulfilled their potential for emancipation while German women had not. The expansion of the American female suffrage movement only occurred because the movement abandoned liberal individualism, rather as German feminism was doing at the same time, and directed its appeal consciously towards white Anglo-Saxon Protestant women who wanted enfranchisement to counter the influence of the growing numbers of male immigrant and black voters — indeed, the American feminists began explicitly arguing for the disfranchisement of these two groups. The increasing appeal of feminism was thus linked with the increasing racism and anti-democratic tendencies of the movement. The parallel with the German case was striking.[75]

Finally, what lies at the root of the models of continuity employed by both Wehler and Zmarzlik is the concept of modernisation: the difference between the two models can in fact be simply expressed by saying that while Wehler believes that Germany's modernisation was retarded (above all through the manipulations of the 'pre-modern' élites), Zmarzlik argues that there were important instances of modernisation taking place in Wilhelmine Germany which Wehler has overlooked (including the rise of feminism). More precisely, both would probably agree that modernisation was taking place in the economy but not in the political system; the dispute arises in the crucial area in between, in the structure of society. It is for this reason (among many others) that these historians have turned to social history rather than political or economic history for solutions to the problem of the pre-history of Nazism. Yet once more, neither argument is really applicable in the case of feminism and female emancipation. Leaving aside for the moment the many problems associated with the concepts of 'modernisation' and 'modernity',[76] it is clear that both models of continuity involve an equation of these concepts with the idea of emancipation. Of the two phases of the feminist movement discussed in the present essay, however, it is indisputable that the latter was the more 'modern'. The liberal individualist plea for equal rights for woman as a free and independent personality was a characteristic not of feminist movements in general, but only of a phase in their development. In Germany as in America this phase ended with the transition of society to industrial maturity. Feminists such as Gertrud Bäumer explicitly argued, like her contemporaries in the United States, that individualist concepts of equal rights were outmoded; what was really modern was a situation in which women did not try to establish their independence from the family, but rather built upon the role they played in family life, dignified it, secured the support of the state for it, and in turn used this role as a base from which to extend a 'motherly' influence over society.[77] These ideas were an initial theorisation of an important part of what later came to be dubbed by its critics as the 'feminine mystique', which was to reach its apogee in the countries of the Western industrial world in the 1950s.[78] Both the women who dominated the German feminist movement in its more radical period before 1908, and the more conservative women who flocked into the movement in the last six years before the outbreak of the First World War, had moved towards a more 'modern' position in endorsing this view. As in America, this turning away from individualism towards collectivism signified that society had entered the era of advanced capitalism, in which pre-industrial elites and 'pre-modern' modes of thought were declining in influence, In this more general sense, then, Zmarzlik's critique perhaps has more to offer than its liberal bias might at first sight suggest.

Notes

I am grateful to David Blackbourn and Geoff Eley for their helpful comments on an earlier draft of this essay, and also wish to acknowledge the help of the archives and libraries which house the material on which this essay is based.

1. Hans-Ulrich Wehler, *Das deutsche Kaiserreich 1871–1918* (Göttingen, 1973), esp. pp. 227–39 ('Eine Bilanz').
2. Thomas Nipperdey, 'Wehlers "Kaiserreich"'. Eine kritische Auseinandersetzung', *Geschichte und Gesellschaft*, Vol. 1, No. 4 (1975), pp. 539–60; Nipperdey's critique is far more subtle and wide-ranging than can be adequately conveyed in these few introductory remarks.
3. Hans-Günter Zmarzlik, 'Das Kaiserreich in neuer Sicht?', *Historische Zeitschrift*, 222 (1976), pp. 105–26; and the same author's 'Das Kaiserreich als Einbahnstrasse?', in Karl Holl, Günther List (eds.), *Liberalismus und imperialistischer Staat. Der Imperialismus als Problem liberaler Parteien in Deutschland 1890–1914* (Göttingen, 1976), pp. 62–71. See also Dieter Düding, *Der Nationalsoziale Verein 1896–1903* (Munich/Vienna, 1972).
4. Zmarzlik, 'Kaiserreich in neuer Sicht?', pp. 118–19.
5. It is perhaps worth noting that women as a group make no appearance whatever in Wehler's book, not even in his discussion of the role of the family (pp. 123–4), which is concerned with the 'father-son relationship'. For Bebel's book, see Hans-Josef Steinberg, *Sozialismus und deutsche Sozialdemokratie* (2nd ed., Bonn, 1972), p. 158, n. 38. For women voters in the Weimar Republic, see Gabrielle Bremme, *Die politische Rolle der Frau in Deutschland* (Göttingen, 1956).
6. Margrit Twellmann, *Die deutsche Frauenbewegung im Spiegel repräsentativer Frauenzeitschriften, Ihre Anfänge und erste Entwicklung 1843–1889* (Meisenheim am Glan, 1972), Vol. I, *passim*; Hugh Wiley Puckett, *Germany's Women Go Forward* (New York, 1930), pp. 139–40; *Jahrbuch der Frauenbewegung 1914* (Berlin/Leipzig, 1914), entry for 'Allgemeiner Deutscher Frauenverein'.
7. Gertrud Bäumer, 'Die Geschichte des Bundes Deutscher Frauenvereine', *Jahrbuch der Frauenbewegung 1921* (Leipzig/Berlin, 1921). The claim of half a million (which seems to be the source of the figure quoted in Zmarzlik, 'Kaiserreich in neuer Sicht?', p. 118), was in fact a wild exaggeration (see note 30, below).
8. Biographies of Auguste Schmidt, Betty Naue, Auguste Förster, Anna Simson,

Marie Stritt, Henriette Goldschmidt, Jeannette Schwerin, in: Deutsches Zentralinstitut fur Soziale Fragen, Berlin-Dahlem, Archiv des Bundes Deutscher Frauenvereine (hereinafter ABDF) 2/I/1−4. Stenographic report of 1902 Congress in ABDF 16/I/2.

9. *Centralblatt des Bundes deutscher Frauenvereine* Vol. 9, No. 7 (1 July 1907), pp. 49−51; ABDF 5/VIII/1:Stritt and Pappritz to Gesamtvorstand, 14 April 1907 (dealing with objections).

10. Stenographic report in ABDF 16/I/5.

11. Ibid., pp. 365−468. The assertion by Ulrich Linse, in his otherwise excellent article 'Arbeiterschaft und Geburtenentwicklung im Deutschen Kaiserreich von 1871', *Archiv für Sozialgeschichte* XII (1972), pp. 233−6, that the BDF supported legalised abortion, is shown by the stenographic report of the debate in the movement's archives in Berlin (which Linse failed to consult) to be erroneous.

12. ABDF 2/I/1: Salomon to Bensheimer, 7 April 1909 (for the description of Stritt as 'one-sidedly radical'; the rest of the file, marked 'not to be shown to outsiders', contains the minutes and correspondence relating to Stritt's enforced resignation).

13. Gertrud Bäumer, 'Was bedeutet in der deutschen Frauenbewegung "jüngere" und "ältere" Richtung?', *Die Frau. Monatsschrift fur das gesamte Frauenleben unserer Zeit*, Vol. 12, No. 6 (March, 1905), pp. 321−9 (one of the earliest statements of Bäumer's views). See also the lucid exposition of these theories by Alice Salomon in *International Council of Women: Report of Transactions of 4th Quinquennial Meeting, held at Toronto, Canada, June 1909* (London, 1910), edited by the Countess of Aberdeen, pp. 212−13.

14. See speeches of Marie Baum (for BDF Vorstand) and Maria Lischnewska, and final accepted resolution, in ABDF 16/I/5, pp. 365−468 (1908 General Assembly); propaganda for 'racial hygiene' (including disfranchisement or even sterilisation of mentally subnormal, cripples, alcoholics, and so on), in Staatsarchiv Hamburg (hereinafter StA Hbg), Politische Polizei, S9001/I: Versammlungsbericht 22 Oct. 1912; *Die Frauenbewegung*, Vol. 17, No. 14, 15 July 1911, p. 110; *Frauenstimmrecht. Monatshefte des Deutschen Verbandes für Frauenstimmrecht*, Vol. 2, No. 5 (August 1913), pp. 93−4; *Zeitschrift für Frauenstimmrecht* (Beiheft der 'Frauenbewegung'), Vol. 6, No. 7, 1 August 1912; *Das kleine Journal*, 5 August 1912 (cutting in Bundesarchiv Koblenz, Nachlass Adele Schreiber-Krieger, Pak. 25). These examples could easily be multiplied.

15. Thus cf. the discussion of arrangements for the 1914 BDF General Assembly in ABDF 5/XVI/2: Baumer to Agnes Bluhm, 4 April 1914.

16. Brief accounts in Auguste Kirchhoff, *Zur Entwicklung der Frauenstimmrechts-bewegung* (Bremen, 1916) and Maria Lischnewska, *Die deutsche Frauen-stimmrechtsbewegung zwischen Krieg und Frieden* (Berlin, 1915).

17. Detailed (but wildly prejudiced) accounts in Regine Deutsch, Francis Sklarek (eds.), *Zur Krise im Bund für Mutterschutz* (Berlin, 1910), and Helene Stocker, *Krisenmache. Eine Abfertigung* (The Hague, 1910). Extensive documentation in Bundesarchiv Koblenz, Nachlass Adele Schreiber-Krieger, Pak. 1−3 (183 numbered Vorstandsprotokolle and 367 numbered letters). Eminent supporters who resigned included Werner Sombart, Anton Erkelenz, Friedrich Naumann, Lily Braun and August Forel.

18. This interpretation is perhaps most accessible in Hans-Ulrich Wehler, 'Industrial Growth and Early German Imperialism', in R Owen and R. Sutcliffe, (eds.), *Studies in the Theory of Imperialism* (London, 1972), pp. 71−92; and the same author's 'Bismarck's Imperialism 1862−1890', *Past and Present* 48 (1970), pp. 119−155. A major aim of social imperialism,

according to Wehler, *Das deutsche Kaiserreich*, p. 173, was to function as a 'conservative policy of diverting and taming attempts at reform which endangered the existing system, such as were incorporated in the emancipatory forces of liberalism or of the organised socialist labour movement, by diverting them abroad'. The discussion in the preceding paragraphs of this essay should have established the potential of the feminist movement as such as 'emancipatory force', and the social and political threat it posed to the existing system. I am following here one of the lines of criticism set out in Geoff Eley, 'Defining Social imperialism: use and abuse of an idea', *Social History*, Vol. 1, No. 3 (October 1976), pp. 265–90, and the same author's 'Social Imperialism in Germany: Reformist Synthesis or Reactionary Sleight of Hand?', in I. Geiss and J. Radkau (eds.), *Imperialismus im 20. Jahrhundert. Gedenkschrift für G.W.F. Hallgarten* (Munich, 1976), pp. 71–86.

19. *Hamburgischer Correspondent*, 7 October 1910 (cutting in Deutsches Zentralinstitut für Soziale Fragen, Berlin-Dahlem, Helene-Lange-Archiv (hereinafter HLA), Box 57); Irmgard Remme, 'Die Internationalen Beziehungen der deutschen Frauenbewegung vom Ausgang des 19. Jahrhunderts bis 1933' (Ph.D., West Berlin, 1955), pp. 37–40.
20. Remme, pp. 50–63. See also Lida Gustava Heymann, in Zusammenarbeit mit Dr. jur. Anita Augspurg, *Erlebtes-Erschautes. Deutsche Frauen kämpfen für Frieden, Recht und Freiheit 1850–1940* (ed. M. Twellmann, Meisenheim am Glan, 1972). For Stritt's views, see Remme, p. 9.
21. ABDF 4/2: Erklärung des Bundes Deutscher Frauenvereine zur Organisation der Gegner.
22. As the *Erklärung* (see previous note) demonstrated. For the 'Anti-League', as it was known, see StA Hbg, Politische Polizei, S18848: cuttings of *Hamburger Nachrichten* 8 June 1912, *Hamburgischer Correspondent* 12 June 1912.
23. Gertrud Bäumer, *Lebensweg durch eine Zeitenwende* (Tubingen, 1933).
24. The Civil Code (*Bürgerliches Gesetzbuch*), which came into force in 1900, was arguably more important, but far from constituting an improvement for women, it actually worsened their legal position in some respects. See Agnes von Zahn-Harnack, *Die Frauenbewegung – Geschichte, Probleme, Ziele* (Berlin, 1928), pp. 39–43; Marianne Weber, *Ehefrau und Mutter in der Rechtsentwicklung* (Tübingen, 1907), pp. 331–41. For the importance of the *Reichsvereinsgesetz* for the feminist movement see *Report of the Fourth Conference of the International Woman Suffrage Alliance* (Amsterdam, 1908), pp. 100–1. For the adverse effects of the *Reichsvereinsgesetz* on other groups in German society, see Alex Hall's contribution to this volume, pp. 255–6. below.
25. Examples of its use against the SPD in *Sozialdemokratische Parteitagsprotokoll 1906*, pp. 404, 409; and against liberal feminists in StA Hbg, Politische Polizei, SA 593/II: Heymann to police, 14 March 1903, 19 February 1908; *Der Abolitionist*, Vol. 6, No. 2, 1 February 1907, p. 18.
26. *Statistik der Frauenorganistationen im Deutschen Reiche* (1. Sonderheft zum Reichsarbeitsblatte, Berlin, 1909), 'Deutscher Verband für Frauenstimmrecht'.
27. Marie Wegner, *Merkbuch der Frauenbewegung* (Leipzig/Berlin, 1908), gives a total of 120,000 individuals belonging to the BDF, but this figure probably includes about 20,000 men. See note 30, below.
28. Archiv des Deutsch-evangelischen Frauenbundes, Hanover, B1: Adelheid von Bennigsen, 'Ausführungen Paula Müllers über die Stellung des DEFB zur Politik' (Vorstandssitzung, 5 February 1913); Zahn-Harnack, pp. 298–301; ABDF 5/IV/5: Bäumer to Vorstand, 5 September 1912, 10 September 1912, 20 October 1912; ABDF 5/IV/5: 'Resolution des Ausschusses des Deutsch-evangelischen Frauenbundes', 13 December 1912.

29. ABDF 16/II/2: Gesamtvorstandssitzung, 7–8 March 1913.
30. The BDF's peculiar method of counting the same members in different categories as if they were different individuals resulted in a claimed membership roughly double the real number of women in the BDF. For the mathematics of this, see my book *The Feminist Movement in Germany 1894–1933* (London, 1976), pp. 193–4.
31. Figures in *Jahrbuch der Frauenbewegung 1912, 1913, 1914* (Leipzig/Berlin, 1912–14); StA Hbg, Politische Polizei, S9001/I: cutting of *Hamburger Fremdenblatt*, 8 October 1911; Universitätsbibliothek Rostock, Nachlass Käthe Schirmacher: Schirmacher to Schleker, 24 March 1911 (I owe this last reference to the kindness of Amy Hackett, *Feminist Studies*, New York).
32. Ludwig Elm, *Zwischen Fortschritt und Reaktion. Geschichte der Parteien der Liberalen Bourgeoisie in Deutschland 1893–1918* (East Berlin, 1968), p. 234.
33. For the Progressives and the BDF, see Zentrales Staatsarchiv (hereinafter ZSA) Potsdam, Fortschrittliche Volkspartei, Nr. 20: II. Parteitag vom 4.–7 Okt. 1912; Nr. 36/I: Geschaftsführender Ausschuss, Protokoll, 4 Nov. 1912; Nr. 37, pp. 203–6: Zentralausschuss Protokoll, 21 Nov. 1910; HLA 57: 'An die liberalen Frauen!' (Flugblatt, Sept. 1912). The South German liberals Conrad Haussmann and Friedrich Payer were especially hostile to female suffrage (see StA Hbg, Politische Polizei, S9001/II: cutting of *Hamburger Fremdenblatt* 10 Okt. 1906; ZSA Potsdam, Nachlass Friedrich Naumann, Nr. 59, pp. 98, 100, 230.). For the National Liberals, see StA Hbg, Politische Polizei, S9001/I: cutting of *Vorwärts*, 11 Okt. 1911; Lischnewska, pp. 15–16, 25; Zahn-Harnack, p. 287.
34. For these reforms, see Puckett, *Germany's Women Go Forward,* and Zahn-Harnack.
35. Eleanor Flexner, *Century of Struggle. The Women's Rights Movement in the United States* (Cambridge, Mass., 1966), pp. 113–30, 156–92, 215–21; Inge Dahlsgard (ed.), *Kvindebevaegelsens hvem-hvad-hvor* (Copenhagen, 1975), entries for Denmark, Norway and Sweden.
36. Zahn-Harnack, pp. 287–9; ZSA Potsdam, Nachlass Naumann, Nr. 59, pp. 247–51 (Protokoll der Vorstandssitzung des Wahlvereins der Liberalen am 8. und 9. Januar 1907), for the Left-Liberals.
37. *Die Frauenbewegung,* Vol. 7, No. 21 (November 1901), p. 161.
38. The admission of women to political life seems to have been accepted practically without discussion by all parties involved in the preparation of the *Reichsvereinsgesetz*; other aspects of the law, such as those dealing with the admission of minors or the use of foreign languages, proved highly contentious.
39. Zahn-Harnack, pp. 298–301.
40. These consisted almost entirely of the wives of local notables (see lists in *Jahrbuch der Frauenbewegung* (Leipzig/Berlin, 1912–14).
41. Ludwig Langemann, Helene Hummel, *Frauenstimmrecht und Frauenemanzipation* (Berlin, 1916) (n.b. the inclusion of a female in the authorship of this anti-feminist tract, issued by the *Bund zur Bekämpfung der Frauenemanzipation*).
42. Archiv des deutsch-evangelischen Frauenbundes, Hannover, B1: Müller to Ortsgruppen, 19 August 1908.
43. See Jürgen Zinnecker, *Sozialgeschichte der Mädchenbildung* (Weinheim/Basel, 1973), esp. 46–8; Helmut Beilner, *Die Emanzipation der bayerischen Lehrerin, aufgezeigt an der Arbeit des bayerischen Lehrerinnenvereins (1898–1933). Ein Beitrag zur Geschichte der Emanzipation der Frau* (Miscellanea Bavarica Monacensia, 40, Munich, 1971).
44. For the vast social and economic gulf between primary and secondary school

teachers in general, see Fritz K. Ringer, 'Higher Education in Nineteenth-century Germany', *Journal of Contemporary History* Vol. 2, No. 3 (July 1967), p. 128.

45. Langemann/Hummel, p. 9.
46. StA Hbg, Politische Polizei, S9001: Bericht, betr. Feststellung des Vorstandes und der Mitglieder des deutschen Vereins für Frauenstimmrecht (21 November 1904).
47. Heymann/Augspurg, *Erlebtes-Erschautes,* chs. 1–3; Else Lüders, *Minna Cauer,* entrie for 1907. Beilner, op. cit., gives information on women schoolteachers' unions, as does Helene Lange, *Lebenserinnerungen* (Berlin, 1921). The archives of the *Allgemeiner Deutscher Lehrerinnenverein* are housed in the Deutsches Zentral-institut für Soziale Fragen, Berlin-Dahlem. On white-collar workers, it is also worth noting that the major white-collar union, the *Deutschnationaler Handlungsgehilfenverband,* was rabidly anti-feminist, and sponsored publications such as the tract by Werner Heinemann cited below, note 51.
48. Thus compare for example the figures for the Suffrage Union given above with the membership of the moderate *Verein zur Vertretung geistiger Interessen der Frau* (later, *Verein für Fraueninteressen*), Munich, which had 516 members in 1902. Of these, only 207 were unmarried. Twenty members were the wives of army officers, fifty-two were members of the nobility. The association also included the wives of the Bavarian SPD leader Georg von Vollmar and of the racist ideologue Houston Stewart Chamberlain, and in the 1890s the poet Rilke also belonged for a time. (Amy Hackett, 'The Politics of Feminism in Wilhelmine Germany 1890–1918', (Ph.D., Columbia, 1976), pp. 298ff.)
49. *Grundlagen des Stimmrechts* (Frauenstimmrechtsverband für Westdeutschland, Solingen, 1911); an attack on universal suffrage by Rhenish-Westphalian branches of the German Union for Women's Suffrage at its 1909 Congress led to Düsseldorf, Köln, Hamm, Duisburg, Hagen, Solingen and other branches forming the equal suffrage *Frauenstimmrechtsverband für Westdeutschland,* which joined right-wing Silesian dissidents in a new national organisation in 1911. See *Frauenstimmrecht!,* Vol. 1, No. 7, (October 1912), p. 158, and Vol. 1, No. 12 (March, 1913), p. 277; *Jahresbericht des Frauenstimmrechts-verbandes für Westdeutschland 1912* (copy in HLA 50); StA Hbg, Politische Polizei, S9001/II: cutting of *Berliner Tageblatt,* 24 October 1909.
50. See note 38 above.
51. The best and most explicit statement of these arguments is to be found in Minna Bahnson, *Ist es wünschenswert, dass der §3 aus den Satzungen des Deutschen Verbandes für Frauenstimmrecht gestrichen wird?* (Bremen, 1912). These arguments were also, of course, much favoured by anti-feminists. See especially Werner Heinemann, *Die radikale Frauenbewegung als nationale Gefahr!* (Hamburg, 1913).
52. Werner Thönnessen, *The Emancipation of Women. The Rise and Decline of the Women's Movement in German Social Democracy 1863–1933* (London, 1973).
53. Cf. comments of workers recorded in StA Hbg, Politische Polizei, S9001/I: Wirtschaftsvigilanzberichte, 3 May 1903, 1 July 1903.
54. Bahnson, op. cit.
55. This was in effect the message put across by Gertrud Bäumer, following Friedrich Naumann (Bäumer, *Lebensweg,* shows Bäumer's strong admiration for Naumann and his ideas).
56. Gertrud Bäumer, 'Frauenbewegung und Nationalbewusstsein', *Die Frau,* Vol. 20, No. 7 (April, 1913), pp. 387–94. See also *Jahrbuch der Frauenbewegung 1913* (Leipzig/Berlin, 1913).
57. Ursula von Gersdorff, *Frauen im Kriegsdienst* (Stuttgart, 1969), pp. 15–37.

58. These arguments were first advanced, in an American context, by Aileen S. Kraditor, *The Ideas of the Woman Suffrage Movement 1890–1920* (New York, 1965).
59. These developments were accompanied by a withdrawal of radical feminists from professional organisations to concentrate on the struggle for the vote. See in general Else Lüders, *Minna Cauer*, and note 47 above.
60. StA Hbg, Politische Polizei, S5466/I: *Hamburgischer Correspondent* 7 June 1895, *Berliner Tageblatt*, 30 June 1896.
61. See my article, 'Prostitution, State and Society in Imperial Germany', *Past and Present* 70 (February, 1976), pp. 106–29.
62. Bundesarchiv Koblenz, Nachlass Adele Schreiber-Krieger, Pak. 1: Referat über den Vortrag von Helene Stöcker am 27 November 1908; Pak. 3, P28a: Flugblattentwurf 'Zur Aufklärung!'; Pak. 3, P49: Vorstand der Ortsgruppe Berlin, 1 November 1908; Internationaal Instituut voor Sociale Geschiednis, Amsterdam, Collection Henriette Fürth: Stöcker to Fürth, 20 October 1905; *Die Frauenbewegung*, Vol. 13, No. 3, 1 February 1907, pp. 20–1.
63. Cf. ABDF 5/XVI/2: Bäumer to Max von Gruber, 13 July 1914; ABDF 5/XII/6: Scheven to Bäumer 10 February 1911, for BDF views on sexual morality in the Bäumer era.
64. StA Hbg, Politische Polizei, S9000/I: *Hamburger Fremdenblatt,* 4 October 1905.
65. See note 14 above.
66. This function of female suffrage was of course familiar in other countries as well. Cf. Kraditor.
67. BDF, *Die Stellung der Frau in der politisch-sozialen Neugestaltung Deutschlands* (1917).
68. As late as the afternoon of 8 November 1918 the introduction of female suffrage was still being resisted by the majority of the *Interfraktioneller Ausschuss.* See *Die Regierung des Prinzen Max von Baden,* bearbeitet von Erich Matthias und Rudolf Morsey (Quellen zur Geschichte des Parlamentarismus und der politischen Parteien, 1.Reihe, Bd.2, Düsseldorf, 1961), pp. 571–3, 593, 598–9, 602, 606–9.
69. See the useful discussion in David Blackbourn, 'The *Mittelstand* in German Society and Politics, 1871–1914', *Social History* 4 (January, 1977), pp. 409–33.
70. For BDF attitudes to the National Socialists in 1932–3, see esp. ABDF 16/II/5, Sitzung des engeren Vorstandes, 13 June 1932, and ABDF 1/A/2, documentation on 'Auflösung des Bundes'.
71. See the discussion in my book *The Feminist Movement in Germany 1894–1933* (London, 1976), pp. 235–75.
72. Cf. Bremme, refuting Hermann Rauschning, *Hitler Speaks. A Series of Political Conversations with Adolf Hitler on His Real Aims* (London, 1939), p. 259.
73. Before 1930 most of the BDF members supported the DDP, DVP or DNVP and there is no reason to suppose that they were any more loyal to these parties than were the men who deserted them by the million for the Nazis in 1930–3. See *Jahrbuch des Bundes deutscher Frauenvereine 1932* (Leipzig/Berlin, 1932), for a discussion of political preferences of BDF member associations in the late 1920s.
74. There is a good discussion of conservative women in Britain in Brian Harrison, 'For Church, Queen and Family: The Girls' Friendly Society 1874–1910', *Past and Present* 61, November 1973.
75. See above all Aileen S. Kraditor, *The Ideas of the Woman Suffrage Movement 1890–1920* (New York, 1965), pp. 7–8, 66–73, 125–38, 202–3 and *passim*.

76. See Dean C. Tipps, 'Modernisation Theory and the Comparative Study of Societies: A Critical Perspective', *Comparative Studies in Society and History*, Vol. 15 (1972), pp. 199–226.
77. Gertrud Bäumer, 'Was bedeutet in der deutschen Frauenbewegung "jüngere" und "ältere" Richtung?', *Die Frau*, Vol. 12, No. 6 (March 1905), pp. 321–9.
78. Cf. Betty Friedan, *The Feminine Mystique* (London, 1963).

9 THE SHAPING OF THE GERMAN LABOUR MOVEMENT: MINERS IN THE RUHR

Stephen Hickey

I

The social history of nineteenth-century Germany is a new and largely untouched field of historical enquiry. Compared with the attention devoted to Britain, France and the United States, nineteenth-century German society remains largely unstudied. Until recently, for understandable reasons, the leading exponents of German history were concerned almost entirely with political history at the highest level, the creation and development of the German State and particularly its foreign relations. In recent years there has been a substantial and sometimes painful shift, as historians have sought to come to terms with the impact of domestic forces on political affairs at the highest level, including foreign policy formulation. Nevertheless, although economic interests and social movements have now been widely recognised as powerful and dynamic factors, the primary focus even of recent writing has tended to remain the political development of the German State, with domestic problems treated essentially as influences on and adjuncts to the major questions of foreign relations.[1]

The tendency to emphasise high politics at the expense of a more broadly based social history has not, however, been limited to studies of German foreign relations. It has often characterised discussions of domestic German history, and nowhere is this more evident than in the writing on the German labour movement. Labour politics, and particularly the political and ideological history of the German Social Democratic Party (SPD), have received considerable attention. Historians have addressed themselves particularly to the problem of why the party moved from a revolutionary theory — expressed in the Erfurt programme of 1891— to a political practice which aimed at relatively limited objectives and could ultimately accommodate itself with the existing political and social system of the Wilhelmine Reich to the extent of supporting the war in 1914.[2] But the history of the working classes themselves, the background from which they came, the physical and social environment in which they lived, their daily experience of work and home life, and all the other factors which formed their experience and which ultimately shaped their responses to political matters have received relatively little attention.[3] Perhaps most surprising is the fact that this has often been true of local as well as national studies of the labour movement.[4] The result has been that the political and ideological history of the SPD has been seen in something of a vacuum, with little reference to the concrete realities faced and exemplified by the millions of workers in whose name it claimed to speak and on whom it ultimately depended.

In this essay we shall look, necessarily briefly, at one group of workers, the coal miners of the Ruhr. This area, stretching between Dortmund in the east and Duisburg in the west, was the heartland of German heavy industry and the centre of its coal and steel industries. We shall look particularly at the social and working conditions which confronted the newly forming working class there, and at the characteristic patterns of industrial protest and conflict which developed in the pits. In conclusion, we shall suggest that these factors decisively shaped both the character of the organised labour movement in the area and the problems which it faced. It is through the history of working people that we may hope to find the most revealing insights into the history of the labour movement.

II

The Ruhr had not been an important industrial centre in the early nineteenth century, although some coal had been mined in the area for many years. But during the century mining techniques advanced and enabled considerably deeper pits to be sunk, thus making new and very rich seams accessible and commercially viable. The availability of coal in turn attracted heavy industry, particularly steel making and engineering. By the end of the century the Ruhr had become one of the most important economic areas of Germany. In 1903 it presented an uncompromisingly industrial appearance:

> Virtually the entire Ruhr mining district between Oberhausen and Dortmund, Duisburg, Hattingen and Recklinghausen already has the appearance of a continuous giant city, its individual parts linked by a thick network of electirc trams, state railways and spurs to individual mines, vibrating above and below ground with the most vigorous industrial and mining activity, and teeming with a giant army of workers. It is the main artery and workshop of the German coal and iron industry. Everything lives from and for these two products and everything is touched by them. Wherever one looks there are winding towers and the broad outlines of waste-tips,

chimneys and smoking furnaces. The whole scene is enveloped and covered by a misty, dusty, dirty veil which often scarcely allows the blue sky to be seen and which falls on the rows of houses, the churches, etc. as a coating of dirt.[5]

The 'giant army of workers' to operate these industries was a new phenomenon in the district, and had to be largely brought in from outside. In 1850 fewer than 13,000 miners were working in the Ruhr, but by 1900 the number reached 227,000 and in 1913 stood at 395,000. The entire population increased sharply: in Bochum (one of the larger towns in the area) and the surrounding *Landkreis* (or county) it rose by over 200 per cent between 1880 and 1910, compared with an increase of 44 per cent in the population of Germany as a whole.[6] The increase came predominantly from migration, so that the vast majority of the workers were first or second generation inhabitants of the area. Some had had experience of urban and industrial life, having come from the Silesian mines or from Berlin, but many came direct from the countryside.

The immigrants came from all parts of Germany and from abroad, and it was estimated that over twenty 'languages and idioms' were spoken in the area.[7] The most distinctive group were the Poles. Because of the partition of the historical kingdom of Poland they were not classified as a distinct national group, and most were in fact German citizens. But the number of Polish speakers in the Rhineland and Westphalia rose from 16 in 1861 to 33,000 in 1890 and 279,000 in 1910.[8] They tended to concentrate around particular pits, where they sometimes formed an absolute majority. Like other immigrants, the Poles sometimes lived in physical isolation from the natives of the area, particularly when they lived in new estates. The situation in some of the company housing estates (known as 'colonies') was described in 1902:

> Of the Polish immigrants at least sixty per cent are in the colonies and have no steady communication with the natives. In my neighbourhood there are great colonies with several hundred households. If anyone wants convincing, let him go there: he would imagine that he was in 'Greater Poland'. Not only the adults but the children too speak Polish. These extensive company colonies are thus Polish enclaves on German soil. The pit managements are naturally aware of this development, but do nothing to alleviate it in an *'alldeutsche'* spirit.[9]

Not only did they do nothing to prevent it, companies often encouraged the isolation of their workers, particularly recent immigrants. Company housing was usually built in the form of closed 'colonies', sometimes virtually self-contained with a school and store, where only company employees lived. The provision of company housing — which was generally relatively cheap and of relatively high quality — was often an attraction to newcomers to the area, and in some parts of the district was a vital necessity if they were to find anywhere to live at all. The fact that they could live in seclusion from others was frequently an attraction; one company, advertising for workers amongst the Masurians in East and West Prussia in 1908, sought to reassure their potential employees that they would not have to mix with outsiders: the new colony, they were told, 'will if possible be populated only with Masurian families, so that they may live entirely amongst each other and need have nothing to do with Poles, East Prussians, etc. Everyone can think he is in his Masurian homeland'.[10]

The very speed of industrialisation thus imposed important character-istics on the newly forming working class. It was socially fragmented, without any broad historical or cultural experience in common. Many had little experience of industry and had been brought up in an environ-ment profoundly hostile to ideas of class conflict and socialism. More-over, the various cultural traditions continued to flourish in the new home. The divisions within the working class were nowhere more marked than in the field of religion. The churches continued to exert very considerable social and political influence. The denominational balance tilted from a Catholic ('black') dominance in Essen and the West to largely Protestant Dortmund in the East. Bochum was virtually evenly divided. Although many were poor church attenders, miners and their families appear to have maintained a strong respect and feeling for religion, fostered to some extent through the dangers of their work.[11] But deep suspicion and sometimes hostility existed between Protestants and Catholics. Otto Hue, the later miners' leader, recalled his childhood in Hörde, outside Dortmund, in the 1870s and 1880s:

> Sectarian hatred is so profoundly imparted to school children that as a school kid I was involved in the most murderous fights with the 'blacks'. Later I and many of these 'blacks' worked together at the foundry in a perfectly friendly spirit, and we looked back with bitter scorn at the time when fanatical self-interested politics had incited us youngsters against each other.[12]

One important channel through which the Churches sustained their influence amongst the workers was the numerous and popular Working Men's Clubs (*Arbeitervereine*) which they sponsored. These had been pioneered by the Catholics in the 1860s and 1870s, despite the doubts of many of the Church hierarchy, and although the Church consistently maintained that their prime aim was the defence of the faith they sometimes provided important social and material assistance to Catholic miners. By the 1880s the Catholic clubs were recognised by some Protestant churchmen and workers as a threat to their denomination — the threat was the stronger since the Protestant Church was identified with the employers of the Ruhr — and Protestant Working Men's Clubs began to appear. Both denominations continued to maintain and expand their clubs, and thus maintain a direct involvement and leadership role within the working class, until the War.[13] The clubs in turn gave very important support to the two dominant political parties in the Ruhr, the Centre (Catholic) and the National Liberals (Protestant), so that on top of the religious division was imposed a political one. A further complication was caused by the Poles who, although Catholic, insisted on having their own priests, formed their own (strongly nationalist) clubs, and eventually put forward their own political candidates. Where all the denominations could agree, however, was in denouncing the socialists for their alleged hostility to religion as such, and there can be little doubt that the charge was immensely damaging to the Social Democrats. The important role of the sectarian organisations in opposing the SPD was recognised by government officials: 'It is above all the patriotic and Christian associations, such as the Protestant workers' and youth clubs, the Catholic workers' and youth clubs and the Catholic apprentices' clubs which offer the possibility of bringing the advance of Social Democracy to an effective halt'.[14] Although the SPD was eventually able to challenge the tradtionally predominant parties and to win elections in the Ruhr, it was never able to break the hold which 'bourgeois' parties exerted over large numbers of workers. Thus, even in the 1912 elections, when the SPD achieved unprecedented triumphs throughout Germany, the Centre and National Liberals were able to make them *lose* the Bochum and Duisburg seats. In this situation, despite the numerical dominance of workers in this highly industrial environment, the obstacles to the creation of a unified working-class movement, particularly under socialist leadership, were very considerable.

III

The factor which had the potential to bring unity to the disparate work force in the Ruhr and perhaps to forge a common trade union or political movement was the experience of work itself. Work in the pits has never been easy, and in the nineteenth century it was extremely arduous and dangerous. Mechanisation had very little impact on the miner's work before 1914. Coal was still extracted in the main by pick and shovel, the use of which is uniquely difficult in the restricted space offered at the coal face. High temperatures and excess water often made the conditions worse. As the mines became deeper and extended further and further underground, and the number of men at each pit grew, the hours a man spent at the pit increased: an extra two hours a day could be spent simply waiting to be wound down at the start of the shift and up at the end, and in getting to the coal face. The employers insisted that the traditional eight-hour shift, which dated back to the eighteenth century, could not be reduced to com-pensate for this. When demand for coal was buoyant, considerable pressure was exerted on the miners to work overtime, on top of the basic shift. Discipline was harsh and often arbitrary: the overman (*Steiger*) might be responsible for anything up to about two hundred men, working in teams of two to twenty at a number of different coal faces, and he was responsible to the higher management of the pit for securing a given quanitity of coal; if he did not achieve it his own earnings suffered, and persistent failure might result in his losing his privileged status. The overman therefore drove the men hard, and bad feeling between them and the miners — from whose ranks they came — was common. Particular resentment was also caused by the *Nullen* system, whereby any coal truck which was sent to the surface and was judged 'impure' because it did not contain sufficient coal or had too much rock, was completely ignored in assessing the team's output for the purpose of calculating their wages, irrespective of the coal which it did in fact contain.[15] The difficult judgements involved gave an essentially arbitrary power to the mine officials which directly affected earnings and was bitterly resented.

The safety of the mines left much to be desired. Accidents were more common in German mines than in other comparable countries.[16] One important reason for the high accident rate was the presence of so many newcomers to the pits, and it was further compounded by the high labour turnover rates which were normal in the area. The official safety inspectorate was inadequate to meet the enormous growth in the industry, and was compromised by personal links

between inspectors and mine managers. The explosion at the
Carolinenglück pit (outside Bochum) in 1898, in which 116 men died,
was widely blamed on inadequate safety inspection, and was followed by
an expansion of the service. It was only after the explosion at the
Radbod pit (near Hamm) in 1908, when no fewer than 348 men lost
their lives, that the government agreed to introduce a system of workers'
safety inspectors: in practice, however, the new system aroused little
enthusiasm and made very little difference to mine safety.[17] The horror
of these large tragedies should not, however, obscure the small
accidents which were reported almost daily in the local press, rarely
involving fatalities but often leaving at least one man with fairly serious
injuries. It was the cumulative effect of these less dramatic incidents,
together with diseases such as pneumoconiosis and the 'worm disease'
which swept the pits in the early 1900s, which constituted the major
danger to miners, and helped to ensure that few of them were still
working underground after forty.

The actual experience of work was common to the great majority of
miners. They followed approximately the same career pattern, starting
as young surface workers and going underground at 16 as pony minders
or brakesmen. They would become hauliers at 18 for two years or so
and then 'apprentice hewers' (*Lehrhäuer*) under the supervision of a
hewer for at least a further year before becoming full hewers themselves.
A certain number might rise to the position of overman, or learn a
specialist skill such as shot-firing (the placing and firing of explosive). But
for the great majority this was the full career pattern, until injury or
failing strength forced them back to surface work for their final years.
The miners differed therefore very considerably from workers in
engineering and manufacturing industry where differences in status and
earning power reflected permanent divisions (sometimes passed on from
father to son) between skilled and unskilled and between one specialist
group and another. Although fit hewers in the pit would earn considerably more than their older colleagues now working at the surface,
this merely reflected their different stage in life. The experience of work
thus offered a strong basis for solidarity and relatively little opportunity
for the development of a limited craft loyalty not encompassing the
aspirations of other fellow workers. This potential solidarity was
further fostered by the daily experience of work underground where
the hewers worked in teams; each depended on the others both for
physical safety and for sufficient output to ensure adequate earnings.

As far as earnings are concerned the Ruhr miners did better than
many other workers, including miners in other parts of Germany. Dr

Jüngst of the employers' association maintained that the highest wages on the Continent were paid in the Ruhr.[18] It is certainly true that there was a long-term improvement after the low wages of the depression years of the late 1870s and the 1880s. During the depression miners had been earning well below three marks per shift; by the end of the 1880s average earnings had risen to over three marks per shift and 1,000 marks per year. After this they continued − with fluctuations − to rise, reaching five marks and over per shift and 1,600 marks a year by the war.[19]

This picture of the highly paid miner needs, however, a number of important qualifications. In the first place price movements reduced much of the value of the money increases, although the incidence of this varied from time to time and place to place.[20] Secondly, both money and real wages were subject to cyclical fluctuations. Wages constituted the largest single factor in production costs (usually between 50 and 60 per cent of the value of production in the Ruhr mines) and this meant that wage cutting was an obvious and perhaps inevitable response to falls in the demand for coal. In fact mining wages appear to have moved more sharply than food prices, both up and down, if one looks at particular cycles. This meant that the long-term upward trend was largely concealed behind relatively short-term ups and downs. Thirdly, increased wages often merely reflected longer hours worked. During slumps in demand for coal the number of shifts worked was usually cut, but when demand picked up overtime shifts were introduced. It was often alleged that not all the extra shifts were actually recorded as such, thereby inflating the apparent pay per shift. Fourthly, and in some ways most important, the average figures conceal very great differences between the earnings of individuals. This was an unsurprising result of the fact that wages were calculated by reference to the amount of coal produced by each particular team of miners. Because the nature of the coal seams differed considerably from one face to another and from one part of the same seam to another the rate of pay for each truck of coal had to be constantly renegotiated to ensure that effort was fairly rewarded. In fact negotiations took place each month between the team leader and the overman and an agreement for the month was made. The money was divided amongst the members of the team. Although there was usually some attempt when the rate was set to ensure that it would provide a fair wage for each member of the team, it is not surprising that the results in practice showed fairly considerable variations. Thus a great deal of uncertainty continued to surround the wage which individual miners could expect to receive, even if their fellows were generally enjoying high earnings.

The work which the miners did was thus hard, dangerous and not out-standingly well paid. The experience of mutual reliance underground, the relative lack of skill differentiation, and common concerns such as improved safety, shorter hours, better pay and other issues thrown up in the daily course of work offered a potential basis for a common movement, transcending the religious and ethnic differences which characterised the working class in the Ruhr. We shall now turn to the forms which miners' protest took.

IV

One simple method adopted by miners of alleviating the unpleasantness of their work was simply to take time off. Absenteeism was particularly common at the beginning of the week —'Blue Monday' — and after the twice monthly pay days. It was particularly common during economic booms. In 1899, for instance, the Bochum Chamber of Commerce complained of the resulting problems for employers:

> This improvement in the workers' standard of living is a very welcome result of the present upswing. Unfortunately, a large number of workers do not take advantage of the improved conditions to get higher wages but cut their work time by repeatedly missing shifts and particularly doing no work on Mondays. There are thus complaints about falling productivity in mining and other industries.[21]

When, on the other hand, demand for coal was low and shifts were being cut and men laid off, absenteeism was not a particular problem for the employer; and without the opportunity to make up earnings through overtime, it could severly depress the miner's income. Absenteeism was a very individualist form of protest. While some were happy to take time off when they could afford to without putting their jobs and income seriously at risk, others preferred to use the favourable economic conditions to earn as much as possible. A similar division emerged in attitudes to overtime: some welcomed it for the extra money while others thought it should be restricted as much as possible.

Job changing was another way in which miners tried to improve their pay and conditions. This was facilitated by the proximity of many of the pits to others so that a man could walk or, increasingly, cycle to another one without having to move his home. The arrival of so many thousands of newcomers to the area, without local ties or indeed reason to be there except to earn as much as possible also encouraged mobility. The very speed of the growth of the mining industry encouraged workers to change their jobs, since outside the troughs of depressions there was always some demand for labour in the area. The miners in turn were able to exploit this fact in their pay negotiations. The need to renegotiate piece rates every month in the light of the prevailing conditions at the face, and the fact that even when an agreement had been reached it could be immediately revised if conditions changed, produced a situation where bargaining over pay was virtually continuous. 'In mining the silent struggle over piece rates never lets up', as one inspector put it.[22] Disputes were common, with the management threatening to sack the men if they did not accept the rate on offer and the men conversely threatening to leave and find better pay at another pit if their demands were not met. Which argument cut more ice depended, of course, on the state of the industry at the time, and in the end agreement was usually reached. One hewer from the *Shamrock* mine (near Herne) reported that in December 1904 he rejected an offer which reduced his rate: 'After this the overman was so constantly on my back that after I had tried unsuccessfully to find work at other pits, I eventually signed the offer'.[23] The ability to move from one pit to another was thus a vital element in pay bargaining for the miners. One mine inspector commented:

> The freedom to change jobs was one of the most important weapons in the miners' struggle with the owners, above all in wage disputes. Through their freedom of movement, the miners were not only in a position to exploit favourable wages at one pit in the area or another, but they could virtually force higher wage rates by whole teams giving notice together.[24]

There are few records of such collective use of the freedom of movement. One mass migration took place from the *Neu Iserlohn* pit near Bochum to the *Deutscher Kaiser* pit near Oberhausen in August 1905: average wages in the Ruhr at the time stood at 4.86 Marks a shift, but 5.50 was offered at *Deutscher Kaiser*. In this case the movement was particularly encouraged by the fact that the director of *Deutscher Kaiser* had formerly been a popular manager at *Neu Iserlohn*.[25] Nevertheless, such mass migrations from one pit to another were very infrequent. Most job changing was done on an individual basis.

The total level of job changing in the pits was high, though again it rose during economic upswings and declined during slumps. In 1900, for example, departures from Ruhr mines represented 52 per cent of the total labour force at the time, and the new hirings 68 per cent. In

1902, when a short depression manifested itself, the proportions fell to 44 and 48 per cent. Labour turnover reached its peak in 1913 when departures represented 69 per cent of the total work force and new hirings stood at 78 per cent.[26] The figures conceal the fact that a number of the changes in any one year were accounted for by some workers — mostly young ones — who changed their mine more than once and perhaps several times in a year. Nevertheless job changing was considerable and posed very important problems for the employers. It tended, as we have seen, to force up wages. It also reduced productivity since it took a new arrival some time to reach his full productive potential in a new pit, particularly since coal seams in the Ruhr varied fairly considerably — for example, in the hardness of the coal. High turnover also reduced safety in the pits. For these reasons the employers did their best to reduce job-changing. One method, adopted particularly in the aftermath of strikes, was simply to refuse to take on men who had left their former mine without what the employer considered to be satisfactory reasons. Such restrictions, however, were sometimes opposed by the government on the grounds of the law of 1860 guaranteeing the miners' freedom of movement. Such attempts also required an iron will from the employers themselves who had to be willing to subordinate their immediate need to recruit labour to their common cause.

The other major method adopted by the employers to reduce labour turnover was the provision of company housing and other social benefits. Despite the increase in the total numbers of miners in the period, the proportion of the miners in the Ruhr living in company homes rose from under 20 per cent in 1901 to 33 per cent in 1912, and about 37 per cent in 1914.[27] These homes were often cheaper and larger than those available to rent privately. They were let only on condition that the men — and often his sons and any lodgers — worked at the mine to which they belonged. If such a man wanted to change his job, therefore, he had to find a new home too. Job changing was, nor surprisingly, considerably lower amongst those living in company houses than amongst the other workers at the same pits. At ten Bochum pits, where the turnover of all the miners (calculated as the total of departures and new hirings) represented between 33 and 75 per cent of the total work force in 1900, the turnover amongst the workers living in their company homes varied from nil to nine per cent. A mines inspector, Robert Hundt, commented in 1902:

The provision of good housing for the workers is the best and only means in the Ruhr coal mining district of settling the workers and of limiting the extremely high labour turnover. The low interest on the capital outlay is only illusory. In reality the higher productivity of a settled work force which understands the character of the coal seams will soon more than compensate for the lack of interest on capital. The building of good housing is thus as much to the economic advantage of the employer as to that of the workers.[28]

Nevertheless, as we have seen, job-changing was if anything still increasing in the years before 1914. Despite the efforts of the employers to restrict it, it continued to provide an important means by which workers tried to find better pay and/or conditions of work. But it remained generally an individualist method of improvement. An individual miner, or at best a group of miners, could secure some advantage for themselves. But others, particularly those who were for one reason or other less mobile, could not use these methods and were left behind. It was an avenue to individual but not collective advancement.

The most dramatic expression of protest was the strike. This was also the means by which *collective* discontent and *collective* solidarity, in contrast to the individualist forms of protest to which we have already alluded, could find expression. It is to miners' strikes that we now turn.

V

In some ways the simplest, and most immediately effective, way in which the miners could exert pressure on their employers was to stop work and call on their colleagues to join them until their demand was met. And in fact strikes were fairly common. In the Bochum area at least 17 strikes are recorded in the 25 years between 1889 and 1914, and doubtless other small ones occured. Most were small-scale stoppages, limited to one or two pits and lasting only a matter of days. Others could affect a number of pits in a district and have quite serious consequences. And three, in 1889, 1905 and 1912, were general strikes, affecting almost all the pits in the Ruhr and lasting for up to a month. It is clear that if we are to understand the miners' strikes, and their relations with the social and work settings which we have already described, we must look not just at the three large ones — as most writers have tended to do — but equally at the more frequent small ones.[29] Major strikes were merely an extreme manifestation of a pattern which extended more widely.

One obvious feature of mining strikes was their cyclical character. With few exceptions they occured in periods when demand for coal was rising, and when the demand for workers and the general level of

earnings were rising with it. The first significant mining strike in the
Ruhr occured in 1872, during the great economic boom which accompanied
the founding of the German Reich. The next great strike was in 1889,
when the long recession of the 1870s and 1880s was giving way to the
boom which lasted until the early 1890s. The 1889 strike was followed by
a veritable wave of strikes and threats of strikes which lasted until the
economy – specifically, demand for coal – slackened off at the end of
1891. Apart from a strike attempt in 1893, which was uncharacteristic
in that it was not overwhelmingly 'spontaneous' in origin, there were few
stoppages until the boom of the late 1890s, which in turn was marked
by some small strikes and the important 'Herne' strike of 1899. The
largest strike of all, that of 1905, also occured at a time when the
economy was particularly strong, and the last major strike before the outbreak of war, that of 1912, also took place when the economy was
sound, and when miners' wages were already moving upwards.

The issues raised by striking miners were virtually always closely
associated with the conditions of work and associated problems, and
reveal something of the way in which strikes arose out of the particular
working environment of the mines. The two leading demands, which were
raised in strike after strike, were for shorter hours of work – specifically,
the introduction of the eight-hour shift *inclusive* of winding time,
and the abolition of overtime – and for higher pay. After these
two demands there usually followed a series of less pressing issues, though
with the same ones frequently reappearing at subsequent strikes.

It is not difficult to see why the question of the hours of work should
have been so burning an issue, or why the resultant strikes should have
been so cyclical in character. The hours of work of a miner fell during
economic recessions and lengthened appreciably during booms. During
recessions – at least in those which did not last too long -- it was an
important goal of mine management to retain the bulk of their labour
force in order to be well prepared for the upturn when it eventually
came: during booms the demand for labour in the Ruhr was too strong
for mines to risk finding themselves without an adequate number of
workers. This did not mean that there were no redundancies during
recessions: advantage was usually taken of the circumstances to dispense
with men who were regarded by their employers as inefficient or in
some way a nuisance. The main response to cyclical recessions, however,
was not to sack men, but rather to reduce the number of hours worked,
by reducing the length and number of shifts, and to transfer men from
coal cutting to repair and preparatory work. There was often also a
certain amount of stockpiling of coal. The effect for the miners was

that both their hours of work and their earnings fell, and they were conscious of the real possibility of dismissal were they to make themselves unpopular with their employers.

During economic upswings, on the other hand, the hours of work lengthened, and pressure was exerted on the men both to lengthen the 'normal' shift and to work overtime. Hewers and hauliers worked 288 shifts on average during the recession year of 1902, but the figure had risen to 315 by 1906 when the boom was in full swing.[30] Overtime usually took the form of an additional quarter or half shift (that is, an additional two or four hours), but it could consist of a full double shift. In theory it was entirely voluntary, but in practice considerable pressure was exerted on the men to stay on for it. The problem for management was that the overheads of keeping the mine running for the additional period were only covered if a fairly large number of men stayed on; and to secure the greatest efficiency and facilitate the book-keeping it was desirable to keep the existing teams of miners together and working at their stalls, rather than put together new combinations. Since the prime purpose of the overtime was to boost production to take advantage of the prevailing demand for coal, it was clearly in the mine's interest to keep as many men working as possible. The management of the *Unser Fritz* mine commented in 1889 that only 'general' overtime – that is, overtime when all the men worked – was of any value.[31] Accordingly pressure was put on men to stay for overtime: men were commonly required to register a day in advance if they did *not* want to work overtime, and anyone who had not so registered would be prevented from leaving the pit until the overtime was complete. Following a complaint from workers at the *Wallfisch* pit about one such incident in 1889, when a number of men 'wet through with sweat' had to wait at the draughty pit bottom for two hours while the overtime was completed, the mines inspector commented that the management had been 'thoroughly correct' in preventing them from leaving, and had followed the 'general custom'.[32] Sometimes men could be fined or have their pay cut for leaving the mine 'early' at the end of their normal shift. And there remained the general threat which hung over any miner who acted against the wishes of his superiors that in one way or another he would be penalised for his lack of cooperation, perhaps by being given work at a place where the opportunities for earning high wages were limited.

It is easy to see how frustration and discontent with the hours of work tended to grow during economic boom, and why in strike after strike the miners called for overtime to be curtailed and for the length of the shift to be limited to eight hours including winding and journey time. When in 1889 Kaiser Wilhelm II agreed to give a personal audience to three of the strikers' delegates, Ludwig Schröder, their spokesman, told him that their overriding aim was, 'what we have inherited from our fathers, namely the eight-hour shift'.[33] In the strikes of 1890, 1891 and 1893 this demand was prominent again. The 1905 strike broke out over an attempt by the management at the *Bruchstrasse* pit, situated outside Bochum, to lengthen the miners' working day, and although by the time the strike had spread to other pits a number of other demands were made, the issue of the hours of work remained a central one in this strike too. In 1912 the eight-hour shift was demanded again, and the issue appeared also in many of the smaller strikes such as those at the *Von der Heydt* and *Barillon* pits in 1900, and at the *Baaker Mulde* and *Oberhausen* mines in 1903.

The second issue of central importance in the great majority of miners' strikes was pay. The reasons why this should have been so frequently raised are not quite so simple, since earnings in any event rose appreciably during booms. The Bochum Chamber of Commerce, for instance called the 1889 wage demands 'completely unjustified' on the grounds that while coal prices had risen by no more than six per cent in the previous year, wages had risen by six to eight per cent.[34] Nevertheless, there were important reasons why the miners should have frequently raised wage demands. One was the low level of wages which had often prevailed in the preceding recession, creating a backlog of resentment which was not necessarily appeased by moderate improvements. Another factor was that the miners knew from the press that if wages were already rising, then so were share values and dividends.[35] Moreover, the higher earnings, particularly at the outset of booms, were to some extent illusory: much of it resulted not from higher basic wage rates but from longer hours and overtime. The level of annual earnings fluctuated considerably more than did the official figures for pay per shift; and the official figures were frequently alleged to understate the number of shifts actually worked, thus understating the extent to which higher earnings merely resulted from longer hours. The tendency of prices to rise during booms further undermined the effect of improved earnings. These factors seem sometimes to have combined to produce a general feeling of disappointed expectations: miners and their families hoped and assumed that with the advent of the boom better times had arrived: instead they found longer hours of work but only limited improvements in wage rates. The resulting frustration made them responsive to suggestions that wages should be substantially raised.

A further factor, which on several occasions provided the actual spark which started the strike, was the special position of the hauliers and other young underground workers who were paid by the shift and not by piece rates. Whereas the wages of hewers were naturally responsive to changes in the economic position of the mine, because of the constant renegotiation to which they were subject, this did not apply to the wages of shift-paid workers. Nor could they threaten so easily as the hewers to leave the mine and find better paid work elsewhere, because their wages were more standardised and their chances of promotion to hewer might be jeopardised. The result was that the wages of hauliers and other shift-paid workers were considerably less flexible than those of the hewers with whom they worked. While this worked to the hauliers' advantage during recessions, when hewers' wages fell more than theirs, during booms the shift-paid workers lagged behind. In the year and a half preceding the 1889 strike, the wages of hewers in the Bochum district were reported to have risen by around 37 per cent, while those of hauliers rose by under 30 per cent, and those for pony-minders by under 20 per cent.[36]

This wage differential meant that booms were frequently accompanied by mounting dissatisfaction amongst the younger hauliers, brakesmen, and pony-minders who also suffered from the lengthening hours of work, but found that their pay lagged behind that of the hewers with whom they worked. Being young and unburdened by family responsibilities probably also played a part in making them particularly willing to take action. The result was that strikes frequently started amongst these young workers, who were followed by the hewers belatedly, if at all. The 1889 strike strated with sporadic stoppages by hauliers at a number of mines around Bochum and Gelsenkirchen, and it was the decision of the management at the *Rheinelbe und Alma* pit to sack 45 striking hauliers which led to rioting in the streets of Gelsenkirchen, the introduction of troops, and the rapid escalation of the strike throughout the district. At pit after pit it was the young underground workers who stopped work first, and it was a pattern which was to be repeated at later strikes: in 1891, for instance, it was the decision of 40 hauliers and pony minders to stop work which precipitated the shut-down at the *Prinz von Preussen* pit.[37]

The hewers did not always follow their young colleagues out on strike. The 'Herne strike' of 1899, which affected a number of pits around Herne and which led to violent clashes between strikers and non-strikers, remained limited mainly to the young (and mainly Polish) workers. In essence the strike — which because of the violence and the important Polish element caused considerable concern in the German press – was an attempt by these young workers to pressure the pits into following what a number of other mines had already done, which was to raise their shift wages; and to protest at the cut in their take-home pay which had just been imposed through an increase in their insurance contribution. A similar though more peaceful strike affected a number of pits in the north Bochum district in 1907; once again the aim was an increase in the shift rates of the young workers, and once again the hewers did not follow them out: at the *Hannover* pit – and no doubt at other mines – hewers took on the hauliers' work.[38]

The result of all these pressures was that calls for wage increases were made in virtually all miners' strikes. In 1889 increases of 15 to 20 per cent were demanded at many mines; in 1890 up to 50 per cent was demanded, in 1891 and 1893 increases of 25 per cent. In 1905 wage demands were put in the form of minimum earnings for the various categories of miners (reflecting concern over the wide fluctuations in miners' earnings), but later this was replaced by the demand for a general 15 per cent increase. In 1912 15 per cent was the main demand. In some strikes 'hidden' wage demands were made: one common one was that the timber pit props should be delivered to the hewers at the coal face – the effect of which would be that the hewer would spend more time actually cutting coal and thus earning money, rather than 'wasting' time on this unpaid chore.[39]

The hours of work and the level of earnings were the two major issues raised by the miners in strike after strike. A third group of demands, less clearly defined but almost as commonly present, related to the miners' desire for reform of the *manner* in which the mines were run. This was expressed most simply in the frequent demand for 'humane treatment' from the mine officials. Calls for the abolition of *Nullen*, and for reform of the system of discipline and punishments also reflected the miners' resentment at the unfettered and often arbitrary power exercised particularly by the junior mine officials. In a number of strikes, however, more far-reaching demands for some degree of formal consultation between the employers and the workers were raised. In 1890 there were demands for the elected miners' delegates at the individual pits to be recognised as the men's representatives with the right to speak on their collective behalf.[40] In 1891 and 1893 there were demands for recognised and freely elected workers' committees.[41] In 1905 the demands included the election of miners' safety officers, the establishment of workers' committees and the recognition of the miners' unions. The 1912 strike was an implicit attempt to compel the

mine owners to recognise the miners' unions. The ending of the unfettered power of the mine owners and their officials was thus, in one
form or another, an important and recurrent issue in mining strikes.
Again, it was natural that such issues should come to the fore during
booms, when the pressure from the overmen and management on the
men was at its most intense.

The mine owners rejected any suggestion that their authority should
be in any way compromised as fundamental challenges to the rights of
property. All attempts to institute collective bargaining were dismissed
on the grounds that the work contract was one between the employer
and the individual worker. Nevertheless, the hard line adopted by the
coal magnates of the Ruhr should not blind us to the fact that the
demands of the striking miners for better treatment and some degree
of collective bargaining were far from extreme, and if implemented
would have meant a greater obligation on management to consider and
discuss the miners' views, but not an overthrow of the fundamental
powers resulting from ownership. Certainly the government considered
this an area where concessions might be made. In 1892 the miners
were given the legal right to appoint a checkweighman, to watch over
Nullen, and in 1905 the government abolished the *Nullen* system
entirely. In 1908, as we have seen, the government gave the miners
the right to elect safety officers, with the right to unfettered inspection
at the request of the workers. Even the demand for workers' committees
was not as radical as it sounded. The idea had first been put forward
during the 1889 strike by the Left-Liberal Reichstag deputy, Dr Baumbach.[42]
In 1905 the government accepted the idea, and legislated for a system
of elected workers' committees at each mine. There were in fact severe
restrictions on the entitlement of the men to vote and to stand for
election — they had to have worked uninterruptedly at the mine for a full
year before they could vote, and since a strike was technically in breach
of the work contract, strikers were at first effectively excluded — and on
the subjects which the committees, which met regularly with management to discuss the affairs of the mine, could deal with: they could not,
for instance, discuss wages. The workers' committees as introduced were
thus very weak bodies, and were at first boycotted by the main miners'
union, the *Alter Verband* (Old Union), until they realised that the rival
Christlicher Gewerkverein (Christian Trade Union) was finding them a
useful platform. The government's view that there was little risk in
granting the miners a voice in mine affairs and a channel through
which they could air their grievances seems to have paid off: the
miners' committees gained increased support as the unions began to

participate fully; nevertheless, they appear not to have threatened the power of the mine owners and managers, but rather to have played a mediating role, accustoming managers and unionists to talk together and resolve potential sources of conflict.[43]

Miners' strikes thus threw up three broad groups of demands: for shorter hours, better wages and greater dignity at work. The strikes and the demands grew directly out of the specific experience of work in the pits, and there were hardly ever demands which were not of immediate and specific relevance to that work. Even the nationalisation of the mines appears not to have been raised. The 'limited' nature of the issues helps explain why so many miners could, on occasion, prove industrially militant while on broader political and social questions remaining deeply conservative. During the 1889 strike miners' meetings frequently finished with a cheer for the Kaiser, and although this particular habit was less marked in later years there was no close relationship between industrial militancy and political radicalism.

As we observed earlier, the strike differed from such methods of protest as job-changing and absenteeism in that it was essentially a collective and not individual action. For success, therefore, a high degree of support and solidarity was needed — even more in mining than in some other, more highly skilled, trades where a stoppage by even a fairly small but crucial group of men could wreak considerable damage to the employer. In mining a partial stoppage in which most of the men at the pit — or men at other pits — continued working spelt almost certain defeat, since the employer was able to continue operations for an appreciable time without severe strain (particularly when he also owned other unaffected mines, or received some support from other employers), and could follow the stoppage by sacking those involved. Moreover, even when a high degree of solidarity was achieved, it had to be capable of lasting for a considerable time, since even a complete shut-down which severely damaged the wider economy might, at least in the short term, raise coal prices and have only a limited impact on the mine owners.

On two occasions — in 1889 and 1905 — there was a high degree of solidarity, and at the peak of these strikes nearly 80 per cent of the Ruhr miners stayed away from work.[44] These strikes demonstrated that the common issue of the workplace could provide unity and solidarity which transcended the social and political divisions within the working class. From 105 strike delegates from the Bochum-Herne area in 1889, for instance, 49 were Protestant, 46 Catholic and the denomination of the remaining ten was unknown; 24 were thought to be liberal, 32 supporters of the Centre Party, and fourteen Social Democrats.[45] In 1905 again miners of all denominations and political views joined in. Nevertheless, 1889 and 1905 were exceptions to the more common pattern, in which only a minority supported the strikers. We have already seen that frequently the hauliers were not supported by the hewers, who even took on the work of their striking colleagues. In several other strikes, the stoppage remained limited to a number of mines, while men at the rest continued at work. The 1890 strike affected a number of pits around Bochum and Gelsenkirchen, but even at those mines the stoppage was far from complete, and after a few days it was clear that further mines were not going to join them.[46] The 1891 strike at its peak involved some 18,000 men (or 13 per cent) at 45 mines, but after reaching this level a drift back to work ensued.[47] The 1893 strike achieved a peak of some 21,000 men, or 14 per cent of the 146,000 miners in the Ruhr at the time.[48] The strikes of 1899 and 1907 — and the various small ones in the meantime — remained severely limited in their scope. And the 1912 strike, although supported at first by around 60 per cent of the Ruhr miners, started to decline after only three days and collapsed after a week.

There were important reasons, of course, why these strikes failed to gain more substantial support: one important factor was the threats to potential strikers from the employers; another was the frequent opposition from the miners' leaders. Nor should we forget the generally conservative attitudes of many miners which made them reluctant to join in such drastic action — particularly when the strike leaders were mere youths. In 1899 anti-Polish feeling also played a part. 1889 and 1905 showed that it was possible to overcome these factors, though even then the stoppages were far from complete. In most strikes, however, the miners failed to show the same level of solidarity.

Nor were miners' strikes particularly successful in securing concessions. They virtually all ended with a return to work with few, if any, concrete gains, and were followed by the sacking of 'agitators'. While wages were sometimes raised in the aftermath of strikes — for example after that of 1889 — it is difficult to attribute more than the timing to the strike, since wages were on an upwards trend anyway. The employers did not hesitate to reduce wages again when the economic situation changed. Nor is there any sign that the employers were persuaded by strikes to shorten the hours of work. Where concessions were made they usually came not from the employers but from the government, intervening as a third party. Thus in 1889 the government — and Kaiser Wilhelm II personally — tried to mediate, and persuaded the strikers to return to work on the promise of legal reforms. Three years later a reform of the mining law required each mine to provide a full set of work rules and gave the miners certain limited new rights — for example, to appoint a representative to oversee the *Nullen* at their mine. The 1905 strike also saw attempts by the government to mediate, and was followed by some important legal concessions: *Nullen* was abolished, to be replaced by a system of fines for 'impure' trucks; the normal shift was, in effect, restricted to 8½ hours including winding time; and the workers' committees to which we have already referred were established. These positive, if limited, government concessions were not paralleled by concessions from the employers themselves. In the majority of strikes, when the government refused to intervene on behalf of the strikers — and sometimes intervened to help force the strikers back to work — the return to work was followed by no concessions at all.

VI

The working class in the Ruhr was a very new creation at the end of the nineteenth century. It was characterised by deep divisions. The potential for unity lay in the common experience of work. But discontent with the harsh experience of work in the pits, while common, found only occasional collective expression: normally it was expressed through individual action such as job-changing and absenteeism, or through uncoordinated spontaneous strikes which usually achieved only limited backing and almost always ended in defeat and failure.

The labour movement in the Ruhr emerged from within this social and industrial setting. It had to grapple with the problems it threw up. The strength of working-class movements and organisations generally lies in collective solidarity and unity, since only this enables individually weak workers and their families to effectively confront the power of employers and governments. In the Ruhr, however, this unity was lacking. The repeated strike failures, particularly in the years between 1889 and 1893, convinced the generation of miners' leaders who emerged in the later 1890s and early 1900s — most notably Hermann Sachse and Otto Hue — that spontaneous industrial militancy alone was not enough. It had to be backed up by coordinated and sustained mass action, and this was only to be achieved through the creation of a numerically strong and well disciplined organisation. It required the cooperation of all miners, and this in turn required that the deeply divisive questions of religion and politics be strictly excluded from the trade union sphere. This was the basis of the doctrine of trade union 'neutrality', which encouraged the trade unions to distance themselves from all political parties, including the SPD, and pursue strictly limited and immediate goals.[49] Although most leaders of the 'free' miners' union, the *Alter Verband*, were Social Democrats (Sachse, Hue and others became SPD Reichstag deputies), they stressed the non-political aims of the union, and used their considerable authority within the SPD itself to discourage leftist activity which might embarrass them in their attempts to work with the large numbers of miners who were vehemently non-socialist, or were politically apathetic.[50] They also sought to prevent the outbreak of unplanned and spontaneous work stoppages, calling instead for restraint and discipline until action could be backed up by strong and all-embracing organisations. In trying to meet effectively the challenges of the social and industrial conditions of the Ruhr the labour movement thus adopted a gradualist, cautious and non-political stance, with a strong emphasis on the need for organisation and discipline.[51]

The hopes of achieving unity and sustained and effective solidarity through disciplined organisation were, however, only partially realised. In 1889, in the aftermath of the first general miners' strike, a united miners' union was established, but within a few months it split over Catholic accusations that it was being used by the Social Democrats for political ends. The Catholic leaders (and some Protestant non-Social Democrats) founded their own rival union (known eventually as the *Christlicher Gewerkverein*), and although the original *Alter Verband* remained numerically the stronger, the split persisted up to the war and beyond. A further division occured in 1902, when Polish nationalist miners formed their own union.[52] Sometimes the various organisations were able to overcome their differences and work together: in the 1905 strike they formed a joint organising commission, which continued in existence for some years afterwards. But at other times – most notably during and after the 1912 strike – there was bitter conflict, particularly between the *Alter Verband* and the *Christlicher Gewerkverein*. But even more damaging to the hope of achieving unity through organisation was the fact that even in 1910 and 1911, when the unions were numerically at their strongest, only around 40 per cent of mine-workers in the Ruhr were members of any union at all.[53] This was in large part due to the high labour turnover, frequent sacking of activists – particularly after strikes – and the constant arrival of newcomers to the area; but it also reflected the failure of the unions to convince an often sceptical and hostile audience of the advantages of trade union membership. The unions also failed to bring the spontaneous miners' strikes under effective control; although unrest at the level seen between 1889 and 1891 was not repeated before the war, the old pattern of industrial conflict persisted, and re-emerged with even greater force at the end of the war. Ironically, when in 1912 the unions with the exception of the *Gewerkverein* did at last resort to officially approved strike action, the stoppage ended in little over a week in failure and defeat.

A strong emphasis on carefully constructed and well disciplined organisation, combined with a fear of spontaneous and precipitate action on the part of the workers were, of course, central characteristics of the labour movement not just in the Ruhr but in Germany as a whole. This study suggests that this approach was adopted, in the Ruhr at least, in direct response to the divisions and contradictions within working-class society, but that it achieved only limited success in dealing with them. Unity was not achieved, and the old pre-organisation forms of individualist and spontaneous conflict continued, beyond the control or direction of organisations. It is probable that the social and industrial problems of the Ruhr were not unique, but were paralleled by similar — though not, of course, identical — features elsewhere in Germany. This is certainly what might be expected in view of the speed of industrialisation and the very rapid growth of the working class generally. Further studies of class relations at this time, particularly in the work setting, would reveal more about these features and their impact on the character of the labour movement. They would lay bare the social and industrial roots of the ambiguous history of the labour movement in Germany before — and after — 1914.

Notes

1. The work of perhaps the outstanding 'revisionist' historians of the 1960s, F. Fischer and H.-U. Wehler, is directed in the main to Germany's role in Europe and the world, although they stress the impact of domestic factors on foreign relations. F. Fischer, *Der Griff nach der Weltmacht* (Düsseldorf, 1961), and *Krieg der Illusionen* (Düsseldorf, 1969); H.-U. Wehler, *Bismarck und der Imperialismus* (Köln, 1969). For a recent discussion of the development of German historiography, see V.R. Berghahn, 'Looking towards England', in *The Times Literary Supplement*, 5 November 1976.
2. The best general history of the SPD is still Carl E. Schorske, *German Social Democracy, 1905–1917* (Harvard, 1955). See also G.A. Ritter, *Die Arbeiterbewegung im Wilhelminischen Reich* (Berlin, 1959); D. Groh, *Negative Integration und Revolutionärer Attentismus* (Frankfurt a.M., 1974); J.P. Nettl, 'The German Social Democratic Party 1890–1914 as a Political Model', *Past and Present*, No. 35, 1965. The history of trade unions has received only limited attention, despite the recognition of their vital role within the labour movement, and, after 1906, their power of veto over party policy; in 1914 the trade unions preceded the SPD itself into an accommodation with the

state.
3. Perhaps the most notable exception is the series of volumes of Jürgen Kuczynski, *Die Geschichte der Lage der Arbeiter unter dem Kapitalismus* (Berlin-Ost). In recent years a number of Americans have begun to address themselves to the social history of the European and German working class, particularly in the pages of the *Journal of Social History*; see also P.N. Stearns, *Lives of Labour* (London, 1975).
4. Studies such as Lützenkirchen's on Dortmund and Moring's on Bremen are strong on the politics of the local labour movement, but reticent about the wider social history of the working classes of their respective areas: K.E. Moring, *Die sozialdemokratische Partei in Bremen* (Hannover, 1968); R. Lützenkirchen, *Der sozialdemokratische Verein für den Reichstagswahlkreis Dortmund-Hörde* (Dortmund, 1970).
5. L. Pieper, *Die Lage der Bergarbeiter im Ruhrgebiet* (Stuttgart & Berlin, 1903), p. 214.
6. W. Köllmann, Die Bevölkerung Rheinland-Westfalens in der Hochindustrial-isierungsperiode', *Vierteljahrschrift fur Sozial- und Wirtschaftsgeschichte* 1971; SAB, Magistrats-Berichte.
7. SAB, 481, Reg. Präsident Arnsberg to Minister des Innern 28 November 1907.
8. H.-U. Wehler, 'Die Polen im Ruhrgebiet' in Wehler (ed.), *Moderne Deutsche Sozialgeschichte* (Köln, 1970), p. 441.
9. 'Frankfurter Zeitung', 1902, No. 35, quoted in Pieper, p. 242.
10. L. Fischer-Eckert, *Die wirtschaftliche und soziale Lage der Frauen in dem modernen Industrieort Hamborn im Rheinland* (Hagen, 1913), p. 61.
11. O. Hue, *Neutrale oder parteiische Gewerkschaften?* (Bochum, 1900), pp. 90–1.
12. Ibid., p. 111. Even in the 1920s children in (mainly Protestant) Witten fought on sectarian lines, and the Catholic streets were known as the Negerdorf. W. Nettmann, *Witten in den Reichstagswahlen des Deutschen Reiches, 1871–1918* (Witten, 1972), p. 104.
13. The numerical evidence is patchy, but in 1909 there were nearly 70 Protestant workers' clubs alone in and around Bochum and Gelsenkirchen, with an average membership of around 180: StA Münster, Oberpräsidium 2694 Bd.2, 'Siegener Volksblatt', 18 May 1909.
14. SAB, 479, Reg. Präsident Arnsberg to Minister des Innern, 26 October 1895.
15. In England at this time output was measured by the weight of actual coal produced.
16. The annual death rate in all German mines, 1897–1911, averaged 2.2 per thousand miners employed. This was worse than Belgium (1.03), Austria (1.28), the United Kingdom (1.32) and France (1.52), but better than the United States (3.31). H. Stanley Jevons, *The British Coal Trade* (London, 1969), p. 374. (Originally published 1915.)
17. H.G. Kirchhoff, *Die staatliche Sozialpolitik im Ruhrbergbau 1871–1914* (Köln & Opladen, 1958), pp. 170–73.
18. M. Metzner, *Die soziale Fürsorge im Bergbau* (Jena, 1911), p. 11.
19. M. Koch, *Die Bergarbeiterbewegung im Ruhrgebiet zur Zeit Wilhelm II* (Düsseldorf, 1954), pp. 148–50.
20. For various estimates of the general movements of real wages in Germany, see A.V. Desai, *Real Wages in Germany* (Oxford, 1968), p. 36.
21. SAB, Handelskammer zu Bochum Jahresbericht, 1898/99 pp. 18–19.
22. Bergassessor Herbig, 'Schwierigkeiten des Lohnwesens im Bergbau', *Glückauf*, 28 December 1907.
23. SAB, 458, Bergwerksgesellschaft Hibernia to Landrat Bochum, 22 February 1905.

24. Bergassessor E. Oberschuir, *Die Heranziehung und Sesshaftmachung von Bergarbeitern im Ruhrkohlenbecken* (Diss. Düsseldorf, 1910), p. 14.
25. StA Münster, RA I 1485, Dortmunder Zeitung , 20 August 1905, 2 September 1905.
26. Koch, p. 24.
27. A. Heinrichsbauer, *Industrielle Siedlung im Ruhrgebiet* (Essen, 1936), p. 44.
28. R. Hundt, *Bergarbeiter-Wohnungen im Ruhrrevier* (Berlin, 1902), pp. 34–5, 39. Company housing was only the more visible manifestation of a broad paternalist approach adopted by many Ruhr employers who sought to develop a strong sense of company loyalty in their workers. See D. Crew, 'Industry and Community: the Social History of a German Town 1860–1914' (Ph.D. thesis, Cornell University, 1975), chapter 3.
29. Recent examples of the tendency of historians to concentrate exclusively on the large strikes include A. Gladen, 'Die Streiks der Bergarbeiter im Ruhrgebiet in den Jahren 1889, 1905 und 1912', in J. Reulecke (ed.), *Arbeiterbewegung an Rhein und Ruhr* (Wuppertal, 1974), and Crew, chapter 6.
30. H. Münz, *Die Lage der Bergarbeiter im Ruhrrevier* (Essen, 1909), p. 55.
31. SAB, 442.
32. SAB, 439.
33. WWA, Handelskammer zu Bochum Jahresbericht 1888 p. 14.
34. Ibid.
35. SAB, 441, 'Die Post', 1 September 1889; *Zur Feier des 25 jährigen Bestehens der Gelsenkirchener Bergwerks A.G., 1873–1898* (Düsseldorf, n.d.); Gladen, p. 119.
36. WWA, Handelskammer zu Bochum Jahresbericht 1888. These increases appear to have been somewhat greater than those in the Ruhr generally, but the disparity between the different groups of workers was general. During the boom of 1902–7 hewers' average wages in the Ruhr generally rose by 31 per cent, while those for hauliers' etc. rose by 25 per cent: Koch, pp. 17, 149.
37. SAB, 447, Gendarm Rose to Landrat Bochum, 23 April 1891.
38. IGBE, Al 19, Deutscher Bergarbeiterverband Jahresbericht 1907/8; StAB, 464. Hewers also did hauliers' work when the latter struck at *Constantin der Grosse* in 1898.
39. It is interesting to note that most of the protest aroused in 1902 and 1903 over the epidemic of worm disease was directed at the lack of sanitation which caused the epidemic, but against the compulsory treatment, lasting several days, since this involved a loss of earnings. SAB, 464, Polizei-Commissar Bochum to Reg. Präsident Arnsberg, 27 July 1903; SAB, 480, Reg. Präsident Arnsberg to Minister des Innern, 8 December 1903.
40. SAB, 462.
41. SAB, 448, Reg. Präsident Arnsberg to Landrat Bochum, 6 February 1893.
42. Koch, p. 38.
43. Kirchhoff, pp. 154–9; E.G. Spencer, 'Employer Response to Unionism: Ruhr Coal Industrialists before 1914', *Journal of Modern History*, Vol. 48 (1976), pp. 397–412.
44. Koch, pp. 142–3.
45. SAB, 442.
46. SAB, 462.
47. Verein für die bergbaulichen Interessen im Oberbergamtsbezirk Dortmund, *Die Entwicklung des Niederrheinisch-Westfälischen Steinkohlen-Bergbaues* (Berlin, 1904), Bd.XII, p. 239.
48. SAB, 440.
49. This view was argued by Otto Hue in his book *Neutrale oder Parteiische Gewerkschaften?*, where he explicitly rejected the notion that the trade

unions were 'recruiting schools for the party', and argued (against Kautsky) that the trade unions were at least as important as political parties. Hue, pp. 130–57.

50. In 1910 the protests of the *Alter Verband* led the SPD to reverse its decision to appoint Konrad Haenisch, the radical editor of the *Arbeiter Zeitung* in Dortmund, to an important party job covering the Rhineland and Westphalia; see K. Koszyk, 'Die sozialdemokratische Arbeiterbewegung 1890 bis 1914', in Reulecke.

51. It is unconvincing to attribute this policy to the 'opportunism' of a class of union functionaries, as does Fritsch. In the 1890s, when the union's policy was adopted, the union had virtually no bureaucracy at all (in 1898 there were only four full-time staff). What needs to be asked is *why* solid organisation was valued so highly, in the Ruhr and elsewhere, by trade unionists and Social Democrats. See J. Fritsch, *Eindringen und Ausbreitung des Revisionismus im deutschen Bergarbeiterverband* (Leipzig, 1967), pp. 19–20.

52. There was in addition a very small (politically liberal) Hirsch-Duncker union.

53. The Ruhr membership figures for the three main miners' unions are published in C. Klessmann, 'Klassensolidarität und nationales Bewusstsein', in *Internationale wissenschaftliche Korrespondenz zur Geschichte der deutschen Arbeiterbewegung* (Juni 1974, Heft 2), p. 154. The Hirsch-Duncker union had around 2,000 members: Koch, p. 122. A number of historians have seriously exagerated the degree of unionisation of Ruhr miners by applying *national* union membership figures to the Ruhr: cf. Kirchhoff, p. 168; W. Köllmann, 'Die Geschichte der Bergarbeiterschaft', in W. forst (ed.), *Ruhrgebiet und i Neues Land* (Köln, 1968), p. 92; Gladen, p. 141. The proportion of underground workers unionised was higher, reaching over a half: O. Hue, *Die Bergarbeiter* (Stuttgart, 1910 and 1913), Bd.II, p. 720.

10 YOUTH IN REBELLION: THE BEGINNINGS OF THE SOCIALIST YOUTH MOVEMENT 1904–1914

Alex Hall

I

From time to time the outward serenity of Wilhelmine Germany was ruffled by events which seemed to well up from the gloomier undercurrents of social and economic change and cast a shadow over the facade of confident optimism. Often the whiff of scandal was never quite absent, providing journalists of all political persuasions, but especially those dedicated to exposing the hollowness of the Wilhelmine *Rechtsstaat*, with ample and attractive news-copy. As the SPD struggled to establish itself as the legitimate voice of the German working class, it seized on such minor calamities as evidence not only of the impending collapse of a system which was rotten to the core, but also as valuable ammunition with which to harass its political antagonists.[1]

It was impossible to overlook the elements of lurid sensationalism which accompanied the discovery, early in June 1904, of the badly bruised and bloodstained body of a sixteen-year-old apprentice locksmith. The corpse was found hanging from a tree in the Berlin suburb of Grunewald, the final act of desperation by a boy who had been systematically ill-treated to the point where suicide offered a tempting release from all his worldly troubles. This incident, by no means the only one of its kind,[2] was to provide a spark which led to the launching of the socialist youth movement.

II

At the turn of the century Wilhelmine Germany was caught in the fever of industrial expansion, drawing on the vast pool of unskilled labour from the land and fashioning characteristically stark skylines in the new urban centres. Those who moved into the old trades in the big cities were often at the mercy of unscrupulous employers, who set the profit motive higher in their list of priorities than adequate standards of hygiene and safety. Youngsters who left their family homes in the country and came to seek their fortune in the cities encountered a strictly hierarchical system within the old craft industries, where the apprentice (*Lehrling*) was subordinate to the journeyman (*Geselle*) and both were directly responsible to the registered masters (*Meister*). These masters were regarded as being *in loco parentis*, so that they were accorded the right, for example, to administer corporal punishment as well as exercising full guardianship. Such were the perils to which young workers were often subjected that the local sickness insurance society in Berlin reported in 1904 that of a total of 1,400 apprentices in the printing industry, some 800 had fallen ill, and of these 307 were afflicted with illnesses directly caused by their work.[3] The dreaded 'proletarian disease' of the time, tuberculosis, annually claimed about 70,000 victims, and young workers were often most at risk.[4]

As in other industrialising countries, child labour had been one of the most profitable sources of employment throughout the nineteenth century. In the Rhineland in particular, it was no exception to find children of five working 12 to 15 hours a day in the spinning and weaving mills, with all the subsequent high child mortality rates.[5] In 1839 the first measure to protect children was introduced in the state of Prussia, forbidding work under the age of nine and 'protecting' those between the ages of nine and sixteen, who were allowed to work up to 10 hours in the factories and pits. Young workers over the age of sixteen did not exist as a separate category. Moreover, this law only came about because the military recruiting stations in the relevant industrial areas had been encountering so many young people totally unfit for military service.[6] In practice little was done to enforce protection, and the very low fines imposed on recalcitrant employers in no way acted as a deterrent.[7] In any case, young people who worked in small businesses and workshop staffed by fewer than ten people were not protected by the industrial code or *Gewerbeordnung*.[8] In their annual report for 1905, the factory inspectors in Minden cited evidence of how many owners attempted to overcome the restrictions imposed upon them by the *Gewerbeordnung* by insisting that apprentices should clear up and clean the machine-rooms after the completion of their ten-hour day. This operation often involved an additional work period of two hours.[9]

Nor were these practices confined to Prussia alone. Reports from an inspectorate in the Upper Palatinate (Bavaria) revealed that children and young workers were found to be at work at four o'clock in the morning and frequently remained at their work-place until nine o'clock at night.[10] The inspectors at Konstanz reported that two or more apprentices were often required to share the same bed and that the standard of cleanliness in such rooms left much to be desired. Inadequate ventilation and lighting in attic rooms, together with narrow stairs without a balustrade, often characterised the sleeping quarters of the young apprentices.[11] In the wake of the Kaiser's concern to portray himself as an *'Arbeiterkaiser'* ('Workers' Emperor'), dedicated to improving the conditions of working people, the *Gewerbeordnung* was changed in June 1891 in order to reduce the working hours of young people between the ages of 14 and 16 to ten hours daily. Children under the age of 13 were not allowed to work in factories at all, and the limit for 13–14-year-olds was set at six hours. Ingenious employers still managed to find ways of circumventing the new regulations, since it was invariably cheaper to employ even several children under age, working in relays at different times of the week, than to engage a full-time adult.

As the industrial sector continued to expand, more and more young people swelled the productive capacity of the factories, whilst others were sucked into commerce and the burgeoning transport industries.[12] By 1900, as the structural changes were taking effect which were to transform Germany from an agrarian state to an industrial power of the first order, German industry employed almost four million young workers. Of these, only about 20 per cent had an officially recognised apprenticeship or course of training which led to an approved qualification.[13] The rest belonged to the group of unskilled workers, who often carried out a myriad of unpleasant and poorly paid jobs. Many were employed, for example, in the guano mills in the port of Hamburg, where phosphorus was extracted and fertiliser produced. This was where the political career of men like Ernst Thälmann – later to play a leading rôle in the German Communist Party (KPD) – began. It was in such places that a new kind of working-class consciousness was born, where the term 'worker' was not only of socio-economic significance for theorists of the class struggle, but also a kind of professional occupation in its own right, conveying its own inherent sense of pride and dignity.[14]

At the same time there still remained a large reservoir of young labour on the land. In 1904, no fewer than 1.8 million children under the age of 14 could be described as rural workers and annual child fairs or markets were not unknown in parts of southern Germany, at which young children could be 'bought' for the summer months, in order to tend the cattle and help on the farms.[15] It was as the agrarian sector began to decline still further in relative economic importance and the drift to the urban centres continued unchecked that those responsible for guiding the fortunes of the Reich began to betray increasing signs of concern. The position of 14 or 15-year-old boys who came from a rural background of close, intimate life in a small village and were confronted with the entirely different sort of life in the towns was fraught with all kinds of dangers. Religion and patriotism as a kind of daily medicine imbibed at the place of work on the land was soon replaced by the hard, bitter tone of the class struggle and the demands of the working class for a greater share in political decision-making. Much more serious was the gap between school and army, a period of susceptibility to new influences, which the Social Democratic Party was increasingly exploiting for its own ends. Young men were drawn into the army when still in an impressionable state of mind. The SPD, for its part, directed its attention to immunising — through appropriate measures of enlightenment, if not actual propaganda — young people against the pressures they would have to face in the barrack-room atmosphere. Social Democrats freely admitted that youth was susceptible to the pomp and ceremony of army life, to the colour and splendour of the marches, parades and uniforms, and had therefore to be alerted to the true significance of the militarist spirit in Germany. From its point of view the establishment sensed a two-fold danger in such proselytising activities: the threat that the troops might be encouraged to offer no resistance not only to the 'external', but also to the 'internal' enemy.

It was to such fears that a leading conservative politician, Count Westarp, gave expression in a speech to the Reichstag in May 1914:

> We must get to the young people, we must persuade our working-class youth how hopelessly wrong it is when they are made to believe in the anti-militarist propaganda of the SPD, that the Fatherland, for which they are to put on the king's uniform, is not their Fatherland. We must enlighten even this section of our youth that our Fatherland is really theirs too, and that it is worth-while to stand up for it with enthusiasm.[16]

Partly for this reason institutions like the school had long been a factor of immense political significance, first in Prussia and then in the newly-created German Reich.[17] As early as February 1874 Count Helmuth von Moltke had declared in the Reichstag: 'I believe that the schools represent the point where we must apply a lever if we wish to protect ourselves from dangers which, no less important than external ones, come from the internal activities of socialist and communist groups'.[18] A decree from Wilhelm II in May 1889 concerned itself with the struggle against socialist tendencies in the schools. The content of school lessons, especially in history and religious instruction, should aim at stressing the ordered nature of German society and emphasising the necessity of the monarchy for the protection and welfare of the working class. This edict represented the initial two-pronged approach of the new reign: hoping to win over the working masses with evidence of a new social conscience, whilst enforcing the existing ideological struggle through all the organs of state.[19] Discussions on new school curricula began late in 1890 and new syllabuses were published in 1892. The immediate effect was a cutback in foreign languages to benefit the teaching of German, and an increase in the range and scope of history lessons.[20]

In 1893 the Prussian Ministry of the Interior issued a circular which, drawing on an earlier Imperial decree, pursued the idea of a form of 'ideological welfare' for the worker. This kind of indirect pressure on local authorities produced a large number of apparently spontaneous, quasi-citizens' action groups, imbued with a wholly patriotic spirit, professing slogans such as 'Love of Kaiser and Fatherland' (*Liebe zu Kaiser und Vaterland*) and dedicated to combating the threat posed by socialism at all levels of society. Thus, in May 1898, the Federation of German Charitable Societies was set up, at the foundation conference of which a leading civil servant described the army as 'the greatest centre for further education for young males'.[21] This organisation was intended to work as a central agency for directing individual and collective efforts in the government's ideological offensives.[22] Such groups played an immeasurable part in providing reports and material on which the Prussian authorities and central government or *Reichsleitung* could make their respective judgments affecting future policy. They were responsible, for example, for the broad content of the package of measures announced by the Prussian government in 1900–1, which banned all Sunday work and introduced earlier closing hours, and which were construed as a reform of working conditions for young people.

Similarly, from 1900 onwards many idealistic academics, clearly influenced by the example of Toynbee Hall in London and inspired by the notions of men like Friedrich Naumann, helped to found welfare societies for apprentices and journeymen. In January 1900 the Prussian Minister of Trade, writing to the heads of the regional administration, urged the building of Sunday recreational centres for young working people.[23] A large part of this work had been the responsibility of the various Church organisations who, irrespective of confession, continued to play a vital role in upholding traditional values amongst young people. Every priest attempted to persuade a confirmed member of the Church to continue a close association through a variety of different clubs and associations. By 1909 some 200,000 youngsters were members of Catholic youth groups, and Protestant organisations numbered 125,000 activists. In any case, children who were not confirmed were liable to suffer disadvantages in their social position and job preferment. Above all, the Catholic Church had large reserves of financial support. It possessed its own meeting-halls and paid wardens, as well as an army of trained youth and social workers.[24] Not surprisingly, these Church groups were strongest in the Rhineland and were so well-organised that many small towns had two clubs, one for boys and one for girls.

Big industry was also involved in the process of winning over the minds of the young. In the Krupp factories in Essen and those of Bayer in Leverkusen there existed a wide range of recreational facilities for the young — libraries, playgrounds, sewing-circles for girls, musical, sports and gymnastics clubs.[25] The state industries, including the Imperial dockyards and the Prussian state railways, also introduced similar measures.

The extent to which the schools were drawn into the government's long-term ideological objectives is demonstrated by a directive from the Prussian Minister of Education and Religious Affairs in November 1903. This document, which was sent to all higher schools, pointed to Germany's new role as a naval power. It included copies of a poster, originally intended not for use in schools but as an instrument of propaganda for 'naval policy' (*Flottenpolitik*), which was nonetheless considered singularly apt in creating a 'favourable climate' amongst those still at school.[26] The period between the last year at school and entry into military service remained a pressing problem, the more so since SPD attacks on the institutions of the State continued unabated, and this led to a major directive from the Minister of Education and Religious Affairs in September 1905. It focused the attention of all regional heads of administration on three urgent tasks: that all existing institutions (employers' advisory groups, guilds, sports clubs and youth sections affiliated to professional organisations) should receive proper official support and financial help from government sources; that local co-ordinating groups should be formed with provision for annual con-ferences and permanent liaison directed from a central office; and that the vocational schools should become one of the main pillars of support in the struggle for the minds of young people between school and the army.[27] His action was given powerful reinforcement by the Kaiser, who instructed members of the *Kronrat* in February 1906 to observe the need to protect German youth from an infection with socialist ideas and to keep them away from all activities directed against the state; otherwise one would experience a situation comparable to that in Russia, where the young belonged to the most impassioned protagonists of the revolutionary movement.[28]

Early in 1911 the Prussian government issued its first grant-in-aid of one million marks for the purpose of youth welfare, and two years later the sum was increased to three million marks.[29] At the same time, the importance of military tradition was never overlooked. In October 1909, the Prussian Minister of War issued a circular to the effect that those still attending school were to be given preferential seats at all public manoeuvres, parades and military celebrations and that an officer should be authorised to act as their guide.[30] At the beginning of 1914, the head of the same Ministry sent to all his colleagues the draft of a law which foresaw obligatory military training for all males over the age of 13 until entry into the army at about the age of 17.[31] It was only the outbreak of war in the summer of 1914 that prevented such a measure from being approved by the Reichstag.

III

This is the background against which the position of the young worker in Imperial Germany must be seen. Faced with the exploitation and misery of life in the industrial towns and the oppressive power of government agencies and anti-socialist coalitions, it needed but a small spark, such as that caused by the suicide of the locksmith apprentice Paul Nähring in June 1904, to trigger off a series of wide-reaching consequences. Since the autumn of 1890 the SPD had slowly been adjusting to a nominal position of legality, after 12 years in which it had been outlawed as a political organisation. The years between 1878 and 1890 had left an indelible mark on the Party's collective consciousness, producing a hardening of Marxian theory within the ranks, as well as cementing a fortress-like position on the far left of the political spectrum, from which the party activists launched their attacks against the institutions of Wilhelmine Germany. For their part, the authorities concentrated their efforts on engineering a series of new legal statutes designed to stem the growing influence of Social Democracy and, where these failed, relied on manipulating existing laws and police regulations.[32] The consequence was that the SPD was subjected to interminable restrictions, and leading members of the party were frequently arrested on the slightest of pretexts. This tended to provoke, on the one hand, an attitude of truculence from the party leadership, which often found its expression in guerilla-war tactics, but which, paradoxically, also accounted for a high degree of measured caution with which the SPD responded to new political developments. The fear of being outlawed once more or being the object of a *coup d'état* from above, or *Staatsstreich*, was never quite dispelled.

By way of compensation, radicalism — albeit often of a purely verbal kind — was given full flow within the columns of the party press. Despite the dangers which journalists courted in their exposés of political and economic realities,[33] an element of brazen outspokenness was seldom missing from party publications. Whether on the left or the right, the radical or revisionist wings of the movement, Social Democratic journalists joined in condemning each new act of oppression against the working-class. It was in a weekly paper published by Eduard Bernstein, the *Neues Montagsblatt*, that an article first drew attention to the death of Nähring and the wider implications behind this desperate act of suicide. Despite an impassioned call for action, it was some weeks before Max Peters, a 17-year-old apprentice in Berlin and later to become one of the leaders of the socialist youth movement,[34] sustained further interest in the case by discussing possible practical initiatives. In the wake of his article there followed a lively correspondence column, which concerned itself with the problems of setting up a viable youth organisation. Thus it was that in October 1904 an association of young workers and apprentices, *Verein der Lehrlinge und junger Arbeiter Berlins*, came into being, attracting at its first public meeting the same month an attendance of 800, of whom 300 immediately joined the association as paid-up members.[35]

The task of the Berlin group was regarded as being three-fold, that of providing information concerning the true economic relationships in the State, acting as an important source of intellectual stimulation and developing the concept of 'moral education'.[36] The latter included a crusade against the perils of alcoholism — widely prevalent amongst a working class which sought comfort and solace from worldly woes in the pleasures of drink — and within a few years the German socialist youth movement was also to declare itself against cinematographic shows, because of their allegedly baneful influence and the 'criminal tendencies' they were purported to arouse. Indeed, in 1914 Kurt Tucholsky gave up his job as film critic of the central party newspaper (*Vorwärts*) because he thought the material being shown — *Schundfilme* as they were widely referred to — was of abominable quality. The Berlin group also set up a complaints centre which gathered information about the violations of the industrial code directly from young workers, with the intention of issuing writs against offending factory-owners. It also set up a separate legal department to help and advise youngsters. By the beginning of 1907 the Berlin group had 1,268 members; of these, 770 apprentices and 277 unskilled workers of both sexes were under the age of 18.

It was not long before the Berlin group was joined by many others in Prussia, in Cottbus, Halle, Königsberg, Kiel, Magdeburg and Rostock. Willi Münzenberg, an activist in the youth movement before the First World War and later a leading member of the KPD, recalls the work of a socialist youth group founded in Erfurt in 1906 under the name *Bildungsverein Propaganda*.[37] It was here that he first came into contact with socialist literature and the works of Ferdinand Lassalle, Bruno Schoenlank and Karl Kautsky. Hitherto most young people of his disposition had read the popular adventure stories of Karl May and knew little about the ideas of Marx or Social Darwinists like Ernst Haeckel. These small youth groups thus fulfilled a vital function in transmitting socialist ideas, together with a specialist socialist vocabulary, in which the exploitation of the working masses and the explanation of individual rights were related to political realities of the day. There had long been a demand for such kinds of youth education. At party conferences voices had repeatedly been heard calling on the party executive to publish material suitable for young people, so that parents could initiate their children into the world of socialist thought and ideas, rather on the lines of a socialist catechism.

Notwithstanding the crucial importance of the 'trigger-mechanism' in the suicide of a Berlin apprentice in the summer of 1904, the first socialist youth group later formed there was neither the first in Europe,[38] nor indeed the first in Germany. As early as October 1903, a founding member of the Austrian socialist youth organisation had formed a similar group in Offenbach. More significant was the part played by Ludwig Frank in setting up his own socialist youth group in Mannheim, during the autumn of 1904. Frank had been a delegate at the International Socialist Conference in Amsterdam, during which attempts had been made – in vain – to bring into being an international socialist youth movement. He resolved to take the first steps towards creating at least the partial German framework of a youth movement allied to the ideals of Social Democracy. This was, for a variety of reasons, more likely to achieve success in the southern German situation than in the North, where the influence of Prussia was all too dominant. The severity of police restrictions in the North and the ever-present threat of official 'consequences' meant that local groups there usually limited themselves to expounding ideas for the protection of young workers, and supporting demands for further education.

In the southern German context, however, groups were able to adopt a much more aggressive line, more socialist in content and much more assertively anti-militarist. The relatively liberal combination laws and regulations governing political assembly in the South meant that groups there did not have to conceal their essentially political nature. By 1907 there were some 72 such groups, all functioning effectively and with a combined membership of 4,500.[39] In February 1906, Ludwig Frank opened a socialist youth conference in Karlsruhe, to which delegates from all the southern states had been invited, but which was attended only by representatives from Baden and Bavaria. Nonetheless, it was unanimously decided to set up a central federation for the southern states,[40] and issue a monthly journal, *Die junge Garde*. This publication played a major role in reporting cases of ill-treatment of soldiers, as well as examples of blatant arbitrary power as exercised by the military authorities. Its radical tone was much welcomed by its readership, which extended well beyond southern Germany. In Saxony alone there were 2,000 subscribers, and at its peak the circulation reached 11,000, much more than the total membership of the South German federation, which at the time of its dissolution in May 1908 numbered only 4,500.

From the very beginning, *Die junge Garde*, which was adroitly edited by Ludwig Frank, aimed at carrying the principles of the socialist struggle for equality and basic humanity into the hearts and minds of the 15–20 age group. In its own commentary on an appeal for new members, issued by the South German federation, the party newspaper *Vorwärts*[41] insisted that the basis of intellectual stimulation in young people of this age was of critical importance for their whole future development. It sharply attacked the attitude of the Catholic and Lutheran Churches which, recognising this fact, had founded innumerable societies and organisations, in order to perpetuate their work of stultification or *Volksverdummung* begun in the elementary schools.[42] At the same time, establishment newspapers seized upon these early attempts at organising the socialist youth as evidence of a further slide into moral decadence. Only a month later the conservative *Hamburger Nachrichten* thundered: 'If the state does not concern itself with the training and moral discipline which parents apparently seem increasingly unable to enforce, if it does not earnestly take upon itself the task of educating its young, then the strength and health of the nation as represented by its youth will go to the dogs', and it boldly asserted: 'youth must become. . . the bodyguard of the nation'.[43]

It was the aggressively strident tone of such editorials, repeated with gusto in a variety of influential publications, which created a climate in which the authorities could move towards a more interventionist policy in the field of youth welfare (*Jugendpflege*), and aided the setting up of a series of recreational centres and the funding of new educational programmes. When the North German groups formed their own federation, the *Vereinigung der freien Jugendorganisationen Deutschlands*, at the end of 1906 and began producing their own regular publication, *Die arbeitende Jugend*, the authorities stepped up their strict surveillance of all socialist activities. Section 8 of the Prussian laws of combination forbade apprentices or schoolchildren membership of a political organisation. The law also required a list of all members of such organisations to be submitted to the authorities, so that any employer was able to check whether any of his young workers were 'with the socialists'. Employers themselves attempted to correct inroads made by the socialist youth movement by giving instructions to various guilds to insert special clauses into the conditions of service for their apprentices. As a result, many youngsters could only attend public meetings with the prior permission of their employer.[44] In the two Mecklenburg states the carpenters' guilds, for instance, directed that apprentices were to be fined for belonging to any association without the consent of their masters.[45]

As part of the constant battle for survival, activists had to contend with police chicanery which often took on quite ridiculous proportions. Max Peters recalls an occasion in Halle when two policemen removed him from a lectern, from which he had been addressing a meeting, and imprisoned him for 36 hours, for daring to utter the word 'freedom'.[46] Meetings were almost invariably banned on occasions when well-known personalities were invited to speak, because of the 'danger to public order'. Above all, any discussion which could be construed as being of a political nature threatened the very existence of the youth groups in the North. In February 1906, for example, the young chairman of the working-men's anti-alcoholic association in Königsberg, himself a member of the SPD, was scheduled to speak to a gathering of young workers on the subject of anti-alcoholism. His connections with organised Social Democracy were cited as evidence of the intended 'political' nature of the meeting and, following an argument with police officers who considered themselves insulted by his remarks, the hapless speaker was hauled into court and received a sentence of imprisonment for his insolence.[47]

Often the youth groups attempted to circumvent the stiff police regulations by announcing that purely factual talks would be given on 'non-political' topics. The police responded by disinterring ancient statutes from the Prussian legal code, which laid down that those intending to transmit knowledge to minors had to possess an official permit from the local authorities. Numerous cases were reported where meetings had to be dissolved, because the speaker in question was unable to produce the desired document.[48] Nor was it uncommon for the police to seize copies of song books used by the youth groups, on the grounds that the sentiments expressed in the songs were of 'a revolutionary nature'. This happened in Berlin in July 1907,[49] and later in Breslau and other large towns. These song books were of considerable importance in the SPD's struggle because, unlike newspapers, books and pamphlets, they were not read merely once but, through the very act of constant repetition, were completely assimilated and thus formed an invaluable cutting edge for party propaganda. By 1910 no fewer than 30,000 copies of the standard song book had been sold or made available through party channels.[50]

Official reaction was especially sensitive to the SPD's frequent, orchestrated attacks on the evils of militarism, in which Karl Liebknecht, the darling of the youth groups, displayed the full force of his rhetorical venom. He wrote many articles for the Party's diverse publications, and in one characteristically vigorous piece[51] referred to the socialist youth movement as 'the praetorian guard' in the struggle against militarism, emphasising the significance of capturing the allegiance of young minds in the celebrated phrase, 'Wer die Jugend hat, der hat die Armee' ('Whoever possesses the youth of the country possesses its army'). It was at the first meeting of the South German federation, held immediately after the SPD's 1906 congress in Mannheim, that a representative from the Belgian socialist youth movement was heard to say that since 1902 no government in his country had dared to send troops out on to the streets against striking workers. He attributed this to the striking successes of their vigorous anti-militarist agitation.[52] At the very same meeting Karl Liebknecht gave an historical review of militarism, and it was the revised and extended text of his speech, published as a pamphlet in February 1907, that resulted in his facing charges of high treason. Under the leadership of the Leipzig youth group thousands of people demonstrated in front of the highest court in the land, the *Reichsgericht*, at the opening of his trial in October 1907, and again at its conclusion two months later. At the hearing Liebknecht rejected all claims by the prosecution that he had deliberately undermined the very foundation of the State, arguing 'My aim is to replace enthusiasm for war with the most intense enthusiasm for peace. That is the nub and consequence of my pamphlet'.[53] Nonetheless, he was convicted and sentenced to 18 months in prison.

IV

Official nervousness had already increased when, in August 1907, at the conclusion of the deliberations of the Second International in Stuttgart, the first constituent meeting of the Youth International took place, with delegates from 13 countries. Because of the difficulties facing the North German groups, only the South German federation was represented at the conference, which decided to establish a permanent international bureau in Vienna, and authorised the publication of a hectographed monthly journal in German and French.[54]

By this time the attitude of the party elders and the trade union leadership to the developments among the younger generation was beginning to crystallise. At the party conference in 1904 several motions urging the establishment of a youth movement had come up for debate, but without the necessary support of a majority of the delegates.[55] In particular, powerful voices from the trade unions, headed by Carl Legien, warned of the dangers of dissipating collective energies and efforts by sanctioning the creation of a separate organisation for young workers. Hermann Molkenbuhr summed up the feelings of many doubters within the SPD at the 1904 conference when, speaking of the possibility of a separate youth movement, he said: 'If we had such a movement we would have to fight against it, since all the efforts of the Party are directed towards centralisation and greater unity'.[56]

Although individual party associations were quite often sympathetic towards young socialist groups,[57] the trade unions repeatedly questioned the wisdom of allowing such initiatives to remain 'uncontrolled' by the party leadership. Indeed, when Ernst Thälmann organised meetings of young people in Hamburg, because of the lack of interest shown by trade unionists in youth problems, he encountered strong hostility, simply because the unions feared Thälmann would lure away potential members. Such was the strength of feeling amongst 14 to 16 year-olds, working in the transport industry in Berlin, that their interests were being ignored by their trade union colleagues during bargaining sessions with the employers, that they called their own strike. This un-precedented action was the first of its kind by unskilled young workers in Berlin and, after a long struggle, the employers eventually gave in to their demands.[58]

Trade union opposition to youth groups was perhaps strongest in the North, since both the unions and the SPD needed every willing able-bodied person for their own work and organisation, whereas in the South the groups impinged much less on trade union areas of competence, and concentrated their energies on awakening interest through the vocational schools. There was also the experience of the Swedish socialist youth movement which had a decidedly salutary effect on SPD attitudes. Here the movement had been in sharp conflict with the party, even tabling a motion at a conference of the Second International, requesting admission as a separate party, and relationships between both sides remained acrimonious for many years.[59]

Three months after the Mannheim party conference in 1906, at which the problems of the young were discussed in depth for the first time, and at which the trade unions had declared their opposition to a central youth organisation, a special union conference reaffirmed this essentially negative attitude. A year later, in December 1907, Robert Schmidt, a leading union organiser and later to become Reich Minister of Economics, attacked in particular the 'internationalist fantasies' of the youth groups, and declared that it was the job of the Party and the unions to concern themselves with international relations. Both Schmidt and Carl Legien published their views in the *Sozialistische Monatshefte*,[60] widely regarded as a haven for right-wing revisionists, which promptly elicited sharp words from the *Leipziger Volkszeitung* and other leading radical party newspapers. Thus began a long and heated debate about the nature of the SPD's commitment to the concept of 'youth welfare', producing a long series of contributions by eminent party figures in leading theoretical journals such as *Die neue Zeit*,[61] as well as in the daily press.

In June 1908 a further conference of the trade unions was held in Hamburg. Once again the leadership reaffirmed its opposition to any form of separate youth organisation, arguing instead in favour of local committees to be run jointly by representatives from the Party, the unions and the membership itself. It was during this conference that Robert Schmidt was to make his highly controversial suggestion that with the 10 pfennigs the young paid as membership dues to the existing youth groups, they would be better off buying 'a piece of sausage'.[62] It is hard to overlook a certain patronising air in this statement and Schmidt's additional claim that the incipient youth movement was merely 'playing at societies' brought a great deal of opprobrium on his head. Such was the strength of emotion amongst

young socialists at this time, fuelled by the feeling that an older
generation was trying to deprive them of a legitimate claim to their
own organisation, that in July 1908 several thousand young people
demonstrated in Berlin against the decisions taken at the trade union
congress.[63]

These further developments engulfed the party at a time when
irritability was already high, as a result of the latest government attempts
to curtail the freedom of political organisations. In May 1908 the new
Imperial Law of Association (*Reichsvereinsgesetz*) came into force. For
the most part it extended to the whole of the Empire a number of
restrictions on political activity, which already existed under the terms
of the Prussian constitution of 1853 and combination laws. It was but
one example of the way in which the Prussian state was often able to force
its legislative practices on the rest of Germany, and so strengthen its
already dominant position. A major bone of contention was section 17
of the new law, which prohibited all young people under the age of 18
from joining political clubs or attending political meetings or any other
public assemblies called for the purpose of discussing political matters.
Those guilty of tolerating such contraventions of the law were
threatened with heavy fines or, in cases of penury, with imprisonment.[64]
It was clear at the time that the original strategy of the authorities, of
relying on existing legislation to impede the organisational growth of
the youth groups, was not succeeding, and establishment papers had
long given up referring *en passant* to 'the saucy youngsters and babes-in-
arms'. These new measures were interpreted throughout the movement
as a kind of anti-socialist law (*Sozialistengesetz*) for the young, and
though they might have been secretly welcomed by the opponents of
a separate youth organisation, they required a fresh policy to be
formulated, which took account of the new circumstances and of the
views of all the parties involved.

What followed was to some extent pre-empted by the action of the
South German federation, which at a hastily called special conference
at Darmstadt voted to disband the existing groups and set up 'local
agitation committees'. This immediately created tension between the
southern and northern groups. The latter, more used to dealing with
official repression, were incensed that the groups in southern Germany
had not offered any opposition to the new law. Following the 1908
party congress at Nuremberg, the SPD Executive Committee met the
General Council of the trade unions in Berlin and drew up a joint
document, which was to form the basis of future youth policy. It
called upon all party and union branches to cooperate in creating

special youth committees or *Jugendausschüsse*. The aim was to provide a
general framework of support for youth activities, with the intention of
drawing young people of age into either full adult membership of the
SPD or a relevant trade union. Problems of organisation became immediately apparent. The new local committees were run by party and
union men who had no pedagogical training and little idea of how to
organise young people, let alone appreciate the aspirations and feelings
of a new generation. They tended to expect automatic respect and un-
questioning acceptance of decisions, and were not always pleased to
discover that their young membership was often unduly rebellious and
unwilling to accept authority for authority's sake. In contrast, non-
socialist youth groups were frequently led by people of intellect,
vision and distinction, who were 'model figures' in every sense. This
tended to encourage the adulation of leadership and foster a hero-
cult, trends which were later to merge into the National Socialist
stream of consciousness.[65]

One important consequence of the decisions arrived at jointly in
the autumn of 1908 was the creation in Berlin of a Central Coordinating
Office (*Zentralstelle*) for the various local youth committees. It was
an indication of the high order of priority that both the SPD and the
unions attached to this Central Office that their nominated representatives were figures of considerable political weight, including Hermann
Müller (later to become Chancellor in the Weimar Republic), Carl
Legien, Robert Schmidt, Luise Zietz and Heinrich Schulz. Friedrich
Ebert ran the day-to-day business, later assisted by Max Peters, and
he devoted himself at once to using the SPD's wealth of experience in
political propaganda in the cause of winning maximum support for
the new youth committees. In a leaflet distributed to school-leavers,
Ebert painted a harrowing picture of the two nations within society,
contrasting the poverty-stricken working-class with the idle rich and
— in a rhetorical flourish which characterised much of the party
propaganda of the period — he averred: 'What comes after school is
certainly life, but not a life with a firmament full of golden fruits, but
rather a life which with every single breath makes severe demands on
you, on your brains, your arms, your earnestness and your sense of
duty'.[66] In a similar leaflet, this time directed at the parents of schoolchildren, Ebert attacked the indoctrination of young people in the
schools and the inculcation of false values, which intensified still
further during the period of military service, so that 'all that remained
of their human dignity and proletarian sense of honour' was driven out.
Again in a rhetorical flight of fancy, he proceeded to whip up parental

emotions:

> With bound hands and in powerless rage you are forced to see how in
> the schools of this state the hearts of your children are gradually
> turned from you, how they are systematically taught to hate what
> you love, to value what you scorn and — flesh of your flesh — to
> disdain everything which is your pride and joy.[67]

By spring 1910, a total of more than 600,000 such leaflets had been
distributed on the authority of the Central Office.[68]

Even more important was the decision of the Central Office to
replace *Die arbeitende Jugend* and *Die junge Garde*, the two publications
of the northern and southern federations, with a new fortnightly paper,
Die Arbeiter-Jugend, under the former editor of the party newspaper in
Kiel, Karl Korn. Previewing the publication, *Vorwärts*[69] said that
its primary objective was to be 'a journal of education (*Bildungsorgan*)
for young workers'. The paper was to take due account of those areas
of knowledge which 'the educational policy of the Class State has with-
held from the young', including the social sciences in their broadest
application. In its first number, Karl Korn wrote:

> The young proletarian is not only a worker, but also a human being:
> he should be informed not only about the economic struggle and
> the historical background of his class situation, but also about the
> connecting strands which form the natural framework in which, as
> a human being, he finds himself.[70]

This new act of provocation did not pass unnoticed by officialdom. In
1911, the Prussian Minister of Education and Religious Affairs issued
instructions to all local inspectors of schools, warning them about
Die Arbeiter-Jugend, whose alleged intention was 'to further the intellectual and economic interests of young working-people', but which
in reality determined 'to train young workers for the cultural mission
of the proletariat and thoroughly drill them for the liberation struggle
of the working-class'. In this way 'the painstaking process of education
through the parental home, school and church was being destroyed'.
Heads of schools were requested to make reports on the current
situation in their areas and to prohibit the sale of any copies.[71] Despite
or perhaps because of the repeated attempts to suppress the publication,
Die Arbeiter-Jugend continued to flourish, and its circulation figures
leapt from 20,000 in 1909 to 65,000 in 1911 and 108,000 in the

summer of 1914. In the first year of its existence it required a subven-
tion from central party funds of 8,000 marks, but in time this was
gradually reduced.[72]

Meanwhile, the youth committees had been extending the scope of
their work. By the middle of 1910, 360 such committees were in
existence. Two years later this figure had risen to 574, and by the
outbreak of war in 1914 the total stood at 837. No fewer than 391
social centres were in operation, providing facilities for amusement
and recreation, with almost as many well-stocked libraries.[73] In 1909
the committee in Cologne was alone responsible for organising a
total of 35 lectures, 2 recitals, a literary evening, 4 public meetings, 6
social evenings, a Schiller commemoration, a Christmas fête, 4 day trips
and 8 half-day excursions.[74] In addition, physical activity and
exercise in the fresh air were always encouraged. In its report for
1912, the committee in Elberfeld-Barmen (later to become the town
of Wuppertal) declared: 'Nothing is more calculated to engage the
hearts and minds of young people than organised rambles and strolls
through the countryside. A spirit of solidarity is promoted to a quite
extraordinary degree by such undertakings'.[75] Not all the original
youth groups had decided to comply with the terms of the 1908 agreement between the SPD and trade-union leadership, and disband themselves. This brought them into immediate conflict with the law. Many,
in the South as well as in the North, simply changed their name to
something as ostensibly harmless, such as 'Educational Association of
Young Workers' (*Bildungsverein junger Arbeiter und Arbeiterinnen*),
and proceeded with a full programme of activities. Others regrouped
themselves as reading or literary circles. A major test case developed
over the original youth group in Berlin, when the local political police
pronounced it a political organisation in October 1909 and ordered
its dissolution the following January. In November 1910 the Prussian
constitutional court upheld this action, on the grounds that members
had been subscribers to *Die Arbeiter-Jugend*. Published by the Central
Office, its political function could not be in question.[76]

Almost immediately the Prussian Minister of the Interior wrote
to all the heads of the regional administration, calling on them to use
the recent judgement as a model, since it showed the way 'in which it
will be possible to counteract successfully the Social Democratic
attempts directed at gaining a hold over our young'. For this reason
it was 'of the utmost importance to make the fullest use of every
possible opportunity for controlling this activity'.[77] As the chief of
police in Cologne made clear in a letter to his superior, the local

Regierungsprasident, in July 1911, since the Berlin judgment the SPD had gone over to making widespread use of the terms 'Free Youth Movement' and 'Free Youth', and had resorted to describing planned meetings as 'large non-political assemblies'.[78] As if to parody this argument over semantics, the local party newspaper, the *Rheinische Zeitung*, declared 'The youth organisation is dead. Long live the youth movement!'.[79] Using the basis of the judgment by the Prussian constitutional court, it was relatively easy to proceed against not only many of the original youth groups, but also the newly-formed youth committees. It was hard to deny the political connections, since SPD party activists were usually on the boards of management. Official disclaimers seldom did any good. If the committees concerned ignored the demands of local state prosecutors for membership lists and copies of the statutes, they risked heavy fines or the threat of dissolution. When this happened, as in Magdeburg for example, the Party responded by issuing statements in the local press declaring that the police had dissolved a political club which had never existed. The authorities then simply pronounced the subscribers to *Die Arbeiter-Jugend* a political association, and fined the delivery agents for contravening the Imperial Law of Association.[80]

Other legal battles followed in different parts of the country. A long correspondence ensued between the chairman of the Cologne youth committee and the Provincial Governor (*Oberpräsident*) of the Rhine Province, who cited subscriptions to *Die Arbeiter-Jugend*, historical talks on political matters, the contents of the local song book, the use of a red flag and financial assistance from central SPD funds as evidence of the committee's essentially political work.[81]

Even when local committees turned their attention to campaigning against the 'penny dreadfuls' of the period, they ran up against opposition from the authorities. It was one such case that caused Ludwig Frank to complain bitterly in a speech to the Reichstag in February 1911:

> It is 'political' when young people are warned about the danger of alcoholism, 'political' when they are invited to attend historical lectures or talks about public health, 'political' when war is waged against obscene literature. But it is not 'political' when in 'Christian' and 'national' youth clubs talks are held about world politics, not 'political' when leading figures in the public eye make election speeches there.[82]

Worse still was the way in which a form of *Berufsverbot* was applied to those whose activities on behalf of the socialist cause were deemed incompatible with employment by the State. In 1912, disciplinary proceedings were instituted against a teacher in Bremen, who wrote under a pseudonym for several SPD publications and helped organise the local youth meetings. A year later he was dismissed.[83] Others were refused permission to sit their matriculation examinations, because of their membership of socialist youth organisations.[84]

While it is undoubtedly true, as Franz Mehring remarked in the spring of 1911, that 'the more the youth movement is put under pressure, the more it will be protected from the danger of degenerating into mere games and trifles',[85] there was not much practical value to be gained from demonstrative martyrdom. Indeed, the Central Office had to remind its youth committees again and again of the need for absolute caution in view of such persistent police practices. A similar point was made by Hermann Müller at the first Reich conference of the youth committees in April 1910, when he said, 'Our whole activity must be influenced by the consideration we have to give to the existing laws and the work of the authorities'.[86]

This caution partly explains the rather muted response of the party leadership to the idealistic enthusiasm of the first few years of the socialist youth movement. It is understandable that the German working class, after its united, determined and bitter struggle against the iniquities of the Anti-Socialist law, was unwilling to see its solidarity and organisational strength crumble away. Any attempt at 'breaking away' and setting up a separate structure was bound to fill the party veterans with horror. The years of ostracism between 1878 and 1890 had convinced them that only by forging a strong bond of togetherness, a spirit of mutual comradeship, could they hope to win the war against capitalism. If once the principle of an all-embracing united organisation were breached, the authorities could pick off the smaller individual units with ease. Moreover, as the SPD, and to a lesser extent the trade unions, continued their respective struggles, the need to draw on reserves of talent from the younger membership loomed large. A separate and independent youth organisation could offer no guarantee of future solidarity within the movement. In any case, the SPD had always regarded itself as more than just a political organisation.[87] It saw its role as providing for the material and spiritual needs of the worker from the cradle to the grave, and in the process immunising him against the ills of the bourgeois world. To this end German Social Democracy maintained a plethora of different organisations –

gymnastics, rowing and athletics clubs, choral societies, swimming and bowling associations, cycling clubs, the working men's theatre (*Volksbühne*), cooperatives, funeral societies and other welfare schemes — over which it continued to exercise firm control.

In seeking to suppress the spontaneous reaction which had attended the birth of its youth movement, the SPD was to create considerable difficulties for itself. It was the left wing of the party which recognised the inherent potential in mobilising young workers, and it was from the leadership of the left wing — from strong personalities like Karl Liebknecht and Rosa Luxemburg — that the socialist youth was increasingly to draw its inspiration. To some extent the radical extremes which became evident after 1914 were due to the purposeful severity with which the institutions of the Reich waged their own war against socialism. Those who had matured under Wilhelmine reaction were later unable or unwilling to differentiate between a semi-autocratic and a democratic State, and thus fought against every kind of State power. The consequences for the Weimar Republic were ominous. But the failure to harness the idealism of the young and give the socialist youth movement its head meant that in 1918 many a fervent young socialist, seeing the collaboration of his former comrades-in-arms with the hated representatives of a police state, rushed to the communist cause.

Notes

1. This point is developed at length in my book, *Scandal, Sensation and Social Democracy* (Cambridge, 1977), which also contains an analysis of the SPD press during the period.
2. The cases of ill-treatment were often spectacular, but courts were notoriously lenient with the well-situated. A Potsdam court, for instance, sentenced a master locksmith to a relatively small fine for applying a burning hot rod to his apprentice's body, and plunging his face into the hot gleeds. Similarly, a court at Kassel acquitted a master of all charges relating to the death of one of his apprentices. Although the lad had fallen to the ground and broken his skull after being beaten by his employer, the master had only been carrying out his lawful right to beat the apprentice; see Johannes Schult, *Aufbruch einer Jugend* (Bonn, 1956), p. 102.
3. Max Peters, *Der Weg zum Licht* (Berlin, 1907), p. 24.
4. Out of every 10,000 inhabitants living in Berlin in 1907, eight children between the ages of 10 and 15, and twenty-nine in the category 15 to 20 succumbed to the disease; see *Geschichte der deutschen Arbeiterjugendbewegung 1904–1945* (Dortmund, 1973), p. 24.
5. Edith Baumann, *Die Geschichte der deutschen Jugendbewegung* (Berlin, 1947), p. 18.
6. Erich Lindstaedt, *Mit uns zieht die neue Zeit* (Bonn, 1954), p. 19.

7. In 1905 the Prussian inspectorate reported a total of 8,015 violations (1904: 7,405), leading to 1,291 convictions (1904: 1,403), requiring the payment of small money fines between 3 and 10 marks. The survey had taken account of 64,325 work-places with a total of 2,318,161 employees; see Peters, p. 28.

8. Of 809,286 apprentices in Germany in 1907, 496,618 were in small businesses and workshops employing only up to 10 people; see *Arbeiter jugendbewegung*, p. 24.

9. Peters, p. 13.

10. Ibid., p. 11.

11. Ibid., p. 15.

12. Amongst the Prussian factory labour-force in 1904, there were no fewer than 124,305 male workers aged 14—16 and 65,392 females of the same age. A year later these figures had risen to 132,597 and 69,054 respectively. Similarly, there were some 51,428 young males and 14,056 young females of the same age in Bavaria; see Peters, p. 9.

13. The *Gewerbeordnung* laid down that the articles of apprenticeship were not terms of work, but represented an undertaking to be trained, a relationship in which the trade-master was given the right to exercise corporal punishment (*Züchtigungsrecht*). In 1907, the number of male and female young workers had risen to 4,326,305, of whom 1,407,652 were in industry and mining, and 1,326,443 still in agriculture and forestry; see Karl Korn, *Die Arbeiter-jugendbewegung* (Berlin, 1922), p. 16. Some sources place the number of young workers at this time as high as 4.8 million.

14. Cf. *Arbeiterjugend gestern und heute*, ed. Helmut Schelsky (Heidelberg, 1955), p. 21.

15. *Arbeiterjugendbewegung*, p. 24.

16. *Stenographische Berichte des Deutschen Reichstages* (hereafter RT), Bd. 295, p. 8571.

17. Cf. Heinz Ernst Brunkhorst, *Die Einbeziehung der preussischen Schule in die Politik des Staates (1808—1918)* (Diss., Köln, 1956).

18. Ibid., p. 53.

19. On the relations between the SPD and the organs of authority in the Wilhelmine Reich, see esp. Klaus Saul, *Staat, Industrie, Arbeiterbewegung im Kaiserreich* (Dusseldorf, 1974); ibid., 'Der Staat und "die Mächte des Umsturzes" ', *Archiv für Sozialgeschichte*, Bd XII (Hannover, 1972); Dieter Fricke, *Bismarcks Prätorianer. Die Berliner politische Polizei im Kampf gegen die deutsche Arbeiterbewegung 1871—1898* (Berlin, 1962); Karl Frohme, *Politische Polizei und Justiz im monarchischen Deutschland* (Hamburg, 1926); Dieter Groh, *Negative Integration und revolutionärer Attentismus* (Frankfurt/M. & Berlin, 1973).

20. Brunkhorst, p. 73ff.

21. Walter Sieger, *Das erste Jahrzehnt der deutschen Arbeiterjugendbewegung 1904—1914* (Berlin, 1958), p. 17. See also Klaus Saul, 'Der Kampf um die Jugend zwischen Volksschule und Kaserne', *Militärgeschichtliche Mitteilungen*, 1/1971; Dieter Fricke, 'Zum Bündnis des preussisch-deutschen Militarismus mit dem Klerus gegen die sozialistische Arbeiterbewegung am Ende des 19. Jahrhunderts', *Zeitschrift für Geschichtswissenschaft*, 1960, Heft 6. Fricke also deals with the work of one of the many citizens' action groups, the 'Reichsverband gegen die Sozialdemokratie', in 'Der Reichsverband gegen die Sozialdemokratie von seiner Gründung bis zu den Reichstagswahlen von 1907', *Zeitschrift für Geschichtswissenschaft*, 1959, Heft 5.

22. For a more detailed examination of this aspect of Wilhelmine policy see my article, 'The War of Words: Anti-socialist offensives and counter-propaganda in Wilhelmine Germany 1890—1914', *Journal of Contemporary History*,

Vol. 11, Nos. 2 and 3 (July 1976).

23. *Arbeiterjugendbewegung*, p. 21.

24. The Protestant social clubs alone had 131 full-time youth workers and 135 recreational centres; see *Rheinische Zeitung*, 22 February 1911.

25. In 1893 the non-socialist *Deutsche Turnerschaft* had 150 members up to the age of 20. By 1914 this had risen to more than 400,000; see *Arbeiterjugendbewegung*, p. 20.

26. Brunkhorst, p. 87.

27. Schult, p. 93. In July 1908 the Prussian Minister of Trade issued a circular concerned with vocational schools. Each such school, whose principal function was to assist in the training of young people for various trades and minor professions, was to be linked to a social centre; see Schult, p. 94.

28. *Archivalische Forschungen zur Geschichte der deutschen Arbeiterbewegung*, ed. Leo Stern, 2, I (Berlin, 1954), p. 211.

29. *Arbeiterjugendbewegung*, p. 79.

30. Ibid., p. 78.

31. Ibid., p. 81.

32. Cf. my article, 'By Other Means: The Legal Struggle Against the SPD in Wilhelmine Germany 1890–1900', *Historical Journal*, Vol. 17, 2 (June 1974), and Part Two of my book, *Scandal, Sensation and Social Democracy*. Vernon T. Lidtke, *The Outlawed Party* (Princeton, N.J., 1966), provides a good introduction to the history of Social Democracy under the *Sozialistengesetz*. More general works on the SPD include Dieter Fricke, *Zur Organisation und Tätigkeit der deutschen Arbeiterbewegung 1890–1914* (Leipzig, 1962); Georg Fülberth, 'Zur Genese des Revisionismus in der deutschen Sozialdemokratie vor 1914', *Das Argument*, March 1971; Peter J. Gay, *The Dilemma of Democratic Socialism* (New York, 1952); Erich Matthias, 'Kautsky und der Kautskyanismus', *Marxismus-Studien*, 2. Folge (Tübingen, 1957); J.P. Nettl, 'The Social Democratic Party 1890–1914', *Past and Present*, 30 (April 1965); Guenther Roth, *Social Democrats in Imperial Germany* (Totowa, 1963); Carl E. Schorske, *German Social Democracy 1905–17* (Cambridge, Mass. 1955); Hans-Josef Steinberg, *Sozialismus und deutsche Sozialdemokratie* (Hanover, 1967); Hans-Ulrich Wehler, *Sozialdemokratie und Nationalstaat 1840–1914*, 2nd edn. (Göttingen, 1971), as well as the works listed in note 19.

33. On the conflict between the authorities and SPD journalists resulting from the law on *lèse-majesté*, see my article, 'The Kaiser, the Wilhelmine State and Lèse-Majesté', *German Life and Letters*, XXVII, 2 (January, 1974).

34. For Max Peters' own recollections of the early years of struggle, see *50 Jahre Arbeiterjugendbewegung 1904–54* (Bonn, 1954), p.21ff., as well as Peters, op. cit. (see note 3).

35. Cf. the recollections of Helmut Lehmann, elected chairman of the association in October 1904, in *Deutschlands junge Garde*, eds. Wolfgang Arlt, Manfred Heinze, Manfred Uhlemann (Berlin, 1959), p. 8ff.

36. Peters, op. cit., p. 35. The statutes of the *Freie Jugendorganisation Kiel*, formed in 1907, stressed the need to protect 'the spiritual, legal and economic needs' of apprentices and young workers.

37. Willi Münzenberg, *Die dritte Front* (Berlin, 1930), p. 17ff., which includes a vivid picture of working conditions during that period.

38. The oldest of all the youth organisations was the Belgian *Fédération des Jeunes Gardes Socialistes de Belgique*, which in 1907, after 22 years, had 13,000 paying members in 12 different associations. The Dutch organisation *De Zaaier* was formed in Amsterdam in 1901, and Denmark, Sweden, Norway, Finland, France and Italy had similar groups.

39. *Hamburger Correspondent*, 16 July 1907. There is a wealth of material, mostly consisting of press cuttings, in StA Hbg, Politische Polizei, S 17290 Bd 2, S 12570, S 14115, S 16640.
40. The *Verband junger Arbeiter und Arbeiterinnen* held its first meeting immediately following the SPD party conference in Mannheim, in September 1906. Fifty-two representatives from 37 local groups with more than 3,000 members attended and the statutes provided for both groups and individual membership. A copy of the statutes is in StA Hbg, Politische Polizei, V 898.
41. *Vorwärts*, 22 March 1906.
42. By early 1907, the whole of the SPD's organisational area 'Oberrhein' had still only enrolled 6,750 youth members, whereas the *Volksverein für das katholische Deutschland* had over 22,000 members in Cologne alone.
43. *Hamburger Nachrichten*, 18 April 1906. Shortly after the Berlin group had held its inaugural meeting in October 1904, the anti-Semitic Christian Social Party organised a counter-demonstration at which the former Court Preacher Adolf Stöcker described the new movement as 'a fiend'; *Deutschlands junge Garde* , p. 14.
44. Baumann, p. 23.
45. *Hamburger Echo*, 18 July 1908.
46. *Arbeiterjugendbewegung* (Bonn, 1954), p. 26.
47. Schult, p. 38. Shortly after its formation, the youth group in Königsberg was dissolved by the local police and the offices of the local party newspaper, which had presumed to criticise the action of the authorities, were raided on the orders of the local state prosecutor; see *Vorwärts*, 27 June 1906.
48. *Deutschlands junge Garde*, pp. 54–5. The extensive efforts of police spies, often employed as *agents provocateurs*, are recalled by Paul Schiller in *Deutschlands junge Garde. 50 Jahre Arbeiterjugendbewegung* (Berlin, 1954), pp. 49–50.
49. *Leipziger Volkszeitung*, 24 July 1907.
50. *Arbeiter-Jugend*, 7 May 1910.
51. *Die junge Garde*, 22 September 1906.
52. Cf. the report in the *Hamburger Fremdenblatt*, 2 October 1906.
53. *Der Hochverratsprozess gegen Karl Liebknecht vor dem Reichsgericht. Verhandlungsbericht* (Berlin, 1957), p. 150.
54. *Deutschlands junge Garde*, p. 29. At the same conference Henrietta Roland-Holst, a leading Dutch socialist, spoke about the aims and purpose of the youth movement, detailing the need to campaign for better conditions of work and continue the struggle against alcoholism and militarism. She suggested a variety of different events and activities, including talks and lectures, the publication of newspapers and pamphlets, the setting up of mobile local libraries, excursions and visits, the formation of study-circles, the organisation of cultural and literary evenings and plenty of physical exercise, in which a team-spirit could be fostered; cf. *Hamburger Echo*, 8 September 1907.
55. Cf. *Protokoll des Parteitages der Sozialdemokratischen Partei Deutschlands* (hereafter PT), 1904 Bremen, pp. 133, 317.
56. Ibid., p. 185.
57. The success of the group in Cologne, formed early in 1907, owed much to the strong support of the local SPD, which provided the organisation with rooms in the party's social club; cf. Helmuth Stoecker, *Walter Stoecker – Die Frühzeit eines deutschen Arbeiterführers 1891–1920* (Berlin, 1907), p. 18.
58. *Deutschlands junge Garde*, pp. 47–8.
59. Schult, p. 44.

60. See esp. *Sozialistische Monatshefte*, 12 Jg., Heft 12 (June 1908), p. 712. In the July 1908 edition, Paul Umbreit refused to countenance the idea that the young should have a say in party affairs and the work of the trade unions, and set himself completely against the idea of a separate organisation.
61. Cf. especially Ludwig Frank in *Die neue Zeit*, 1907/08, II, Nr 33, p. 233ff; Anton Pannekoek, Nr 42, p. 557ff.; Max Peters, 1911/12, I, Nr 7, p. 17ff.; and Paul Schiller, 1912/13, II, Nr 50, p. 942ff.
62. Münzenberg, p. 39.
63. Cf. *Hamburger Fremdenblatt*, 28 July 1908, and reports in StA Hamburg, Politische Polizei, S 14115.
64. For a more detailed discussion of this law, see Section 2.2 of my book, *Scandal, Sensation and Social Democracy*. Shortly before the new law took effect several thousand young workers held a protest demonstration in Berlin, which had to be forcibly broken up by police using dogs. For another, more positive aspect of this law, see above, pp. 193–4.
65. A comparison with 'bourgeois' youth movements is beyond the confines of this study, but in many respects their importance dwarfed the activities of their socialist counterparts. In the introduction to Walter Z. Laqueur's excellent survey, *Young Germany* (London, 1962), Richard Crossman describes them as 'the German analogue to the public school system'.
66. A copy is in StA Hbg, Politische Polizei, V 965, Bd 1.
67. Ibid.
68. *Arbeiter-Jugend*, 7 May 1910. On other aspects of the work of the *Zentralstelle*, see Korn, p. 177ff.
69. *Vorwärts*, 9 January 1909. See also StA Hbg, Politische Polizei, which has innumerable press cuttings on the *Arbeiter-Jugend* 1909–18.
70. *Arbeiter-Jugend*, 30 January 1909.
71. *Hamburger Schulzeitung*, 20 November 1911, in StA Hbg, Politische Polizei, S 16640.
72. Cf. Korn, p. 176.
73. Cf. Schult, p. 104ff.
74. Stoecker, p. 25.
75. *Elberfelder Freie Presse*, 6 June 1913.
76. Cp. Schult, p. 98; Korn, p. 205ff.
77. *Arbeiterjugendbewegung*, p. 75. Cf. the correspondence between the *Landrat* of Harburg and the *Regierungspräsident* in Lüneburg on the political nature of youth groups in the area: StA Hbg, Politische Polizei, S 17290, Bd 3, Bl 68.
78. HStA Düsseldorf, Bestand Reg. Köln, Nr 8077, Bl 215.
79. *Rheinische Zeitung*, 24 October 1910, quoted ibid.
80. Cf. Korn, p. 220ff. and Schult, p. 100.
81. HStA Düsseldorf, Reg. Köln Nr 8077, Bl 129ff.
82. Quoted in *Rheinische Zeitung*, 22 February 1911.
83. Korn, p. 218.
84. Ibid., p. 219. Two young men who had attended meetings of one of the youth groups had their high school diplomas rescinded by the authorities; Schult, p. 100.
85. *Die neue Zeit*, 1910/11, I, p. 859.
86. Stoecker, p. 31; also Korn, p. 188ff. At the same conference representatives of the different Rhine committees expressed a wish for greater independence and freedom from trade union control and influence. They especially sought parity of representation for the membership on the *Jugendausschüsse*, but encountered strong opposition from the party leadership.
87. In one of the propaganda works published by the Central Office the author

declared: 'What the cosy family circle cannot be for the worker of today must be provided by the bigger family of his comrades-in-arms. The workers have formed a new community to replace the old family circle: that is the Organisation, the union of all like-minded men, of the many – weak as individuals, but strong together'; Heinrich Schulz, *Gehörst du zu uns?* (Berlin, 1911), a copy of which is in HStA Düsseldorf, B1 138.

11 RADICALISM AND THE WORKER: METALWORKERS AND REVOLUTION 1914–23

Dick Geary

I

The revolutionary events that took place in Germany between 1918 and 1923 (the November Revolution, the foundation of several Soviet Republics in 1919, the activities of the Red Army in the Ruhr in 1920, the creation of a mass communist party and its attempts at insurrection in 1921 and 1923) present something of a problem for a widely held view of the earlier history of the German labour movement, which believes that by 1914 the German working class had become 'integrated' into the society of the Second Reich.[1] In consequence the regeneration of working-class radicalism is attributed to a number of problems generated by the four years of war: food shortage, inflation, increasing pressure of work in the factory and a resultant desire for peace. As part of this picture the November Revolution then appears as nothing more than a temporary movement to bring an end to the war, although most historians will also admit that the democratisation of the Reich constituted the other important demand of the November revolutionaries. This view is at odds with some significant facts: it makes little sense to talk of the entirety of the German working class or even its political leadership being 'integrated' into Wilhelmine society in 1918. Secondly, the social crisis of 1918 to 1923 and the related emergence of a mass revolutionary movement cannot be dismissed as a transient product of war. For some sections of the German labour force far more was at stake than the admittedly important issues of peace and democracy.

To begin with the question of 'integration' and the supposed embourgeoisement of the pre-war labour movement in Germany: constraints of space dictate that little can be said here, but important points to counter the thesis of increasing reformism can be made at a general level. In the first place we know next to nothing about the views of the great majority of Germany's industrial work-force before the outbreak of war in 1914. For most workers at this time remained outside the ranks of organised labour. Yet it is far from clear that this failure to organise reflected any satisfaction with either the industrial or the political status quo. Indeed it is clearly not without significance that many of those who were active in the councils' movement in

1918–19 were precisely those workers who lacked previous traditions of organisation.[2]

As far as the organised pre-war labour movement is concerned the situation is still far from clear. Since Robert Michels it has been widely argued that the creation of a huge trade union and socialist bureaucracy led the Free Trade Unions and the Social Democratic Party down the road to reformism; whilst Roth, Mitchell and Stearns have gathered much information to demonstrate the non-radical stance of the working-class rank and file.[3] Yet this is only part of the story and there is evidence of a contrary nature. It is by no means true that the views of SPD parliamentary candidates or party functionaries necessarily reflected those of their constituents. Left SPD officials sometimes represented right-wing party branches and vice versa. In several places, left and right wingers succeeded one another with the minimum of fuss; and this may be taken as testifying to the existence at the base of the party of a general social-democratic consciousness, for which the ideological debates of the leadership were not of paramount importance.[4] What is certainly true is that the radical wing of the SPD was grossly underrepresented at national party congresses and complained about this vigorously.[5] Further evidence of pre-war SPD radicalism I have given elsewhere.[6]

A final point on the situation of German Social Democracy before the First World War, and one which will be taken up later, is that there seems to have been more and not less dissatisfaction with the cautious policies of party and trade union leaders in 1913 than there had been in many a previous year. This is clear if one looks at the records of the SPD congress of the year: not only did Rosa Luxemburg gain more support at this congress than at any other, but also several speakers from the floor attacked the party executive and spoke of discontent and disillusionment in the factories.[7] Karl Kautsky also mentioned the same problem in his correspondence with other socialists,[8] and the issue was discussed widely in the party press.[9] Rank and file discontent was to be further exacerbated during the war, as we shall see.

II

To turn now to the central issue of the nature of the German Revolution of 1918 and its aftermath, it is possible to demonstrate that it was far from being solely concerned with bringing an end to war and the demo-cratisation of the constitution. It is true that many of the soldiers' councils which appeared in 1918 renounced any radical socialist aims,[10] and that many commentators have described the workers' councils in a similar way.[11] Yet this is only one side of a far more complicated story. In fact a great many aspects of and evidence for radical aspirations on the part of some workers are rarely mentioned or often completely overlooked by many modern commentators. In the first place, the rhetoric adopted by the workers' councils in some places went much further than demands for democratic reform. The new revolutionary regime was hailed as a 'socialist republic' by the provisional workers' and soldiers' council in Berlin[12] and by the workers' and soldiers' council of Cologne.[13] At Cuxhaven, the most radical of the North Sea ports and one which Noske contemplated bombarding at one stage, demands were made on 7 November for the recognition of the social and political power of the councils;[14] whilst the executive of the Hamburg councils declared: 'This is the beginning of the German Revolution. The World Revolution. Long live Socialism. Long live the Workers' Republic'.[15] Again in November 1918 the workers' and soldiers' council of Brunswick envisaged nothing less than the end of the capitalist order and insisted that power should remain in the hands of the councils, even after the new national assembly had been elected.[16] The regional conference of workers' and soldiers' councils held at Remscheid on 20 November 1918 also stated:

> The workers' and soldiers' councils of the Lower Rhine will tolerate no policies or measures which are aimed at preventing the development of the revolution and depriving the people of its rights. The counter-revolutionary plan to save capitalist society by a national assembly before the aims of the revolution have been realised is totally rejected by the workers' and soldiers' councils of this district.[17]

No less militant in tone was a declaration made by delegates of the workers' and soldiers' councils of Dresden, Leipzig and Chemnitz, who proclaimed that 'the capitalist system is destroyed. The bourgeois monarchical regime is overthrown. The revolutionary proletariat has assumed power'; and who went on to demand socialisation and the arming of the workers.[18] Thus demands for socialisation did appear in some places, even in the early days of the revolution, and can be detected in Bremen and at the Berlin Factories of the German Motorworks, Fritz Werner AG, von Flohr, Siemens-Schukert and others.[19]

What is true, however, is that it was only in the early months of 1919 that a massive socialisation campaign developed amongst the Ruhr miners[20] and in Central Germany (especially in Thuringia and Saxony),[21] in the course of a process of radicalisation which will be described below. To some extent these radical demands relate to the fact that in some parts of Germany it was left-wing socialists who managed to seize power as early as November 1918. Radicals were dominant in Bremen, Halle, Leipzig and Düsseldorf from the start; whilst the workers' and soldiers' councils of Brunswick, Berlin, Chemnitz, Munich and Stuttgart were under the direction of left-wingers.[22] In some towns the old institutions of government were dissolved, as at Bremen, Chemnitz, Gotha, Leipzig and Königsberg;[23] in others the old police forces were dissolved.[24] Where this happened armed groups of workers were then formed both to preserve law and order and the gains of the revolution.[25]

To record radical declarations, of course, is not sufficient to make any statement about exactly how many workers were radical or subscribed to such positions. Indeed, one of the main problems of the present article is the difficulty of obtaining hard quantitative data. Having said this, however, it will not do to point to the fact that in most cases the councils were dominated by representatives of the SPD and claim that in consequence one is dealing with a basically 'moderate' German working class in 1918. This becomes clear if one looks at the Congress of Workers' and Soldiers' Councils that assembled in Berlin in December 1918. At that congress the SPD delegates were by far the largest single contingent: they constituted 288 of the total number of delegates, whereas there were only 80 Independent Socialists and 10 Spartacists in attendance.[26] What is more, no fewer than 164 of the delegates were paid functionaries of the Majority Social Democratic Party.[27] Not surprisingly, therefore, the conference voted for the calling of a National Assembly, and for the SPD leadership's position, rather than for the more radical slogan of 'all power to the workers' and soldiers' councils'. But what is equally important in this context is that the same conference passed a resolution calling for the democratisation of the army, proposed the establishment of an executive committee of the councils to oversee governmental actions and called for the immediate socialisation of those industrial sectors deemed right for such treatment. Now on each of these last three issues the delegates at the conference of councils were proposing courses of action which were deemed inappropriate by the SPD central leadership in 1918; and this demonstrates quite clearly that a majority of Social Democrats were not simply sheep in the hands of their party executive. The point is that the precise relationship between the attitudes of party leaders and those of their supposed followers is by no means easy to gauge and it certainly is worth examining that relationship in times of great and rapid social upheaval. In fact, just as in Russia in mid-1917 one could find Menshevik party members carrying Bolshevik slogans, so in Germany in 1918–19 one can find similar happenings. We know that the campaign for socialisation in the Ruhr in 1919 involved SPD members as well as their more left-wing colleagues, for the general strike of April of that year is reckoned to have involved no less than 75 per cent of the total work-force in the mines.[28] SPD members also took part in the insurrectionary activities of the Red Army in the Ruhr in the wake of the Kapp putsch, manifestly against the desires and indeed policies of their ostensible leadership.[29] Some SPD members of the Executive Committee of the Berlin Councils voted for a radical proposal made by the Independent Ernst Däumig for rule by the councils and against the immediate calling of a national assembly, whereas the Social Democratic leadership did desire immediate elections.[30] The dissolution of some councils caused anger on the part of many Majority Socialists;[31] whilst the policies of the SPD leaders in Munich by no means met with the automatic acceptance of the rank and file.[32] There were other SPD members who objected to the SPD government's dismissal of the radical Berlin chief of police.[33]

In fact in many places workers seemed to have difficulty in making a clear distinction between the policies of the different socialist factions. Hence the extraordinary slogan heard in Kiel at the very beginning of the Revolution: 'Scheidemann for President, Liebknecht for Minister of Defence';[34] and the fact that in the same town mutinous sailors both invited Hugo Haase and Georg Ledebour, two of the most prominent members of the USPD, to represent them *and* were prepared to propose the Majority Socialist Gustav Noske, later to earn the title of the 'bloodhound of the revolution', for mayor.[35] Later, in early 1919 at Essen, the workers' and soldiers' council sent a telegram to the Ebert-Scheidemann government condemning its repressive actions; and that telegram was signed not just by KPD and USPD members, but also by Majority Socialists.[36] In fact at Essen the SPD, USPD and KPD joined together to demand the socialisation of the mines.[37] As we have seen, this was by no means uncommon in the Ruhr in 1919. Furthermore the relationship between the different political organisations of the left varied enormously from place to place. For example, in July 1919 the SPD and the USPD joined forces for strike action in Bautzen, Kiel and Nuremberg, yet in Berlin, Dresden and Wilhelmshaven relations between the two parties were far less cordial. In Brunswick, Hanover and Wilhelmshaven the USPD and the KPD cooperated with one another, as they did in Duisburg and Düsseldorf, whereas there was considerable tension between the two organisations in Dresden, Hamburg and Stuttgart.[38] Rosa Luxemburg wrote to Clara Zetkin in December 1918, complaining that the SPD and the Independent Socialists had fused in some localities;[39] whilst Bock tells us that many Ruhr miners had no idea of the difference between the Communist Party on the one hand and the various anarcho-syndicalist organisations on the other. In fact some workers are believed to have belonged to both movements.[40]

That this should be the case is none too difficult to understand. In the first place the splitting of the old socialist movement was a new phenomenon and it was to take some time before a process of clarification set in. This was especially so as the division between the SPD and the USPD was not a clear split of left from right: for although most radicals did belong to the latter organisation, it was far from ideologically homogeneous, including not only Rosa Luxemburg and Karl Liebknecht of the far left, but also Eduard Bernstein, the theorist of revisionism. Furthermore, the fact that the USPD served in a coalition government with the SPD between 10 November and 27 December did not serve to make any more evident the difference between the two parties. It is also true that the USPD had a decentralised administrative structure allowing considerable autonomy to party branches;[41] whilst in its early years the KPD was no more monolithic in its structure or ideology.[42] It is also significant that the oppositional movement within the Free Trade Unions, which was based upon the Revolutionary Shop Stewards Organisation and of which more will be said later, refused to become too closely associated with any particular political faction as it feared losing its factory base; and this despite the fact that many of its members were members of the USPD. Thus in the great strike of January 1918 the shop stewards insisted on parity representation for the two socialist parties on the strike committee; and Richard Müller, perhaps the most prominent member of the Revolutionary Shop Stewards, went out of his way to prevent internal factional disputes.[43] Similarly, after the events of 6 December, when troops had fired on leftist demonstrators and when some suspected Ebert's complicity in a counter-revolutionary coup, the workers of the AEG factory at Hennigsdorf downed tools in protest and yet refused to let that protest be interpreted as support for any particular socialist faction.[44]

In fact at the level of the factory floor it is clear that many workers resented factionalism and desired the reunification of the socialist movement in Germany at the end of the war. At the national congress of workers' and soldiers' councils in Berlin in December 1918 some soldiers' delegates called for a joint socialist election campaign;[45] whilst in the previous month at the congress of Berlin councils there had been frequent calls for 'unity' from the floor and Spartacist speeches were attacked as divisive rather than for their specific content.[46] Even during the Spartacist rising, after bitter internecine war, workers at the Schwarzkopf and AEG concerns in Berlin passed resolutions calling for socialist unity;[47] and some actually declared 'Down with fratricide! Workers' unity *without the leaders*'.[48] Thus although the SPD tried to exploit the idea of working-class solidarity to gag opposition from the left[49] the concept of unity was clearly one which had a genuine appeal to many workers who disapproved of some aspects of SPD policies in government. As Rosa Luxemburg said herself at the founding conference of the German Communist Party at the end of December 1918: 'the primary illusion of the workers and soldiers who made the revolution was their belief in the possibility of unity under the banner of what passes by the name of socialism'.[50] Thus one may postulate that the attitudes and aspirations of socialist leaders and those of their rank and file were by no means necessarily identical; and although few have ever doubted that the numerical following of the Spartacists in January 1918 was minute and that they were incapable of determining the course of events, it is no less true that the SPD and the USPD had enormous difficulties in dictating to their respective memberships. Often the parties worked together in the localities, as we have seen.

III

So far it has been shown that some workers did have radical aspirations, even in the early days of the revolution, and furthermore that membership of the SPD was no guarantee of 'moderation' or satisfaction with the status quo. A further and perhaps even more telling criticism of what might be described as the moderate interpretation of the German Revolution is that it often ends in early 1919 with the defeat of the Spartacists and huge SPD electoral successes. In fact neither of these things denoted the collapse of working-class radicalism in Germany. Quite the opposite is the case: for they came at the very beginning of an extremely rapid process of radicalisation that was to affect large numbers of German workers and led to the emergence of a mass communist movement.

In part this process of radicalisation was a direct product of the enormous economic dislocation in Germany at the end of the First World War, hardly helped by the fact that the Allied blockade continued well into 1919 until the final signing of the peace treaty. The scene was characterised by a high rate of inflation and enormous food shortage. Not surprisingly therefore the harsh winter brought starvation and disease: in January 1919 it has been estimated that no fewer than 800 Germans died each day as a result of dietry deficiences. In the first three months of 1919 about a third of all new born children died within a few days of birth; whilst in Düsseldorf, where there was an extreme shortage of food, the figure for child deaths rose to a catastrophic 80 per cent.[51] A further problem was that of unemployment as a consequence of demobilisation, the running down of the war industries and to a certain extent industrial rationalisation. In fact the total number of unemployed in Germany at this time hardly begins to compare with the situation of the early 1930s, despite the human misery entailed. From 300,000 out of work (figures for the state-assisted unemployed) on 1 December 1918, the figure rose to 1,100,000 by the end of the next February. What this aggregate figure does not disclose, however, is that most of the unemployed were concentrated in areas that were already politically volatile. In Hamburg there were 40,000 totally without work in January 1919 and 60,000 in the next month, with over 100,000 more men only partly employed. Most striking of all, over a quarter of the unemployed were living in Berlin.[52]

There is some evidence to suggest that the Spartacists and other left radical groups recruited from the ranks of the unemployed. Eduard Bernstein maintained that the base of Spartacist strength in North-East Berlin lay in deserters and the unemployed,[53] and more modern commentators have argued similarly.[54] It was the KPD which led the strikes of the unemployed in Leipzig[55] and the same party was always to retain a high percentage of those without work.[56] Yet it was not just the unemployed who suffered in the early months of 1919. With inflation outstripping wage increases other groups of workers resorted to strike action, despite the existence of an ostensibly socialist government. Engineering workers in Berlin and miners in the Ruhr and Silesia went on strike when the regime was less than a month old; and when they went on strike they found themselves faced with a hostile reaction from both the SPD Government and the Free Trade Unions, who were intent on preserving a moderate socialist regime. In this way economic grievances could easily lead to political radicalism and discontent with the Majority Socialists. Bock, Lucas and von Oertzen have all shown how demands for higher wages, a shorter working week and guarantees against unemployment in the Ruhr mines led gradually and spontaneously to demands for socialisation and some form of workers'

control; and how the introduction of troops into turbulent areas led
not only to bloody conflicts but also to the creation of the Red Army
and the formulation of radical political and social goals. Indeed, after
the failure of the general strike of April 1919 many miners even turned
to various forms of anarcho-syndicalism.[57] Between April and June 1919
in the Ruhr the old union organisations lost no less than half their
membership as a result of disillusionment.[58]

The relative failure of the USPD compared to the SPD in the January
elections of 1919 has often been regarded as a clear indication of the
non-radical nature of the German working class: whereas the Independent
Socialists won only 7.6 per cent of the total vote, the SPD polled
37.9 per cent. What this actually tells us about working-class attitudes,
however, is far from clear. The SPD began the election campaign with
an organisation far superior to that of the Independents and furthermore
gained many non-proletarian votes (witness its poll of over 30 per cent
of the total in rural Schleswig-Holstein). We have also seen already that
some workers had difficulty distinguishing between the different
socialist factions and that some SPD members, let alone voters, had
attitudes well to the left of their cautious leaders. The January elections
of 1919 also took place only at the beginning of a process of radicalis-
ations. Finally, a close analysis of the voting statistics succeeds in
revealing a far more complicated pattern of working-class support. In
Berlin the SPD gained 36.4 per cent of the vote compared to the 27.6
per cent of the USPD, but in the working-class areas of Wedding and
Friedrichshain the two parties did equally well. In Düsseldorf, which
was to become a centre of anarcho-syndicalism, the Independents won
22.5 per cent of the votes cast, as against 34.6 per cent for the Majority
Socialists; and there were even places where the USPD did better than
its parent party. At Leipzig it gained 38.6 per cent of the poll compared
to the 20.7 per cent of the SPD; and in Halle-Merseburg no less than
44.1 per cent as against the 16.3 per cent of the SPD. Thus the voting
statistics of the large industrial towns reveal a much greater degree of
working-class support for the USPD than is suggested by the aggregate
voting figures; and this makes it unsurprising that in the elections of
1920, after the radicalisation process had fully set in, the USPD did
especially well in the heavy industrial areas. Now the Independents
gained 18.8 per cent of the total number of votes cast, whereas the
Majority Socialists fell back to 21.6 per cent, clearly having lost some of
its previous non-proletarian support. In many industrial centres the
USPD was actually stronger than the SPD, winning 45.2 per cent of
the vote (SPD 8.8 per cent) in Halle-Merseburg, 42.7 per cent in Berlin

(SPD 17.5 per cent) and 42.1 per cent (SPD 9.1 per cent) in Leipzig.[59]

What is equally important is that at the same time as the USPD was threatening to become Germany's largest proletarian party, it was also moving to the left, as increasing pressure from the rank and file culminated in the decision by the party to affiliate to the Third International in 1920.[60] The USPD also had a good deal of success within the trade union movement and by October 1919 had taken control of the metalworkers' union, the largest in Germany.[61]

Only by examining this process of radicalisation can one begin to understand that fatal split between social democracy and communism that doomed the German labour movement to failure in the 1920s and destruction in the 1930s. By 1919 we have seen that at least some sections of the working class had embarked upon a revolutionary course and this is further testified by a large number of events in the next three years. As well as the Spartacist rising in Berlin and the socialisation movement in the Ruhr in early 1919, socialist republics were proclaimed at Cuxhaven on January 11, at Bremen and Brunswick in the same month and in Munich in April as well as at Mannheim in February. These were also often accompanied by massive demonstrations against the Ebert-Scheidemann government, as in Brunswick, Stuttgart and Halle, which also saw a campaign for socialisation and workers' control.[62] There was a bloody uprising in Berlin in March 1919, the formation of a Red Army and insurrectionary strikes in the Ruhr and Central Germany after the Kapp putsch of 1920 and later attempts at communist uprisings in the March Action of 1921 and in Hamburg, Saxony and Thuringia in 1923.[63] Of course it would be wrong to claim that the majority of the German working class was involved in these activities but there can be little doubt, as evidenced by the numerical growth of the USPD, that, the theory of integration and embourgeoisement makes little sense for a significant section of the German labour movement. What is true, of course, is that it was specific sections of the German working class who participated in the councils' movement of 1918 and the later revolutionary activities. It seems to have been the case that radical initiatives were restricted to particular parts of Germany, namely and predictably the large industrial towns; and to workers in specific industries. The workers from the traditional craft industries who had long dominated the SPD and Free Trade Union organisations seem to have remained loyal to the Majority Socialists and to have played only a small part in the radical movement.[64] On the other hand, the councils' movement appears to have developed most strongly in those industrial sectors where there had been little or no union organisation before 1914, for example in textiles and the railways, or in those into which there was a massive influx of new labour in the course of the war, for example, metallurgy, chemicals and mining.[65] For workers in these industries the council was clearly a natural consequence of the need for representative institutions in a time of social upheaval and no mere imitation of a Russian example.

Having said this, however, it is essential to realise that not all sectors that participated in the proliferation of workers' councils were militant revolutionaries. On the contrary, railway and textile workers played little part in insurrectionary activities and had only a small representation in the ranks of the KPD.[66] Far more volatile were the mining, metallurgical and chemical industries, which had undergone a massive expansion in the course of the war and in consequence had recruited a mass of young workers, who, unlike their elder and craftsmen contemporaries, had no previous traditions of trade union organisation or history of attachment to the social democratic movement. All commentators agree that youth was a major determinant of radicalism in this period; it certainly applied to left voting in the USPD and to membership of the Communist Party.[67] Eduard Bernstein claimed that the Spartacists were young and that the Ruhr strikers were composed of the young and backward.[68] Similarly Gustav Noske complained in November 1918: 'the most turbulent and disobedient element in Kiel were the very young'.[69] Now one would expect Majority Socialists to make such statements in an attempt to discredit the left. Yet leftists themselves often made the same point, although this time with no implied criticism. Karl Retzlaw, a former Spartacist, tells us in his autobiography that the older workers in the engineering firm for which were loath to join the left for fear of losing their jobs,[70] whilst other communist veterans have claimed that Wilhelm Pieck made contact with young workers in Berlin in 1915[71] and that it was amongst the young in Hamburg that the Spartacists gained a following.[72] We also know that it was young workers who became involved in the anti-war and pro-Leibknecht demonstrations of 1916.[73]

IV

All this is hardly surprising. Militant activity and youth often accompany one another. But as well as temperament there were important historical and structural reasons why the young worker|should have been particularly susceptible to leftist propaganda. Such workers had no traditional commitment to the SPD, and hence it is not surprising that radicalism should be most marked in areas of new industry, for example, the Leuna works outside Halle,[74] or areas where there had been a quite spectacular expansion of the labour force, for example, the Thyssen mines at Hamborn where a strong syndicalist movement developed.[75] Otto Braun, at one time Minister of Agriculture for Prussia and a Majority Social Democrat, claimed that it was in precisely such places that a young and previously indifferent work force formed the core of the left.[76] Furthermore these new workers were often engaged in a new type of industrial production, working in large concerns on flow techniques which had been introduced into the optical and metallurgical industries in the course of the war.[77] Indeed both Richard Comfort and Peter von Oertzen have seen in precisely such workers the rank and file of the left.[78] Certainly this is true to some extent, though an analysis of the role and activities of metalworkers in the course of the revolution will serve to qualify this picture.

In many ways the history of the German Revolution is the history of the acts of workers in the metallurgical industries, which is hardly surprising given the dominance of that sector in the German industrial structure during the war. In Stuttgart a large part of the Spartacist following was to be found in the Daimler factory, as was also true in Friedrichshafen of the munitions workers at the Zeppelin factory.[79] In the great demonstrations of 9 November 1918 in Berlin it was workers from the great armaments factories in the north of the city who were first prominent, whilst munitions workers, often imported from the North played a significant role in the seizure of power in Munich.[80] Many of the strikes during the war were organised by the Revolutionary Shop Stewards Organisation, as to a certain extent was the so-called Spartacist rising of January 1919; and that organisation was based upon the turners' branch of the Berlin Metalworkers' Union.[81] Again it was the workers of the Schwarzkopf machine factory who supported the radical Berlin Chief of Police Emil Eichhorn against the SPD government that was trying to remove him from office.[82] Metalworkers were also prominent in the later communist movement: in the 1920s 145 of 285 known KPD functionaries worked in the metallurgical industries.[83]

Having claimed such preeminence for the German metalworker, it has to be admitted that the initial impetus for the revolution came from a naval mutiny rather than working-class demonstrations and strikes. In fact whereas soldiers played a fundamentally moderating role on the course of the revolution, the same cannot be said of their naval counterparts. It was a group of sailors who triggered off the revolution at Kiel[84] and then spread revolutionary initiatives throughout the length and breadth of Germany with mobile flying squads. One such led the revolution in Essen,[85] another the revolution in Brunswick;[86] and the same happened in Frankfurt am Main.[87] Furthermore, throughout the early months of the revolution in Berlin the People's Naval Division (*Volksmarine*), led by Heinrich Dorrenbach, a Spartacist sympathiser, gave its support to Emil Barth, one of the Revolutionary Shop Stewards, and fought several pitched battles with the forces of reaction.[88]

There can be no doubt, therefore, that sailors played a significantly greater role in the revolutionary initiatives of 1918 than did the soldiery, and there seems to have been a number of different reasons for this. In the first place the gap between the officers and men of the High Seas Fleet was not bridged by joint action against a hostile power: the navy, apart from its submarines, was inactive in the last two years of the war. The sailors therefore had plenty of time to reflect on their bad treatment and some were clearly open to USPD propaganda.[89] Another and rather different explanation of sailor militancy may be found in the social composition of the naval reserve and technical staff. For these were recruited from the skilled sections of the working class and often from workers in the engineering industry. Again, therefore, we are often dealing with metalworkers.[90]

It is important to realise that the militancy of metalworkers was not simply the product of physical deprivation engendered by four years of war. There were several indications of a swing to the left in the years immediately prior to the war. From 1905 onwards in the metallurgical industries, at this time undergoing rapid expansion, a series of struggles developed in several places between the leadership of the DMV (German Metalworkers' Union) and its rank and file membership. The background to this struggle is not difficult to understand. The trade-union leaders were becoming increasingly cautious at this point in time as they had suffered a number of defeats at the hands of the well organised employers' associations which had been formed to combat the threat of industrial action. In consequence they were fearful of unproductive conflicts which might lead to a considerable wastage of union funds and hence they tried to ward off impetuous and unofficial actions. For example they opposed a number of wild-cat strikes among their membership at Mannheim in 1908, which generated amongst the local shop stewards a marked hostility to the central union leadership.[91] There were numerous similar struggles in 1910, but it was to be in 1913 that the greatest bitterness arose between the rank and file and the leadership of the DMV. In some places there were demands for more power to be given to the local branches. In others the union leadership was forced to support actions as a result of rank-and-file pressure.[92]

Such tensions became most evident in the great strike in the Hamburg docks in 1913, which principally involved members of the DMV. After a large strike, the union executive decided to put an end to industrial action but the call to return to work was not heeded by the local membership. As a result the DMV executive decided to take the unpopular step of refusing to pay out from strike funds; and this in turn led to demands for local control of union funds, decentralisation and limitations on the powers of the central executive.[93] This is the background of disillusionment with the party and trade union hierarchies that Kautsky mentioned in his correspondence with Viktor Adler, the Austrian Social Democrat,[94] and to the remark of one contemporary that there was a growing syndicalist undercurrent amongst the tradeunion membership. As an article in *Die neue Zeit* claimed: 'the trade union is not successful enough for the man on the shop floor; the tactic is too cautious, the leadership too circumspect . . . he is readily prepared in meetings to be excited into opposition to the leaders'.[95]

It would be arrant nonsense to claim that what was involved in these struggles was a real threat of revolution in Wilhelmine Germany; but the widespread discontent with the official bureaucracies of the labour movement before the outbreak of the First World War did lead to demands for more control at the level of the shop floor and such demands may constitute one explanation of why the councils' movement found such fruitful soil in the metallurgical industries, in so far as it constituted an alternative to the traditional trade-union structure. Furthermore, the emergence of a radical left in the course of the war may be more closely related to disputes within the Metalworkers' Union than political factionalism in the higher ranks of the SPD: for the areas of greatest USPD strength were precisely those areas in which there had been strong rank and file opposition to the leadership of the DMV.[96]

There can be no doubt that certain developments in the four years of war served to increase the alienation of some metalworkers from their union leadership. This was partly because the central officials of the union, and for that matter those of other unions, made a number of important gains between 1914 and 1918. Union leaders were exempted from conscription, were given a representation in the procedures of collective bargaining in the terms of the Auxiliary Service Law of 1916, and were allowed for the first time to recruit in areas which had previously been forbidden, namely amongst state employees.[97] As a result of these concessions from the State many union leaders reconsidered their position and adopted a position of positive support for the German war effort. Adolf Cohen, who headed the German Metalworkers' Union, was prepared to state that the coming of war in August 1914 was nothing less than a godsend to his union, as otherwise there would have been widespread unemployment in the winter of that year.[98]

At the same time as trade unions were beginning to look more favourably on the State, however, the situation of the working-class rank and file was undergoing a marked deterioration. To support the war effort workers were having to work longer hours at increased pace in a situation in which protective labour legislation wassuspended andl when therefore there was a high accident rate. Even more important, however, was the fact that rising prices more than outstripped wage increases, even for the relatively prosperous skilled engineering workers. According to Kuczynski the price index rose from 100 in 1900 to 130 in 1913, 221 in 1916, 329 in 1917 and a disasterous 407 in the following year.[99] Furthermore, the provisions of the Auxiliary Service Law, which attempted to prevent labour mobility from factory to factory without the permission of the employer, were greatly resented by skilled metalworkers, who could make a great deal of money by moving from one firm to another at a time of labour scarcity.[100]

As a result of this situation, and perhaps with some relation to their pre-war discontents, German metalworkers were to prove increasingly hostile to the cautious policies of their leadership. From the very beginning of the war, the turners' branch of the Berlin Metal Workers' Union refused to accept the general policy of industrial peace for the duration.[101] In 1915 amongst some sections of the union there were objections to the pro-government line of the union and party newspapers[102] as there were also at the party congress of that year;[103] and by 1917 the opposition within the union was explicitly identifying itself with the Independent Socialists.[104] It was also metalworkers who played a major role in the strikes of 1916, 1917 and January 1918, as they did in the course of the revolution, as we have seen.

Why was this the case? One model of explanation, provided by Comfort and Oertzen,[105] argues that it was the young worker in large factories, lacking any prior connection with the craft traditions of Social Democracy and its affiliated unions, who formed the radical rank and file. This clearly fits the evidence adduced by Comfort, explains radicalism in the Ruhr and at Halle and is supported by Ruth Fischer's contention that the USPD decision to affiliate to the Third International was the product of the votes of the unskilled and semi-skilled members.[106] It also gains some credence from the autobiography of another radical, Toni Sender, who claimed that the rapid growth and radical nature of the DMV in Essen could be related to an influx of wild young elements.[107]

This picture is confronted with a number of problems. In the USPD the branches of Remscheid and Solingen, bastions of skilled craft cutlers, voted far more heavily in favour of joining the Bolshevik International than did the branches of Düsseldorf and Hagen, where machine building and steel refining were concentrated,[108] although it is significant that the USPD was strong in all four towns. Furthermore, the Revolutionary Shop Stewards' Organisation was based upon the turners of the engineering industry, that is, highly skilled workers, a point which was repeated at length by Richard Müller, the leading shop steward.[109] In fact the radicalism of metalworkers was not simply restricted to new industrial areas,[110] although it does seem clear that those metalworkers who were radical worked in the large factories.[111] In short there seem to be two models of explanation of militancy. One concentrates on the emergence of a new semi-skilled work-force with no attachments to craft traditions (according to Oertzen a work-force which approximates more closely to the Marxian model of the proletarian);[112] the other on the activities of skilled craftsmen facing the threat of downward mobility as a consequence of technological innovation. This is what Wheeler suggests as a possible cause of radicalism in Remscheid and Solingen;[113] and clearly relates to the usual interpretation of the movement for workers' control which developed in Great Britain at the end of the First World War.[114] Certainly the little evidence we have of the social composition of the Spartacist leadership in the localities reveals a skilled working-class affiliation rather than anything else.[115] In any case, much of this is pure speculation, in so far as contemporaries spoke in terms of *Metallarbeiter* rather than in more differentiated terms; and if one has evidence of radicalism on the part of the work-force of certain engineering firms this still tells one little about exactly which specific group of workers were the real activists. In part the evidence suggests that both some of the new work-force, especially in Central Germany and the Ruhr, constituted the rank and file militants; yet amongst the Berlin workers a radical tradition and more skilled workers may have played a role. In fact it may be best to let Richard Müller have the last word on this subject: for he claimed that the originators of the revolutionary movement were the skilled workers of the large concerns but that they also had some success in mobilising their less skilled colleagues working on serial production who had no previous traditions

of SPD membership.[116]
All of this must remain tenative at this stage until more research has been done on the structure of militancy amongst the working class. Yet it does seem clear that working-class radicalism did form a significant part of the German revolutionary experience in 1918 to 1923; that that militancy had structured roots; and that it cannot simply be dismissed as a product of the war that has so often come to be regarded as a watershed in working-class history.

Notes

1. Dieter Groh, *Negative Integration und revolutionärer Attentismus* (Frankfurt am Main, 1973); Harvey Mitchell and Peter N. Stearns, *Workers and Protest* (Itasca, Illinois, 1971); Guenther Roth, *The Social Democrats in Imperial Germany* (Totowa, N.J., 1963); Hedwig Wachenheim, *Die deutsche Arbeiterbewegung* (Cologne, 1967).
2. R. Comfort, *Revolutionary Hamburg* (Stanford, 1966), pp. 91f. and *passim;* P. von Oertzen, *Betriebsräte in der Novemberrevolution* (Düsseldorf, 1963), p. 119 and p. 276.
3. See note 1.
4. T. Nipperdey, *Die Organisation der deutschen Parteien* (Düsseldorf, 1961), p. 337.
5. SPD *Protokolle* 1905 to 1912.
6. Dick Geary, 'The German Labour Movement', *European Studies Review*, Vol. 6, no. 3, 1976, pp. 297–330.
7. *Protokoll 1913*, pp. 246, 287.
8. Kautsky to Heinrich Schlüter 4 December 1913 in International Institute for Social History, Kautsky Nachlass, c 624; and to Viktor Adler in *Viktor Adler. Briefwechsel mit August Bebel und Karl Kautsky* (Vienna, 1954), p. 52.
9. *Die Neue Zeit*, 32, pp. 55–9; *Sozialistische Monatshefte*, 19, iii, pp. 1155–62.
10. On soldiers' councils see Ludwig Lewinsohn, *Die Revolution an der Westfront* (Charlottenburg, 1920); Ulrich Kluge, *Soldatenräte und Revolution* (Göttingen, 1975).
11. The essential moderation of the revolutionary demands is a central theme in F.L. Carsten, *Revolution in Central Europe 1918–1919* (London, 1972); A.J. Ryder, *The German Revolution* (Cambridge, 1967); G.A. Ritter and S. Miller, *Die deutsche Revolution* (Frankfurt, 1969).
12. Ritter and Miller, p. 76.
13. W. Sollmann, *Die Revolution in Köln* (Cologne, 1918), p. 11.
14. D. Woodward, *Mutiny in the High Seas Fleet* (London, 1973), p. 160.
15. Eberhard Büchner, *Revolutionsdokumente*, Vol. I (Berlin, 1921), pp. 75f.
16. Karl Anlauf, *Die Revolution in Niedersachsen* (Hanover, 1919), p. 99.
17. *Illustrierte Geschichte der Novemberrevolution in Deutschland* (Berlin, 1968), p. 195.
18. E. Bernstein, *Die deutsche Revolution* (Berlin, 1921), p. 59.
19. J.S. Drabkin, *Die Novemberrevolution in Deutschland* (East Berlin, 1968), p. 120.
20. See the article by von Oertzen in *Vierteljahreshefte für Zeitgeschichte*, vi,

1968, pp. 231–62.
21. *Illustrierte Geschichte der Revolution in Deutschland* (Berlin, n.d. 1929?), pp. 373–7.
22. E. Kolb, *Die Arbeiterräte in der deutschen Innenpolitik* (Düsseldorf, 1962), pp. 94ff.
23. *Zeitschrift fur Geschichtswissenschaft*, 1956, no. 3, p. 548.
24. For Berlin see *Ill. Gesch.*, 1968, p. 193; for Thuringia, Carsten, pp. 163ff.
25. For example in Bremen, Brunswick, Frankfurt, Düsseldorf, Halle and Hamburg: P. Broué, *Révolution en Allemagne* (Paris, 1971), p. 167.
26. Eric Waldman, *The Spartacist Uprising 1919* (Milwaukee, 1955), p. 129n.
27. Ibid.
28. H.M. Bock, *Syndikalismus und Linkskommunismus von 1918–1923* (Meisenheim an Glan, 1969), p. 120.
29. J. Reulecke, *Arbeiterbewegung an Rhein und Ruhr* (Wuppertal, 1974), p. 245; Broué, p. 349.
30. Kolb, p. 131; Drabkin, p. 240.
31. Carsten, p. 67.
32. Gerhard Schmolze, *Räterepublik in München* (Düsseldorf, 1969), p. 24.
33. Rosa Meyer-Leviné, *Leviné* (Munich, 1972), p. 109.
34. Gilbert Badia, *Le Spartakisme* (Paris, 1966), p. 132.
35. Bernstein, p. 16.
36. Drabkin, p. 534.
37. R. Müller, *Der Bürgerkrieg in Deutschland* (Berlin, 1925), p. 130; *Ill. Gesch.*, 1929, pp. 313–16.
38. R.F. Wheeler, *USPD und Internationale* (Frankfurt am Main, 1975), pp. 95–8; D.W. Morgan, *The Socialist Left and the German Revolution* (London, 1975), *passim*.
39. G. Badia, *Les Spartakistes* (Paris, 1967), p. 183.
40. Bock, pp. 154ff.
41. Morgan, *passim*.
42. For the ideological debates at the founding congress of the KPD see H. Weber (ed.), *Die Gründungsparteitag der KPD* (Frankfurt am Main, 1969); for lack of central control, see Bock, p. 117.
43. R. Müller, *Vom Kaiserreich zur Republik* (Berlin, 1924), pp. 66, 103.
44. Badia, *Les Spartakistes*, p. 166n.
45. Bernstein, p. 96.
46. Ibid., p. 46ff.
47. Ibid., p. 154.
48. Quoted in Drabkin, p. 498 (my italics).
49. *Vorwärts*, 10 November 1918.
50. Quoted in M.A. Waters (ed.), *Rosa Luxemburg Speaks* (New York, 1970), p. 415.
51. David Mitchell, *Red Mirage* (London, 1970), p. 93.
52. Badia, *Le Spartakisme*, p. 277.
53. Bernstein, p. 71.
54. Kolb, pp. 319ff.; Badia, *Le Spartakisme*, p. 214.
55. *Vorwärts und nicht vergessen* (Berlin, 1958), p. 411.
56. H. Weber, *Die Wandlung des deutschen Kommunismus* (Frankfurt am Main, 1969), Vol. 2; O.K. Flechtheim, *Die Kommunistische Partei Deutschlands* (Frankfurt am Main, 1969).
57. Bock, esp. p. 105; Oertzen's article and book; E. Lucas, *Märzrevolution im Ruhrgebiet* (Frankfurt am Main, 1970).
58. Bock, p. 133.
59. Drabkin, pp. 538–50; Broué, pp. 290–2.

60. Wheeler, *passim*.
61. F. Opel, *Der deutsche Metallarbeiterverband* (Hanover, 1957).
62. Drabkin, pp. 520–33; A. Remmele, *Staatsumwälzung und Neuaufbau in Baden* (Karlsruhe, 1925), pp. 60–7; A. Mitchell, *Revolution in Bavaria* (Princeton, 1965).
63. Bock and Lucas *passim* for the activities of the Red Army. For the communist risings see W.T. Angress, *Stillborn Revolution*, 2 Vols. (New York, 1972).
64. This is the basic structure of analysis to be found in Comfort. In Munich Kurt Eisner also claimed that German printers were difficult to mobilise: see Schmolze, p. 50.
65. The best structural analysis of the councils is in Oertzen, pp. 275–80.
66. Ibid; and for the composition of the KPD see Weber, *Wandlung*, Vol. 2.
67. For SPD voting see Wheeler, p. 253; for KPD Weber.
68. Bernstein, pp. 70, 179.
69. Quoted in Woodward, p. 150.
70. Karl Retzlaw, *Spartakus* (Frankfurt, 1972), pp. 54, 65.
71. *Unter der roten Fahne* (Berlin, 1958), p. 92.
72. *Vorwärts und nicht vergessen*, p. 235.
73. Opel p. 54; G. Mergner, *Arbeiterbewegung und Intelligenz* (Starnberg, 1973), p. 88f.
74. Wilhelm Koenen in *Vorwärts und nicht vergessen*.
75. Lucas, p. 28.
76. O. Braun, *Von Weimar zu Hitler* (2nd. edn., New York, 1940), p. 95.
77. J. Kocka, *Klassengesellschaft im Krieg* (Gottingen, 1973), p. 27.
78. Comfort *passim*; Oertzen, esp. pp. 47, 54.
79. For Daimler see *Schwäbischer Merkur* 5 November 1918; for Zeppelin, Badia, *Le Spartakisme*, p. 176.
80. Büchner, pp. 128f.
81. Müller, *Vom Kaiserreich*, pp. 125ff.
82. Bernstein, p. 132.
83. Weber, Vol. 2.
84. Woodward; D. Horn, *The German Naval Mutinies of World War I* (New Brunswick, 1969).
85. Büchner, p. 124.
86. Anlauf, p. 97.
87. Büchner, p. 119.
88. H. Ströbel, *The German Revolution and After* (London, 1940), *passim*.
89. Bernstein, p. 21.
90. Ströbel, p. 48 and p. 53.
91. Wachenheim, p. 567.
92. *Metallarbeiterverband*, 1913, pp. 254–79.
93. *Die Neue Zeit*, 32, i, pp. 59, 704, 988.
94. *Adler Briefwechsel*, p. 582.
95. *Die Neue Zeit*, p. 988.
96. Oertzen, pp. 47n, 281; Opel, p. 47.
97. For a full treatment of the unions in the war see G.D. Feldman, *Army, Industry and Labor 1914 to 1918* (Princeton, 1966).
98. Emil Barth, *Aus der Werkstatt der Revolution* (Berlin, 1919), p. 11.
99. Jurgen Kuczynski, *Die Geschichte der Lage der Arbeiter*, Pt. I, Vol. 4 (Berlin, 1967), p. 350.
100. Feldman, *passim*.
101. R. Coper, *Failure of a Revolution* (Cambridge, 1955). p. 55.
102. *Deutsche Matallarbeiterzeitung*, 1915, no. 29, p. 122.
103. *Protokoll der ordentlichen Generalversammlung des DMVs* (Stuttgart, 1915),

pp. 129ff.
104. *DMZ*, 1917, 27, pp. 113ff.
105. See note 2 above.
106. Ruth Fischer, *Stalin and German Communism* (Cambridge, Mass., 1948), p. 146.
107. T. Sender, *Autobiography of a German Rebel* (London, 1940), p. 147.
108. Wheeler, p. 255.
109. R. Müller, *Vom Kaiserreich*, pp. 125–31.
110. Oertzen, p. 281.
111. Müller, p. 131; Oertzen, p. 268; Leviné claimed that the radicals in Munich were recruited from the large factories: T. Dorst, *Die Münchener Räterepublik* (Frankfurt am Main, 1966), p. 149.
112. Oertzen, p. 47.
113. Wheeler, p. 255.
114. J. Hinton, *The First Shop Stewards' Movement* (London, 1973).
115. Badia, *Le Spartakisme*, pp. 280ff.
116. Müller, p. 56.

NOTES ON CONTRIBUTORS

David Blackbourn was born in Spilsby, Lincolnshire in 1949 and was educated in Leeds. He read History at Christ's College, Cambridge and was elected to a Research Fellowship at Jesus College, Cambridge in 1973. From 1974 to 1975 he was a Research Fellow at the Institute of European History in Mainz. He is currently Lecturer in European History at Queen Mary College, University of London. Dr Blackbourn has published articles and reviews in a number of journals and is completing a book on local politics in Imperial Germany.

Terry Cole was born in Malmesbury, Wiltshire in 1944 and studied Philosophy at the University of Sussex before going on to write his dissertation on Imperial Chancellor Bernhard von Bülow and the politics of the 'Bülow Block' at the same university. Since 1970 he has been Lecturer in History at the University of Edinburgh. He is currently engaged on a biography of Bülow.

Geoff Eley was born in Burton-on-Trent, Staffordshire in 1949 and read History at Balliol College, Oxford, before going on to the University of Sussex to write a dissertation on 'The German Navy League in German Politics 1898–1914'. He was a Research Student of the Volkswagen Foundation in Germany from 1972 to 1973 and a Research Fellow at the University of Swansea from 1973 to 1974. After spending 1974–5 as Lecturer in History at the University of Keele, he was appointed College Lecturer and Director of Studies in History at Emmanuel College, Cambridge in 1975. He has published a number of articles in various journals and is now completing a book on the German right between the 1880s and the 1920s.

Richard J. Evans was born in Woodford, Essex in 1947 and studied at Jesus and St Antony's Colleges, Oxford. From 1970 to 1972 he was Hanseatic Scholar of the FVS Foundation at Hamburg University and in Berlin, and from 1972 to 1976 he was Lecturer in History at the University of Stirling. Dr Evans is the author of *The Feminist Movement in Germany 1894–1933* (London, 1976) and articles and reviews in a number of journals. Since 1976 he has been Lecturer in the School of European Studies at the University of East Anglia, Norwich, and he is currently working on a study of Social Democracy, women and the family in Imperial Germany.

Ian Farr was born in Nuneaton, Warwickshire in 1951 and studied Modern History at Durham University. In 1972–3 he was Research Assistant at the University of Wales. After spending 1974–5 in Bavaria as a Research Scholar of the German Academic Exchange Service he took up a post as Lecturer in the School of European Studies at the University of East Anglia in 1976. His continuing work on peasant society and politics includes a paper on charivaris in late nineteenth-century Bavaria to be published in the proceedings of the Paris conference on charivaris held in April 1977.

Dick Geary was born in Leicester in 1945 and read History at King's College, Cambridge, where he also wrote a dissertation on Karl Kautsky. From 1970 to 1973 he was Research Fellow of Emmanuel College, Cambridge. Since 1973 he has been Lecturer in French and German Studies at the University of Lancaster. A regular contributor of reviews to the *Times Higher Education Supplement* and the author of a number of articles in various journals, Dr Geary is now completing a book on Marxism and German Social Democracy.

Alex Hall was born in Hamburg in 1948 and was educated in England and Germany. He studied at St Catharine's College, Cambridge and the University of Hamburg. In 1972–3 he was a Research Student of the Volkswagen Foundation. Dr Hall is the athor of *Scandal, Sensation and Social Democracy: The SPD Press and Wilhelmine Germany* (Cambridge, 1977) and articles in a number of journals. He now lives in Hamburg, where he is *Studienrat* at a *Fachoberschule* and part-time *Lektor* in English at the University. He is currently engaged on a study of the Social Democratic Youth Movement.

Stephen Hickey was born in Oxford in 1949 and studied at Corpus Christi and St Antony's Colleges, Oxford. From 1972 to 1973 he was a Research Student of the Volkswagen Foundation in Bochum. He now works in government service and is completing a dissertation on the social history of miners in the Ruhr before 1914.

Robin Lenman was born in Dorking, Surrey in 1945. After studying at Merton and St Antony's Colleges, Oxford, he was Michael Foster Scholar at the University of Marburg in 1969–70 and Lecturer in History at the University of Hull in 1970–1. Since 1971 he has been

Lecturer in History at the University of Warwick. Dr Lenman has published a study of Julius Streicher and the origins of the Nazi Party in Nuremberg and is now working on a book about artistic and literary life in Munich between 1885 and 1914.

Richard Owen was born in Aberdyfi, North Wales in 1948. He studied History and French at the Universities of East Anglia and Geneva. In 1974–5 he held a Research Scholarship at the Institute for European History in Mainz. He now works in government service and has been preparing a doctoral dissertation at the University of East Anglia on the relationship between German heavy industry and the Imperial Navy Office before the First World War.

INDEX

abortion law reform 190, 192, 194,
  199, 203
absenteeism in industry 33, 223, 233,
  235
academics 165, 167, 169–71, 197,
  199; *see also* universities
accidents (mines) 220–1
Adenauer, Konrad, West German
  Chancellor 14
Adler, Viktor, Austrian Social
  Democrat 280
administration *see* bureaucracy
Agrarian League 19, 28, 56, 73,
  119–22, 124, 129, 131, 134n35,
  136, 139, 144–5, 151–2
agrarians *see* Junkers
Agricultural Association, Bavaria 137,
  148–9
agriculture 20, 119, 128, 136–59,
  161, 164, 176; *see also* Junkers,
  peasants
Agriculture, Prussian Ministry of 55,
  278
alcoholism 203, 248, 251, 259,
  264n54
Alexander VI, Pope 95
Algeciras Conference 52–3, 66
Allen, William S., historian 130
Allgemeine Elektrizitäts-Gesellschaft
  (AEG), industrial firm 272–3
Allgemeine Rundschau, magazine
  102
Alliance of Conservative Women 196
Alliance of Free Youth Organisations
  of Germany 251
Allotria artists' club (Munich) 91–2
Alsace-Lorraine 58, 165
Altena-Iserlohn 62–3
Altona 198
America, United States of 14–15,
  88n58, 195, 206–8, 215
Amsterdam 249, 263n38
anarchism 103
anarcho-syndicalism 272, 275, 278
Antrick, Otto, SPD Reichstag deputy
  176
anti-clericalism 146, 150–1
Anti-Jesuit Law 183n43
anti-modernism 115–16, 143, 153,

167
anti-Prussianism 120, 138, 152
anti-semitism, Anti-semitic Parties 29,
  114, 119–21, 129, 131, 134n24,
  138, 140, 143–4, 151, 154, 264n43
anti-socialism 116, 127, 131, 152
Anti-Socialist Law 17, 21, 164, 247,
  255, 260
apprentices 164, 221, 241, 247–8,
  251; *see also* guilds
Arenberg, Prince Franz von, Catholic
  Centre Reichstag deputy 42–3
aristocracy 16, 20, 42–3, 104, 130,
  138, 142–3, 146, 149–50, 170–2,
  177–9, 186, 199; *see also* Junkers;
  and under individual names
  (Arenberg, Bismarck, Bulow, etc.)
armaments industry 18, 20, 26–7,
  71–89, 162, 186, 278
army 16–17, 19–20, 49, 55–6, 63,
  78, 83, 126, 155, 160, 174, 178,
  199, 206, 230, 244–7, 252, 270;
  see also militarism; pacifism
Arnsberg 133; *see also* Ruhr
art 31, 90–111, 169
Artillery Commission 84–5
artisans, craftsmen 28, 97, 118–19,
  164, 166, 177, 197, 221, 241–2;
  see also guilds; petty-bourgeoisie
Artists' Guild, Munich 91–3
Assembly of German Catholics 163,
  170
Assiette au Beurre, French satirical
  magazine 98
Association for Commercial Clerks
  122
Association for Women's Interests,
  Munich 212n48
Association of Apprentices and
  Young Workers in Berlin 248
Association of German Commercial
  Assistants 122
Association of German Technicians
  122
Association of Traders 119
Augsburg 142
Austria 16, 58, 91, 145, 249
autarky 114
Auxiliary Service Law (1916) 280–1